MW01620987

Unlocking
The King James Bible's
Common Words and Phrases –

A Dictionary For Today's Reader

Compiled and Edited by R. Scott Giberti

Published in the United States by
First Stone Publishing, Inc.
PO Box 5310
Tucson, Arizona 85703

www.firststonellc.com

First Stone book titles may be purchased in bulk for education, business, fund-raising, or sales promotional use. For information, please email tlc@dakotacom.net or sales@firststonellc.org.

All Scripture quotations, unless otherwise indicated, are taken from the King James Version.

Library of Congress Catalog-in-Publication Data

Giberti, R. Scott.
Unlocking The King James Bible's Common Words and Phrases – A Dictionary For Today's Reader / R. Scott Giberti.
p.cm.
Includes bibliographical references.
ISBN 13: 978-1-4276-2093-4 (pbk.)
1. Bible—Dictionary. 2. Religious—Christian. 3. Historical—Religious. I. Title. II. Title: Unlocking The King James Bible's Common Words and Phrases.

Library of Congress Control Number: 2007905615

Printed in the United States of America
06 07 08 09 10 RRD 9 8 6 7 5 4 3 2
First Edition

Foreword

Since its first appearance, this little "Notebook" has gone through numerous editions, revisions and at least two different authors. This edition is the fruition of much previous labor.

I wish to express my profound gratitude to Robert Lee Turner (1910-2007) for his generosity in funding this project and assisting in its overall scope, design and intent. Thanks to my wife Tina without whose patience, support and editorial skills this project would not have happened. Special thanks go to the individuals that read through the entire Bible, providing the project with "fresh eyes." These readers recorded the commonly unknown or misunderstood words and phrases that formed the basis of this book.

To God alone be all the glory. May the Lord add many souls from this generation who will receive blessing and salvation from using *"Unlocking the King James Bible's Common Words and Phrases – A Dictionary For Today's Reader"*.

R Scott Giberti
First Stone Publishing, LLC
May 2007

Note: Beyond the Genesis chapter, throughout the notebook wherever a certain name of/for God is used we have not provided an individual definition, rather we have included a section (Appendix C) entitled ***The Names of God – His Identity & Character*****).**

Dear Friends,

As many of you know, my father Robert Turner had a great passion for the King James Bible. He also understood, however, that mnay young or newly converted believers mght not understand the language of King James. So, it became in his last years, a personal project of his to create a dictionary/thesaurus of the the King James Bible. He began marking, compiling and defining these difficult words and phrases. These notes took the basic form of what my dad affectionately called the "notebook", which would be used side by side with the Bible to aid the reader.

In an effort to make my father's dream come true, Mr. Giberti and RLT Foundation picked up where he left off. It was during the final editing phase of this project when my father was called home to be with his Lord & Savior. I am pleased to say that the work is now completed. I believe this book will be helpful to you personally and in your service to God.

Sincerely,

Virginia Turner Rezetko
August 2007

Old Testament

GENESIS

1:1	in the beginning	before time; thought-then reality
1:2	without form	empty, chaotic
	void	without life, empty, barren
	face of the deep	earth's surface
1:2+	God	El, Elohim; self-existing, Almighty
1:3, 14	light	sun, moon, stars
1:4	moved	brooded, incubated
1:6,7,8 14,15,20	firmament	expanse, sky, land envelope of air around the earth
1:7	above	sun, moon, stars in sky
1:11	bring forth	come to life
1:11,12	grass	vegetation, plants
1:14	signs, and seasons	day, night, spring, summer, fall, winter
1:16	great lights	sun
	lesser light	moon
1:20	abundantly	a lot, plentiful, extra
	creature	life form
1:20,22	fowl	feathered, for food
1:21	winged fowl	feathered birds and fowl small and large
1:25	after their kind	species, type e.g. dogs breed dogs
1:26	Our image	spiritual & bodily representation
	Our likeness	essence, similtude
1:26,28	dominion	authority
1:27	image	spiritual & bodily representation
1:28	replenish	repopulate e.g. infers that the earth had been destroyed prior to this time
	subdue	conquer, rule over
1:29	seed	descendants, offspring, children
1:29,30	meat	food, a meal
1:30	life	breath of life
2:1	host	groups of angels
2:2+	God	El, Elohim; self-existing, Almighty
2:3	sanctified	blessed, dedicated, holy, special
2:6	mist	vapor, light moisture
	face	earth's surface

GENESIS

2:7	breath of life	breath, air, life force
	soul	form – being, a living person
2:9	the tree of life	God in a spiritual body (ref. Rev 2:7, JN 11:25)
	tree of knowledge	Satan in a spiritual body (ref. Ezek 28:13-15)
	midst	middle, center
2:10	went	flowed
	four heads	rivers, 4 branches
2:11,13	compasses	go about, surround, encamp, encircle
2:14	Hiddekel	Tigris
2:15	dress	cultivate, tend, care for
2:18,20	help meet	helper suitable, companion
2:21	instead thereof	in place of it
2:24	cleave unto	joined, united
	one flesh	intimate, form a special, deep bond
3:1	subtil	crafty, sneaky, tricky
3:1+	Lord God	Jehovah Elohim, the self-existing God now interacting with mankind
3:1+	God	El, Elohim; self-existing, Almighty
3:3,4	die	physically and spiritually
3:7	aprons	Loin coverings, skirts
3:13	beguiled	tricked, deceived, seduced
3:15	enmity	hostility
	you	Satan, Serpant
	seed	offspring, children, heirs
	bruise your head	crush, i.e. deadly wound
	bruise your heel	less than deadly wound
3:16	conception	pregnancy, child bearing
	desire	attraction, longing, physical/ sexual/emotional hunger
3:17	harkened	listened, yielded to suggestion
	in sorrow…you eat	troubles, not easy
3:19	sweat of face	work hard, labor
	eat bread	for wages, pay check
	return to the ground	after death, dust to dust, decompose, rot
3:20	Eve	life or living, mother, life producer
3:21	coats of skins	slaughter a lamb to make leather garments
3:22	as one of us	loss of innocence, not child-like
3:24	Cheru-bims	special angels

GENESIS

	flaming sword	consuming, dangerous weapon to attack/defend a.k.a. God's Word
	keep the way of	The way of the tree of life is Divine revelation. God shows a Person what His Word means, it Is hidden to man's logic
4:1	knew	had intercourse with, sexual relations
	conceived	pregnant, with child, gotten one
4:1+	Lord	Jehovah; God in relationship to mankind
4:2	tiller	one who cultivates, farmer
4:4	firstlings	first born
	had respect	approved, accepted, pleased with
4:5	wroth	exceedingly angry, furious
4:6	countenance fallen	face downcast, sorrowful
4:7	sin lies at the door	unconfessed, rebellious attitude
4:8	slew	killed, murdered
4:11	from your hand	because of your action
4:12	till	cultivate, farm
4:12,14	vagabond	wanderer, nomad
4:15,24	sevenfold	seven times
4:16	Nod	wandering, separated from God
4:17,18	Enoch	dedicated; teacher, instill wisdom
4:20	cattle	livestock
4:22	artificer	metal craftsman, coppersmith, blacksmith
4:23	hearken	listen to, hearken, pay attention
	to my wounding	for wounding me
4:25	seed	offspring, children, heirs
	God	El, Elohim; self-existing, Almighty
4:26	began men	started, had children, produced
5:1+	God	El, Elohim; self-existing, Almighty
5:3	begat	started, had children, produced
	son in own likeness	looked and acted like his father
5:22,24	walked	believed and was obedient, lived as God's close friend
5:24	he was not	died, God took him, he disappeared, was translated to Heaven without physically experiencing death
6:2,4	sons of God	lineage, offspring of Adam & Eve

GENESIS

	daughters of men	lineage, offspring of Eve & Serpant (an upright, talking creature before it was cursed to go upon its belly – Genesis 3:14)
6:4	renown	famous, heroic, popular
6:5	wickedness	sinfulness, cruelty
	continually	all the time
6:6,7	repented	grieved
6:6+	Lord	Jehovah; God in relationship to mankind
6:7	Me	God
6:9	perfect	mature, complete, developed
	walked	lived, obedient
6:9+	God	El, Elohim; self-existing, Almighty
6:13	end	end-times, destruction of all
6:14	pitch	seal/coat with tar inside and out, waterproof
6:18	covenant	agreement, contract, promise
6:20	fowls	larger feathered birds
6:20	after its kind	species, type e.g. dogs breed dogs
7:1	house	family
	righteous	obedient, guiltless
7:3	seed	offspring, children, heirs
7:4	substance	thing, property, possessions
7:5+	Lord	Jehovah; God in relationship to mankind
7:6	was	came
7:11	windows	clouds
7:16	God	El, Elohim; self-existing, Almighty
7:17	bore up	carried
7:18	went	floated, traveled
	face	earth's surface
	prevailed	won, champs, overcame, defeated
8:1+	God	El, Elohim; self-existing, Almighty
8:1	assuaged	subsided
8:2	fountains	springs, natural water well
	windows of heaven	rain clouds
8:3	returned	receded
8:3,8,11	were abated	decreased, lessened, disappeared
8:9	face	earth's surface
8:20+	Lord	Jehovah; God in relationship to mankind
8:21	sweet savor	soothing aroma, smell of satisfaction

	for	though
8:22	While	as long as
	seedtime	planting season
9:1+	God	El, Elohim; self-existing, Almighty
9:3	meat	food
9:4	life=blood	spirit, force
9:7	be fruitful	have a lot of children
	multiply	increase population
9:9+	covenant	unconditional agreement, contract, promise
9:9	seed	offspring, children, heirs
9:12,13,17	token	sign, pledge, testimony
9:12	perpetual	long, long time; forever
9:13,14,16	bow	rainbow
9:19	overspread	populated, with inhabitants
9:20	husbandman	farmer
9:21	uncovered	undressed, naked, nude
9:23	went	walked
9:26	Lord God	Jehovah Elohim, the self-existing God now interacting with mankind
9:27	enlarge	prosper, add to his wealth
10:5	isles	distant lands, maritime nations, coastland
	Gentiles	non-Jewish people
	tongue	language, dialect, e.g Spanish, French
10:9	Lord	Jehovah; God in relationship to mankind
10:18	spread abroad	spread out, make bigger
10:25	earth divided	people became separated
10:31,32	after	according to
10:31	in	by
11:1	one speech	common language, all understood eachother
11:2	journeyed	traveled, went out
11:3	slime=mortar	sticky material that holds bricks together
11:3,4,7	Go to	come, ambition to glorify self over God
11:5+	Lord	Jehovah; God in relationship to mankind
11:6	restrained	held back, control, tame
11:7	confound	confuse, put to shame
11:9	Babel	Confusion
11:27	fathered, begat	made babies, had kids
11:28	before	in the presence of

GENESIS

	nativity	place of birth
11:30	barren	not able to have children
12:1+	Lord	Jehovah; God in relationship to mankind
12:1	kindred	relatives, family
12:5	substance	wealth, property, possessions, belongings, stuff
	souls	people, lives
	gotten	acquired
12:7	seed	offspring, children, heirs
12:8	pitched	set up, put up, made
	called upon	prayed to, invoked the Lord by name
12:9	sojourn	temporarily stay, visit
12:10	famine	time, period with food
	sojourn	temporarily stay, visit
	grievous	grief, sad, painful, hurtful
12:13	my soul	inner person, heart, emotions, feelings
12:14	beheld	saw, looked upon
12:15	Pharoah	head ruler of the Egyptians
	commended	praised, brag about
12:16	entreated	treated, dealt with
12:17	plagued	disease, sickness, disaster
13:1,3	south	Negev
13:4+	Lord	Jehovah; God in relationship to mankind
13:5	which	who
13:6	bear	support
	substance	property, possessions, belongings, stuff
13:7,8	strife	quarreling, fighting, tension
13:7	cattle	livestock
13:8	brethren	relatives, kin, family
13:10,11	plain	valley of Oak trees
13:15,16	seed	offspring, children, heirs
13:16	as dust of the earth	beyond number, a lot, a large amount
13:18	removed	moved, went away, left
	in the plain	by the oaks
14:3,8,10	vale	Valley, now covered by the Dead Sea
14:3	salt	Dead Sea
14:4	rebelled	disagreed, refused, fought against
14:5,7,15	smote	attacked, strike, hit, punish
14:9	with	against

GENESIS

14:10	slime	tar
14:11	victuals	food supply, flocks and herds
14:13	in the plain	by the oaks
	confederate	allies, friends, military/political partners
14:14,16	brother	nephew, close relative
14:14	pursued	went after, chased, followed
14:16,21	goods	possessions
14:17	dale	valley, low land
14:18	Salem	a.k.a. Jerusalem
14:18+	Most High God	El Elyon
14:20	tithes of all	ten percent of money or things
14:21	persons	people
14:22	lifted up my hand	pledged, vowed, promised, gave an oath
	Lord	Jehovah; God in relationship to mankind
14:23	shoe lace	sandal thong
14:24	save	except
15:1+	Lord	Jehovah; God in relationship to mankind
15:2+	Lord God	Jehovah Elohim, the self-existing God now interacting with mankind
15:2	go	remain
	steward	manager, personal assistant
15:3,5,13,18	seed	offspring, children, heirs
15:3	one born in my	one of my servants, slave
	house	temple, place of worship, religious building
15:4	bowels	body, your own body
15:5	tell the stars	count the stars
15:9	heifer	female cow
15:12	horror of darkness	nightmare, fear, scared
15:13	surety	to know, be sure, be certain
	stranger	temporary resident
	land	Egypt
15:14	substance	property, possessions, belongings, stuff
15:15	go to your fathers	die, end of life
15:16	here	to this place
	iniquity	sins, crime, evildoing, immorality
15:17	burning lamp	blazing torch
15:18	covenant	unconditional agreement, contract, promise
16:1	handmaid	slave girl

16:2	obtain	build a family through, have children
	hearkened	listen to, hearken, pay attention
16:4	despised	hated, rejected, disrespected
16:5+	Lord	Jehovah; God in relationship to mankind
16:6	hardly	harshly, cruelly
	face	presence
16:9,10,11	angel	messenger, supernatural being
16:9	submit	obey, listen, yield
16:11	affliction	sickness, disease
16:12	wild man	stubborn, unruly, lack self-control, impulsive
	dwell	live, encamp
16:13	God	El, Elohim; self-existing, Almighty
16:14	Beer-la-hai-roi	the living one who sees me
17:1	Almighty God	El Shaddai
	perfect	blameless, obedient
17:2+	covenant	unconditional agreement, contract, promise
17:2	multiply	increase
17:3+	God	El, Elohim; self-existing, Almighty
17:4	many	a multitude of, lots
17:6	exceeding	very, much, great
17:7,8,9,12	seed	offspring, children, heirs
17:8	stranger	temporary resident, country to which you have migrated, foreigner, exile
17:10	circumcision	medical surgery that cuts off skin that covers the tip or head of the penis; a religious act
17:11	foreskin	excess skin covering the tip or head of the penis
17:13	needs	necessarily, shall
17:17	fell upon his face	bowed down, worshipped out of respect, knelt
17:23,27	house	family
17:26	selfsame	same
18:1+	Lord	Jehovah; God in relationship to mankind
18:1	in the plains	by the oaks, strong trees
18:2	bowed	humbled, gracious greeting
18:3	pass not away	do not pass by, don't leave or go away
18:5	morsel	small piece of food, snack
	comfort	refresh and strengthen
18:6	hastened	hurried up, sped up, went faster
	knead	squeeze bread dough

GENESIS

	hearth	fireplace, an open oven e.g. like a pizza oven
18:7,8	dress, dressed	prepare, prepared
18:12	am waxed	have grown, worn out
	have pleasure	have enjoyable sex
18:13	Wherefore	why
18:15	Nay	no
18:19	household	family of descendants, posterity
18:20	grievous	burdensome, bad, grave
18:21	the cry of it	complaint, distressing cry
18:25	Judge	God, i.e. Jesus
18:27	dust and ashes	a simple, worthless man
18:28	peradventure	suppose. Guess, assume
18:33	communing	talking, deep conversation
19:1,15	angels	messengers, supernatural beings
19:1	at evening	in the evening, sundown, sunset
19:2	tarry	wait, delay, put off
19:3	pressed upon	urged them
	unleavened	yeast free
19:4	compassed	go about, surround, encamp, encircle
	quarter	area, districts, parts of the city
19:5,8	know, known	sexually, homosexual conduct, rape, abuse
19:8	shadow	protection
19:9	sojourn	temporarily stay, visit
	needs	necessarily
	sore	hard, harsh, difficult
19:10	shut to	securely shut
19:11	smote	struck, defeated, killed
	wearied	tired out, frustrated, annoyed
19:13	waxed	has become
19:13+	Lord	Jehovah; God in relationship to mankind
19:14	mocked	joked, ridiculed
19:15	hastened	hurried up, sped up, went faster
	consumed	waste away, dried up, spent, used up, engulfed
	iniquity	sins, crime, evildoing, immorality
19:16	lingered	wait, delay, put off
	grace in our sight	acceptance, grace, mercy
	magnified	honored, made important, exalted
19:20	soul shall live	life shall be spared

GENESIS

19:21	overthrow	defeat, beat, destroy
19:22	haste	hurry up, speed up, go faster
19:24	brimstone	God's judgment/anger, sulphur (matchstick)
19:25	overthrew	defeat, beat, destroy
19:26	pillar of salt	judgment and warning, post, large pile of salt
19:29	God	El, Elohim; self-existing, Almighty
19:32,34	seed	offspring, children, heirs
19:33	perceived	knew, recognized, understood
19:34	morrow	tomorrow, next day
20:1	sojourned	temporarily stay, visit
20:3+	God	El, Elohim; self-existing, Almighty
20:3	a man's wife	married, belongs to another
20:4+	Lord	Jehovah; God in relationship to mankind
20:5	innocency	not guilty, not responsible, not at fault
20:6	integrity	honesty, innocence, goodness
	sinning against Me	commit a sin
20:8	sore	greatly, exceedingly
20:9	offended	sin, done wrong, hurt someone
20:10	saw you	encountered, what was your purpose
20:11	fear	revered, respected, trembled, dread
20:16	covering of the eyes	veil, protection, glory
	reproved	rebuke, correct, chasten, punish, warn
20:18	closed up wombs	not able to have children
21:1	Lord	Jehovah; God in relationship to mankind
21:2+	God	El, Elohim; self-existing, Almighty
21:7	given children suck	nursed children, breast-fed
21:8	weaned	grown up, no longer breast-fed
21:9	mocking	ridiculing, teasing
21:10	bondwoman	female slave, a companion that is not a wife nor a prostitute
21:12	hearken	listen, grant all that she asks
21:12,13	seed	offspring, children, heirs
21:15	spent	used up, gone
	cast	placed, laid
21:16	bowshot	a long distance away, out of sight
21:17	ails	troubles, bothers, irritates
	angel	messenger, supernatural being
21:23	deal falsely	cheat, trick, not be honest

GENESIS

21:25	reproved	corrected, scold, got them in trouble
21:26	wot not	know not
21:27,32	covenant	unconditional agreement, contract, promise
21:33	grove	a group of trees, an orchard
21:33	Everlasting God	El Olam
22:1+	God	El, Elohim; self-existing, Almighty
22:1	tempt	tried, tested, searched, examined, known
22:2	offer	present, sacrifice
22:3	clave	split
22:5	yonder	over there, another location
22:11	angel	messenger, supernatural being
22:11+	Lord	Jehovah; God in relationship to mankind
22:12	fear	revered, respected, trembled, dread
22:13	thicket	a thick group of bushes, undergrowth
22:14	Je-ho'vah-ji'reh	Jehovah, the Lord will provide
22:16	Myself	Lord, God
22:17,18	seed	offspring, children, heirs
22:17	possess	own, control, master
	gate	entrance, position of administration
22:18	nations	people, groups, descendants
22:24	concubine	a sexual partner that is not a wife nor a prostitute
23:2	mourn	cry, be sad about, depressed
23:4	sojourner	temporarily stay, visitor
23:6	mighty prince	prince of God
	sepulchers	tombs, burial sites
23:8	entreat	plead, beg, to sincerely request
23:10,13,16	audience	hearing, gathering, crowd
23:11	Nay	No
23:15,16	hearken	listen, pay attention
23:16	current rent money	land/deed money, purchase price
23:17,20	made sure	deeded over
24:1	well stricken	far advanced in years
24:1+	Lord	Jehovah; God in relationship to mankind
24:3,8,37	swear	promise under oath, vow
24:3	God	El, Elohim; self-existing, Almighty
24:5	needs	necessarily
24:7+	Lord God	Jehovah Elohim, the self-existing God now interacting with mankind

GENESIS

24:8	oath	pledge, promise, give one's word
24:12	send me good speed	grant me success
24:7,60	seed	offspring, children, heirs
24:7,40	angel	messenger, supernatural being
24:8	oath	sworn promise
24:11	draw water	fill buckets of water from the well/fountain
24:12	send me good speed	grant me success, prosper the way before me
24:14+	damsel	young girl, virgin
24:14	let down…pitcher	a person would come to a well, which was a deep hole in the ground with water, and would either get their own water or sometimes an employee of the well would fill it for them (for money or a favor)
24:16	known	had relations with her
24:20	hasted	hurried
24:21	held his peace	kept quiet, watched her
	wit	see
	prosperous	successful, wealthy
24:24,32	provender	feed, straw and fodder
24:27	left destitute	forsaken, broke, ghetto
24:32	ungirded	unloaded, unpacked
24:33	meat	food
	errand	job, task, assignment, chore
24:38,20	house	family
24:38,40,41	kindred	relatives
24:41	clear	free, absolved
24:53	raiment	clothing
24:56	Hinder me not	don't detain me, stop me or get in the way
24:57	inquire at her mouth	consult her wishes
24:60	possess the gate of	be victorious over, inherit the cities
	seed possess the gate	descendants be victorious; ownership, ruler
24:63	meditate	think deeply, pray, focus attention
24:64	lighted off	dismounted, got off
24:65	veil/vail	scarf, piece of material that covered the head and most of the face
25:1	took a wife	choose, pick up, buy, get
25:6	concubines	secondary wives, sexual partner not a wife or prostitute

GENESIS

25:7	threescore	sixty (a score equals 20, 3x20)
25:8	gave up the ghost	died, quit breathing, not alive
25:11	God	El, Elohim; self-existing, Almighty
25:12,19	generations	descendants, offspring, children
25:16	castles	walled camps, encampments, settlements
25:21	barren	not able to have children
25:21	entreated	pleaded with, prayed earnestly
25:21+	Lord	Jehovah; God in relationship to mankind
25:23	Two nations	two families, 2 rival peoples (Esau and Jacob)
	bowels	body, womb
25:26	threescore	60 (3 x 20)
25:27	cunning	skillful, an expert, experienced
25:28	venison	wild animal meat e.g. deer, antelope
25:29	sod pottage	cooked lentil stew
25:30	pottage	stew, red soup
25:32	at the point	about
25:33	swear	pledged, vowed, promised, gave an oath
25:33,34	birthright	first born privileges, inheritance
26:2+	Lord	Jehovah; God in relationship to mankind
26:3	sojourn	temporarily stay, visit
	oath	pledge, pact
26:3,4,24	seed	offspring, children, heirs
26:8	sporting with	caressing, fondling, showing endearment to
26:9	of a surety	certainly, clearly
26:10	lien, lain	have sex with
	guiltiness	sin, trouble, punishment
26:11	charged	warned
26:12	sowed	planted seeds, invested
	received	reaped
26:13	waxed	became, grew
26:14	great store	a great number
	envied	jealous, greedy, wanting
26:17	pitched his tent	camped, set up, established
26:19	springing	flowing, well, running, artesian well
26:20	did strive	quarreled, struggled, contention, argument
26:20,21,22	strove	struggled, quarreled, disputed
26:24	God	El, Elohim; self-existing, Almighty

GENESIS

26:27	wherefore	why
	hate	despise
26:28	certainly	plainly, definitely, without a doubt
	oath	pledge, pact
	covenant	unconditional agreement, contract, promise
26:29	hurt	harm, injure, damage
26:31	betimes	early
	swore	exchanged oaths, pact
26:35	were a	brought
27:1	eyes were dim	growing old, eyesight failing (possibly having cataracts)
27:2	take	get
27:4+	savory	tasty, likable
27:3	quiver	shoulder-held arrow holder
27:4	savory	spicy, full-flavored, salty
27:4,25	soul	inner person, emotion, life-force, being, life
27:7+	Lord	Jehovah; God in relationship to mankind
27:12	deceiver	liar, dishonest person, false
27:15,27	raiment	clothing
27:19	bid	asked
27:20+	God	El, Elohim; self-existing, Almighty
27:28	dew of heaven	mist, early morning moisture, fog
	fatness	richness, the best
27:30	scarce gone	just left, recently gone
27:33	taken	hunted, brought
27:36	supplanted	cheated, tricked, beat out of deal
27:37	sustained	supplied, fed, strenghtened
27:40	yoke	harness, farm tool that attached to the neck/shoulder of an animal used to pull things
27:41	hated	held a grudge, purposed evil
27:42	touching	concerning, regarding
27:43	obey my voice	do what I say, comply with command
27:43	flee	run, escape, get away
27:44	tarry	stay, wait
27:45	deprived	bereaved, lose, dead
28:1,6	charge	command, order
28:3	God Almighty	El Shaddai
28:4	a stranger	foreigner, visitor, guest

GENESIS

28:4+	God	El, Elohim; self-existing, Almighty
28:8	pleased	happy, glad, excited
28:9	to	in addition to
28:11	lighted upon	came to
28:12	ladder	stairway
	angel	messenger, supernatural being
28:13+	Lord	Jehovah; God in relationship to mankind
28:13	Lord God	Jehovah Elohim, the self-existing God now interacting with mankind
28:13,14	seed	offspring, children, heirs
28:15	keep	watch over
28:17	dreadful place	awesome holy place
28:17,22	house	temple, holy place
28:17	gate	main door, the place to enter a house or town
28:19	Beth'-el	house of God
28:20	raiment	clothing
28:22	tenth	tithe, 10%
29:3	mouth	opening
29:7	high day	early in the day
29:13	embraced	hugged, greeted
	tidings	news, report, update
29:15	wages	paycheck, money
29:17	tender eyed	weak, unattractive
	well favored	loved, honored, respected
29:21	days are fulfilled	job finished, work done, contract fulfilled
	go in to her	have sex, lie with her, slept with, cohabitated
29:23	came to pass	happened, fulfilled, occurred
29:24	handmaid	a female servant, personal assistant
29:25	beguiled	deceived, cheated, duped
29:26	It must not be done	i.e. it is not the practice
29:27	fulfill her week	be newlyweds, have sexual relations on a regular basis for a week
29:31+	Lord	Jehovah; God in relationship to mankind
29:31	opened her womb	enabled her to have children
29:33	hated	heard, despised, unloved, slighted
29:34	joined	attached, closely united, knit, bound
29:35	left	stopped
30:2	kindled	started, began, aroused

GENESIS

	in God's stead	in the place of God
30:3	bear upon my knees	when the child is being delivered/born it will be immediately placed in her lap as if it were hers
30:6+	God	El, Elohim; self-existing, Almighty
30:6	Dan	Judge
30:8	wrestlings	struggle, concern, worry
30:11	Gad	Troop
30:13	Ash'er	Divinely favored, "Happy"
30:14,15,16	mandrakes	herb causing sexual desire (like Viagra)
30:17,22	hearkened	listen to, hearken, pay attention
30:18,32,33	hire	wages, reward
30:20	endued	given, supplied, awarded
	dowry	money, goods given by the brides family to the groom's (husband) family
30:21	daughter	offspring, fruit/by-product of behaviors
30:24+	Lord	Jehovah; God in relationship to mankind
30:28	Appoint	name
30:33	time to come	the future, later
30:37	strakes	streaks, stripes
30:39,40	ringstraked	striped, streaked
30:40	cattle	animals, cows
30:42	feeble	weak, not strong, sickly
31:1	glory	abundance, wealth
31:2	toward	friendly to
31:3	Lord	Jehovah; God in relationship to mankind
31:5+	God	El, Elohim; self-existing, Almighty
31:6	power	strength, best of my ability
31:8,9,12	ringstraked	striped
31:8	hire	wages, pay
31:10	grisled	spotted
31:11	angel	messenger, supernatural being
31:13	vowed a vow	made a pledge, promised, oath
31:15	devoured	consumed, spent
31:19,34,35	images	household idols, items worshiped as gods
31:20	unawares	by surprise, off guard, suddenly
31:25	pitched	camped, set up, established
31:27	steal	sneak
	mirth	laughter, joy, glad

GENESIS

	tabret	tambourine, a small hand-drum
31:29	hurt	harm, punish
31:30	needs	necessarily, require
	sore	greatly homesick, miss alot
	wherefore	why
31:32	discern you	point out, make search
31:34	furniture	saddle, camel cushion
31:35	custom of women	period, menstrual cycle
31:36	chode	contended, reprimanded, find fault, argued
	hotly	quickly, aggressively, fast
31:37	stuff	goods, possessions
31:38	ewes	female sheep
31:39	torn of beasts	attacked by wild animals
31:40	drought	heat, lack of water
	sleep departed	sleepless, unable to sleep
31:42	with	for
31:42	rebuked	corrected, criticized, yelled at
31:44	covenant	unconditional agreement, contract, peace pact
31:46,48,51	heap	pile, mound
31:50	afflict	mistreat, are harsh to
31:53	swore	pledged, vowed, promised, gave an oath
	sware by the fear	promised solemnly
32:1	angels	messenger, supernatural being
32:1+	God	El, Elohim; self-existing, Almighty
32:2	host	group, crowd, gathering, army
32:4	lord	master, ruler, boss
	sojourned	lived some time, visit, temporarily dwell
32:5	tell	inform, sent message
32:8,11	smite	attacked, strike, hit, punish
32:9	Lord	Jehovah; God in relationship to mankind
32:10	bands	companies, camps, armies
32:12	seed	offspring, children, heirs
32:15	milk	nursing, females
32:16	drove	herd, group
32:20	appease	make happy, satisfy, please
	accept	receive me kindly, show me favor
32:24	wrestled a man	struggled, fought, held on to

	day	dawn
32:28	Is'ra-el	name changed, Jacob to Israel
	Prevailed	overcome
32:31	halted	limped
33:3	bowed	showing respect, went down on his face
33:11	dealt graciously	treated nicely, kindly or generous
	urged	cheered, supported, encouraged
33:5+	God	El, Elohim; self-existing, Almighty
33:8,10	grace	favor
33:13,14,15	lord	master, referring to Esau
33:13	tender	weak, frail
	overdrive	overwork, make walk too much
33:14	softly	gently, leisurely, slowly
33:17	booths	temporary shelters
33:20	erected	construct, build, set up
34:2,5	defiled	violated, raped, dishonored
34:3,8	soul	inner person, emotion, life-force, being, life
34:3	clung	was drawn, attracted, attached
34:3,4,12	damsel	young woman
34:5	held his peace	remained silent, said nothing, took no action
34:6	commune	spoke, talked with, discussed
34:7	grieved	painfully displeased, outraged, wounded
	wrought folly	done a disgraceful thing, committed an outrage
34:12	dowry	in old times, man paid pledge to bride, therefore girls had much jewelry. In other cases, the girl's family paid her husband.
34:15	consent	agree to, okay, say yes to
34:17,24	hearken	listen, pay attention, heed
34:19	deferred	preferred, delayed
34:21	peaceable	friends, not a threat, not at war
34:22	herein	on this condition
34:25	slew	killed, slaughtered, massacred
34:27,29	spoiled	looted, plundered
34:30	troubled	ruined, embarrassed, disgraced, shamed
	to stink	odious, given me a bad name
	house	family
34:31	deal…as a harlot	abuse, misuse, treat like a prostitute

GENESIS

35:1+	God	El, Elohim; self-existing, Almighty
35:1,15,16	Beth'-el	House of God
35:4	strange gods	foreign, false, heathen/pagan
35:7	El'Bethel	the God of Bethel
35:8	Al'lon-bach'uth	Oak of Weeping
35:11	God Almighty	El Shaddai
	out of your loins	come from you, be your offspring, children
35:12	seed	offspring, children, heirs
35:16	travailed	labor, pain in child birth, struggled
35:18	soul	inner person, emotion, life-force, being, life
	Ben'ja-min	Son of the Right Hand
35:22	concubine	a sexual partner that is not a wife nor a prostitute
35:29	gathered to…people	memorial service, gather to honor and remember
36:7	bear	sustain, support
36:24	mules	water springs, oasis
35:34	stead	in place of, substitute, replace
36:43	habitations	homes, cities, where they come from
37:2	evil	bad, untrue, harmful
37:4,8	hatred	despised
37:4	peaceably	be friendly, not threatening, not warlike
37:7	sheaves	bundle, stack, group of wheat plants
37:8	dominion	rule, lord over
37:9	made obeisance	bowed down in homage, reverence, respect
37:11	envied	jealous, greedy, wanting
	observed	remembered, pondered over
37:14	vale	valley
37:18	conspired	scheme, provoke, work together against
37:22	rid	rescue
37:25	bread	a meal, snack
37:26	conceal	hide, cover up, stash
37:27	were content	agreed, satisfied
37:28	merchantmen	businessmen, shop owners
37:29,33,34	rent	tore as an act of grief
37:30	child	boy
37:32	no	not
38:24	whoredom	illegallon sex outside of marriage, immoral, prostitution or worse; also describes unfaithfulness to God/His rules (sin)

GENESIS

38:7+	Lord	Jehovah; God in relationship to mankind
38:7	wicked	evil, offensive
	slew him	took his life, killed
38:8,9	seed	offspring, children, heirs
38:9	spilled	ejaculated, sexually climaxed
	it	male sperm
38:15	harlot	hooker, prostitute, call girl
38:16	Go to	Come now
	come in to me	Intercourse, have sex with
38:24	whoredom	illegallon sex outside of marriage, immoral, prostitution or worse; also describes unfaithfulness to God/His rules (sin)
38:18,25	signet	sealing-ring, ring bearing seal with which official documents were stamped
38:28	travailed	gave birth
39:2+	Lord	Jehovah; God in relationship to mankind
39:4	overseer	boss, head man, top authority
39:9	God	El, Elohim; self-existing, Almighty
39:10	hearkened	listen, pay attention, heed
39:13	fled forth	ran away, escaped, got away
39:15	lifted up	raised, shouted
39:19	kindled	started, began, aroused
40:1,7	lord	master, ruler, boss
40:3,4,7	ward	confinement, in custody
40:3	bound	imprisoned, confined
40:7	Wherefore	why
40:8	interpreter	tell the meaning of something
40:14	think on house	remember, keep me in mind
40:17	bakemeats	baked goods
41:1,2,3	river	i.e. Nile
41:3+	ill favored	ugly
41:4	lean fleshed	skinny, thin, unhealthy looking
41:5,7	rank	plump, large, full, healthy
41:6	blasted	damaged, blasted
41:6	sprung up	arose, came after, blew in
41:10	ward	confinement, in custody
41:14	hastily	hurried, speedy, fast, quickly
	raiment	clothes

GENESIS

41:16+	God	El, Elohim; self-existing, Almighty
41:19	badness	ugliness
41:24	devoured	ate up, consumed, destroyed
41:23,27	blasted	scorched
41:32	doubled	repeated
	established	determined, has decreed
41:33	discreet	discerning, intelligent, shrewd
41:34	officers	commissioners, overseers
	plenteous	a lot, extra, a whole bunch
41:39	discreet	careful, crafty, shrewd, trustworthy
41:40	over	in charge of
	word	command
41:42	vestures	garments
41:42	arrayed	clothed, dressed, put on
41:43	bowed the knee	worship, reverence, pay respect to
41:44	you	your permission
	without you	without your permission
41:46	stood before	entered the service of
41:47	by handfuls	abundantly, plenty, in excess
41:51	toil	work, labor, put effort into
41:49,57	corn	grain
41:54	dearth	famine
41:56	waxed sore	grew severe, worsened
41:57	so sore	severe, bad, aweful
42:1+	corn	grain
42:7	strange	as a stranger
42:9,12	nakedness	unprotected parts, weak points
42:17	ward	confinement
42:18	fear	revered, respected, trembled, dread
42:18+	God	El, Elohim; self-existing, Almighty
42:21	verily	surely, truly, honestly, yes, correct
	anguish	grief, heartache, misery
	besought	asked, pleaded, begged
42:22	child	boy
42:24	communed	spoke, talked with, discussed
42:26	laded	loaded
42:27	provender	fodder, food for animals
	espied	saw

GENESIS

42:28	lo	behold
42:30,33	lord	head man, boss, ruler
42:30	roughly	harshly
42:34	traffic	trade, do business
42:36	bereaved	sorrowful, troubled, mournful
42:38	mischief	harm, trouble
42:38	grey hairs to grave	broken heart, die of sadness, heart-attack
43:1	sore	severe, fierce, grievous
43:2	corn	grain
43:3	solemnly	serious, not joking, sincerely
	protest	warn, threaten
43:6	wherefore	why
43:7	straitly	particularly, strictly, specifically
	tenor	general idea
43:9	surety	guarantee, replacement
43:11	balm	medicinal cream, lotion
43:14	God Almighty	El Shaddai
43:14	bereaved	sorrowful, troubled, mournful
43:16	slay	kill an animal
43:18	bondmen	slaves, servants
43:19	communed	spoke, talked with, discussed
43:23+	God	El, Elohim; self-existing, Almighty
43:24	provender	fodder, food for animals
43:28	made obeisance	paid him honor, bowed in respect
43:30	bowels	heart, emotions, feelings
43:31	refrained	hold back, resist, stop from doing
43:32	set on for	served
	an abomination	loathsome, pollution, disgrace
43:33	birthright	rights by birth
43:33	marveled	act surprised, be amazed, shocked
43:34	messes	portions, meals, servings of food
44:4,7	Wherefore	why
44:4	rewarded	repaid
44:5	divineth	foretells the future, makes predictions
44:7+	God	El, Elohim; self-existing, Almighty
44:8,9,24,33	lord	master, boss, ruler
44:12	left	ended
44:13	rent	tear, ripped, shred, pull apart, open

GENESIS

44:15	divine	foretell the future, predict
44:29	grey hairs to grave	broken heart, die of sadness, heart-attack
44:32	surety	guarantee, deposit
44:33	abide	dwell, live, stay, make a home
	bondman	slave
44:34	evil	misery, harm, ill effect
	come on	overtake
45:5	grieved	distressed, upset
45:5+	God	El, Elohim; self-existing, Almighty
45:6	earing	plowing
45:7	posterity	children, future generations, offspring
45:8,9	lord	master, boss, ruler
45:9	tarry	delay, stay longer, wait
45:11	poverty	become poor, bankrupt, broke
45:16	fame	news, report
45:21	provision	food and supplies, stocked them up
45:22	raiment	garments, clothes
45:23	laden	loaded, packed up
	corn	grain
	meat	food
45:24	fall not out by	quarrel not on, have no argument
45:27	spirit	hope, energy, enthusiasm
46:1+	God	El, Elohim; self-existing, Almighty
46:4	put his hand upon your eyes	be with you when you die
46:6,7	seed	offspring, children, heirs
46:15+	souls	persons, people, living beings
46:26	loins	reproductive organs, sex parts
46:27	threescore and ten	70 (3 x 20 + 10)
46:29	made ready	prepared
46:31	Pharaoh	a title given to the rulers of Egypt
46:34	an abomination	loathsome, despised, hated, detestable to God
47:4	sojourn	temporarily stay, visit, live
47:4,13	sore	severe, harsh, bad
47:6	men of activity	capable men, competent men
47:9	pilgrimage	life journey, lifetime
	days…few and evil	lived hard times, life hasn't been easy
47:14	corn	grain

GENESIS

47:15,17,19	bread	provisions, food, grain
47:18	lord	master, boss, ruler
	not ought	nothing
47:19	Wherefore	why
	desolate	destroyed, ruined, empty
47:31	swear, swore	pledged, vowed, promised, gave an oath
48:2	strengthened	raised up, picked up, revived
48:3	God Almighty	El Shaddai
48:4,11,19	seed	offspring, children, heirs
48:6	issue	offspring, children, offspring
48:11+	God	El, Elohim; self-existing, Almighty
48:14	guiding	crossing
	wittingly	intentionally, on purpose
48:16	Angel	messenger, supernatural being
48:19	become a people	multiply in number, a big tribe
49:2	hearken	listen, pay attention, heed
49:3	beginning	first fruit, start
49:3	dignity	pride, self-respect, poise
49:4	my couch	bed, bedroom
49:5	their habitations	weapons of violence
49:6	dug down a wall	destruction, ruined
49:8	the neck	control over
49:9	whelp	cub, baby lion, young, small prince
49:10	scepter	rod-staff-stick that symbolized power/authority
	from between his feet	descendants
	Shil'loh come	Jesus Christ
	gathering	obedience, respect
49:13	haven	safe port/harbor
49:14	couching down	weighted, burdened, struggling under
	burdens	packages, load, sacks of stuff
49:15	bowed his shoulder	worked hard, labored, not afraid to work
49:17	adder	poisonous snake
49:20	dainties	expensive, exotic foods, fancy foods
49:22	bough	tree branch, limb, long twig
49:23	archers	enemies
	sorely grieved	badly hurt, injured
	hated	despised, detested, loathed
49:24+	God	El, Elohim; self-existing, Almighty

GENESIS

49:24	shepherd	leaders, caretaker
	stone	rock, strength
49:25	blessings	fortunes, luck, wealth, good things
49:26	progenitors	ancestors, forefathers, family line
	everlasting hills	very old, ancient, been around a long time
49:27	raven	greedily devour, eat up, consume
49:33	yielded up the ghost	expired, died, quit breathing
50:3	mourned	wept, cried
	threescore and ten	70
50:5,6	swear	pledged, vowed, promised, gave an oath
50:10	threshing-floor	work area where the shells/skin were beaten/broken off wheat, barley grain
	lamentation	cry, be sad about, agonize
	sore	great, badly, aweful
50:11	grievous	painful, great, severe
50:15	hate	abhor, despise, loathe, detest, loathe
	requite us	pay us back in full, avenge
50:18+	God	El, Elohim; self-existing, Almighty
50:21	nourish	provide for, take care of

EXODUS

1:5	souls	people, individuals, living beings
1:7,20	waxed	grew, increased
1:10	there falls out	occurs, happens, arises
1:11	taskmasters	boss, ruler, master, foreman
1:13,14	rigor	harshness, severely
	serve with rigor	work under cruel circumstances
1:14	bondage	slavery, captivity, prisoner
1:16	stools	childbirth seats
1:17,21	feared	revered, stood in awe, submissive obedience
1:20	midwives	women that assisted in the delivery and birth of children
1:21	houses	families, households
2:3	took	made, tar, calked it
	slime and pitch	clay and tar
	bullrushes	reeds, willows, water plants
	daubed	coated, smeared, brushed on
2:3,5	flags	reeds, tall water plants
2:4	to wit	to know, understand
2:11	spied	saw, beheld, observed
2:11,13	smiting, smite	attacked, strike, hit, punish
2:13	strove	struggled, quarreled
2:15	face	presence, proximity, location
2:23	sighed	groaning, sadness, despair, emotional pain
	bondage	slavery, severe oppression
2:24	covenant	unconditional agreement, contract, promise
2:25	had respect to	paid attention, noticed and was concerned about
3:2	consumed	vanish, waste away, dried up, spent, used up
3:5	holy ground	sacred, special, respected
3:7,17	affliction	misery, distress, oppression
3:7	sorrows	pains, sufferings, grief
3:9	oppression	abusive, controlling, harsh, cruel
3:12	token	sign, evidence, proof
	this mountain	Sinai
3:18	hearken	listen, believe, obey
	beseech	beg, plead, ask

EXODUS

3:19	mighty hand	strong, powerful, skillful
3:20	smite	attacked, strike, hit, punish
3:22	sojourns	lives, temporary stay
	spoil	take the wealth of, plunder, goods
4:1,8,9	hearken	listen, heed, obey
4:6	bosom	chest, breast, inside robes, under shirt/coat
4:6	leprous	skin disease (flesh rotted)
4:10	heretofore	before, earlier, at times past
	eloquent	good speaker, clear speech
4:10	of a slow tongue	not eloquent, speech impediment (stutter?)
4:11	dumb	mute, unable to speak
4:13	him whom You will send	some other person, another
4:16	instead of	spokesman, representative
4:21	wonders	miracles, marvels
	pestilence	disease, fungus, mildew, disaster, crop failure
5:4,14,15,22	Wherefore	why
5:7,8	heretofore	previously
5:8,18	tale	number, amount, quota
5:8	idle	lazy, slow, worthless, slacker
5:9	vain	false, deceitful, worthless
5:11,19	diminished	reduced, reduce, lessened
5:13	hasted	pressed, harassed
5:18	tale	number
5:19	evil case	bad off, not in a good position, trouble
5:21	our savor to be abhorred	offensive, loathsome
5:22	evil entreated	brought harm to, afflicted
6:4,5	covenant	unconditional agreement, contract, promise
6:6	with a stretched out arm	powerfully, forcefully, vigorous action
6:8	swear	pledged, vowed, promised, gave an oath
6:9,12	hearkened	listen to, hearken, pay attention
6:9	anguish	impatience, distress, misery
6:12,30	uncircumcised lips	unclean, unworthy, impure
6:13	charge	command, commission
6:26	armies	masses of soldiers, ranks, troops
7:4,13	hearken	listen, pay attention, heed

EXODUS

7:4	armies	masses of soldiers, ranks, troops
7:11	enchantments	deception, spell, witchcraft
7:15	against he come	to meet him
7:18	loathe	be grieved, disgusted
7:19	vessels	cups, bowls, vase, holder
7:22	enchantments	secret arts, witchcraft
7:23	neither did he set his heart to do this also	no concern even for this, paid no attention
8:2	smite	strike, i.e. bring upon a plague
8:3	troughs	bowls, vessels, basins
8:9	glory over me	the honor is yours to tell me
8:15	respite	relief, an interval of delay
8:17,18	lice	gnats, sand fleas
8:18	enchantments	secret arts, witchcraft
8:19	hearkened	listen to, hearken, pay attention
8:22	sever	separate, set apart
8:23	put a division	establish a redemptions
8:26	meet	fitting, proper, acceptable
	abomination	detestable things, filthy, unclean
8:28,29,30	entreat	intercede, plead, pray fervently
9:3	grievous murrain	severe pestilence, great plague
9:4	sever	make a distinction, set apart
9:7	sent	inquired, asked for a report
9:9,10	blains	blisters, boils, i.e. sores, ulcers
9:12	hearkened	listen, pay attention, heed
9:18	grievous	heavy, severe
9:20,30	feared	revered, stood in awe of, submissive obedience
9:24	mingled	flashing continually, darting in between
9:25	smote	struck, laid in ruins
9:28	Entreat	pray to, beseech, intercede
9:31	in the ear	ripening
	bolled	in bud, in bloom
10:5	residue	what's left over, excess, surplus
10:7	be a snare to	bring us trouble, endanger, menace
10:14	coasts	territories, borders, natural boundaries
	grievous	numerous, many, overbearing
10:15	herbs	plants
10:18	entreated	pleaded with, begged, asked

EXODUS

10:19	coasts	territory, boundary, border
10:28	heed	listen to, obey, pay attention to
11:2	borrow	ask, claim, accept
11:3	favor in the sight	approval, respect, mercy
11:3	great	esteemed, well honored
11:5	mill	stones used to grind grain (wheat, etc.)
12:3	congregation	group of people, gathering, crowd
12:4	souls	persons, individuals, living beings
12:7	upper door post	lintel, over the door
12:8	unleavened	yeast-free (Uncontaminated), illustrates the absence of evil
12:9	sodden	boiled, cooked
	purtenance	entrails, inner organs of an animal
12:11	loins girded	prepared, dressed for a journey
	passover	an event where God's angel of death would "Passover" any person/house marked by blood
12:13	token	sign, badge, mark, proof
12:14	feast	ceremony, memorial
	ordinance	rule, statute, important tradition
12:15,17,18,39	unleavened	yeast-free
12:15+	leavened	yeast, a symbol of corruption and evil
12:15	cut off	outlawed, eliminated, perish
12:16	convocation	holy assembly, gathering
12:17,51	armies	masses of soldiers, ranks, troops
12:22	hyssop	a common weed/plant
12:22	lintel	upper door post, crosspiece at the top of the door
12:32	bless	pray for, doing a favor
12:35	borrowed	asked
12:36	spoiled	took away the valuables of, plundered
12:39	victual	provisions, food
12:49	homeborn	someone born in Israel
12:48,49	sojourn	temporarily stay, visit, live
13:2	sanctify	dedicate, consecrate, set apart for God
	openeth the womb	the first child born
13:3	bondage	slavery, prison
13:3,7	leavened	yeast-containing
13:6,7	unleavened	yeast-free
13:7	leaven	yeast, a symbol of corruption and evil

EXODUS

13:8	show	tell, explain
13:10	ordinance	rule, authoritative law
13:12	matrix	womb
13:12,13	firstling	firstborn
13:13,15	redeem	spare by offering a substitute, reclaim, restore, deliver from sin and its consequences
13:16	token	sign, pledge, testimony, mark
	frontlets	a type of forehead ornament, pendant, symbol, memorial symbol
13:18	up harnessed	armed, equipped, in military order
13:19	straitly sworn	solemnly placed under an oath
	visit	take care of, remember, come to
13:20	encamped	surrounded, circled, set up a perimeter
13:21	pillar of a cloud	a smoky, dusty whirlwind (tornado)
13:21	pillar of fire	a fiery whirlwind (tornado)
14:2	encamp	camp
14:6	made ready	prepared, yoked, hitched
14:8	high hand	boldly, defiantly, proudly
14:9	encamping	camping
14:10	sore	very, greatly
14:13	salvation	deliverance, victory
14:14	hold our peace	be silent, remain quiet
14:15	Wherefore	why
14:17	get me honor upon	my honor and authority will be sustained
14:24	troubled	confused, caused panic, panicked
14:27	returned to his strength	flowed back, turned back, normal depth
	overthrew	defeated, beat, destroyed
14:31	feared	revered, respected, trembled, dread
15:1	triumphed	won, beat, were victorious, defeated
15:7	consumed	vanish, waste away, dried up, spent, used up
15:8	congealed	thickened, became solid
15:14	sorrow	anguish
	Palestina	Philistia, land of the Philistines (Palestine was the name the Romans gave to Israel in the Second century AD)
15:24	murmured	complain, fuss, whine, grumble
15:25	statute	law, rule, commands, decrees, directives

EXODUS

15:26	Lord that heals	Jehovah Rophi
16:2	murmured	grumbled, complained, criticized
16:4	prove	tried, tested, searched, examined, known
16:7,8,9,12	murmurings	grumbling, complaints
16:14	hoar	white, old age, ancient
16:15	manna	edible substance provided by God, white, and flaky, with the taste of honey
16:18	mete	measure, count
16:21	waxed	grew, became
16:23+	Sabbath	rest day, 7th day consecrated to the Lord
16:28	keep	obey, follow, do, practice
16:36	ephah	a measurement for dry items (flour etc.)
17:1	pitched	camped, put up tents, encamped
17:2	chide	quarrel, find fault
	tempt	test, challenge
17:3	murmured	grumbled, complained
	Wherefore	why
17:5	smote	attacked, strike, hit, punish
17:7	chiding	scold, rebuke, correct
17:11	prevailed	was victorious, won
17:12	stayed up	supported, held up
17:13	discomfited	disabled, i.e. routed, weakened, defeated
17:15	Je-ho'vah-nis'si	The Lord is my banner (symbol, family crest)
18:3	alien	foreigner, outsider, visitor
18:7	did obeisance	bowed down, greeted, treated respectfully
18:8	travail	hardship, weariness, distress, trouble
18:14	yourself	alone as judge
18:19,26	causes	disputes
18:21	fear	revered, respected, trembled, dread
	covetousness	envious, greedy, wants what others have, lust
18:22	seasons	times
18:26	causes	disputes, questions
19:4	bore	carried, taken you up
19:5	covenant	unconditional agreement, contract, promise
	peculiar	special, unique, chosen
19:7	laid	set, placed, presented
19:10+	sanctify	consecrate, set apart to serve God
19:17	nether	bottom, base, lower

EXODUS

19:19	waxed	grew, became
19:21	charge	warn, admonish
20:2	bondage	slavery, servitude
20:4	graven	molded, carved, sculptured
20:5	down yourself	worship, pay homage
	visiting the iniquity	bringing punishment, suffering, or judgment
	hate	abhor, despise, loathe, detest
20:7	vain	empty, shallow, proud
20:10,11	sabbath	rest, 7th day consecrated to the Lord
20:13	kill	murder, kill, end a life
20:14	adultery	a married person that has sex with someone beside their partner
20:16	witness	accuse, blame, charge
20:17	covet	envy, greed, lust, wanting what is not yours
20:18	removed	moved away, fell back, trembled
20:20	fear	revered, respected, trembled, dread, submission
20:24	record	put, mention
20:25	hewn	cut by man, dressed, cut
21:5	free	as a free man, take leave
21:6	aul, awl	ice pick, sharp metal rod
21:8	strange	foreign, outsiders
21:9	betrothed	engaged, soon to be married
21:14	presumptuously	willfully, boldly, arrogantly, overconfidently
	guile	deceit, craftily, treacherously
21:15,26,27	smites	strikes, kills
21:16,20	steals	kidnaps, abducts
21:18	strive	fight, struggle, work hard at
21:18	keepeth his bed	is badly injured, bedridden
21:19	smote	attacked, strike, hit, punish
	be quit	go unpunished, be let off
21:22	her fruit depart from her	she suffers a miscarriage, the child is stillborn
21:22	lay upon	judgment, penalty, restitution
21:22,23	mischief	further injury, damage
21:26	perish	lost, badly damaged, destroyed
21:28	gore	poked with horns
	quit	free or clear of blame, guiltless
21:29	were wont	accustomed (as a habit), has tried before

EXODUS

	stoned	killed by being hit with rocks
21:30	laid	placed, put on
21:34	make it good	pay back, restore, replace
22:2	breaking up	in, breaking into
22:3	risen upon him	a new day, the day after the crime
	theft	robbery, stolen, ripped off
	sold	as a slave
22:5	vineyard	where grapes are grown
22:6	corn	grain
22:8	put his hand to	laid his hand on
22:16	entice	tempt, tease, lure, draw away
	endow	pledge, make, pay for
22:17	utterly	completely, fully, totally
22:18	witch	a person that practices magic, uses spells
22:20	save	except
22:21	vex	terrify, trouble, plague, confuse, dismayed
	strangers	foreigners, resident aliens
22:23	wise	way, fashion, manner
22:24	wax hot	be kindled, flare up
22:25	usurer	person who loans, creditor, loans with interest
	usury	interest, loan with high interest
22:26	take to pledge	payment on a debt, down payment, deposit
22:26,27	raiment	in what else, clothing, garment
22:28	revile	speak against, criticize, bad mouth
22:29	liquors	juice, alcohol, wines
22:30	dam	mother
22:31	holy	dedicated, consecrated
23:2	decline	follow, turn aside, yield to
23:3	neither . . .	see a poor person and do nothing to help
	countenance	not be partial to, not prefer
	cause	dispute, quarrel
23:5	hates	abhor, despise, loathe, detest
	forbear	hesitate, refrain
23:6	pervert	corrupt, twist, change for the worse
23:8	gift	bribe, reward
23:9	oppress	burden, beat down, crush, harass
23:11	olive yard	olive grove
23:12	stranger	foreigner, employer, alien

EXODUS

23:13	be circumspect	be on guard, take heed, be cautious
23:15	unleavened	yeast-free
23:18	sacrifice	offering
	leavened	yeast, a symbol of corruption and evil
23:19	seethe	boil, cook
23:21	transgressions	misdeed, sin, wrong-doing, violation
23:22	adversary	enemy, foe, opponent, competitor
23:24	quite	completely, thoroughly
23:26	cast their young	miscarriage, premature birth of a child
23:31	bounds	boundaries, borders
	sea of the Philistines	a.k.a. Mediterranean Sea
23:32	covenant	unconditional agreement, promise, treaty
24:7	audience	hearing, listening people
24:7,8	covenant	unconditional agreement, contract, promise
24:10	paved work	closely fit together bricks of sapphires
24:13	minister	servant, assistant, aide, attendant
25:7	ephod	robe, cape, coat hung over the shoulders
25:9	tabernacle	sacred building, holy site, shrine
25:9	instruments	furniture, utensils
25:10	cubit	about 18 inches
25:11	crown	border, molding, rim
25:13,14,15,28	staves	poles, shafts
25:14	borne	carried, bore
25:17	mercy seat	throne where mercy could be found, a seat where blood was sprinkled
25:22	commune	spoke, talked with, discussed, convey
25:24	crown	border, edge, rim of gold
25:25	a hand breadth	3-4 inches
25:27,37	Over against	on the opposite wall
25:28	borne	carried, lifted
25:29	cover withal	overlay with, coating of
25:38	tongs	snuffers
26:1	cunning	inventive, inwrought, skillful, expert craftsman
26:4	selvedge	woven edge, border
26:6,11,33	taches	hooks, device for fastening parts together, clasps
26:11	tent	covering
26:12	remnant	leftover, remains, survivors

EXODUS

26:17,19	tenons	clasps, handles
26:24	coupled	joined, pairs
26:30	rear up	erect, set up, build
26:31	cunning	tricky, sneaky, smart
26:33	holy place	2nd most sacred place in the Jewish holy site; contained candlesticks, table of bread and incense
	most holy	the 1st holiest place in the Jewish holy site; contained 10 commandments, ark of covenant, manna & Aaron's rod
26:36,37	hanging	screen, veil
27:3	fleshhooks	a many-pronged fork used by priests to separate meat from bone
27:5	compass	edge, rim, ledge
27,6,7	staves	poles for carrying rods
27:7	bear	carry, haul
27:9	court	courtyard, compound, campgrounds belonging to the tabernacle
27:10,11	fillets	bands connecting the posts, threads
27:17	filleted	joined, hooked together, attachment
27:19	vessels	utensil, instruments
27:21	order	case, keep
	order it	keep it burning
28:2	holy	special, sacred, separated
28:3	consecrate	dedicate, honor, respect
	wise hearted	skillful, craftsmen
28:4,6,8,12	ephod	priestly 2-piece sleeveless garment
28:4	miter	turban, head covering, fancy hat
28:6	cunning	inventive, inwrought, skillful, expert craftsman
28:8	curious girdle	embroidered, interlaced belt, woven band
28:9	grave	engrave, inscribe
28:11	signet	seal, stamp
28:11,13,14	ouches	settings, frames, sockets
28:12	memorial	remembrances, to remind
28:14	wreathed	braided, twisted, entwined
28:15	breastplate	originally battle armor was placed over the chest area; this breastplate was ornamental/decorative – instead of metal or leather, it was made up of

EXODUS

		expensive jewels
	cunning	inventive, inwrought, skillful, expert craftsman
28:15+	ephod	priestly garment
28:16	span	9 inches, palms length
28:17	carbuncle	emerald, a crystal
28:19	ligure	jacinth, zircon
28:20	inclosings	settings, mountings
28:21	signet	seal, stamp
28:22,24,25	wreathen	braided, twisted, thick band
28:25	ouches	settings for jewels, sockets
28:27,28	curious	embroidered, made beautifully
28:30	U'rim and Thum'mim	translated as "lights and perfections" or revelation and truth" — were a divination, medium or process used by ancient Hebrews/Israelites in revealing the will of God on a contested point of view or other problem
28:32	habergeon	coat of mail, protective armor
	hole of an habergeon	neck opening in a garment
	rent	tear, ripped, shred, pull apart, open
28:36	signet	seal, stamp
28:37,39	miter	turban, headdress
28:38	hallow	set apart, sanctify, dedicate
28:40	bonnets	headpieces, caps
28:42	nakedness	bare flesh, private parts
	loins	male reproductive organs
28:43	bear not iniquity	do not incur guilt, blamed
	statute	law, rule, commands, decrees, directives
	seed	offspring, children, heirs
29:1	bullock	young male cow, steer, bull
29:1	blemish	defect, impurity, deformity
29:2,23	unleavened	yeast-free
29:4	tabernacle	tent, dwelling place, sacred building
29:5	ephod	priestly garment, dress, sleeved tunic
	curious	embroidered, made beautifully
29:6	miter	turban, headdress
29:7	anointing oil	special oil, sacred oil
29:9	girdles	vest, sash, belt & suspenders

EXODUS

29:13,22	caul	fatty appendage on liver
29:14	dung	refuse, manure, waste, poop
29:17	inwards	entrails, inner organs
	to	upon
29:18,25,41	sweet savor	soothing aroma, sweet fragrance
29:20	great	big
29:21	hallowed	respected, revered, sacred, holy
29:22	rump	butt, rear end
	caul	appendage on the liver
29:27	wave offering	an offering given (to earth) by moving it side to side - horizontal
	heave offering	an offering given (to heaven) by moving it up and down - vertical
29:28	by a statute	as their portion, perpetual obligation
29:31	seethe	boil, cook
29:33,34	holy	set aside, sanctified, sacred
29:36,37	atonement	a sacrifice, gift offered to forgive sins (sin separated man from God, the gift forgave the sin/united them: at-one-ment, to become one again)
29:39	even	twilight, sunset, dusk
29:41	meat	grain, meal
30:3,4	crown	molding, rim
30:4,5	staves	poles, rods
30:4	bear	carry, lift with
	withal	with
30:8	evening	twilight, dusk
30:9	meat	meal, food
30:10	upon	for
30:12,15	his soul	inner person, emotion, life-force, being, life
30:14	offering	contribution, sum set aside for God
30:16	atonement	a sacrifice, gift offered to forgive sins (sin separated man from God, the gift forgave the sin/united them: at-one-ment, to become one again)
	memorial	reminder, remembrance
30:18	laver	tub, wash basin
30:21	statute	law, rule, policy, decrees, an order

EXODUS

	seed	offspring, children, heirs
30:25,35	apothecary	perfumer, druggist
30:27	vessels	utensils, furnishings
30:29	sanctify	consecrate, anoint
30:32	man's flesh	human body
30:33	compounds	mixes, prepares
	cut off	destroyed, rooted out
30:34	like weight	equal part, equal amount
31:4	cunning	inventive, inwrought, skillful, expert craftsman
31:5	cutting	engraving
31:6	as wise hearted	have good judgment, able men
31:13	Verily	surely, truly, honestly, yes, correct
	keep	obey, follow, do, practice
	sanctify you	set apart, dedicated to God
31:13,14,15,16	sabbath	rest days, sacred day
31:14	defileth	to dirty, dishonor, disgrace, spoil
	soul	inner person, emotion, life-force, being, life
31:16	covenant	unconditional agreement, contract, promise
32:1	Gods	Elohim (i.e. an image of God or a god)
32:4,8	These be your gods	Egyptians wore earrings as amulets and/or small portable idols, so Aaron took the earrings and said they were their gods
32:7	corrupted themselves	done wrong, disgraced themselves
32:9	stiffnecked	obstinate, stubborn, headstrong
32:10	consume	vanish, waste away, dried up, spent, used up
32:11,19,22	wax	grow, become, be provoked to
32:12	Wherefore	why
	mischief	evil interest, bad intent
	repent	relent, renounce and go the other way
32:13	swore	pledged, vowed, promised, gave an oath
	seed	offspring, children, heirs
32:14	repented	relented, reconciled
	evil	harm, calamity
32:15,16,19	tables	pieces of flat stone to carve upon, tablets
32:20	strawed	scattered, spread
32:25	made them naked	nude, unclothed, sexual activity
32:29	bestow	give, hand out, award
32:32	blot	wipe away, remove, take away

EXODUS

32:35	plagued	smote, made the people suffer
33:1	seed	offspring, children, heirs
33:2	angel	messenger, supernatural being
33:4	ornaments	jewelry, fancy clothes
33:3,5	stiffnecked	stubborn, hard-headed, proud
33:5	ornaments	jewelry, finery
33:14	rest	pause, lighten your burden
33:18	beseech	beg, pray
33:22	clift	cleft, cave, hollow opening
33:23	back parts	the back parts of a person
34:1+	Lord	Jehovah; God in relationship to mankind
34:1	Hew	cut out, carve, chip
34:1,4	tables	pieces of flat stone to carve upon, tablets
34:5	proclaimed	made known, announced
34:7	iniquity	sin, wickedness, evil, wrongdoing
34:9	stiffnecked	obstinate, stubborn
34:10+	covenant	unconditional agreement, contract, promise
34:10	terrible	fearful, marvelous, awesome
34:12	snare	trapped, imprisoned, tripped up, stumbling block
34:13	images	idols, engravings, carvings of pagan gods
	groves	(Heb:Asherah) either a living tree or a tree-like pole, set up as an object of worship, being symbolical of the female or productive principle in nature. Every Phoenician had an asherah near them. Both the "May Pole" and "Christmas Tree" (Jer.10:3-5) originate with this Asherah. The word is often translated "green trees" or "grove." This "nature worship" became associated with sexual immorality.
34:15,16	whoring after their gods	worshipped, revered carvings, statues, idols
34:17	molten gods	melted, poured, cast-metal idols
34:18	unleavened	yeast-free
34:19	matrix	womb
34:19,20	firstling	firstborn
34:21	earing	plowing, seeding
34:23	Thrice	three times
	Lord God	Jehovah Elohim, the self-existing God

		now interacting with mankind
34:25	leaven	yeast, a symbol of corruption and evil
34:26	seethe a kid	boil a young goat
34:27	tenor	essence, rough translation, basics
34:28,29	tables	pieces of flat stone to carve upon tablets
35:2,3	sabbath	rest day, sacred day
35:10	wise hearted	skillful man, able, expert, craftsman
35:11	his taches	its hooks, clasps
35:12,13,15,16	staves	poles, shafts
35:14	furniture	utensils, instruments, vessels
35:18	pins	pegs, nails
35:25	wise hearted	skilled, able, expert
35:27	ephod	priestly garment
35:29	willing	free will, voluntary
35:32	curious	artistic, skillful
35:33,35	cunning	inventive, inwrought, skillful, expert craftsman
35:35	embroiderer	tailor, seamstress, person that sews
36:1,2,8	wise hearted	skillful, artistic, talented
36:2	stirred	inwardly moved, prompted
36:3	free	free-will, voluntary
36:4	wrought	work, labor, build, produce
36:8	cunning	inventive, inwrought, skillful, expert craftsman
36:11	selvedge	woven extreme edge
36:13,18	taches	clasps, hooks
36:17	coupling	first coupling, set
36:22,24	tenons	pins, handles, sockets
36:29	coupled	joined, linked
36:33	shoot	pass, run right along
36:38	chapiters	tops, capitals
37:2,11,12,26,27	crown	moulding, wreath, rim
37:4,5,14,15,27,28	staves	poles, shafts
37:7,8,9	cherubims	special angels, plural
37:8	cherub	special angel, singular
37:12	border of a handbreadth	three inch rim/band
	border	rim, band
37:15,27	bear	carry, lift
37:16	withal	everything

EXODUS

37:19,20	almonds	blossoms
37:19	another	one
38:4	brasen, brazen	the metal brass (symbolically used to identify judgment)
	compass	ledge, fire hearth
38:5,6,7	staves	poles
38:7	bear	carry, lift
38:8	looking glasses	mirrors
38:9	twined	twisted, wrapped, braided
38:10+	fillets	bands, rods
38:17,19,28	chapiters	top for silver columns, posts
38:18	answerable	corresponding, like that of, just the same as
38:23	engraver	craftsman, artisan
	cunning	inventive, inwrought, skillful, expert craftsman
39:2,5,7,8,18, 19,20,21,22	ephod	high priest's priestly garment worn over the shoulders and hanging down both front and back, the breastplate was attached to it
39:3	wires	threads, braids, fine strings
39:3,8	cunning	inventive, inwrought, skillful, expert craftsman
39:4	curious girdle	skillfully woven band
39:6,13,16,18	ouches	settings for a broach worn as jewelry
39:6,14	signets	seals, stamps
39:9	span	unit of measure or the distance from thumb to little finger on an outstretched hand (9 inches)
39:10	sardius	ruby
39:15,18	wreathen	braided, twisted
39:20	coupling	connection, joint, seam
39:20,21	curious girdle	woven band
39:23	habergeon	coat of mail, garment
	band	woven binding to keep it from tearing
	rend	tear, ripped, shred, pull apart, open
39:26,41	minister	serve, perform his sacred office
39:28,31	miter	turban, head covering, hat
39:33	taches	clasps, hooks
39:34	covering	screen, wrapper
39:35,39	staves	poles
39:36	showbread	holy bread of Presence
39:39	laver	large bowl, basin used for washing

EXODUS

	foot	stand, base
40:3,5	testimony	witness, decrees, pact
40:3	cover	screen, veil
40:5,8	hanging	veil, drapes, curtains
40:7,11	laver	large bowl, basin used for washing
40:10,13	sanctify	consecrate, set apart for God
40:10	most holy	consecrated, sacred, dedicated only for God
40:11	his foot	its stand, base
40:13	anoint	to bless, dedicate, consecrate by pouring or applying an oil, lotion or spirit/force
40:17,18,33	reared	raised, erected
40:20,21	testimony	witness, i.e. tablets of the Law, pact

LEVITICUS

1:4	atonement	a sacrifice, gift offered to forgive sins (sin separated man from God, the gift forgave the sin/united them: at-one-ment, to become one again)
1:5	bullock	young male cow, steer, bull
1:6	flay	skin, peel off skin
1:9,13	inwards	innards, entrails, internal organs
	sweet savor	soothing pleasing aroma
1:15	wring, wrung	choke, strangle, twist
1:16	crop	gullet, remove
1:17	cleave	split, tear, divide
	asunder	in two parts
2:1	meat	grain
	holy	sanctified, set apart
2:1	frankincense	spice, incense, perfume
2:1+	meat	grain
2:2,9,16	memorial	token part, token sacrifice
2:3	remnant	rest, leftover, extra
2:4,7,12,13	oblation	offering, gift
	suffer	allow, tolerate, accept
2:4,5	unleavened	yeast-free
2:5	mingled	mixed, blended
2:11	leaven	yeast, a symbol of corruption and evil
2:13	salt	preservation, flavoring, seasoning
2:14	corn	grain
3:1	oblation	offering, gift
3:3,9,14	inwards	innards, entrails, internal organs
3:4,10	flanks	loins
3:4,10,15	caul	lobe of fat
3:3:5,16	sweet savor	soothing aroma
3:9	hard by	close, narrow
3:17	perpetual	forever, everlasting
4:2	soul	inner person, emotion, life-force, being, life
4:4	before the Lord	as to the Lord
4:8,11	inwards	entrails, internal organs
4:12	without	outside, away

LEVITICUS

4:13	somewhat	something, any of the things
4:20	an atonement	a sacrifice, gift offered to forgive sins (sin separated man from God, the gift forgave the sin/united them: at-one-ment, to become one again)
4:22	ruler	leader, boss, chief
4:22,27	somewhat	something, a little
4:23	to his knowledge	is made known to him, becomes conscious of
4:27	sin through	With so many complicated ignorance laws, the Jews often "sinned" mistakenly or by accident
4:28,32	blemish	mark, defect
4:31	sweet savor	soothing aroma
5:1,2	souls	inner person, emotion, life-force, being, life
5:2	unclean	unfit, ceremonially defiled
5:3	it be hid from him	he is unaware of it, unknown
5:4	soul swear	person make a vow, utters an oath
5:5	guilty	responsible, answerable
5:6+	Lord	Jehovah; God in relationship to mankind
5:7	turtledoves	timid, small type of dove used in some types of sacrifices
5:8	asunder	in two parts, breaking it off completely
5:10	manner	law, ordinance
5:12	memorial	reminder, represent
5:13	touching his sin	related, belonging, connected to
5:15	soul…trespass	person sins, does wrong/bad things
5:17	iniquity	sins, crime, evildoing, immorality
	bear his iniquity	responsible for his sin, accountable, guilty
5:18	estimation	valuation of, price of
6:2	soul	inner person, emotion, life-force, being, life
6:2	fellowship	pledge of partnership, friendship
	thing	deposit, security
	taken away by violence	robbery, stolen article
6:5	sworn falsely	lied about, took a false oath
	appertains	belongs
6:10	linen breeches	long, boxer style underwear
6:11	without	outside
6:14,15,20,21	meat	grain

LEVITICUS

6:15	memorial	reminder, token part
6:16	unleavened	yeast-free
6:17	leaven	yeast, a symbol of corruption and evil
	portion	possession, share, amount, cut, take
6:18,22	statute	law, rule, commands, decrees, directives
6:18	holy	set apart, sacred
6:20	perpetual	long, long time; forever
6:21	sweet savor	soothing aroma
6:22	wholly	completely, fully, totally, all
6:28	sodden	boiled, cooked
	scoured	brush, clean, scrub
6:30	reconcile	resolve, make up, bring peace
7:1	trespass	guilt, wrong doing
7:3	inwards	innards, entrails, guts
7:5,7	trespass	guilt, violation, break the law
7:7,11	law	procedure, code of behavior, rules
7:8	to	for
7:9,10,37	meat	grain
7:12	unleavened	yeast-free
	mingled	mixed, blended
7:13	leavened	yeast, a symbol of corruption and evil
7:14	oblation	offering, sacrifice, various offerings beyond obligation
7:16	vow	promise, contract, oath, pledge
7:18	imputed	blame, accuse, indict
	abomination	offensive thing, unclean, destestable to God
7:18,20,21,25,27	soul	inner person, emotion, life-force, being, life
7:20	pertain	relates/applies to, connected with
7:29,38	oblation	offering, sacrifice
7:32	heave-offering	an offering given (to heaven) by moving it up and down - vertical
7:34	by a statute	as their due, by a law
8:2,26	unleavened	yeast-free
8:7	ephod	priestly robe, sacred apron
	curious girdle	artistic band, ribbon, skillfully woven cords attached to the girdle
8:8	U'rim	
	Thum'mim	translated as "lights and perfections" or

		revelation and truth" — were a divination, medium or process used by ancient Hebrews/Israelites in revealing the will of God on a contested point of view or other problem
8:9	mitre	turban, headdress
	forefront	beginning, at the front, start
8:11	laver	it was a "basin" (pot) for boiling in, cooking, baking or roasting, and the sacred wash-bowl used by priests in religious work
	foot	base, pedestal
8:13	bonnets	headpieces, caps
8:15	reconciliation	atonement, purged
8:16,21,25	inwards	innards, entrails
8:21,28	sweet savor	soothing aroma
8:22,31	consecration	ordination, for sacrifice
8:23,24	great	big, large
8:27	wave-offering	an offering given (to earth) by moving it side to side - horizontal
8:29	consecration	dedicate, honor, respect
8:34	atonement	a sacrifice, gift offered to forgive sins (sin separated man from God, the gift forgave the sin/united them: at-one-ment, to become one again)
8:35	charge	obey the ordinances, carrying out the Lord's prescription
9:4,17	meat	grain
9:4	mingled	mixed, blended, joined
9:8	himself	his own sins, his own faults
9:14,19	inwards	entrails, guts
9:16	manner	procedure, process
10:1	censer	something that held incense and hot charcoal
10:1	strange	unlawful, unholy, profane, illicit
10:3	glorified	honored, exalted, famous
10:6	bewail	cry, weep, moan
10:9,11	statute	law, rule, commands, decrees, directives
10:10	unholy	unacceptable, unclean, dirty
10:12	meat	grain
	leaven	yeast, a symbol of corruption and evil

LEVITICUS

10:13,14	due	share, portion, amount, yours legallonly
10:15	heave shoulder	thigh
10:17	Wherefore	why
10:19	befallen	happened to
11:3,7	clovenfooted	split hoofed, two distinct hoofs
11:4	cud	regurgitated food that is chewed over and over to help digestion
11:4+	unclean	unfit, unacceptable
11:8	carcass	corpses, dead bodies
11:10+	abomination	detestable to God, unclean, filthy, dirty
11:11	have their carcasses in abomination	detest their carcasses, declare unclean
11:13	ossifrage	bearded vulture, black vulture
11:14	kite	hawk, falcon
11:28,40	bears	carries
11:32	raiment	clothing, garment
11:34	meat	food, grain
11:35	ranges	hearth, stove, cooking furnaces
11:36	fountain	spring, natural well
	pit	cistern, large man-made container to hold water
11:44	sanctify	consecrate, set apart
12:2	infirmity	sickness, illness, disease
12:2,5	unclean	unfit, unacceptable
12:5	maid	female
	three-score and six	66
12:7	issue	menstrual period, outflow, time of the month
12:8	clean	fit, acceptable, proper
13:2	rising	swelling, growth
13:3	pronounce	declare, decree, testify
13:2+	plague	disease, catastrophe, disaster, infection
13:3+	unclean	unfit, unacceptable
13:4,31,33,50	shut up	isolate, set apart
13:5	be at a stay	has not changed, not spread
13:5,11,21	shut him up	isolate him, keep seperate
13:10,24	quick	sensitive, raw, inflamed, ulcer forming
13:11	old	chronic, established case
13:19,28	rising	swelling, inflammation
13:23	burning boil	puss-filled sore, blister, skin rash

LEVITICUS

13:30+	scall	scale, scab, ringworm
13:38,39	bright spots	pimples, blemish
13:39	freckled spot	eczema, flaking skin
13:43	rising	swelling
13:44	utterly unclean	dirty, filthy, unacceptable
13:45	rent	tear, ripped, shred, pull apart, open
13:45	covering upon upper lip	a veil or mask made of material
13:46	dwell	live
13:48+	warp, or woof	weaving or texture, woven, knitted
13:57	warp	up & down threads in material
	woof	sideways threads in material
13:51	fretting	contagious, spreading
13:55	fret inward	eaten away within, infected
13:56	rend	tear, cut, separate from rest
14:3+	plague	infection, disease, disaster, infection
14:4	hyssop	a common plant (Oregano?)
14:7	pronounce	declare, make known, reveal
14:8	tarry abroad	delay outside, stay outside his tent
14:10	he	male
	ewe	female
	deals	portions, parts
	mingled	mixed, blened
14:10,12,21,24	log	pint
14:12,14,21	trespass	guilt
14:14,17,25,28	great	big, large
14:18,19,20, 21,29,53	an atonement	a sacrifice, gift offered to forgive sins (sin separated man from God, the gift forgave the sin/united them: at-one-ment, to become one again)
14:18	remnant	leftover, remains, survivors
14:20,31	meat	food
14:21	deal	portion, share
14:23	to	in front
14:32	whose hand is not able	who cannot afford, unable
14:36,44,46,57	unclean	unfit, contaminated
14:37	strakes	steaks, strips, patches, marks

LEVITICUS

	lower than the wall	deeper than the surface
14:38,46	shut up	quarantine, separate, isolate
14:41	within round about	all around inside
14:44	fretting	spreading, corrosive
14:52	cleanse	in a ceremonial way, purge
14:54	scall	scale, scab
14:56	rising	swelling
	bright spot	pimple, blemish
14:57	clean	fit, acceptable
15:2+	running issue	discharge, chronic flow
15:2+	unclean	unfit, contaminated, unacceptable
15:6	bathe	wash, clean, take a bath
15:16,17,18	seed of copulation	seminal emission, sperm, sexual discharge
15:19+	issue	discharge
15:19	put apart	keep separate, in a state of impurity
15:24,33	flowers	monthly period, menstrual cycle
15:29	turtles	turtledoves
15:30	atonement	a sacrifice, gift offered to forgive sins (sin separated man from God, the gift forgave the sin/united them: at-one-ment, to become one again)
15:31	uncleanness	unfit, contaminated, unacceptable
15:32	law	regulation, ritual, procedure
16:4	miter	turban, headdress
16:6,10,11,16, 17,18,27,32,33,34	an atonement	a sacrifice, gift offered to forgive sins (sin separated man from God, the gift forgave the sin/united them: at-one-ment, to become one again)
16:8	cast lots	predictions; like flipping a coin; paper, rock, scissors, throw dice
	scapegoat	substitute; one that takes the blame
16:12	censer	incense holder, pan full of glowing coals
16:16,19	uncleanness	defilements, contamination
16:19	hallow it	consecrate, render it clean and holy, dedicate it only for God
16:20	reconciling	atoning for, making peace, forgiveness
16:21	confess	admit guilt, say aloud
16:21,22	iniquities	sins, crime, evildoing, immorality

LEVITICUS

16:26	scapegoat	victim, sacrifice, anything that takes the blame
16:29,34	statute	law, standing rule, ordinance
16:29	stranger	visitor, guest, foreigner
	sojourns	temporarily stay, visit, live
16:29,31	afflict you souls	humble yourselves, practice self denial
17:3	out of	outside
17:4	imputed	reckoned, answer for, counted against
17:4,9,14	cut off	destroyed, outlawed from family & nation, executed, excommunicated
17:6	sweet savor	pleasing aroma, smell
17:7	devils	demons, evil spirits
	gone a whoring	prostituted themselves, lowered standards
	statute	law, rule, commands, decrees, directives
17:8,10,12,13	sojourn	temporarily stay, visit, live
17:10,11,12,15	soul	person, individual, living being
17:11	atonement	a reconciliation, expiation
17:14	the blood of it is for the life thereof	its blood sustains its life; the blood was believed to contain the force of a person
17:15	of itself	naturally, natural cause
17:16	iniquity	sins, crime, evildoing, immorality
18:3	doings	ways, manner, practices
18:4	ordinances	laws, rules
18:5,26	statutes	law, rule, commands, decrees, directives
18:5	judgments	ordinances, laws, policies, decisions
18:6	kin	family, direct relative, blood
	uncover their nakedness	sexual intercourse, look at sexual organs
18:12	kinswoman	female family, direct relative, blood
18:17	wickedness	sinful, lewdness, depravity
18:18	vex	terrify, trouble, plague, confuse, dismayed
18:20	lie carnally	have intercourse, sex
18:21	pass through fire	children were sacrificed by fire to Moloch, and other pagan gods
	seed	offspring, children, heirs
18:22,26,27,29	abomination	detestable, i.e. grossly sinful, loathsome, enormous sin
18:23	lie before a beast	have sex with an animal

LEVITICUS

18:23	confusion	perversion, foul thing
18:25	visit the iniquity	bring judgment for its sins
18:26	keep	obey, follow, do, practice
	stranger	alien, foreigner, visitor, guest
	sojourns	temporarily stay, visit, live
18:28	spue	spit, vomit, throw up
	nations	groups of people, tribe or selection
18:29	souls	such persons
	cut off	destroyed, separated, isolated
19:2,24	holy	set apart, pure, acceptable
19:3,14	fear	revered, respected, trembled, dread
19:3,30	sabbaths	rest days, dedicated time
19:4	molten gods	images, metal gods, cast metal
19:6	ought	whatever
19:7	abominable	detestable, repulsive
19:8	avenge	get even, pay back, revenge
	iniquity	sins, crime, evildoing, immorality
	soul	person
19:9	gleanings	leftovers, what's left after the first pick
19:13	defraud	cheat, use extortion, defraud
19:15	respect	show partiality, favor
19:16	stand against the blood	act against life, jeopardize your neighbors life, fail to help when a neighbor's life is in danger
19:17	rebuke thy neighbor and not suffer sin upon	rebuke your neighbor for his wrongdoings, thereby clearing yourself of his guilt, incur sin because of, bear sin
19:18	avenge	retaliate, revenge
	grudge	hard feelings, rivalry, resentment
19:19	keep	obey, follow, do, practice
	statutes	law, rule, commands, decrees, directives
	gender	breed, mate
	mingled	mixed, blended, joined
19:20	carnally	sexually
	betrothed to	engaged, designated for
	scourged	whipped, punished

LEVITICUS

19:22	atonement	a sacrifice, gift offered to forgive sins (sin separated man from God, the gift forgave the sin/united them: at-one-ment, to become one again)
19:23	uncircumcised	forbidden, ceremonially defiled
19:26	enchantment	divination, fortune telling or witchcraft
	observe times	soothsaying, astrology
19:27	mar corners	trim, cut, shave
19:28	print any marks upon you	tattoo, cut yourself as the Pagans do
19:30	reverence	pay respect to, admire
19:31	them that have familiar spirits	mediums, fortune tellers
	wizards	diviners, magicians, males who practice witchcraft
19:32	hoary head	aged, grey
	fear	revered, respected, trembled, dread
19:33	sojourn	temporarily stay, visit, live
	vex	terrify, trouble, plague, confuse, dismayed
19:34	stranger	foreigner, visitor, guest
19:35	meteyard	measurements, take dimensions
19:36	just	fair, true, honest
19:37	statutes	law, rule, commands, decrees, directives
20:2	strangers	foreigner, visitor, guest
	sojourns	temporarily stay, visit, live
20:2,3,4	seed	offspring, children, heirs
20:3	cut him off	destroy him, ban him
20:4	hide their eyes	ignore, pretend not to know
20:5	whoring	lust, go after, want badly
20:6	soul	person, individual, living being
	familiar spirits	mediums, ghost, spirits
20:6,27	wizards	diviners, magicians, males who practice witchcraft
20:8	keep	obey, follow, do, practice
	sanctify	set you apart, make holy
20:8,22	statutes	law, rule, commands, decrees, directives
20:10	adulterous	unfaithful, cheating, disloyal
20:12	wrought	worked, made

LEVITICUS

20:13	abomination	a detestable act, evil, filthy
20:18	having her sickness	in her monthly menstrual period, time of month
	cut off	destroyed, isolated, banished
20:21	unclean thing	impure deed, unacceptable
20:22	spew	vomit, spit out
20:23	abhorred	abhor, despise, loathe, detest
20:24	separated you	made a distinction between you and other people
20:25	abominable	detestable, dirty, unclean
20:26	severed	separated, chosen out
20:27	familiar spirit	medium, ghost, spirits
21:2	but	except
	kin	relative, family, blood
21:5	corner	side growth, edges
21:7	put away	divorced, parted from
21:8	sanctify	set apart, hold him as holy
21:9,12,15	profane	defile, play the harlot
21:11	go in to	have sex with, intercourse
21:14	harlot	prostitute, hooker, paid sex
21:15,17,21	seed	offspring, children, heirs
21:17,18,21,23	blemish	defect, fault
21:17	offer	serves as priest, present
21:18	superfluous	extra, leftover, too much
21:20	crookbacked	hunchbacked
	scabbed	skin disease, boil scarred
	stones	testicles, balls
21:20	scurvy	itchy, scabby, scaly disease
21:23	go in to the veil, nor come near to the altar	serve as a priest, approach the altar
21:23	profane	defile, dirty, make unclean
22:2	hallow	to respect, revere, make sacred, holy
22:3,4	seed	offspring, children, heirs
22:4	leper	a person with an incurable skin disease(s)
22:4	running	bodily discharge
22:4,5,6	unclean	defiled, dirty, unacceptable
22:6,11	soul	person, individual, living being
22:6+	holy things	sacred offerings, dedicated to God
22:9	keep	obey, observe, follow, do
	ordinance	requirements, my charge, laws, rules

LEVITICUS

22:10	sojourner	guest, temporarily stay, visit, live
22:11,13	meat	food
22:13	stranger	foreigner, visitor, guest
22:15,32	profane	desecrate, make unclean, violate
22:16	iniquity	sins, crime, evildoing, immorality
22:18	oblation	offering
22:19,20,21	blemish	defect, fault, impurity
22:19,21	beeves	beef cattle, bullocks
22:22	maimed	permanently injured, handicapped
	wen	running sore, discharge
	scabbed	skin disease
22:23	any thing superfluous	deformed, deformity, too long or too short
	vow	required offering
22:27	dam	mother
22:29	at	of
22:31	keep	obey, follow, do, practice
22:32	hallowed	sanctified, revered
23:2+	convocations	sacred assemblies
23:3+	sabbath	rest day, day off from work
23:3	dwellings	homes, palces to live
23:6	unleavened	yeast-free
23:7	servile	slavish, strenuous, work at your occupation
23:10,11,12,15	sheaf	bundle (of grain)
23:11	wave	present, lift up
23:12,18	blemish	defect, fault, impurity
23:13,16,18,37	meat	food
23:13	deals	parts, portions
23:13,18	sweet savor	soothing aroma, smell
23:14	parched	dried
	corn	grain
23:14	statute	law, rule, commands, decrees, directives
23:15,16,32,38	sabbaths	rest days
23:17,20	wave	to gain acceptance, held up to the Lord
23:17	deals	parts, portions
23:21,31,41	statute	law, rule, commands, decrees, directives
23:21,25,35	servile	slavish, strenuous
23:21	convocation	assembly, large meeting, big get-together
23:22	clean riddance	complete removal, illiminate

LEVITICUS

23:27	afflict your souls	humble yourselves, abstain and fast
23:27,29,30	souls	people, selves, individuals
23:36	solemn	serious, no joke, sincere
23:38,39	sabbaths	rest days, a day off from work
23:42,43	booths	rugged shelters, temporary shelter, tent
23:44	feasts	festivals, appointed seasons
24:3	testimony	ark, sacred/holy container
24:3,9	statute	law, rule, commands, decrees, directives
24:4	order	prepare, keep, see to, arrange
24:5	deals	portions, parts, share
24:6	pure table	pure gold, ritually clean, table of pure gold
24:7	memorial	remembrance, oblation
24:8	sabbath	rest day, day off work
	covenant	unconditional agreement, contract, promise
24:10	strove	fought, go after, worked hard at
24:11	blasphemed	dishonor, act disgracefully
24:12	ward	custody, under guard
24:15	bear his sin	be held responsible
24:16	blasphemies	curses, uses God's name without purpose
	stranger	foreigner, visit, guest
24:19,20	blemish	an injury, disfigures, permanent injury
24:20	breach	broken place, crumbled walls, holes, gap
25:2,4,6,8	sabbath	rest day, day off work
25:3	prune	clip, cut, to trim a tree/bush
25:5	reap	harvest, collect, gather, pick/pluck
25:6	sojourns	temporarily stay, visit, live
25:6,7	meat	food
25:9,11,12,13,15, 28,30,31,33,40	jubilee	every 50th year freedom, Day of Atonement, release
25:14,17	oppress	cheat, take advantage
25:17,26,43	fear	revered, respected, trembled, dread
25:18	statutes	law, rule, commands, decrees, directives
	judgments	ordinances, laws, policies, decisions
25:23,35,47	strangers	foreigner, visit, guest
25:23,35,40,45,47	sojourners	tenants, settlers
25:30	shall not be out	shall not be returned to the original owner
25:31	fields of country	outside city limits, suburbs
25:34	field of the suburbs	pasture land, common land

LEVITICUS

25:35	be waxed	has become, reduced to
	decay	hard times, debt, money problems
25:36,37	usury	interest on loans
25:37	give victuals	food, supplies, needs
25:39	be waxed	has become, reduced to
	be sold	sells himself, sells his own liberty
25:42	bondmen	loan sharks, money/payday lenders
25:43,47,53	rigor	ruthless severity, harshness, severity, oppression
25:44	heathen	nations, non-Jew, pagan
25:43	rigor	harshness, severity, cruelty, mean
25:47	wax	grow, become
25:50	year of jubilee	every 50th year freedom, Day of Atonement, release
26:1	graven	carved, chiseled, sculpted, hand-made
	rear	erect, set up
26:2	keep	obey, follow, do, practice
26:3,15	statutes	law, rule, commands, decrees, directives
26:3	keep	obey, follow, do, practice
26:6	the sword	war, fighting
	neither shall the sword go	there will be no war
26:9+	covenant	unconditional agreement, contract, promise
26:10	store	food supply
26:11	abhor	hate, disgusted by, dislike
26:13	bondmen	slaves, contracted servant
	go upright	be free, walk erect as free men
	bands…yoke	set free, let go, deliver
26:14,18,21,27	hearken	listen, pay attention, heed
26:15	soul abhor	heart reject, disregard, reject
26:16	consumption	wasting diseases
	burning ague	fever
26:16,20	in vain	foolishly, uselessly
26:17	hate	abhor, despise, loathe, detest
26:18	hearken	listen, pay attention, heed
26:19	brass	judgment
26:21	plagues	afflictions, blows
26:25	avenge the quarrel	execute punishment
	pestilence	disease, fungus, mildew, disaster, crop failure

LEVITICUS

26:28	chastise	punish, rage in opposition
26:30	high places	shrines, incense altars, cult places
	images	idols, heathen statues of their gods
	carcasses	bodies
	My soul	inner person, emotion, life-force, being, life
26:31	will not smell the savor of your sweet odors	aroma, will not accept your offerings
26:33	heathen	non-Jewish people/nations, did not serve the one true God
26:36	faintness	fear, worry, anxiety, dread
26:39	pine	waste away, perish
26:39,40,41	iniquities	sins, crime, evildoing, immorality
26:44	cast them away	reject them, spurn them
	abhor	despise, loathe, detest
27:2	singular	special, explicit
27:2+	estimation	evaluation, calculate, figure out
27:9,10,14,30	holy	only for this use, consecrated, sacred
27:11	unclean	ceremonially unfit
27:14+	sanctify	consecrate, dedicate
27:15,19,20,27,29,33	redeem	buy back, rescue, claim
27:18	abated	deducted
27:26	firstling	first born
27:28	not withstanding	nevertheless, however
27:28,29	devoted	dedicated (to God), sincerely committed
27:30,31,32	tithe	tenth portion, one out of every ten

NUMBERS

1:2	take the sum	take the census, count the people
	by their polls	each one individually, account
1:3	number	count, record
1:16	renowned	outstanding, reputable, select, chosen national representative
1:17	expressed	designated, identified
1:18	pedigrees	ancestry, families
1:27	threescore	sixty (a score equals 20, 3x20)
1:44	princes	leaders, chiefs, rulers, influential men
1:47	levites	a descendant of the tribe of Levi; used as the title for religious workers
1:50	encamp	surround, set up temporary camp (home) outside the holy area
1:51	sets forward	is to move, take down
1:51,52,53	pitch	set up, camp, establish
1:52	standard	flag, camp, assigned position
1:53	charge	custody, responsibility
2:2,3,5,12,34	pitch	set up, camp
2:2+	standard	flag
2:2	ensign	tribal banner or flag, emblem, logo
	about	around, against
2:9,16	set forth	go, march
2:24	rank	group, line of battle
2:27	encamp	make camp, surround, defensive position
2:31	hindmost	last, behind, tail-end
3:3	consecrated	ordained, installed
3:3,4,6	minister	serve, work, labor
3:4	strange	unholy, irregular, improper, alien
3:8	instruments	furnishings, articles, utensils
3:10	wait on	care for, attend to, entrust, have charge
3:12	matrix	womb
3:13	hallowed	respected, revered, sacred, holy
3:15,40	number	count, review, take a census
3:16,22	numbered	counted, made a register
3:23,29,31	pitch	camp, encamp
3:24,35	chief	leader, boss, head

NUMBERS

3:25,31,38	charge	duties, responsibilities
3:32	the charge	custody, watch
3:38	encamp	camp, make camp, surround, defensive position
3:41	firstlings	firstborn
3:46	redeemed	buy/win back, pay ransom, purchased
3:48	odd number	remainder, excess
3:50	shekel	a weight of silver
4:2	take the sum of	count, take a census
4:3	enter into the host	enter the service, begin week
4:6,8,11,14	staves	carrying poles
4:6	badger	a small meat-eating animal known for its fierce, violent nature when provoked; symbolically used to represent the fallen, human nature inside us
4:7	showbread	consecrated bread, holy bread
4:9	snuffdish	bowls in which the used, burnt-up candles were placed before throwing them away
4:10	bar	a carrying frame
4:12	instruments	furnishings, articles, utensils
4:12,14	minister	serve, work, labor
4:14	censers	firepans
	basins	bowls
4:15	holy	sacred, special, dedicated
	burden	responsibility, duty, care, concern
4:16	anointing	an oil, lotion or spirit/force used to bless, dedicate, or consecrate by pouring or applying
4:19	appoint	assign, give responsibility to
4:24,31,32	for burdens	carrying, to carry when moving or on march
4:26,32	instruments	tools, accessories
4:27	appoint	assign, give responsibility to
4:28	hand	direction, oversight, supervision
4:31,32	charge	duty, assignment
4:33	whoredoms	illegallon sex outside of marriage, immoral, prostitution or worse; also describes unfaithfulness to God/His rules (sin)
5:2	an issue	a discharge, flow from his body
5:3	defile	contaminate, make unclean
5:7,8	recompense	pay for, restore, make full restitution

NUMBERS

5:8	kinsman	relative, next of kin, blood, near-family
	atonement	a sacrifice, gift offered to forgive sins (sin separated man from God, the gift forgave the sin/united them: at-one-ment, to become one again)
5:10	hallowed	sacred, holy, consecrated, respected
5:12	a trespass	unfaithfulness, treachery, does wrong
5:13	know carnally	have sex with, intercourse
	close	secret, undetected
	taken with	caught in the act, busted
5:17	recompense	pay back, payment, reward or punish
5:18	the curse	bad things that would happen as a result of adultery or sexual behavior outside of marriage (re: "thigh to rot" meant that the woman would get sexual disease in/around her vagina)
5:22	bowels	inward parts, stomach
5:27	a curse	an outcast, reject
5:31	iniquity	sins, crime, evildoing, immorality
6:2	Nazarite	separated from others and consecrated to God; they did not drink alcohol or cut their hair
6:2	separate to	
	vow a vow	pledge a pledge, make special vow, promise a solemn vow
6:3	liquor	any drink with alcohol in it
	moist	fresh
6:4	vine tree	grapevine
6:5,8	holy	separated, consecrated, dedicated
6:6	come at	come close to (i.e. touch), go near
6:7	make unclean	dirty, unacceptable, unable to do religious work
6:10	turtles	turtle doves; small, ceremonially clean birds
6:11	atonement	a sacrifice, gift offered to forgive sins (sin separated man from God, the gift forgave the sin/united them: at-one-ment, to become one again)
6:12	consecrate	make holy, rededicate
6:14	blemish	defect, fault, impurity
	ewe	female
6:15,17,19	unleavened	yeast-free

NUMBERS

6:15,17	meat	grain
6:19	sodden	boiled, roasted
6:20	wave	swing, shake, present, gesture of offering
6:21	vowed	pledged, promised, vowed
6:26	countenance	"face" - influence, personal attention, blessings
6:27	put	invoke, link, call down
7:5	do the service	do the work, put to use in affecting the work
7:13+	charger	platter, bowl, large dish
7:13+	mingled	mixed, blended, combined
7:13+	meat	grain
7:21	bullock	young bull
7:44	spoon	bowl with a handle
7:73	shekels	the term for Jewish money, like our "dollar"
8:2	over against	in front of
8:4	beaten	hammered, thinned out, flattened
8:8	meat	grain
	mingled	mixed, blended, combined
8:11	execute	do, perform
8:14	Mine	for God's special purpose
8:17	smote	attacked, strike, hit, punish
	sanctified them for myself	set them apart, consecrated, made them mine
8:18	for	instead of
8:19	plague	deadly disease (as a punishment)
8:21	purified	cleansed, washed
8:26	charge	duties, assignments
	touching their charge	concerning their charge, assisted in their duties, concerning their responsibilities
9:6,7	defiled	unclean, dirty, spoiled
9:7	kept back, that we may not offer	restrained from sharing, prohibited from presenting
9:8	Stand still	wait, be patient
9:10	posterity	descendents, offspring, children
9:11	unleavened	yeast-free
9:12	ordinances	regulations, rules
9:13	forbeareth	neglects

NUMBERS

	soul	person, individual, living being
	cut off	destroyed, wiped out
	its appointed season	at the appointed time
9:14	sojourn	temporarily stay, visit, live
	ordinance	rule, statute, important tradition
9:15	reared	raised, erected
9:17	taken up	lifted, raised
9:17,18,20,21,22	abode	dwell, live, stay, make a home, settled
9:18	pitched	camped, set up defenses
9:19	tarried	waited, delayed, put off
9:19,23	charge	order, command, direct
10:6	take their journey	set out, break camp
10:8	an ordinance	a rule, law
10:10	solemn days	appointed times, festivals, fixed seasons, feasts
10:13,18,22,25	standard	banner, flag, tribal colors
10:13+	host	army
10:17,21	bearing	camping, carrying
10:21	against they came	in anticipation of their arrival
10:22	armies	masses of soldiers, ranks, troops
10:25	which was rearward	which was the rear guard
10:28	journeyings	travels, order of march, order of departure
10:29	spoken	promised, given an assurance
10:31	encamp	make camp, set up defenses
10:32	what goodness	whatever good, blessing
11:1	kindled	started, began, aroused
11:2	quenched	put out, died out, abated
11:4	fell a lusting	had greedy desires, strong craving
11:5	freely	at no cost, for the asking
11:6	our soul	our body
	is dried away	is dissatisfied and discouraged up
11:10	was kindled	was burned, blazed hotly, exceedingly angry
11:11	wherefore	why
	burden	responsibility, care
11:12,14,17	bears	carries, supports
	sucking	nursing, breastfeeding
11:13,18,21	flesh	meat
11:15	deal thus with me	treat me this way
	out of hand	at once, right away

NUMBERS

11:18	Sanctify	consecrate, purify, hollow
11:20	loathsome	disgusting, nauseating
	despised	rejected, spurned
11:22	slain	killed, slaughtered
	suffice	be enough for, fulfill your promise
11:23	waxed short	become short, i.e. limited, lost its power
11:25	prophesied	foretell, make a prediction, speak for God
11:29	envy for my sake	jealous, protective, defending
11:30	gat	returned, went
11:33	smote	attacked, strike, hit, punish
12:3	meek	humble, gentle
12:8	apparently	openly, clearly
	in speeches dark	in riddles, in parables, difficult to understand
	similitude	visible likeness, appearance, image
12:11,13	beseech	beg, pray
12:14,15	shut out from	outside of
12:16	pitched	camped, set up defenses
13:18	see	assess, see what the land is like
13:20	fat or lean	fertile or barren
13:23	brook	valley, wadi, gorge, dry riverbed
	bore	carried, supported
13:30	possess	take, occupy, conquer
13:32	eats up	devours, destroys
13:32	great stature	very tall, giants
14:1	lifted up their voice	made loud lament, cried out
14:2	murmured	grumbled, complained, whine
	Would God	we wish, hope
14:3	wherefore	why
	fall by the sword	die in war, slain
14:6	rent	tear, ripped, shred, pull apart, open
14:10	bid	said, asked, told
14:11	provoke	spurn, insult, treat with contempt, disrespect
	signs	miracles, marvelous deeds
14:12	pestilence	deadly disease, plague
14:17,19	beseech	beg, plead, ask
14:18	long-suffering	patient, merciful, understanding
14:20	pardoned	forgive, excuse, let go, not hold against
14:27,29,36	murmur	grumble, muttering, complained, whine

NUMBERS

14:29,32	carcasses	corpses, dead bodies
14:30	swore	pledged, vowed, promised, gave an oath
	save	except
14:31	know	enjoyed, appreciate
	despised	rejected, spurned
14:33	wander	be shepherds, nomads
	whoredoms	illegallon sex outside of marriage, immoral, prostitution or worse; also describes unfaithfulness to God/His rules (sin)
14:34	breach of promise	opposition, enmity
14:36	search	spy out, recon, snoop around
	slander	bad report, rumor
14:37	plague	pestilence, disease
14:38	Wherefore	Why
	prosper	succeed
14:39	mourned	cried, be sad about, depressed
14:41	transgress	misdeed, sin, wrong-doing, break the law
14:42	smitten	defeated, struck down, decimated
14:44	presumed to go	heedlessly went, recklessly, stubbornly
14:45	smote	attacked, strike, hit, punish
	discomfited	thrashed, punished, made unhappy
15:2	habitations	dwelling-place
15:3,7,10,14,24	sweet savor	soothing aroma, smell
15:4,24	meat	grain, cereal
15:6	deals	portions
15:8	performing a vow	fulfilling a promise
15:13	born of the country	native born, native Israelite
15:14	stranger	alien, foreigner, visitor, guest
	sojourn	temporarily stay, visit, live
15:15	one ordinance	the same rule, same regulation
15:15,16	sojourns	temporarily stay, visit, live
15:20	heave	lifted
15:22	erred	make a mistake, messed up, did the wrong thing
15:24,25,26,27	ignorance	error, without knowledge
15:24	manner	regulation, as the ordinance prescribes
15:27,28,30	soul	person, individual, living being
15:28	atonement	a sacrifice, gift offered to forgive sins (sin

NUMBERS

		separated man from God, the gift forgave the sin/united them: at-one-ment, to become one again)
15:29	sojourns	temporarily stay, visit, live
15:30	presumptuously	defiantly, through pride, deliberately
	cut off	destroyed, outlawed
15:32	sabbath	rest, day off from work
15:34	in ward	in custody, jail, captivity
	declared	revealed, announced
15:38	ribband	cord
15:39	go a whoring	play the harlot, go away from God
16:2	renown	famous, popular, had a reputation
16:6	censers	incense burners
16:7	holy	set apart, consecrated, dedicated
16:11	murmur	grumble, conspire, complain
16:29	visited	punished, avenged, judgement
16:30	appertain	concerning, relates to, in reference to
	quick	alive, energetic, active, powerful
	provoked	spurned, defiled, rejected
16:31	clave asunder	split apart, split open
16:35	consumed	vanish, waste away, dried up, spent, used up
16:38	souls	heart, person, living being
16:14	memorial	reminder
	seed	offspring, children, heirs
16:41	murmured against	grumbled against, complained, railed
16:46,47,48,50	plague	fatal sickness, disease
16:48,50	stayed	stopped, restrained, ceased
17:5,10	murmurings	grumblings, complaints
17:6	apiece	each
17:8	yielded	produced, borne
17:10	token	pledge, memorial, a sign, special pass
	testimony	Ark of the Covenant
	take away	put an end to it
18:1	bear the iniquity of	be responsible for, be answerable for offenses
18:2	witness	testimony
18:3,4	keep your charge	guard your responsibility, attend to all duties
18:5	charge	responsibility, duties
	wrath	anger, fury, punishment, judgment

NUMBERS

18:6	gift	given freely, a present
18:9	oblation	offspring, offering
	meat	grain
18:10	holy	separated, consecrated, dedicated to God
18:11	statute	allotment, perpetual allowance
	clean	cleansed from sin
18:15	everything that opens the matrix	every firstborn male
	matrix	womb
	unclean	unfit, unclean, defiled, impure
18:17	firstling	firstborn
18:19	covenant of salt	an unbreakable promise, permanent contract
	seed	offspring, children, heirs
18:21	an inheritance	their share, their heritage
18:23	do	perform, discharge
	statute	law, rule, commands, decrees, directives
18:24	inheritance	share, cut, take
18:27	corn	grain
18:30	heaved	lifted up
	threshingfloor	an area used to separate grain from its skin
	winepress	an area used to press/squeeze the juice from grapes, to be used in wine-making
18:31	reward	wages, salary, money from work
19:2	spot	defect, imperfection
	blemish	defect, imperfection
19:6	hyssop	an aromatic plant used for purging and cleansing, common plant
19:9	waters of separation	used along with the ashes of a red heifer for the ceremonial cleansing of persons defiled by contact with a dead body
	purification for sin	sin-offering, removal of sin
19:10	stranger	foreigner, visitor, guest
	sojourns	temporarily stay, visit, live
19:10,20	statute	law, rule, commands, decrees, directives
19:13,20,22	soul	person, individual, living being, heart
20:3	chode	contended, argued
	Would God	we wish
20:5	wherefore	why

NUMBERS

20:11	smote	attacked, strike, hit, punish
20:12	sanctify Me	hold Me in reverential honor
20:13	strove	contended, argued, rebelled
20:14	travail	labor, pain, work hard, toil, difficulty
	befallen	happened, taken place, occurred
20:15	vexed	terrify, trouble, plague, confuse, dismayed
20:16	uttermost	outermost, edge
20:24	gathered to his people	buried, reunited
20:24	rebelled	disagreed, refused, fought against
20:29	house	family
21:1	heard tell	heard what it said
21:2	vowed a vow	make a pledge, promise, contract
21:2,3	utterly	completely, fully
21:4	compass	go about, encamp, encircle, make a circuit
	soul	heart, person, living being
21:5	Wherefore	why
	Soul loathes	people detest or are disgusted with
21:11	toward the sunrising	by the eastern border
21:18	staves	staffs, poles, sticks
21:23	suffer	permit, allow, tolerate
	went out against	attacked, went out to meet
21:24	possessed	took over, seized
21:27	they	the poets, sacred text writers
21:29	undone	beaten, trashed, ruined, fell apart
21:30	laid them waste	demolished them, destroyed
21:35	smote	attacked, strike, hit, punish
22:1	pitched	camped, set up defenses
	on this side	on the eastern side
22:3	sore	very, utterly, badly
22:4	lick up	defeat in battle, consume, devour
22:5	over against me	in front of me, opposite me
22:6,28,32	smite	attacked, strike, hit, punish
	wot	know
22:7	rewards of divination	fees for fortune telling

NUMBERS

22:13	leave	permission, let me go
22:22	adversary	enemy, foe, opponent, competitor
22:25,27	smote	attacked, strike, hit, punish
22:27	staff	rod, stick
22:29	mocked	make fun off, laugh at, imitated
	would	wish, if only
22:30	wont to do so	in a habit, failed to serve you
22:32,37	Wherefore	why
22:32	withstand	oppose, stop
	perverse	contrary, wrong, troublesome
22:36,41	utmost	farthest, extremity of boundary
22:41	morrow	tomorrow, next day
23:3	peradventure	perhaps, maybe, possibly
23:7	took up his parable	began his discourse, declaimed his poem
23:9	reckoned	known, counted, a part of
23:10	dust	descendants, offspring, children
23:12	take heed	listen to, obey, pay attention to
23:13	utmost	farthest, end
23:21	perverseness	mischief, trouble, wretchedness
23:22	unicorn	wild bull, wild ox, buffalo
23:23	enchantment	sorcery, witchcraft
	divination	fortune telling, predicting, spiritualist
	wrought	done, executed
24:1	enchantments	omens, signs in the natural world
24:3	parable	story, myth, riddle/puzzle
24:4	Almighty	Shaddai
	trance	daydream, under a spell
24:5	goodly	attractive, lovely
24:8	unicorn	wild bull, buffalo
24:9	couched	knelt, bowed down, bent down
24:10	smote	struck, hit, slapped, punished
24:14	advertise	counsel, let you know, tell you
24:18	do valiantly	grew strong, be triumphant
25:1	commit whoredom	illegallon sex outside of marriage, immoral, prostitution or worse; also describes unfaithfulness to God/His rules (sin)
25:3	kindled against	aroused against, blazed, flared hot
25:7	javelin	spear

NUMBERS

25:8,9,18	plague	slaughter, pestilence
25:8	stayed	stopped, ended, put on hold
25:11	zealous	excited, ambitious, energetic, hyper
	wrath	anger, zeal, jealousy
	consumed	vanish, waste away, dried up, spent, used up
5:12	covenant	unconditional agreement, contract, promise
25:13	seed	offspring, children, heirs
	atonement	a sacrifice, gift offered to forgive sins (sin separated man from God, the gift forgave the sin/united them: at-one-ment, to become one again)
	zealous	excited, ambitious, energetic, hyper
25:17	vex	terrify, trouble, plague, confuse, dismayed
25:18	wiles	tricks, underhandedness, treacherous deceit
	beguiled	deceived, tricked, scammed
26:2	the sum	a census, count the people
26:9	strove against	rebelled against, contended against
26:10	earth opened mouth	earthquake, earth split open
	swallowed	fell in, collapsed
26:61	strange	profane or foreign, unauthorized
27:4	done away from among his family	lost to his clan, family line ended
27:13	shall be gathered to your people	will die
27:14	sanctify Me	make My holiness apparent
27:18	lay your hand	transfer authority
27:19,23	give him a charge	commission him as your successor
27:21	U'rim	translated as "lights and perfections" or revelation and truth" — were a divination, medium or process used by ancient Hebrews/Israelites in revealing the will of God on a contested point of view or other problem
28:2+	sweet savor	soothing aroma, pleasing fragrance, smell
28:3	spot	defect, blemish, imperfection
28:6	ordained	instituted, offered
28:8+	meat	grain
28:9+	deals	portions, part, piece
28:10	sabbath	rest day, day off from work

NUMBERS

28:13,21,29	several	separate
28:17	unleavened	yeast-free
28:18	holy convocation	sacred assembly
28:18,25	servile	slavish, hard
28:19,31	blemish	defect, imperfection
28:22,28	an atonement	a sacrifice, gift offered to forgive sins (sin separated man from God, the gift forgave the sin/united them: at-one-ment, to become one again)
28:25,26 29:1,7,12	holy convocation	sacred assembly, special religious gathering
29:1	servile	slavish, bought worker
29:2,6,8,13	sweet savor	soothing aroma, pleasing smell
29:2+	blemish	defect, imperfection
29:3+	meat	grain
29:3,9,14	mingled	mixed, blended
29:3+	deals	portions, part
29:6	month	new moon
29:7	ye shall afflict your souls	a day of solemn fasting, soul searching, prayer, and repentance of all known sin
29:10	several	separate
29:12	servile	slavish, hard
29:17	spot	defect, imperfection
29:24,27,30,33	manner	ordinance, procedure
29:35	solemn	sacred, serious, holy, reverent
29:39	do	present
	set feast	appointed times, scheduled
30:2+	vow a vow	pledge, promise, vow
30:2	bind his soul	obligation, an oath to abstain from something
30:4+	her soul	herself
30:4	hold his peace at	say nothing to, keep silence
30:5	disallow	forbid, raise objection
30:7,11,14	held her peace at	said nothing to
30:8	disallowed	rejected, resisted, not allowed
30:12	void	invalid, nullify
30:16	statutes	law, rule, commands, decrees, directives
31:2	be gathered to	

NUMBERS

	your people	die
31:11,26,27	prey	plunder, treasure, wealth
	spoil	plunder, rob, robbery
31:16	plague	sickness, disease, illness
31:20	raiment	garments, clothes
31:21	ordinance	law, rule, commands, decrees, directives
31:23	abide	dwell, hang out, inhabit, live
	purified	ceremonially cleaned, ready
31:28+	tribute	tax
31:28,50	soul	person, individual, living being
31:28,30,33,38,44	beeves	cattle, cows
31:28	levy	make pay, tax, toll
31:29	for a heave offering	presented to the Lord as a sacrifice
31:32	booty	plunder, spoils, stolen goods
31:36	portion	quota, ration, share, piece of the pie
31:39	tribute	an assessment, taxes
31:42	warred	fought, battled
31:47,49	charge	responsibility, duties
31:49	sum	count, accounted for
31:50	oblation	offering
	tablets	necklaces, beads
31:51	wrought	worked, artful, craftsman
31:53	spoil	plunder, rob, robbery
31:54	memorial	remembrance, reminder
32:4+	Lord	Jehovah; God in relationship to mankind
32:4	smote	attacked, strike, hit, punish
32:7	wherefore	why
32:7,9	discourage	frustrate, restrain, turn the minds
32:10,13	was kindled	burned, inflamed, blazed, incensed
32:11,12	followed	obeyed, remained loyal
32:12	saved	except
32:14	an increase	a brood, many, a bunch
	augment	increase, add to
32:16	sheepfold	a pen/cage for sheep, where sheep were kept
32:17,36	fenced	fortified, walled
32:18	inherited	received, got
32:19	forward	beyond, past
32:22	subdued	conquered, ruled over, beaten down

NUMBERS

	guiltless	free of obligation
32:39	dispossessed	drove out, kicked out
33:2	goings out	starting places, beginning
33:3	with a high hand	confidently, triumphantly
33:5+	pitched	camped, surrounded, set up defenses
33:10+	encamped	camped, surrounded, set up defenses
33:16+	removed	left, residue
33:52	pictures	carved figures that were worshipped, stone idols
	quite pluck down	completely destroy, demolish
	high places	places where shrines for idol worship were erected – these places eventually came to mean the shrines themselves
33:54	the more	a larger
33:55	pricks	spots, cinders, barbs, stings
	vex you	trouble you, be your mortal enemies
34:3,12	Salt Sea	Dead Sea
34:5	circle around	take a turn, walk around
	bring a compass	take a turn toward
34:5,9	goings out	and, termination, beginnings, start
34:6,7	Great Sea	Mediterranean Sea
34:8	goings forth	extend to
34:11	Chin'ne-reth	Gallonilee
35:2,3,5,7	suburbs	open land, common land surrounding a town, pastureland
35:6	manslayer	a person that killed accidentally or on purpose
35:6	to them	in addition
35:11	refuge	safely, sanctuary
35:11,15	unawares	unintentionally, unwittingly
35:12	avenger	a punisher of those that break the law, torturer
35:15	stranger	foreigner, visitor, guest
	sojourner	temporarily stay, visit, live
35:16,17,18,21	smite	strike, hit, attack
35:20,22	thrust	push, stab
35:20	lay of wait	deception, trickery, set a trap
35:21	enmity	hatred, bad blood, bitterness
35:26	come without	go outside
35:27	without	outside
35:29	statute	law, rule, commands, decrees, directives

NUMBERS

35:30	mouth of witnesses	several people must agree, testify
35:31,32	satisfaction	ransom, blood money
35:33	pollute	spoil, stain, make dirty, corrupt
36:1	chief fathers	heads, family head

DEUTERONOMY

1:7	vale	valley, low land
1:8	seed	offspring, children, heirs, descendents
1:12	bear your cumbrance	endure, handle your problems, strife, bickering, disputes, weariness from pressures
1:12	strife	controversy, disagreement, dispute, fight
1:14	have spoken	purposed, suggested
1:15	made	appointed, suggested
	heads	chiefs, rulers
1:16	charged	commanded, ordered, commissioned
1:16,17	cause	problems, issues, complaints
1:22	search	spy, explore
1:26	notwithstanding	regardless, despite, nevertheless
1:27	murmured	grumbled, sulked
	hated	abhor, despise, loathe, detest
1:29	dread	fear, awe, worry, scared
1:34,35	swore	pledged, vowed, promised, gave an oath
1:36	save	except, besides, other than
	has trodden	walk, trampled, stepped on, beaten, defeated
	wholly followed	fully obeyed, followed unreservedly, been true
1:39	should be a prey	would be taken captive, carried off, seized
1:41	girded	equipped, fastened, fortified, held up
1:42	smitten	defeated, routed
1:43	presumptuously	arrogantly, foolhardily
2:1,3	compassed	went around, circled around
2:4	take you good heed	be cautious, watch yourself, be careful
2:5	meddle	interfere, interrupt, get in the middle of
2;6,28	meat	food
2:9	Distress not	Do not create a problem
2:9	contend	argue, fight, dispute, oppose
2:13	wadi, brook	a small river (stream)
2:14	wasted out	wadi, valley, perished, passed away, died
2:14,15	host	company, camp, men of war of that generation
2:18	coast	boarder, territory, frontiers

DEUTERONOMY

2:20	old time	formerly, long ago
2:30	obstinate	stubborn, uncooperative, rebellious
2:33	smote	defeated, attacked, strike, hit, punish
2:34	for a prey	as a prize of war, along with the plunder
	spoil	plunder, booty, treasure
2:36	brink	edge, shore, bank
3:3	smote	struck, destroyed, dealt a terrible blow
3:5	fenced	fortified, well-defensed, protected
3:7	spoil	plunder, booty, treasure
	prey	prize of the war
3:11	bedstead	bed, couch, place to sleep or lie down
3:11	nine cubits	13.5 feet long
	four cubits	6 feet wide
3:17	coast	territory, boundary, border
	Salt	Dead
3:18	meet	fit, men of valor, stouthearted, qualified to fight
3:24	Lord God	Jehovah Elohim, the self-existing God now interacting with mankind
3:27	behold	look well at what you see
3:28	charge	commission, orders, imbue him with strength
4:1	statutes	law, rule, commands, decrees, directives
4:1,14,22	possess	live in, own, control
4:2	diminish anything	take away, subtract from it
	keep	obey, follow, do, practice
4:5,6,8,14,45	statutes	law, rule, commands, decrees, directives
4:8,14,45	judgments	ordinances, laws, policies, decisions
4:9	take heed	be careful for, take utmost care
	your soul	watch yourselves
4:10	fear	revered, respected, trembled, dread
4:12,15,16	similitude	form, shape, figure
4:13,23	covenant	unconditional agreement, contract, promise
4:13	tables	tablets
4:15	heed	listen to, obey, pay attention to
4:16,25	corrupt	spoil, pollute, change for the worse
4:19	divided	allotted, provided, rendered available
4:26	prolong	extend, long endure
4:27	heathen	nations, non-Jew, pagan

DEUTERONOMY

4:30	tribulation	distress, anguish
	latter	later
4:34	assayed	ever tried, ventured, intervened, attempted
	temptations	trials, a series of tests
4:37	their seed	their offspring, children, heirs
	in His sight	by His presence, by His mighty power
4:40	prolong your days	live long, have long enjoyment
4:41	severed	separated, set apart
4:42	unawares	accidentally, unintentionally
	hated	malice, standing feud
4:46	smote	attacked, strike, hit, punish
5:1,31	statutes	law, rule, commands, decrees, directives
5:1	judgments	ordinances, laws, policies, decisions
5:1,10,29	keep	obey, follow, do, practice
5:2,3	covenant	unconditional agreement, contract, promise
5:5	show	declare to, convey, announce
5:6	bondage	slavery, forced labor
5:9	visiting the iniquity	pay back, payment, reward or punish
5:9	hate	abhor, despise, loathe, detest
5:14,15	sabbath	rest, day off from work
5:15	mighty	powerful, sheer strength
5:21	coven	crave, lust after, desire
5:29	fear	revered, respected, trembled, dread
6:1,2,17,20,24	statutes	law, rule, commands, decrees, directives
6:1,20	judgments	ordinances, laws, policies, decisions
6:2,13,24	fear	revered, respected, trembled, dread
6:3	observe	be careful, be attentive
	increase mightily	multiply greatly, have a lot of kids
6:7	teach them diligently to your children	impress them on your children, drill them into diligently to your children
6:8	frontlets	headband, a small scroll tied around forehead
6:10,13,18,23	swore	pledged, vowed, promised, gave an oath
6:16	tempt	test, challenge, try
6:17	keep	obey, follow, do, practice
6:21	bondmen	slaves, forced labor
	mighty	powerful, sheer strength

DEUTERONOMY

6:22	sore	terrible, ominous, horrifying
7:2	smite	attacked, strike, hit, punish
7:2,9,12	covenant	unconditional agreement, contract, promise
7:5	groves	woods, forest, a group of trees
	graven	carved, chiseled, sculpted, hand-made
7:6	special people	special treasure, people peculiarly his own
	above	out of
7:8	oath	promise, vow, contract
	bondmen	slaves, forced labor
7:9	thousand	future generations
7:10	hate	abhor, despise, loathe, detest
	slack	slow, delay
7:11	statutes	law, rule, commands, decrees, directives
7:13	fruit of thy womb	children
	fruit	crops
	corn	grain
	kine	cattle, cows
	swore	pledged, vowed, promised, gave an oath
7:15	evil	horrible, malignant
7:16,22	consume	vanish, waste away, dried up, spent, used up
7:16,25	snare	trapped, caught, imprisoned, tripped up, lure
7:20	sent the hornet	punished, caused hornets to attack
7:25	graven images	idols & carvings, statues of pagan gods
7:25,26	abomination	hated thing, detested, hated
8:2,16	prove	tried, tested, searched, examined, known
	know	learn, discover
8:4	raiment	garment, clothes
8:5	consider	remember, bear in mind
	chastens	discipline, punish, rebuke, reprimand, scold
8:6	fear	revered, respected, trembled, dread
8:9	scarceness	having plenty, excess, abundant
8:9	brass	bronze, copper
8:12	full	satisfied, content
8:13	multiplied	increased, prospered, enriched
8:14	your heart be lifted	become proud, arrogant
8:15	flint	a type of very, very hard rock
8:16	manna	edible substance provided by God, white, and flaky, with the taste of honey

DEUTERONOMY

8:18	establish	confirm, set up
	covenant	unconditional agreement, contract, promise
9:1	fenced	walled, fortified
9:3	your face	you, countenance, personal presence/power
9:5	perform the word	accomplish His promise, confirm His Word, fulfill His oath
9:6,13	stiffnecked	stubborn, obstinate, headstrong, hardened
9:7	rebellious	disobedient, quarreling, defiant
9:8,22	wrath	anger, vengeance, punishment
9:9,11,15	covenant	unconditional agreement, contract, promise
9:9	abode	dwell, live, stay, make a home, settled
9:12	corrupted	corruptly perverted, broken faith, done a disgraceful thing
9:16	molten	liquid, fluid, melted metal (i.e. volcanic lava)
9:19,23	hearkened	listened, ear was open
	a mighty hand	strength, power, force
9:28	land	people, nation
	hated	abhor, despise, loathe, detest
10:1,3	Hew	cut, carve
10:6	stead	place, succeeding him
10:8	separated	set apart, dedicated, consecrated
10:11	take	proceed on, go in and possess
10:12,20	fear	revered, respected, trembled, dread
10:13	soul	inner person, emotion, life-force, being, life
10:14	good	benefit, good not in this passage
10:15	seed	offspring, children, heirs
10:16	circumcised therefore the foreskin of your heart	the physical symbol of Israel's separation and circumcision was to be a symbol of their love and loyalty to God
	stiffnecked	stubborn, obstinate, hardened
10:17	terrible	awesome, fearful, dangerous
10:18	raiment	clothing, garments
11:1	Lord	Jehovah; God in relationship to mankind
	statutes	law, rule, commands, decrees, directives
	judgments	ordinances, laws, policies, decisions
11:2	chastisement	punishment, judgment

DEUTERONOMY

11:6	opened her mouth	split like a chasm, yawned
11:9	swore	pledged, vowed, promised, gave an oath
11:10	your foot	a treadmill, your own labors
11:11	drinks	received, soaks up
11:12	cares	provides, watches over
11:13	diligently	hard-working, busy, steady
	soul	inner person, emotion, life-force, being, life
11:14	first rain	autumn rain (after planting season)
	latter rain	spring rain (before harvest, to bring maturity)
	corn	grain
11:17	wrath	anger, fury, judgement
	kindled	burn, flare up
	shut up	close
	perish	die
11:18	frontlets	badge, memorial symbol
11:20	gates	city gates, door posts
11:21	fathers	ancestors
	as the days of heaven upon the earth	forever, long as the heavens are above the earth
11:22	cleave	hold fast, cling to
11:24	uttermost sea	Mediterranean Sea
11:25	stand before	resist, hold his own
11:29	go	are entering
11:30	the champaign over against Gilgallon	Arabah, the flat open country opposite Gilgallon
	plains	oaks
11:32	statutes	law, rule, commands, decrees, directives
12:1	judgments	ordinances, laws, policies, decisions
12:2	possess	conquer, control, rule over, dominate
12:3	groves	(Heb:Asherah) either a living tree or a tree-like pole, set up as an object of worship, being symbolical of the female or productive principle in nature. Every Phoenician had an asherah near them. Both the "May Pole" and "Christmas Tree" (Jer.10:3-5) originate with this Asherah. The word is often translated "green trees" or

DEUTERONOMY

		"grove." This "nature worship" became associated with sexual immorality, re: May Pole
12:3	hew	axe, chop, cut, chisel, sculpt
12:5	habitation	dwelling, home
12:6	tithes	ten percent, one out of every ten
12:9	rest	resting place, allotted haven
	inheritance	possessions, heritage
12:11,17,26	choice vows	special pledges, special offering
11:15,17,18,21	gates	city gates, towns
12:15	lusts after	desire, hunger, crave, want badly
12:15,24	hart	stag, deer
12:15:22	roebuck	gazelle
12:19	heed	care, keep constantly in mind
12:19	forsake	abandon, leave, betray, walk away
12:20,23,27	flesh	meat
12:20,21	your soul lusts after	to your heart's desire, whenever you wish
12:26	holy	consecrated, sacred
12:29	cut off	destroy, remove, exterminate, put to death
12:30	snared	trapped, caught, imprisoned, tripped up, lure
12:31	abomination	detestable, abhorrent act
	hates	abhors, despises, disregards
12:32	observe	be careful, follow, keeps
	diminish	take away, do less
13:3	proves	tests, challenges, makes sure
13:4	walk	follow, obey, do
	fear	revered, respected, trembled, dread
13:5,10	thrust	push, draw, allure, make one leave
13:5	house of bondage	(Egypt) slavery, prisoners
13:6	bosom	chest, breast, heart
	entice	tempt, tease, lure, draw away
13:7	Namely	specifically, precisely, particularly
13:8	consent	yield, give way
13:13	children of Be'lial	worthlessness, destruction, wicked people who oppose the love of God and prefer evil
13:14	abomination	detestable thing, disgusting thing
13:15	smite	attacked, strike, hit, punish
13:16	spoil	plunder, stolen goods, booty
	whit	peace

DEUTERONOMY

13:17	fierceness	menacing, raging, savage, violent
	multiply	increase your numbers
13:18	hearken	listen, pay attention, heed
	eyes	sight, vision
14:1	cut	disfigure, gash, tattooed patterns in the skin
	make	shave
	make any baldness	shave their head as a sign of sorrow
14:2	holy	consecrated, dedicated
	be a peculiar people unto Himself	be a treasured possession, be dedicated people not conformed to worldly standards but living to please God
14:3	abominable	detestable, unclean
14:5	hart	stag
	roebuck	gazelle
	pygarg	antelope
	chamois	mountain sheep
14:7	cloven	split
	unclean	unfit for, impure, unacceptable
14:8	swine	pig, hog
14:11	clean	fit, without fear of defilement
14:12	ossifrage	vulture, gier eagle
	ospray	black vulture, bearded vulture
14:13	glede	buzzard
	kite	falcon
14:15	cuckow	sea-mew, seagull
14:17	gier eagle	carrion vulture, white vulture
14:19	creeping	teeming, swarming
14:21	gates	community, town
	seethe	boil, cook in a pot
14:22	increase of your seed	produce from what you sow
14:23	fear	revered, respected, trembled, dread
4:25	turn	exchange
14:26	bestow	spend, give, provide
	soul	inner person, emotion, life-force, being, life
14:28	lay it up	deposit it, leave it
	gates	city gates, community, settlement
15:1,2	release	remission of debts, grant of forgiveness

DEUTERONOMY

15:4	save	except
15:5	hearken	listen, pay attention, heed
15:7,22	gates	city gates
15:7	shut	close
15:9	be evil	is hostile, loveless
	cry	appeal, plead, ask
15:10	grieved	grudging, have no regrets
15:11	open your hand wide	give freely, be open-handed
15:12	sold to you	obligated economically
15:13	empty	empty handed, nothing
15:14	furnish liberally	excess, plenty, abundant, plentiful
	floor	threshing floor
15:15	bondman	slave, forced labor
15:16	with you	off
15:18	hard	a hardship, with reluctance
15:19	sanctify	consecrate, dedicate, commit
15:21	blemish	imperfection, impurity, defect
	sacrifice	slaughter, blood offering
15:23	roebuck	gazelle
	hart	stag
16:2,5,6	sacrifice	slaughter, blood offering
16:3,4	leavened	yeast, a symbol of corruption and evil
16:3,8,16	unleavened	yeast-free
16:3	affliction	distress, humiliation
16:4	coast	territory, boundary, border
16:5,11	gates	city gates, townships
16:7	turn	return, start back, set out
16:9	sickle	reap, harvest, gather crops
16:10	tribute	portion, share, gift
16:12	bond	slave, forced labor
	statutes	law, rule, commands, decrees, directives
16:12,13	observe	follow carefully, keep
16:13	corn	grain
16:19	wrest judgment	pervert justice, dishonest, corrupt
	gift	bribe, pay off, cheat
	pervert	subvert, jeopardize, twist
16:22	image	idolatrous stone, sacred pillar

DEUTERONOMY

	hates	abhor, despise, loathe, detest
17:1	evilfavoredness	defect
	blemish	imperfection, impurity, defect
	abomination	detestable, abhorrent
17:2,5	gates	city gates, communities
17:2	transgressing His covenant	violation of His agreement
17:4	abomination is	detestable thing is, foul deed
	wrought	done, accomplished, completed
17:8	controversy	dispute, doubtful case
17:11	sentence	words, terms, instruction
17:12,13	presumptuously	arrogantly, proud, big-headed
17:12	hearken	listen, pay attention, heed
17:15	set	make, appoint, commission
	stranger	foreigner, guest, visitor
17:17	multiply	take many, amass
17:19	fear	revere, respect, honor, worship
	statutes	law, rule, commands, decrees, directives
18:3	due	right, proper
	maw	stomach, inner parts, guts
18:4	corn	grain
18:6	gates	city gates
	sojourned	temporarily stay, visit, live
18:8	like portions	equal portions, fair shares
	patrimony	fathers' estates, family property
18:9,12	abominations	detestable things, unclean, filthy
18:10	pass through the fire	practice the pagan rite, be burned alive as an offering or sacrifice to the god Molech
	divination	fortune telling, spiritualist
	enchanter	magician, sorcerer
18:11	familiar spirits	ghosts, demons, supernatural beings
	wizard	medium, spiritualist, make witch
	necromancer	consulter of the dead, séance leader
18:13	perfect	blameless, absolutely true
18:14,15,19	hearkened	listen, pay attention, heed
18:14	diviners	fortune tellers
18:22	presumptuously	arrogantly, proud, big-headed
19:3	prepare	build, survey

DEUTERONOMY

	way	road, area of the land
19:3,8	coast	borders, boundaries, territory limits
19:4	ignorantly	unintentionally, by mistake
19:5	hew	cut, chop, hack
	head	iron
	helve	handle
	lights	strikes
19:6	long	too great
	hated him not	had no malice, no beef
19:11	hate	abhor, has a feud against him
	lie in wait	plot to kill
19:14	landmark	property line, boundary marker
19:18	make diligent inquisition	investigate thoroughly, look into with care, investigate
20:11	tributaries	forced laborers, enslaved subjects
20:14	spoil	plunder, bounty, treasures, stolen goods
20:18	abominations	detestable ways, sin, wickedness
20:20	meat	food
20:20	bulwarks	fort, fortress, wall, defense
23:3	wrought	worked, created, made, crafted
21:4	rough valley	valley with running water
	eared	ploughed
	strike off	break, end
21:5	controversy	dispute, strife
	stroke	assault, violence case
21:12	bring her home	take her captive, prisoner
	shave her head	shave all her head in a ritual of purification & cleansing
	pare	trim, cut
21:13	raiment	clothing, garment
	bewail	mourn, cry, be sad
21:15,15,16,	hated	abhor, despise, loathe, detest
21:18	stubborn, rebellious	unruly, lack self-control, uncooperative
21:20	glutton	overeater, pig, hog
	drunkard	over drink alcohol, wino, drunk, partier
21:21	stone	execute, kill, capital punishment
21:23	his	the criminal's

DEUTERONOMY

	the tree	the place of his hanging
22:1	your brother	one of their own people
22:3	raiment	clothing, garments
	hide yourself	avoid responsibility, indifferent, turn away
22:4	way	road, path, direction
22:5	abomination	detestable ways, sin, wickedness
22:6,7	dam	mother
22:8	battlement	parapet, guard railing
22:9	divers seeds	various seeds, more than one kind of seeds
22:11	divers sorts	various fabrics
22:12	quarters	corners
	vesture	cloak, robe
22:13,16	hate	turns against, dislikes
22:13,17	maid	virgin
22:14	speech against	tell a lie, slander, false accusations
22:15+	damsel	young woman
22:19	amerce	punish with a fine, penalty
22:21	wrought	committed, done
	evil	wickedness, sin, wrong-doing
22:24	she cried not	didn't complain, didn't fight back, allowed
	he has humbled	taken her virginity, shamed, ruined reputation
22:25	force her and lie with her	rape her
22:30	discover	uncover, see naked body
	discover his father's skirt	commit adultery with his father's wife
23:1	stones	testicles, balls
23:2	illegitimate	child fathered out of marriage
23:2,3	congregation	assembly, gathering, main group of people
23:5	hearken	listen, pay attention, heed
23:7	abhor	despise, detest
23:13	paddle	spade, stick, peg
23:16	likes	pleases, makes happy
23:17	Sodomite	a homosexual, gay, same gender sexual activity
23:19	victuals	food, snacks, meals, grub, chow
23:19,20	upon usury	with high interest, (like payday loans)
23:21	vow a vow	make a pledge, promise, oath
23:22	forbear to vow	refrain from pledging/promising

DEUTERONOMY

23:23	vowed	pledged, spoken promise
23:25	move	wield, put
	corn	grain
24:1	favor	acceptance, liking
24:3	hate	abhor, despise, loathe, detest
24:4	abomination	detestable, abhorrent, nasty, unholy
24:6	nether	lower, bottom
24:7	makes merchandise	sells him into slavery
24:8	plague	infection, disease
	observe diligently	be cautious, be careful
24:10,11	to fetch his pledge	to carry off his security or collateral
24:11	stand abroad	wait outside
24:12	not sleep with his pledge	not to keep it overnight
24:15	hire	wages, salary, payment
24:17	raiment	clothing, garment
	to pledge	as security or collateral, in pawn
24:18,22	bondman	slave, forced laborer
24:20	beat	shake, knock off the fruit
25:1	controversy	dispute, argument, disagreement
	to judgment	to court
25:4	tread	walking, smashing, stamping
	corn	grain
25:5	without to a stranger	outside the family
25:8	stand to it	still refuses, won't accept
25:11	secret	genitals, private parts
25:13	divers	different, two kinds
25:16	an abomination	detestable, unclean, unholy, impure
25:18	smote the hindmost	struck down those who were weary or feeble
	feared	revered, respected, trembled, dread
26:5	sojourned	temporarily stay, visit, live
26:6	evil entreated us	mistreated us, dealt ill with us, treated us harshly
	bondage	forced labor, slavery
26:10	set	offer, brought
26:14	mourning	distress, ceremonially defiled
	aught	any
	hearkened	listen, pay attention, heed
26:16	statutes	law, rule, commands, decrees, directives

DEUTERONOMY

	judgments	ordinances, laws, policies, decisions
26:17	avouched the Lord	openly declared the Lord
26:18	avouched	made an agreement with
	peculiar people	treasured possession, special, valued
26:19	make you high	set you up, honor, make great & powerful
	holy	consecrated, dedicated, obedient
27:10	statutes	law, rule, commands, decrees, directives
27:11	charged	commanded, ordered
27:15	an abomination	a detestable thing, unclean, impure
	Amen	So be it, It is true
27:16	sets light by	disgraces, dishonors, insult, despises, slights
27:17	removes his neighbor's landmark	move the property boundary mark
27:19	perverts	distorts, denies
27:24	smites	strikes, kills, murders
27:25	takes reward	accepts a bribe, cheats, dishonest, corrupt
27:26	confirms	uphold, observe
27:30	father's skirt	private parts, nakedness; specifically, not to have sex with his father's wife
28:2	hearken to	listen, pay attention, heed, obey
28:4,18,53	fruit	offering
28:5	store	kneading trough or bread bin
28:7,25	smitten	struck, defeated, attacked
28:10	called by the name of the Lord	see the Lord's name proclaimed over them
28:11	plenteous	abound, overflow, fertile, abundant
28:12	good treasure	storehouse, bounteous store
28:13	head	chief, most important, on top, rising
	tail	underneath, downward
	observe	take note, obey
28:13,15	hearken	listen, pay attention, heed
28:14	go inside	deviate, turn aside
28:20	vexation	confusion, trouble, frustrations, distresses
28:21	pestilence	disease, plague
	consumed	vanish, waste away, dried up, spent, used up
28:22	consumption	tuberculosis, a wasting away disease of the lungs
	mildew	paleness, anemia, white blood cell disease
	blasting	blight

DEUTERONOMY

28:23	shall be brass	solid, not emitting rain
	shall be iron	unproductive
28:24	make	give, provide
28:26	fray	frighten, scare off
28:27,35	botch	boils, sores
28:27	emerods	tumors, ulcers
28:28	madness	insanity, crazy, mentally ill
	astonishment of heart	bewilderment, terror of heart
28:29	grope	feel for, grab, search for, fumble around
	spoiled	robbed, exploited and plundered, oppressed
28:32	fail with longing	yearn, ache continually for, pine after
28:33	eat up	take away, remove, consume
28:38	consume	vanish, waste away, dried up, spent, used up
28:40	coasts	territory, boundary, border
	cast	lose, drop
28:41	go into captivity	taken as slaves
28:42	consume	vanish, waste away, dried up, spent, used up
28:43	inside you	in your midst
28:44	head	chief, important one
28:46	wonder	miracle, proofs
	seed	offspring, children, heirs
28:48	a yoke of iron	oppression, dominated, ruled over
28:49	tongue	language, dialect
28:50	regard	noticed, heeded, observed, attended to
28:52	besiege	surround, attack
	fenced	fortified, unscalable
28:53	fruit	offspring, child
28:53,55,57	straitness	hardship, distressing confinement
28:54	tender	soft, gentle, sissy, lightweight
28:55	distress	oppress, trouble, bother
28:56	tender	young, most refined
	delicate	weak, dainty
	evil	hostile, angry, cruel
28:57	between her feet	give birth, have a child, deliver a baby
28:58,66,67	fear	revered, respected, trembled, dread
28:58	fearful	awe-inspiring, amazing
28:59,61	plagues	diseases, afflictions

DEUTERONOMY

28:67	evening	night
28:68	bondmen	male slaves
	bondwomen	female slaves
29:1,9,12,14,21	covenant	unconditional agreement, contract, promise
29:3	temptations	trails, challenges, tests
29:4	perceive	know, understand
29:7	smote	defeated, attacked, strike, hit, punish
29:11	hewer	axe-man, chopper, cutter, chisel, sculptor
29:17	abominations	detestable things, disgusting images
29:18	wormwood	bitter, hard to take, painful to swallow
29:19	bless himself	congratulate himself
29:20	smoke	burn
29:22	stranger	foreigner, visitor, guest
	plagues	desolations, diseases, sicknesses
29:23	brimstone	judgment, damnation, hellfire
29:25	forsaken the covenant	broken the agreement
29:28	indignation	anger, wrath, fury
29:29	secret	hidden, concealed things
30:1	call them to mind	remember, reflect upon them
30:2	return	turn again
30:3	turn your captivity	restore you from captivity
30:4	outmost parts	to the ends of earth
30:7	hate	persecuted, punished, cruel
30:9	plenteous	prosperous, wealthy, rich
	fruit	offspring, children, heirs
30:10	hearken	listen, pay attention, heed
	statutes	law, rule, commands, decrees, directives
30:18	denounce	speak against, declare, put down
30:19	record	witness, give testimony
	seed	offspring, children, heirs
31:3	possess	take possession of, exterminate, supplant
31:8	dismayed	afraid, alarmed, shocked
31:9,16,20,25,26	covenant	unconditional agreement, contract, promise
31:10	solemnity	appointed time, prescribed time, fixed time
31:12	stranger	alien, visitor, guest
31:12,13	fear	reverence, be careful to practice
31:13,23	charge	commission, orders, job, duty

DEUTERONOMY

31:16	go a whoring	be unfaithful to God
31:17	devoured	consumed, destroyed
31:18	wrought	done
31:20	flows honey	honey was scarce, and used to sweeten (like sugar), so for it to "flow" means the land would be full of good things
31:21	seed	offspring, children, heirs
31:21,23	swore	pledged, vowed, promised, gave an oath
31:27	rebellion	disobedience, defiant, arrogance
	stiff neck	stubbornness
31:28	ears	hearing, listening, obey
32:2	doctrine	teaching, instruction
	distil as the dew	gentle, unforced, regularly appear
32:3	publish	proclaim, report, tell, testify
32:5	crooked	twisted, underhanded, crafty
32:6	requite	repay, settle debt
32:8	Most High	El Elyon
32:10	waste howling	empty, ruined, occupied by beasts
32:11	flutters	hover over, flap wings over, protect, guard
32:13	flinty	very hard, sharp
32:15	Jeshurun	Israel
	waxen fat	became successful, prsoper, become rich
	esteemed	well favored, loved, honored, respected
32:17,27	feared	revered, respected, trembled, dread
32:18	unmindful	forgetful, inconsiderate, unthinking, unthankful
32:19	abhorred	spurned, filled with loathing
32:20	froward	perverse, unfaithful, disloyal
32:21	vanities	worthless idols
32:28	void	without life, empty, barren
32:30,31	Rock	foundation, strength
32:33	venom of asps	this means that what his enemies produce or make will not be a good thing if the Jews eat, drink or use them; the enemies "stuff" is cursed
32:35	shoes of iron	figuratively this blessing means that Asher shall "step on" or defeat his enemies
	vengeance	get even, pay back, revenge, punish
	recompense	pay back, payment, reward or punish
	calamity	disaster, misfortune, accident, bad luck

DEUTERONOMY

	make haste	are coming soon, near is the day of their fate
32:41	whet	sharpen, take up
32:42	drunk	overflow with, drench
32:44	Ho-she'a	Joshua
32:51	sanctified	honored, displayed holiness
33:8	Thum'mim	
	U'rim	translated as "lights and perfections" or revelation and truth" — were a divination, medium or process used by ancient Hebrews/Israelites in revealing the will of God on a contested point of view or other problem
33:9	observed	watched, kept watch, heeded
	covenant	unconditional agreement, contract, promise
33:15	lasting	everlasting, timeless
33:17	unicorns	wild oxen
	push	gore, butt
33:28	corn	grain
33:29	tread upon	trample down, walk on/over
34:2	utmost sea	Mediterranean
34:3	south	Negev
34:4	seed	offspring, children, heirs
34:6	sepulcher	grave, burial
34:7	natural force	strength, youthfulness, vigor, energy
34:7	abated	lessened, impaired
34:9	hearkened	listen, pay attention, hee
34:12	great terror	awesome deeds, mighty power

JOSHUA

1:1	minister	assistant, attendant, religious worker
1:4	great	Mediterranean Sea
	coast	territory, border, boundary
1:8	depart out	be removed from, leave
1:11	victuals	provisions, food, supplies
1:14	valour	bravery, courage, daring, heroism
1:15	rest	peace, security
	sunrising	east
1:17	hearkened	listen, pay attention, heed
2:6	flax	a type of plant, after beaten, would be used for fine clothes (linen, gauze)
2:6	laid	arranged, set up, planned
2:15	upon	built into, a terrace/balcony
2:16	pursuers	trackers, bounty-hunters
2:17	blameless	free, not responsible
	swear	pledged, vowed, promised, gave an oath
2:19	guiltless	free, not responsible
	on our head	our responsibility, burden
2:20	quit	free, rid of
2:23	befell	came about, occurred, took place, transpired
3:4	heretofore	before, earlier, at times past
3:3,6,11,14,17	covenant	unconditional agreement, contract, promise
3:7	magnify	glorify, honor, increase, enlarge, praise
3:8	bear	carry, support
3:10	know	understand, comprehend
3:16	Salt	a.k.a. the Dead Sea
	against	opposite
3:17	were passed clean over	had finished crossing
4:5	pass	cross, journey
4:6	sign	memorial, physical reminder, monument
	mean	is signified
4:7	cut off	held back, separated
	memorial	reminder, monument
4:7,9,18	covenant	unconditional agreement, contract, promise
4:10	hasted	hurried, sped up

JOSHUA

4:11	clean passed	finished crossing
4:13	prepared	equipped, trained, ready
4:14	magnified	exalted, praised, spoke highly of
4:14,24	feared	revered, respected, trembled, dread
4:16	bear	carry, support, lift up
4:18	soles	bottom of the feet
4:20	pitch	set up, prepare, establish camp
5:1	their heart melted	they lost their courage, gave up
5:8	whole	healed, made better, restored
5:9	reproach	shamed, ruined reputation, humiliation
5:10	at	in the
5:11	old corn	previously harvested, gathered & stored up
	morrow	next day
	unleavened	yeast-free
	parched	roasted
5:12	corn	grain (like corn, wheat, barley)
6:1	straitly	tightly, completely
6:3,4,7,11,14,15,19	compass	go around, circle, surround
6:4	bear	carry, support, lift up
6:5	scend	go up (i.e. to battle), move out, proceed
6:6,8	covenant	unconditional agreement, contract, promise
6:9,13	rearward	rear guard
6:19	consecrated	set apart, dedicated, live holy
6:23	kindred	relatives, family
6:26	adjured them	required an oath of them, pleaded, begged
6:27	noised	spread, published, braodcasted
7:1	accursed thing	banned, forbidden, illegallon, cursed
7:1	kindled	burned
7:2	view	spy out
	viewed	spied out, observed, watched
7:5	in the going down	on the descent or slope, downhill
7:6	rent	tear, ripped, shred, pull apart, open
	put dust upon their heads	mourned, grieved, humbled
7:7	would to God	if only, I wish, hopeful
7:9	evniron us	surround us, guard, protect
7:10	Get you up	stand up
7:11	covenant	unconditional agreement, contract, promise

JOSHUA

	dissembled	deceived, complained, created divisions
7:13	sanctify	consecrate, clean up, make holy
7:15	accursed	banned, forbidden, illegallon
	transgressed the covenant	violated the agreement, broke contract
7:18	taken	chosen, picked
7:20	thus and thus have I done	this is what I did
7:21	garment	mantle, clothes, threads
	coveted	wanted, lusted, desired badly, craved
7:26	great heap of stones	monument, memorial, marker
	A'chor	Trouble
8:10	went up	marched, proceeded, attacked
8:11	pitched	camped, set up, established
8:13	their liers in wait	ambushers, attackers
8:14	liers in ambush	hidden, camouflaged, highwaymen
8:19	ambush	trapped, mugged, intercepted, hijacked
8:19	hasted	hurried, sped up, rushed
8:22,24	smote	attacked, strike, hit, punish
8:24	made an end	finished, completed
	fallen on	killed by, deadly assault, attack
8:26	wherewith he stretched out the spear	did not call a halt, continued
8:28	desolation	destruction, ruin, emptiness
8:29	carcass	corpse, body
8:33	this side the ark and on that side	both sides of the ark
	covenant	unconditional agreement, contract, promise
9:1	great sea	Mediterranean Sea
9:2	accord	purpose, in agreement, harmony
9:4	wilily	craftily, deceptive, tricky
	bottles	skins, containers to hold wine/liquid
9:4:13	rent	torn, busted, ruined
9:5	clouted	patched, repaired
9:6,7,11,15,16	league	treaty, compact, alliance, accord
9:9	name	name, reputation
9:11,14	victuals	provisions, food

JOSHUA

9:13	bottles	wineskins
9:14	counsel	advice, opinion, guidance, instructions
9:15,18,19	swore	pledged, vowed, promised, gave an oath 9:18
	smote	attacked, assaulted, punished
	murmured	grumbled, complained, whined
9:20	wrath	God's judgment, anger, fury
9:21,23,27	hewers of wood	woodcutters
9:22	beguiled	deceived, tricked, played
9:23	drawers of water	without plumbing (sinks, toilets, etc.), water had to be "drawn" or scooped up with buckets, pitchers from wells and rivers by "drawers" or people (usually women and children)
9:24	certainly	clearly, plainly
	Sore	very, much, a lot, badly
10:4,26,28,33,37,40	smite	attacked, strike, hit, punish
10:6	Slack	relax, lazy, ease up
10:7	mighty	brave, valiant, courageous
10:8+	Lord	Jehovah; God in relationship to mankind
10:10	discomfited	overthrew, confronted
10:11	hailstones	frozen rain drops, balls/chunks of ice
10:13	Ja'sher	not considered for the Holy Bible
	hasted not	delayed, put off
10:14	hearkened	listen, pay attention, heed
10:16	fled	ran away, escaped, got away
10:18	keep	guard, protect, watch over
10:19	hindmost	rear
10:20	slaughter	slain, killed, butchered, massacred
10:20	consumed	vanish, waste away, dried up, spent, used up
	fenced	fortified, walled
10:21	coved his tongue	didn't utter a word, silent
10:24	necks	conquer, as a symbol of mastery
10:25	dismayed	afraid, alarmed, shocked
10:28,30,32,35,37	souls	people, individuals, living beings
10:40	vale	foothills
11:4	hosts	army
11:5	were met together	agreed to meet
	pitched	camped, set up, established
11:6,9	hough	hamstring

JOSHUA

11:11	smote	attacked, assaulted, punished
	souls	people
12:1	smote	attacked, assaulted, punished, i.e. defeated
12:3	Chin'ne-roth	a.k.a. Gallonilee
	Salt	a.k.a. the Dead Sea
12:7	a possession	their own, property
13:1	dismayed	afraid, alarmed, shocked
13:13	expelled	kicked out, run off, booted, banished
13:22	soothsayer	diviner, fortune teller
13:25	coast	territory, boundary, border
13:32	distribute	divide, deal out, pass out, divvy up
14:4	save	except, besides
	suburbs	pasture lands, non-developed area
14:7	espy	spy, watch, closely observe
14:8	wholly followed	obeyed wholeheartedly, dedicated
14:9	swore	pledged, vowed, promised, gave an oath
14:9	trodden	trampled, crushed or broken, stepped upon
14:12	fenced	fortified, well-defended, protected
14:15	rest	peace, safety, relaxed
15:2,5	Salt	a.k.a. the Dead Sea
15:4	goings	extremities
15:4,12	coast	territory, boundary, border
15:5	uttermost	furthest, limits
15:6	stone	marker, boundary point
15:8	valley of giants	an area where the Nephalim & Rephaim (giants-very tall people 7-10 feet tall) lived
15:10	compassed	included, circled
15:12,47	Great	a.k.a. Mediterranean
15:18	lighted off	dismounted from, got off
15:19	nether	lower
16:1	fell	went
16:3	coast	territory, boundary, border
	nether	lower
16:3,8	goings out thereof	borders
16:6	out toward	Westward at
16:10	under tribute	slaves, as forced laborers
17:1	man of war	great soldier, warrior, decorated combat veteran
17:7	coast	territory, boundary, border

JOSHUA

	lies	was
17:13	waxed	grew, increased
	tribute	slaves, forced labor
17:15	narrow	small
17:17	lot	allotment, portion, share
17:18	wood	forest, trees
	outgoings	borders
18:4,6,8,9	describe	diagram, map out, record
18:5,11,20	coast	territory, boundary, border
18:6	cast lots	predictions; like flipping a coin; paper, rock, scissors, throw dice
18:8	charged	commanded, ordered
18:9	parts	divisions, groups
18:10	divisions	family groups, clans
18:12	goings out thereof	its outer limits
18:14	compassed	covered, included
18:14,15	quarter	portion, part, area
18:17	was drawn	extended, established, survey lines
	the going up	the ascent
	stone	marker, boundary point
18:19	outgoings	limits
	Salt	a.k.a. the Dead Sea
19:10	border	territory
19:14	compasses	go about, surround, encamp, encircle
19:14,22,29	outgoings	limits
19:22,29,34,47	coast	territory, boundary, border
19:34	sunrising	east
19:35	fenced	fortified, walled
19:49	made an end of dividing	finished apportioning
	their coasts	by its territory, boundary, border
20:2	Appoint out for you	designate, separate, divide
20:3	unawares	unintentionally, accident
20:3,5	unwittingly	without premeditation, chance
20:3	refuge	hideout, safe place, sanctuary, shelter
20:4	declare his cause	state his case, explain, give an account
20:5	hated him not	without malice, not a plot
20:9	stranger	foreigner, alien, guest

JOSHUA

	sojourns	temporarily stay, visit, live
	at unawares	by accident, off guard, snuck up on
21:1	heads	leaders, bosses, chiefs
21:2+	suburbs	pasture lands, unpopulated areas
21:4,20	lot	share, portion, take, cut
21:9	mentioned	called, named, identified
21:27,32,38	refuge	safe, sanctuary, security
22:2	kept	obey, follow, do, practice
22:3	kept the charge	carried out the missions, fulfilled, honored
22:5	soul	living being, person, individual
22:8	raiment	clothing, garments
22:9	were possessed	had acquired, took ownership
22:10	to see to	in appearance, look at, watch
22:11	say	heard it said, utter
22:12	gathered	assembled, brought together
22:16,20	trespass	wrong doing, violate law
22:17	plague	sickness, disease, curse, judgement
22:19	notwithstanding	However
	unclean	unfit, impure, not acceptable
	beside	in addition to, also
22:20	accursed	banned, devoted, dedicated
22:23	meat	grain
	require	answer, call us to account
22:24,25	fear	revered, respected, trembled, dread
22:27	part	share, portion, cut, take
22:29	meat	grain
23:1	waxed	grew, increased, became
23:4	cut off	destroyed, defeated, punished
	Great	a.k.a. Mediterranean
23:5	expel	kick out, run off, booted, banish
23:6	courageous	brave, gutsy, fearless, heroic
23:7	make mention	speak about, speak of, utter, talk about
23:7	swear	pledged, vowed, promised, gave an oath
23:9	stand before	withstand, go against
23:12	go in to	associate with (business, personal, sexual)
23:13	snares	trapped, caught, imprisoned, tripped up, lure
	scourges	whip lashes, stripes, beatings
23:14	am going the way	

JOSHUA

	of all the earth	will die
24:2,3,14,15	flood	river (i.e. Euphrates)
24:3	seed	offspring, children, heirs
24:5	plagued	afflicted, troubled, tormented
24:7	covered	drowned
24:10	hearken	listen, pay attention, heed
24:14	fear	revered, respected, trembled, dread
24:17	wherein	in which
24:19	transgressions	misdeeds, sins, wrong-doing, violations
24:20,23	strange	foreign, visitor, guest
24:20	do you hurt	bring disaster, plague, trouble
	consume	vanish, waste away, dried up, spent, used up
24:23	incline	yield, listen
24:25	covenant	unconditional agreement, contract, promise
	statute	law, rule, commands, decrees, directives
24:25	ordinance	rule, statute, important tradition
24:31	outlived	survived
24:33	pertained	belonged, relates to, associated

JUDGES

1:6,7	great	big
1:7	meat	scraps
	requited	repaid, avenged
1:10,11	went	advanced, attacked
1:14	lighted	got down, got off, dismounted
1:15	nether	lower, bottom
1:20	expelled from there	kicked out, drove from it
1:22	house	family, estate
1:23	descry	spy out, observe, watch
1:27	would dwell	persisted in living, reside
1:28	tribute	forced labor, servant, slave
1:30,33,35	tributaries	forced laborers
1:35	house	family, estate
1:36	coast	territory, boundary, border
2:1,10	covenant	unconditional agreement, contract, promise
2:2	league	treaty, alliance, partnership
	throw	tear, breakdown
2:3	snare	trapped, caught, imprisoned, tripped up, lure
2:10	gathered to their fathers	died
	bowed themselves	worshiped, humbled
2:13	Baal	principal male god of the Babylonians, sun god
	Ashtoroth	a goddess in the Canaanite religion, fertility (sex) goddess (a.k.a. Ishtar and Easter)
2:14	spoilers	robbers, thieves, vandals
2:15	distressed	bothered, bummed out, troubled, shook up
2:16	judges	a governor or ruler, the name given to those rulers who presided over the affairs of the Israelites during the interval between the death of Joshua and the first "King"
2:16	spoiled	plundered, robbed, ripped off
2:17	went a whoring	prostituting themselves, unfaithful to beliefs
2:18	repented	grieved, upset, felt sorry
2:19	corrupted	perverted, spoiled
2:22	prove	tried, tested, searched, examined, known
3:1,4	prove	tried, tested, searched, examined, known

JUDGES

3:1	known	understand, comprehend
3:7	groves	(Heb:Asherah) either a living tree or a tree-like pole, set up as an object of worship, being symbolical of the female or productive principle in nature. Every Phoenician had an asherah near them. Both the "May Pole" and "Christmas Tree" (Jer.10:3-5) originate with this Asherah. The word is often translated "green trees" or "grove." This "nature worship" became associated with sexual immorality.
3:10	prevailed	win, champs, overcame, defeated
3:13	gathered	recruited, collected
	smote	defeated, beat, conquered
3:16	dagger	knife, small sword
	gird	fasten, hitch, hook up
	raiment	cloak, garment, threads
3:18	made an end	finished presenting
	offer the present	tribute, gift
	bore	carried, lifted
3:19	quarries	caves or pits where large stones/blocks were cut, chiseled
	errand	job, task, assignment, chore
	by	at
	Keep silence	leave us alone
3:22	haft	knife blade
	dirt	poop, excrement
3:24	covers his feet	urinating, pissing, is relieving himself
3:25	tarried	waited, delayed, put off
3:27	before	led
3:29	lusty	healthy, hearty, powerful, go-getter
3:30	subdued	defeated, beat, conquered
3:31	goad	push, fire up, motivate, encourage, urge
4:2	sold them into the hand	made them become slaves
4:7	draw	lure, tempt, entice
	deliver	give
4:11	severed	separated, cut-off, isolated
	pitched his tent	camped, set up, established

JUDGES

4:12	was	had
4:13	Gen'tiles	non-Jews, heathen nations
4:14	gone out	gone ahead, led, advance
4:15	discomfited	routed, beat-up, whipped
4:16	host	army
	fell upon the edge of the sword	were killed
4:18	Turn	Come
	mantle	rug, thick coverlet
4:21,22	nail	tent peg
4:21	smote	attacked, strike, hit, punish
4:23	subdued	defeated, beat, conquered
5:2	the avenging of	bringing victory to, pay back, retribution
5:4	clouds also dropped water	rain
5:5	mountains melted	ran away, fled, tried to hide
5:6	highways	large roads, streets (for horses, carts, chariots)
	byways	small roads, paths, trails (for walking)
	unoccupied	empty, abandoned, vacated, no one at home
5:7	ceased	disappeared, vanished, ended (the small towns that were outside walled cities became unsafe)
	mother	woman leader
5:10	ride on white asses	hold public office
5:11	go down to the gates	defend themselves
5:13	nobles	rich, wealthy, royalty, blue-bloods
5:14	root	few, small number, remnant, left over
	handle the pen	writers, scribes ("literate" and able to make letters, words etc.)
5:15	princes	leaders, chiefs, rulers, influential men
	searches of heart	knows the true intent, nothing is hidden
5:18	jeopardized	risked, took a chance
5:21	ancient	very old, well known, revered, famous
5:26	pierced	stabbed, poked, rammed
5:28	lattice	grate, grill, mesh, a woven pattern
5:30	sped	found, discovered, come upon
	divers	various, different
6:1	into the hand	under the control, captivity
6:3	came up against	

JUDGES

	them	invaded the country, attacked
6:4	increase	produce, crops
	sustenance	food, supplies
6:11	angel	messenger, supernatural being
	hide	save
6:12,20,21,22	angel	messenger, supernatural being
6:13	befallen	happened to, occured
	miracles	wonders, supernatural events
6:16	smite	strike down, beat, defeat
6:19,20,21	unleavened	yeast-free
6:20,21	flesh	meat
6:28,30	groves	(Heb:Asherah) either a living tree or a tree-like pole, set up as an object of worship, being symbolical of the female or productive principle in nature. Every Phoenician had an asherah near them. Both the "May Pole" and "Christmas Tree" (Jer.10:3-5) originate with this Asherah. The word is often translated "green trees" or "grove." This "nature worship" became associated with sexual immorality.
6:30	cast	broken, destroyed, torn up
6:32	plead	contend, beg, discuss
6:33	pitched	camped, set up, established
6:35	gathered	called together to follow, recruited, enlisted
6:36	by my hand	through me, personally
6:37	fleece of wool	the hairy skin/hide of a sheep
6:38	morrow	next day
6:38	wrung, wringed	twist, squeeze
7:1	pitched	camped, set up, established
7:2	vaunt	boast, brag, talk big, act tough
7:3	ears	hearing, presence, audience
	fearful	trembling, scared, worried
	return	turn back, go away, leave
7:4	try	tried, tested, searched, examined, known
7:7	place	home, house, hang out
7:8+	host	army
7:13	along	flat, against the ground
7:14	save	less than, except, other than

JUDGES

7:16,20	lamps	torches, lights made with fire/flame
7:17	likewise	the same
7:22	his fellow	each other
7:23	gathered them-selves	were summoned
8:1	chide	argued, verbally fought, disagreed
	sharp	angrily, strongly, bitterly, wildly
8:3	was abated	subsided
8:7	tear your flesh	thrash your bodies, rip, shred
	briers	stickers, thorns, weeds
8:9	peace	triumph, victory
8:10,11	hosts	army, crowd, horde, legion
8:11	smote	attack, struck, engage in battle
8:12	discomfited	routed, defeated
8:15	upbraid	reproach, defy, taunt, yell at, scold
8:20	feared	was afraid, scared, worried
8:21	ornaments	crescents, decorations
8:24,25	earring of his prey	spoil, loot, booty
8:26	collars	pendants
	raiment	clothing, garment
8:27	ephod	priestly garment
	snare	trapped, caught, imprisoned, tripped up, lure
	house	family, estate
8:27,33	whoring	worshipping false gods, unfaithful to beliefs
8:28	lifted up their heads	were a force, strong, powerful
8:31	concubine	a sexual partner that is not a wife nor a prostitute
8:32	sepulcher	tomb, grave
9:1	communed	spoke, discussed, talked with
9:2	bone and your flesh	relative, kin, blood
9:4	vain and light	worthless and reckless, insignificant
9:6	plain of the pillar	monument, memorial (that Joshua established)
9:7	Hearken	listen, pay attention, heed
9:8	trees went forth	symbolically trees represented men, so "men went out to…"
9:9	leave my fatness	strength, fertility, vitality
	to be promoted	exalted, lifted up, made more important
9:14	bramble	thorn bush

JUDGES

9:17	adventured	risked, gambled, took a chance
9:20	fire	fiery destruction
	devour	eat up, consume, destroy
9:25	liers in wait	men in ambush, hidden, concealed
9:27	made merry	celebrated, rejoiced
9:30	was kindled	burned, incensed, furious
9:32	up	arise
9:35	wait	ambush, sneaky, deception
9:38	mouth	boasting, bragging, arrogance
9:40	entering	entrance
9:41	thrust	drove, threw out, kicked out, booted
9:42	morrow	next day
9:44	entering	entrance
9:45	sowed with salt	to spread salt over the farm land, causing barrenness and infertility (nothing will grow)
9:49	bough	tree branch, limb, long twig
	hold	chamber, jail, secure area
9:50	encamped against	besieged, attacked
9:52	went hard to	approached, attacked
9:53	all to break	crushed, smashed
9:55	place	home, house, residence
9:56,57	rendered	returned, avenged, got even
10:6	forsook	left, abandoned, dumped
10:8	vexed	terrify, trouble, plague, confuse, dismayed
10:9	sore	greatly, badly, aweful
10:14	cry	call, plead, beg
	tribulation	distress, trouble, woe, punishment
10:16;11:2	strange	foreign, heathen, non-Jew
10:17	gathered	summoned, joined, united
10:18	head	leader, chief, boss
10:23	dispossessed	taken away, seized, lost control of
11:3	vain	worthless, unimportant
11:3	in process of time	after a while
11:7	hate	abhor, despise, loathe, detest
	distress	trouble, problems
11:8	turn again	return, come back
11:8,11	head	leader, chief, boss
11:17,28	hearken	listen, pay attention, heed

JUDGES

11:18	compassed	go about, surround, encamp, encircle
11:20	coast	territory, boundary, border
	pitched	camped, set up, established
11:21	possessed	took over, conquered, rule
11:22	coasts	territory, boundary, border
11:23	dispossessed	driven out, kicked out, booted
11:30	vowed a vow	make a pledge, promise, oath
11:31	peace	triumph, victory
11:33	smote	attacked, strike, hit, punish
11:34	timbrels	tambourines
11:35	rent	tear, ripped, shred, pull apart, open
11:35,36	opened your mouth	spoke, utter, talk
11:37	bewail	lament, mourn, be sad
11:37	bewail my virginity	be sad, mourn, feel sorry for her self because she'll never be married
11:39	vowed	pledged, vowed, promised
12:1	gathered themselves	summoned, united, joined
12:3	passed	crossed, travelled
12:4	fugitives	hunted person, outlaw, on the run
12:5	passages	pathways, trails, roads
12:6	frame	enunciate, form the words/sounds
13:1	evil	sinned, wrong-doing, bad behavior
13:4	beware	be careful, watch out, pay attention
	unclean	unfit, dirty, unworthy, impure
13:5	Nazarite	one who is separated from others and consecrated
13:6	terrible	awesome, amazing, supernatural
13:8	entreated	pleaded, begged, sincerely requested
13:9	hearkened	listen, pay attention, heed
13:9,13,16,17,21,22	angel	messenger, supernatural being
13:10	showed	told, instructed, commanded
13:13	let her beware	consider, listen to, pay attention to
13:15,16	detain	keep, hold, secure
13:15	kid	young male goat
13:16	bread	food
13:18	secret	beyond understanding, mystery, hidden
13:19	meat	grain
13:19	did wondrously	did an amazing thing, performed unbelievably

JUDGES

13:20	ascended	went up, rose
14:4	occasion against	opportunity to confront
14:4	dominion	authority, command, power over
14:6	rent	tear, ripped, shred, pull apart, open
14:12,13	sheets	linen wrappers, clothing
14:13	declare	tell
	garments	clothing
14:14	meat	food
	expound	explain, interpret, clarify
14:15	entice	tempt, tease, lure, draw away
14:16	hate	abhor, despise, loathe, detest
14:17	lay sore upon	pressed, pressured, bugged, harrassed
14:19	expounded	explained, described, taught
15:1	verily	surely, truly, honestly, yes, correct
	hated	dislike, abhor, despise, loathe, detest
15:3	displeasure	harm, hurt, damage, anger
15:4	firebrands	torches, burning objects
	corn	grain
15:8,11	top	cleft, cave, cliff
15:9	pitched	camped, set up, established
15:10	bind	capture, detain, hold
15:12	Swear	pledged, vowed, promised, gave an oath
15:15	new	fresh
15:16	heaps upon heaps	a lot, many, a whole bunch
15:17	Ra'math-le'hi	the High place of the jawbone
15:18	sore	very, badly, a lot
16:5	afflict	subdue, punish, torment
16:7,8,9	green withes	fresh cords/ropes, vines
16:9	tow	straw
16:11	fast	tightly, secure
	occupied	used, not new
16:12	liers in wait	ambushers, hidden, concealed
16:16	vexed	terrify, trouble, plague, confuse, dismayed
16:21	fetter	chains, shackles, restraints
16:25,27	make us sport	amuse us, entertain, perform
17:3	wholly	completely, fully, totally
17:3,4	graven	carved, hand-made idol/statue
	molten	cast

JUDGES

17:4	image	idol, statue of false god
17:5	ephod	priestly garment
	teraphim	household idols, statue of false god
17:7,9	sojourned	temporarily stay, visit, live
17:10	victuals	food, snacks, meals, grub, chow
18:2	coasts	territory, boundary, border
18:5	Ask counsel	guidance, wisdom, instruction, teaching, advice
18:9	still	sitting around, not active, relaxing, kick back
	slothful	lazy, slow, worthless, slacker
18:12	pitched	camped, set up, established
18:14,17,20	ephod	priestly garment
	teraphim	household idols
18:14,30,31	graven	carved, hand-made idol/statue
18:14,17	molten image	cast idol
18:15	saluted	greeted, talked with, formal address
18:17,20	graven image	carved statue, man-made idol
18:21	carriage	riches, wealth
18:24	gods	idols, statues of false/various heathen deities
18:27	quiet	peaceful, untroubled
	smote	attacked, strike, hit, punish
19:2	played the whore	wasn't faithful, left him even though she was in a relationship with him
19:3,4,5,6,8,9	damsel	young woman
19:3	retained	detained, kept, had a guest
19:6	let your heart be merry	enjoy yourself, have fun, relax, chill
19:9	tarry	wait, delay, put off
	home	your tent, home, house
19:10,11	Je'bus	the name of the old city before Jerusalem
19:11	day far spent	nearly over, evening time, very late
19:17	wayfaring	traveling, journeying
19:19,21	provender	food, grub, chow, provisions
	washed	bathed, cleaned up
19:22	beset	assault, attack, surround, come against
19:22,25	know him	have sex, was physically intimate
19:23	folly	silly, foolish, stupid, idiotic
19:24	vile	disgusting, evil, filthy, nasty, sickening
19:25	spring	dawn, sunrise, start

JUDGES

19:29	coasts	parts, territory, boundary, border
19:30	advice	guidance, wisdom, instruction, teaching, advice
20:2	footmen	a foot soldier; an infantryman
20:5	forced	raped, ravished
20:6	lewdness	sexually obscene, vulgar
20:10	folly	disgraceful, foolishness, stupidity
20:13	Be'li-al	followers of, or actually *the* fallen angel/demon "Bel." Be'li-al is translated "lawlessness"— and follows a rabbinical tradition which interpreted it as "beli 'ol" the one who has thrown off the yoke of heaven. Belial was accordingly considered the opponent of the rule of God; that is, Satan, or the antagonist of God.
20:16	hair-breadth	a small space, narrow margin, very little
20:29,33,36,37,38	liers in wait	men waiting in, an ambush
20:34	sore	heavy, sore, bad, aweful
20:35	drew the sword	war veterans, experienced soldiers
20:37	sign	signal
20:40	flame	big blaze, fire & smoke, holocaust
	ascended up to heaven	went up in smoke, rose
20:41	amazed	terrified, frightened, scared
20:42	turned their backs	fled, ran away
20:43	trampled them down	overran them, stomped
	sunrising	east
20:45	gleaned	caught, captured, held
20:46	fell	died
	men in valor	valiant warriors, brave soldiers, decorated
21:4	morrow	next day
21:5	congregation	assembly, gathering
21:6,15	repented them	were sorry, sad, remorseful, felt guilty
21:7	to wives	in marriage
21:9	numbered	census, count the people
21:10	valiantest	bravest, gutsiest, fearless, heroic
21:13	call peaceably	proclaim peace
21:15	breach	broken place, crumbled walls, holes, gap
21:20	lie	hide, conceal
21:23	repaired	rebuilt, fixed

RUTH

1:1	sojourn	temporarily stay, visit, live
1:2	continued	lived, stayed, remained
1:5	left	was left with, only had, remaining
1:6	fret	upset, worry, fret, bothered with/by
1:8	the dead	their dead husbands
1:13	grieves	saddens, upsets, depresses, bothers
1:14	clung	stuck with, stayed with, held tightly
1:16	Entreat	ask, plead, beg
1:18	steadfastly	courageous, brave, determined, committed
	minded	determined, decided, committed
1:19	moved	concerned, wormed
1:20	Almighty	God
1:21	testified	witnessed, acted against
2:1	kinsman	family member, direct relative, blood
2:2+	glean	gather (leftover), pick up scraps
2:2	corn	grain
2:3	her hap to light	she was lucky, got a break, fortunate to see
2:6	damsel	young woman
2:7	tarried	waited, delayed, put off
2:8,21,23	fast	close to, near
2:9	charged	commanded, ordered, gave instructions
	touch	molest, bother, trouble
2:11	nativity	place of birth
2:12	recompense	reward, payment
2:13	fleshhook	a many-pronged fork used by priests to separate meat from bone
2:14	morsel	small piece of food, snack
2:14	sufficed	satisfied, content
2:15	reproach	insult, put down, yell at
2:16	of	on
2:19	worked you	did you work
2:20	kinsmen	relative, close family member, blood
2:23	maidens	virgins, unmarried women
3:1	rest	peace, security
3:2	winnows	the process of throwing the parts of wheat in the air to separate the grain from the husk/skin

RUTH

3:3	raiment	mantle (loose sleeveless cloak or cape), garment
3:4	mark	notice, point out, observe, identify
3:6	floor	threshing floor
3:7	corn	grain
	heap	a pile, a big bunch, plenty
3:8	afraid	startled, surprised, shocked
3:9,13	kinsman	relative, close family member, blood
3:11	virtuous	honorable, decent, having good character
3:15	vail/veil	cloak, cape, shawl
3:18	thing	discussion, conversation
4:1	Ho, such a one!	hey you, excuse me, hello there
4:3	parcel	piece of ground, parcel
4:4	advertise	inform, advertise, give notice
	after you	next in line, the next choice
4:5	of	from
4:6	mar	ruin, endanger, risk
4:7	changing	the exchange of land, transfer, title exchange
	plucked off his shoe	a universal symbol of respect when entering a holy, sacred location or act – therefore the act of "redeeming" or buying back a lost relative was a holy or sacred act – NOT a business deal
4:11	worthily	be great, successful
4:12	seed	offspring, children, heirs
4:14	famous	notable, famous, remembered

I SAMUEL

1:3	Lord of hosts	(Jehovah Tsebaoth) – commander of angels
1:10	sore	bitterly, badly, painful
1:11	vowed a vow	make a pledge, oath, promise
1:12	marked	notice, point out, observe, identify
1:15	poured out my soul	prayed earnestly
1:17,27	Him	Godhead, Father
1:21	vow	pledge, oath, promise
1:23	suck	nurse, breastfed
1:18	lent	dedicated, used by
2:1+	Lord	Jehovah; God in relationship to mankind
2:1	horn is exalted	influence, power is greater than before
	mouth is enlarged	same as above (symbolic of being able to "eat" more or gobble up enemies)
2:3	weighed	judged, measured
2:4	girded	lifted up by, strengthened, held up
2:5	waxed	grows, become more
2:6	grave	Hell, death, sickness
2:9	feet of the saints	protect, guard, watch over
	silent in darkness	powerless, without influence
2:10	thunder upon them	shake them, make them tremble or be afraid
2:10	horn	strength, leadership, influence, power
2:13	seething	boiling, cook in a pot
	fleshhook	fork
2:14	cauldron	cooking pot, large bowl
2:15	flesh	meat
	sodden flesh	boiled meat
2:16	presently	first, immediately, now
	your soul	inner person, emotion, life-force, being, life
2:18,28	ephod	priestly garment/clothes
2:20	seed	offspring, children, heir
2:23	dealings	wicked deeds, behavior, interaction
2:25	hearkened	listen, pay attention, heed
2:29	kick	rebel, be disobedient
	chiefest	best, first
2:30	esteemed	well favored, loved, honored, respected

I SAMUEL

2:31	cut off your arm	break you strength, lose power/control
2:33	consume their eyes	take away sight, make them blind (a curse)
	flower	prime, strength, youth
	crouch to him	to bow down, prostrate oneself, humbled
2:36	morsel	loaf, crust
	Put	assign, give, place in
3:1	precious	rare, valuable
	open vision	no known prophet or person that could see/foretell the future
3:2	wax	grow, increase, become
3:11	tingle	ring (in amazement), perk up
3:14	purged	atoned, forgiven, cleansed
3:18	whit	word, a bit
3:20	established	confirmed, successful, proven
4:1	pitched	camped, set up, established
4:2,10	smitten	defeated, beaten
4:3	Wherefore	why
4:3,4,5	covenant	unconditional agreement, contract, promise
4:4	cherubims	angel, archangel, heavenly being
4:7,8	Woe	trouble, danger, look out! – a warning
4:9	quite	act, behave
4:12	rent	tear, ripped, shred, pull apart, open
	earth upon his head	sign of grief, mourning, shame, guilt
4:14	tumult	commotion, excitement, pandemonium, riot
4:15	dim	weak
5:2	Dagon	the fish-god; the national god of the Philistines. This idol had the body of a fish with the head and hands of a man
5:4	threshhold	doorstep, doorway, entrance
5:6,9	smote	attacked, strike, hit, punish
5:6,12	emerods	tumors
5:7	sore	severe, harsh, badly
5:11	slay	kill, murder
5:12	smitten	afflicted, disengaged
6:2	diviners	soothsayers, fortunetellers
6:3	empty	without a gift
6:4,5,11,17	emerods	tumors

I SAMUEL

6:5	lighten	ease, lift, remove
6:6	wrought	worked, done, accomplished
6:7	cart	wagon, transport, moving table
6:8,11	coffer	cash box, chest, small portable safe
6:9	coast	territory, boundary, border
6:18	fenced	fortified, walled
6:19	smote	struck down, beaten, defeated
	flagon	bottle, flask, container to hold liquid
7:1	sanctify	set apart, consecrated, purify, cleanse
7:2	abode	dwell, live, stay, make a home, settled
7:2	lamented	cried, was sad about, mourned, depressed
7:3	strange	foreign, heathen, non-Jew
	deliver	save, rescue, defend
7:10	discomfited	overwhelmed, badly beaten
7:11	smote	destroyed, struck down, defeated
7:14	coasts	territory, boundary, border
	the hands	from the power, strength
8:3	lucre	money, cash, wealth, riches
8:7,9,22	hearken	listen, pay attention, heed
8:6	goodliest	best, finest, nicest, choice
8:13	confectionaries	makers of perfumers, ointments, salves
8:17	servants	slaves, forced laborers
8:20	go out before	lead, go ahead
8:21	rehearsed	repeated, spoke again
9:5	leave	cease, stop, end
9:7	spent	gone, finished
9:11,18,19	seer	prophet, foreteller, spokesman for God
9:13	bidden	invited, asked, requested
9:13	against	toward
9:15+	Lord	Jehovah; God in relationship to mankind
9:22	parlor	hall, waiting room
9:24	shoulder	leg, thigh
9:25	commune	spoke, talk with, converse
9:26	the spring of the day	daybreak, dawn, sunrise
9:27	bid	tell, ask
10:1	vial	flask, small bottle/tube
10:2	sepulcher	tomb, grave
	left care of	stopped worrying about, relaxed

I SAMUEL

10:4	salute	greet, say hello
10:5	psaltery, lyre	a musical instrument, a harp with twelve strings
	tabret	tambourine, a small hand-drum
10:9	another	changed, converted
10:19	tribulations	difficult times, hardships, suffering
10:22	inquired	asked, sought
	stuff	baggage, goods, belongings
10:23	higher	taller
10:23	shoulders and upwards	very tall, stood out above the crowd
10:27	Be'li-al	followers of, or actually *the* fallen angel/demon "Bel." Be'li-al is translated "lawlessness"— and follows a rabbinical tradition which interpreted it as "beli 'ol" the one who has thrown off the yoke of heaven. Belial was accordingly considered the opponent of the rule of God; that is, Satan, or the antagonist of God.
11:1	encamped	besieged, arrayed against, set up
11:1,2	covenant	unconditional agreement, contract, promise
11:3	respite	relief, rest
11:3,7	coasts	territory, boundary, border
11:5	tidings	news, reports
11:7	hewed	hacked, chopped, cut, chiseled, sculpted
11:7	fear	dread, worry, dread
	with one consent	unanimous, all agreed, as one man
11:9	help	deliverance, save, rescue
11:11	host	camp, army
12:1	hearkened	listen, pay attention, heed
12:3	defrauded	cheat, con, rip-off, double-cross
12:5+	Lord	Jehovah; God in relationship to mankind
12:5	He	Samuel
12:6	advanced	appointed, set up
12:7	stand still	take your stand, defend
12:14,18	fear	revered, respected, trembled, dread
13:3,4	smote	attacked, strike, hit, punish
13:4	abomination	detestable, unacceptable, filthy
13:6	strait	critical situation, dilemma, difficulty
13:10	salute	greet, say hello, address

I SAMUEL

13:12	made supplication to	prayed to, asked the favor of
13:13	foolishly	acted stupidly, didn't think, was unwise
13:13,14	kept	obeyed, followed, did
13:16	encamped	made camp, set up, established
13:17	spoilers	raiders, robbers, bandits
13:19	smith	a metal worker; maker of swords, knives
13:20	share	plowshare
13:20,21	coulter	farm tool
	mattock	hoe
13:21	goads	sharp pointed stick
14:1,6	bore	carried, hauled
14:2	uttermost	outmost, outskirts, borders
14:3	ephod	priestly garment, clothes, robes
14:5	situate	situated, located
14:6	restraint	limitation, requirement
14:7	armor bearer	a soldier's assistant, someone that helped carry heavy weapons & armor (helmet, shield, body armor, swords, etc.)
14:8	discover	reveal, expose, show
14:15	trembling	afraid, worried, shake, scared, shiver
14:15	spoilers	raiders, robbers, bandits
14:19	noise	commotion, disturbance, ruckus
14:20	discomfiture	destruction, beat down
14:25,26	woods	forest, groves of trees
14:27	charged	bound, ordered, commanded
14:27,29	enlightened	brightened, sparkled
14:28	straitly charged	strictly bound, bothered, demanded
14:30	haply	only
	spoil	plunder, booty, stolen goods
14:32	them with the blood	not drained from
14:33	transgressed	broken faith, sinned, commit wrongdoing
	roll a great stone	possibly this means that they should set up an altar to the Lord, on which the animals might be properly slain, and the blood poured out upon the earth
14:41	a perfect lot	the right answer, correct, precise
14:45	wrought	worked, did, accomplished
14:47	vexed	terrify, trouble, plague, confuse, dismayed

I SAMUEL

14:48	spoiled	plundered, robbed, ripped off, jacked
14:52	sore	severe, harsh, painful
14:52	took him unto	recruited him, drafted, picked him, conscripted
15:1,22	hearken	listen, pay attention, heed
15:3	smite	attacked, strike, hit, punish
15:11,29,35	repents	sorrows, grieves, feels sorrow & changes
	performed	carried out, accomplished, fulfilled
15:14	lowing, bleating	an animal noise(s) that sheep or cattle make (like a dog's bark or cat's meow)
15:19	fly	rush, hurry to, chase
15:19,21	spoil	plunder, booty, stolen goods
15:23	witchcraft	divination, fortune telling, spells
15:27,28	rent	tear, ripped, shred, pull apart, open
15:32	delicately	carefully, gently
15:33	hewed	cut, chopped, hacked
16:1	mourn	grieve, feel sad
	reigning	king, ruling, leading
	provided	selected, chosen, picked
16:3	name	choose, elect, designate
16:4	peaceable	in peace, friendship, not to attack, not enemies
16:5	sanctify	consecrate, dedicate, make clean
16:7	countenance	"face" - influence, personal attention, blessings
16:12	ruddy	reddish, sun-tanned, healthy glow
	goodly	pleasant, valuable, worthwhile
16:18	comely	handsome, rugged
17:2	set the battle in array	arranged their battle lines, set military positions
17:4	six cubits & a span	nine feet nine inches tall (9'9")
	span	a unit of measure or distance from the thumb to little finger on an outstretched hand (9 inches)
17:5	armed	clothed, outfitted, equipped for battle
	mail	armor
17:6	greaves	leg guards, battle-dress
	target	short sword (covering)
17:7	weaver's beam	a very thick, long pole (the tip weighed 15 pounds)
17:8	in array	and line up for battle, formation
17:10	defy	challenge, go against
17:12	went	passed

I SAMUEL

17:17	corn	grain
	wench	female servant, slave
17:18	pledge	token of receipt, promise, down payment
17:20	trench	entrenchment, circle the camp, enbankment
17:22	carriage	baggage, ancient suitcases
	saluted	greeted, said hello, addressed
17:24	sore	greatly, badly, terrible
17:25	free	tax free, no added cost
17:26	reproach	disgrace, embarrassment, humiliation
17:28	naughtiness	wickedness, bad behavior
17:31	rehearsed	told, informed, reported
17:35	smote	attacked, strike, hit, punish
17:38	armed	clothed, arrayed, outfitted
17:39	girded	equipped, fastened, put on, got dressed up
	assayed	wanted
	proved	tried, tested, searched, examined, known
17:40	scrip	pouch, bag, small money purse
17:42	disdained	abhor, despise, loathe, detest
	ruddy	red-complexioned, flushed, fresh, healthy
17:43	staves	staffs, sticks
17:46	smite you	strike you down, defeat
17:53	spoiled their tents	plundered their camps, robbed, looted
17:56	stripling	youth
18:1	make an end of	finished, conclude
	was knit	buddies, became fast friends
18:3	covenant	unconditional agreement, contract, promise
18:6	tabrets	tambourines, small hand-drum
18:8	ascribed	credited for, blamed for, famous for
18:9	eyed Da'vid	looked at David with suspicion
18:10	morrow	next day
	prophesied	foretell, make a prediction, speak for God
	javelin	spear, lance, pointy stick thrown as a weapon
18:11	avoided	escaped
18:13	removed	sent, picked out, seperated
18:15	was afraid	stood in awe, feared, worried
18:21	snare	trapped, caught, imprisoned, tripped up, lure
	in the one of two	a second time
18:22	commune	speak, talk, discuss

I SAMUEL

18:23	esteemed	well favored, loved, honored, respected
18:25	fall	killed, die, be defeated
18:26	expired	gone, passed by, used up, time still left
18:27	tale	number, ancient measurement
18:29	continually	the rest of his days, always
18:30	set by	valued, esteemed
19:3	commune	speak, talk, discuss
19:4	good	positive, in your best interests
19:5	wrought	worked, accomplished, performed
19:13,16	bolster	head place
20:3,4,17	soul	inner person, emotion, life-force, being, life
20:6,28	leave	permission, allow, tolerate
20:8,16	covenant	agreement, promise, contract
20:12	sounded	questioned, checked out, tested
20:16	house	family, estate
20:17	swear	pledged, vowed, promised, gave an oath
20:19	business was in hand	conference, held a secret meeting
20:24,34	meat	food
20:26	unclean	ceremonially unfit, dirty, unclean
20:30	perverse	Saul was hurt, and basically Saul called Jonathan a "son of a bitch" or "bastard" in anger because his loyalty was with David, over family & throne. Saul, in anger, goes on to accuse Jonathan of being gay (a homosexual).
	to thy own confusion	Saul accuses Jonathan of homosexuality
20:32	Wherefore	why
20:33	javelin	spear
	smite	strike him down, hit, kill
20:34	grieved	sorry, felt bad, guilt
20:37	stay not	do not stop
20:40	artillery	weapons
20:42	seed	offspring, children, heirs
21:4,6	hallowed	consecrated, dedicated, set apart
21:4	kept themselves	stayed pure, virgins, not had sex
21:5	sanctified	made holy, cleaned, purified
21:7	chiefest	leader, boss
21:8	required haste	desperation, was urgent
21:13	feigned	pretended to be demented, acted, faked

I SAMUEL

	scabbed	scratched, scribbled, itched
	spittle	spit, saliva
21:14,15	mad	demented, crazy, insane
22:3	come forth, and be	come and stay
22:4,5	hold	stronghold, fortified, defenced
22:8	league	treaty, agreement
22:10,17,21	Lord	Jehovah; God in relationship to mankind
22:10	victuals	provisions, food and supplies
22:13,15	inquired of God	prayed to God
22;14	honorable	respected, revered
22:18	fall upon	attack, kill, slay, fight
	a linen ephod	priestly garments, robes
22:19	smote	attacked, strike, hit, punish
22:22	house	household, estate
22:23	in safeguard	safe
23:6	an ephod	a priestly garment, robes
23:7	shut in	surrounded, trapped, enclosed
23:9	mischief	plotted evil, schemed
23:11	beseech	beg, plead, ask
23:12	deliver	surrender, give up
23:13	forbore to go forth	stopped going out
23:14,18,25	abode	dwell, live, stay, make a home, settled
23:15,16,18,19	wood	forest, trees
23:16	strengthened his hand	encouraged him, supported
23:18	covenant	unconditional agreement, contract, promise
23:20	soul	person, individual, living being
23:22	haunt	hang out, hiding place, camp
	subtiley	cunningly, tricky, sneaky
23:25	into a rock	to the rock
23:26	compassed	go about, surround, encamp, encircle
24:3	cover his feet	urinate, piss, relieve himself
	sides	recesses, indentations
24:7	stayed	stopped, persuaded
24:9	Wherefore	why
24:10	bid	urged, asked, requested
24:11	skirt	edge
	soul	emotions, person, individual, living being
24:21	swear	pledged, vowed, promised, gave an oath

I SAMUEL

	seed	offspring, children, heirs
24:22	hold	stronghold, fort, secure camp
25:3	churlish	harsh, cruel
25:7	shepherds	wandering sheep herders, nomads, Bedouin
25:11	flesh	butchered meat
25:13	abode by the stuff	stayed with the baggage, possessions
25:14	salute	greet, say hello, acknowledge
25:16	wall	protection, defense
25:17,25	son of Be'-li-al	followers of, or actually *the* fallen angel/demon "Bel." Be'li-al is translated "lawlessness"— and follows a rabbinical tradition which interpreted it as "beli 'ol" the one who has thrown off the yoke of heaven. Belial was accordingly considered the opponent of the rule of God; that is, Satan, or the antagonist of God.
25:20	covert	shelter, hiding place
25:21	requited	returned, payed back, avenged
25:23	lighted	dismounted, got off
25:23	churlish	cowardly, lacking honor
25:28	sure	lasting, secure
25:29	soul	inner person, emotion, life-force, being, life
25:35	hearkened	listen, pay attention, heed
25:37	heart	mind, memory
	stone	paralyzed, stunned, shocked
25:39	wickedness	evil, sin, wrong-doing
	communed	talked, discussed, dialogue
25:42	damsels	young women
	went after	attended, accompanied
26:3,5	pitched	camped, set up, established
26:3	abode	dwell, live, stay, make a home, settled
26:5,7	trench	circle of the camp, fortification
26:7,11,12,16	bolster	head place
	smite	attacked, strike, hit, punish
	at once	immediately, with one stroke
26:1,12,16	cruse	jug, container, small bottle
26:15,18	wherefore	why
26:15,16	kept	guarded, protected
26:20	before the face	away from the presence

I SAMUEL

	seek a flea	nobody, unimportant, not threatening, harmless
26:21	soul	inner person, emotion, life-force, being, life
26:24	set by	valued, appreciated
27:9	smote	attacked, strike, hit, punish
28:3,9	wizards	necromancers, conjurers, magicians
28:4	pitched	camped, set up, established
28:6+	Lord	Jehovah; God in relationship to mankind
28:6	U'rim	translated as "lights and perfections" or revelation and truth" — were a divination, medium or process used by ancient Hebrews/Israelites in revealing the will of God on a contested point of view or other problem
28:7,8,9	has familiar spirit	is a medium, talks with demons
28:9	snare	trapped, caught, imprisoned, tripped up, lure
28:15	disquieted	disturbed, bothered, troubled
28:15,20,21	sore	greatly, badly
28:18	executed	carried out, accomplished, performed
28:20	all along	full length
28:21,22,23	hearkened	listen, pay attention, heed
28:22	morsel	piece, scrap
28:23	compelled	urged, told, made
28:24	hasted	hurried, sped up, quickly
	unleavened	yeast-free
29:1	pitched	camped, set up, established
29:2	in the rearward	behind, in back
29:3	fell to me	deserted to me, came to me
29:6	favor you not	do not approve, disagree
29:9	angel	messenger, supernatural being
30:6	encouraged	strengthened, supported, lifted up
30:7	ephod	priestly garment, robes
30:15	swear	pledged, vowed, promised, gave an oath
30:16,19,20,22,26	spoil	plunder, stolen goods, booty
30:17	smote	fought, attacked, strike, hit, punish
30:21	saluted	greeted, said hello, addressed
30:22	save	except, alone, just
30:24	hearken	listen, pay attention, heed
	part	share, cut, take, portion

I SAMUEL

	stuff	supplies, goods
30:25	statute	law, rule, commands, decrees, directives
30:31	were wont to haunt	had lived
31:2	hard	closely, near by
31:3,4	sore	severely, badly
31:4	abuse	make sport of, torture, torment

II SAMUEL

1:2	rent	tear, ripped, shred, pull apart, open
	did obeisance	showed respect, revere
1:9	upon	by
	is yet whole in me	still lingers in me, not dead yet
1:11	rent	tear, ripped, shred, pull apart, open
1:15	fall upon him	attack him, ambush, waylay
	smote	attacked, strike, hit, punish
1:18	bid	urged, asked, invited
2:4	house	family, estate
2:14	play	hold a military contest, compete, skirmish
2:15	of	for
2:17	sore	severe, bad, violent
2:18	light of foot	fast, quick, speedy, good runner
2:22	wherefore	why
2:22,31	smite	attacked, strike, hit, punish
2:25	one troop	unified, joined, combined forces
2:26	sword devour	keep killing, keep fighting, stay feuding
2:32	sepulcher	tombs, graves, crypts
3:1,2	house	family, estate, clan
3:1	waxed	grew, increased, became
3:9	sworn	pledged, vowed, promised, gave an oath
3:12,13,21	league	agreement, treaty, alliance
3:14	espoused	engaged
	foreskins	the excess skin that covers the tip or head of the penis – (taking a "foreskin" in these days meant cutting off a man's penis and bringing in the tip as a trophy – like the Native American "scalp")
3:16	along weeping	weeping as he went, crying
3:22	spoil	plunder, booty, stolen goods
3:27	quietly	privately, in confidence
	smote	attacked, strike, hit, punish
3:28	guiltless	innocent, not responsible
3:29	house	family, estate, clan
	leans on a staff	old age, weak, no longer young
3:31	rend	tear, ripped, shred, pull apart, open
	bier	casket, coffin

II SAMUEL

3:39	hard	difficult, cruel, mean
4:1	feeble	weak, not strong, sickly
4:2	bands	military units
	reckoned	considered part of
4:3	sojourners	travelers, visitors, non-citizens
4:6	though they would have brought wheat	pretended to get wheat
	smote	attacked, strike, hit, punish
4:8	seed	offspring, children, heirs
4:12	sepulcher	tombs, graves, crypts
5:3	league	treaty, agreement, alliance, gang
5:8	gets up to the gutter	goes through the water tunnel (the cities walled for protection, yet would have left them without water had not Zechariah built a tunnel from the outside valley to the well inside – all underground. This gutter was a tunnel that could be crawled through and the well's vertical shaft had to be climbed)
5:12	perceived	realized, understood, comprehended
5:17	seek	search for, look
	hold	stronghold, secure room
5:21	images	idols, statues of heathen gods
	burned them	carried them away, remove
5:24	going	marching
5:25	smote	attacked, strike, hit, punish
6:4	accompanying	with, join
6:5	psalteries	lyres, a stringed instrument
	timbrels	tambourines
6:8	breach	violent outburst, breakthrough
6:10	remove	take, transfer
6:14	ephod	priestly garment, robes
6:16	despised him in her heart	hated, resented
6:17	pitched	prepared, camped, set up, established
6:19	flagon	bottle, flask, container to hold liquid
6:20	vain	worthless, undignified, common, course
6:21	play	celebrate, rejoice merry
7:2	curtains	a tent, a canvas building

II SAMUEL

7:6,7	walked	traveled, moved
7:8	sheepfold	pasture
7:9	cut off	destroyed, defeated, beaten
7:10	beforetime	previously, earlier
7:11,19	house	family lineage, estate, clan
7:12	seed	offspring, children, heirs
7:13	name	reputation, fame
7:14	stripes	lashes; marks caused by being whipped/beaten
7:19	manner	custom, tradition
7:23	terrible	amazing, mighty, powerful
7:24	confirmed	established, set up, built
8:1,2,3	smote	attacked, strike, hit, punish
8:2	measured…line	tape measure, survey (David "measured" and then divided the Moab land into three sections – destroying 2/3 and keeping one intact or "alive")
8:3	border	portion, land, property line
8:4	houghed	hamstrung
8:5	succor	help, support, give strength
8:6	garrisons	military outpost/barracks, occupying force
	gifts	tribute, offering
8:8	exceeding	very, great
8:10	salute	greet, say hello
8:13	name	reputation, fame
	smiting	killing, slaying
8:14	preserved	saved, rescued
8:15	executed	administered, gave
8:16	recorder	secretary, stenographer, transcriber, someone that wrote down the events that happened
9:8	dead dog	worthless person, loser, bum
9:10	till	cultivate, dig up the ground, farm
10:4	shaved beard	something done to a enemy to shame/embarrass
	cut garments in middle	
10:5	ashamed	humiliated, embarrassed, "dissed"
	Tarry	wait, delay, remain
10:6	stunk before	had greatly offended
10:16	river	a.k.a. Euphrates
10:18,19	smote	attacked, strike, hit, punish
10:19	served	were subject to, made to work for

II SAMUEL

	feared	were afraid, scarred, worried
11:1	after the year has expired	in the spring
	besieged	surround, attack over and over, blockade
11:7	demanded	asked, required an answer
11:8	wash your feet	refresh yourself (a ritual where the visitor's feet were washed – which would be dirty/smelly after walking on the dirt roads where animals had also walked and eliminated their waste)
	mess of meat	portion of food
11:15	retire	withdraw, pull back, leave
12:3	ewe	female
	meat	food
12:4	spared	was unwilling, would not
	dressed	prepared, killed, cooked & served
12:4	wayfaring	surround, attack over and over, blockade
12:5	shall surely die	will die, be killed
12:7	delivered	rescued, saved, preserved
12:8	such and such	more, additional
12:10	sword…never depart	never know peace, keep fighting, stay at war
12:11,12	in the sight of this sun	publicly, openly
12:14	blaspheme	curse, show disrespect
12:16	besought	appealed to, pleaded, begged
12:18	feared	were afraid, terrified
12:18	vex	anger, annoy, bother, harass, frustrate
12:20	required	asked, questioned
12:23	I shall go to him	David to go heaven at death, child cannot return to earth
12:27	city of waters	the royal city of the Ammonites, was called the city of waters, from being surrounded with waters (lakes)
12:30	a talent	100 pounds, approx. weight of a person
12:31	put them under	made them work with, labor
	pass through	work at, labor in
13:1	love	was infatuated with, lusted for, desired
13:2	vexed	miserable, lustful
	hard	impossible, difficult
13:4	lean	thin, depressed

II SAMUEL

13:5	make	pretend
	meat	food
13:5,7	dress him meat	prepare the food
13:12	force	degrade me, rape
	folly	disgusting thing, foolish
13:14	exceedingly	intensely, a lot, much
13:16	hearken	listen, pay attention, heed
13:18	garment	full length robe
	divers	various, many, multi, different
13:19	rent	tear, ripped, shred, pull apart, open
13:22,32	forced	degraded, raped
13:25,27	pressed	urged, pushed, pleaded
13:25	chargeable	burdensome
13:32	appointment	plan, conspiracy
13:36	sore	bitterly, a lot, loudly
13:39	soul	inner person, emotion, life-force, being, life
	comforted	consoled, at peace
14:2	feign	pretend
14:3	on this manner	in this way, like this
14:4	did obeisance	showed respect
14:6	strove	fought, wrestled
	smote	attacked, strike, hit, punish
14:7	quench my coal	destroy the last of my family
	countenance	"face" - influence, personal attention, blessings
14:8	charge	instruction, recommendation
14:11	revengers	avengers, bounty hunters
14:13,32	wherefore	why
14:13	faulty	guilty, to blame, responsible
14:14	expelled	cast out, put away
14:17	angel	messenger, supernatural being
14:22	request	word, petition
14:25	blemish	defect, imperfection
14:26	polled	shaved, cut hair (the practice of taking the hair in a fist, at the base of the neck and cutting what was below the hand – this was done once a year)
14:27	countenance	"face" - influence, personal attention, blessings
14:32	see the king's face	meet with the king, confer with

II SAMUEL

15:3	deputed of	representing, appointed
15:5	do him obeisance	bow before him, show him honor
15:7	pay	fulfill, honor, keep
	vow	pledge, oath, promise
15:8	vowed a vow	pledged a pledge, given my word, oath
15:10	spies	secret messengers, scouts
15:11	simplicity	innocence
15:13	after	with
15:14	else	otherwise
	smite	attacked, strike, hit, punish
15:16	concubines	sexual partners that are not wives nor prostitutes
15:17	tarried	stayed, waited, remained
15:18,23	passed	traveled, moved, went
15:24	covenant	unconditional agreement, contract, promise
15:28	certify	inform, let me know, report
15:32	rent	tear, ripped, shred, pull apart, open
15:33	pass	travel, accompany, journey
15:35	out of	from
16:4	pertained	belonged, related
	beseech	beg, plead, ask
	grace	favor, mercy, kindness
16:7	come	get
	man of Be'li-al	followers of, or actually *the* fallen angel/demon "Bel." Be'li-al is translated "lawlessness"— and follows a rabbinical tradition which interpreted it as "beli 'ol" the one who has thrown off the yoke of heaven. Belial was accordingly considered the opponent of the rule of God; that is, Satan, or the antagonist of God.
16:8	bloody man	man of bloodshed, professional soldier
16:9	take	cut, hack, chop
16:10	wherefore	why
16:11	bowels	insides, loins, reproductive organs
16:18	abide	dwell, live, stay, make a home, settled
16:23	counsel	guidance, wisdom, instruction, teaching, advice
17:2	weak handed	exhausted, without strength
	make him afraid	terrify him, scare
	smite	strike down, attacked, hit, punish

II SAMUEL

17:7	counsel	guidance, wisdom, instruction, teaching, advice
17:8	chafed	fierce, angry, furious
	whelps	cubs
	lodge	spend the night
17:10	valiant	brave, courageous, mighty
17:14	appointed	ordained, planned
17:16	Lodge not	do not spend
17:17	wench	maid, maid-servant, slavegirl
17:19	corn	grain
17:2122,24	pass	travel
17:22	light	dawn, sunrise, daybreak
17:23	sepulcher	tomb, grave, crypt
17:26	pitched	camped, set up, established
17:28	basins	bowls
	pulse	seeds
17:29	is	are
18:3	succor	provide help for
18:5,12	charge	orders, commands, directions
18:6,7	wood	forest, group oftrees
18:8	devoured more people	claimed more lives
18:9	taken up between heaven and earth	off the ground, in the air
18:14	tarry thus	waste time
	darts	lancets, arrows, shanks
18:15	compassed about	go about, surround, encamp, encircle
	smote	attacked, strike, hit, punish
18:18	pillar	monument, memorial, grave marker
	dale	valley
18:22	howsoever	whatever happened
	overran	passed by
18:25	there is tidings in his mouth	he is bringing news, report
18:26	porter	gatekeepers, guards, butlers
18:31	avenged	payback, got even, recompensed
19:3	stealth	secretly, covertly, unseen
19:6	regard	respect, care about, concerned with
19:7	comfortably	kindly, encouraging, supportive

II SAMUEL

19:7	there will not tarry one	not one will remain
19:19	impute iniquity to me	consider me guilty, hold me accountable
19:23	swore	pledged, vowed, promised, gave an oath
19:24	dressed	cared for, wrapped, covered
19:26	to	with
19:27	an angel	a messenger, supernatural being
19:28	cry	complain, whine
19:32	sustenance	help, financial aid, support, allowance
19:36	recompense it	pay back, compensate
19:38	require	choose, ask, want
19:40	conducted	accompanied, went with, journied
19:41	stolen thee away	took as hostage, captured, prisoner
19:43	fiercer	harsher, angrier
20:1	Be'li-al	followers of, or actually *the* fallen angel/demon "Bel." Be'li-al is translated "lawlessness"— and follows a rabbinical tradition which interpreted it as "beli 'ol" the one who has thrown off the yoke of heaven. Belial was accordingly considered the opponent of the rule of God; that is, Satan, or the antagonist of God.
20:3	went not in unto	didn't have sex with them, no intercourse
	shut up	"womb" remained "shut", didn't have children
20:8	girdle	belt that held the sword (like a gun holster)
20:9	took by beard to kiss him	pretended to greet to get close enough to kill
20:15	in the trench	by the rampart, fortified wall
20:18	wont	accustomed
21:9	days of harvest	a few weeks dedicated to harvesting crops that are grown outdoors (grains, fruits, olives)
21:10	sackcloth	rough clothing, burlap material, rags - humility
21:14	sepulcher	tomb, grave, crypt
	was entreated	heard the prayer, acted on behalf
21:15	waxed	became, grew, increased
21:17	succored	helped. Assisted. suppoortied
	smote	attacked, strike, hit, punish
	light not go out	inspiration, leadership, spiritual/emotional guide
21:19	weaver's beam	thick, long pole (the tip weighed 15 pounds)

II SAMUEL

21:21	defied	taunted, made fun of, mocked
22:3	horn of salvation	influence, power, force that keeps safe
	high tower	influence, power, force that keeps safe
22:5,6	compassed	go about, surround, encamp, encircle
22:6,19	prevented	confronted, hindered, stood up to
22:10	darkness under his feet	(speaking of God) came down to fight at or during the night
22:11	wings of the wind	circuits of the wind, wind currents
22:12	darkness pavilions around him	most people were afraid of the nighttime, but God made the night his palace and ruled over it like an empire/kingdom
22:16	discovered	laid bare, opened up
22:23	statues	laws, rules, principles
22:25	recompensed	rewarded, payed, given
22:27	froward	perverted, arrogant, proud
	unsavory	twisted, dirty, crude, ghetto
22:30	run thru a troop	broke thru enemy lines, crashed thru
22:31	buckler	shield

II SAMUEL

22:32	save	except, otherwise
22:34	hinds	deer's
22:35	to	for
22:41	hate	abhor, despise, loathe, detest
22:43	mire of the street	dust, dirt, trash in the street a person walks on
22:44	heathen	nations, non-Jew, pagan
22:45	be afraid out of their close places	come trembling out of their fortresses
22:51	seed	offspring, children, heirs
23:1	psalmist	singer
23:6	Be'li-al	followers of, or actually *the* fallen angel/demon "Bel." Be'li-al is translated "lawlessness"— and follows a rabbinical tradition which interpreted it as "beli 'ol" the one who has thrown off the yoke of heaven. Belial was accordingly considered the opponent of the rule of God; that is, Satan, or the antagonist of God.
	taken with hands	grabbed, picked, plucked with hands
23:7	fenced	armed, protected, defended, guarded
23:10	spoil	plunder, booty, stolen goods
23:11	lentils	herb/plant grown for its edible flattened seeds that are cooked like peas/beans and also ground into meal
23:13	pitched	camped, set up, established
23:14	a hold	the stronghold, fort, safe room
23:18	name	reputation, fame, bragging rights
23:21	goodly	an impressive, important, powerful
23:23	attained	succeeded, received honor
23:30	brooks	streambeds, small river
24:1+	Lord	Jehovah; God in relationship to mankind
24:1	was kindled	burned, ignited, started a fire
24:9	valiant	mighty, famous, battle-decorated, warrior
24:10	heart smote him	felt guilty, remorseful, felt badly
24:10	beseech	beg, plead, implore
24:13	advise	consider, contemplate, think about
24:14	strait	distress, dilemna
24:16	angel	messenger, supernatural being
	repented	relented, softened, changed mind

	stay	hold back, stop, cease
24:22	other instruments	the yokes, equipment

I KINGS

1:2,4	cherish	attend, nurture
1:6	goodly	handsome, strong
1:12	counsel	guidance, wisdom, instruction, teaching, advice
1:13	swear	pledged, vowed, promised, gave an oath
1:16	would you	do you wish
1:19	called	invited, asked
1:41	made an end	finished, completed
1:42	valiant man	mighty, famous, battle-decorated, warrior
1:43	verily	surely, truly, honestly, yes, correct
1:50	feared	was afraid, scared, troubled
	caught	took, captured
2:1,2,43	charged	commanded, requirements, ordered
2:3	statutes	law, rule, commands, decrees, directives
2:4	continue	carry out, fulfill
2:5	girdle	waistband, belt
2:6,9	hoar head	gray hair, old age, respectability
2:7	because of	from
2:8	swore	pledged, vowed, promised, gave an oath
2:12	greatly	firmly, exceedingly, mighty
2:14	somewhat	something, a little
2:17,20	nay	no
2:19	seat	seat (of honor) throne
2:25,29,31,32,34,46	fell upon	attacked, struck
2:33	seed	offspring, children, heirs
2:35	room	place, chamber
2:42	swear	pledged, vowed, promised, gave an oath
	protested	solemnly warned
2:44	privy to	secret, personal, private, confidential, hush-hush
3:1	affinity	an alliance, league, group, gang
3:14	keep	obey, follow, do, practice
	lengthen	prolong, extend, delay
3:18	save	except, other than, besides
3:19	overlaid	lay on it, cover
3:23	Nay	no
3:26	bowels	emotions, feelings, heart
4:4	host	army, gathering of soldiers

I KINGS

4:6	tribute	slaves, gifts of treasures
4:7,27	victuals	provisions, food & supplies
4:13	pertained	belonged, related to
4:21	river	a.k.a. Euphrates
	presents	tribute, gifts
4:23	harts	stag, male deer, antelope
	roebucks	small, graceful male deer
4:25	under his	with his own
4:28	horses	chariot horses, war horses
	dromedaries	camels
	charge	responsibility, care
5:1	anoint	elect, choose, dedicate
5:3	the soles of his feet	his control, ownership, possession
5:6,18	hew	cut, hack
5:6	skill	know how, expertise, talent, ability
5:9	floats	rafts, small boats
	appoint	direct, hire, delegate
5:12	league	treaty, agreement, alliance, gang
5:13,14	levy, muster	make pay, tax, toll
5:14	by courses	in relays
5:18	stone squarers	someone that made a stone "square" and ready to be used as a building block, or large brick
6:5+	oracle	inner sanctuary
6:6	nethermost	lowest, rear
	narrowed rests	ledges, offsets
6:12	statutes	law, rule, commands, decrees, directives
6:15	both	from
	and	to
6:31	entering	entrance, going in
	a fifth part of the wall	wood, five-sided
6:33	a fourth part of the wall	four-sided
6:34	leaves	panels, sections
	folding	pivoting
7:6,7,8,12	porch	hall
7:9,11,12	hewed	cut, hacked
7:9	coping	eaves, overhang
7:14	cunning	inventive, inwrought, skillful, expert craftsman

I KINGS

7:15,24	did compass	go about, surround, encamp, encircle
7:16+	chapiter	capitals, lattice work
7:17	nets	netting, lattice work
7:20	belly	projection, outcropping
7:23,33	molten sea	a large wash basin/sink made of brass
7:25,39	sea	a large wash basin/sink
7:26	two thousand baths	c.15,000 gallonlons
7:28,29,36	ledges	joinings, uprights
7:30	plates	axles
7:30,34	undersetters	supports
7:31,36	engravings	engraved, etchings, markings
7:33	axle-trees	hubs
	naves	rims
7:35	compass	band
7:36	borders	surfaces
	proportion	size, dimension
7:37	one	the same
7:40	made an end	finished, complete
7:44	12 oxen under the sea	in the holy temple, there was a large wash basin/sink made of brass, the brazen "sea" was for the priest to wash in before they performed their jobs – the basin was set up off the ground and the oxen were statures that sat "under" the sea
7:49	oracle	inner sanctuary
7:50	censers	firepans
8:1,6,9,21,23	covenant	unconditional agreement, contract, promise
8:6,8	oracle	inner sanctuary
8:7	staves	poles
8:13	settled	kingly, established, well-founded
8:20	promised	spoke, vowed, gave his word
8:28	You respect	regard, revere, honor
8:28,29,30,52	hearken	listen, pay attention, heed
8:45,47,49	supplication	prayer, appeal, plea, beg, ask, petition
8:31	oath	pledge, vow, promised
	swear	pledged, vowed, promised, gave an oath
8:40	fear	revered, respected, trembled, dread
8:45,47,49,54,59	supplication	prayer, appeal, plea, beg, ask, petition

I KINGS

8:47	bethink themselves	change their minds
	perversely	iniquity, wickedly
8:58	incline	turn, lean towards
	statutes	law, rule, commands, decrees, directives
8:59	at all times	each day, always, regularly
8:61	perfect with	wholly devoted to, consecrate, committed
9:3	supplication	prayer, appeal, plea, beg, ask, petition
	hallowed	consecrated, dedicated, holy
	mine eyes and heart shall be there	God is saying that he will always watch over, keep an eye on, and love Israel (the Jew)
9:4	statutes	law, rule, commands, decrees, directives
9:7	cut off	destroy, end, bring down
	proverb & byword	made an example of; become ancient history, has been, like a fairy tale or story
9:8	hiss	scoff, mock, ridicule
9:13	Ca'bul	Binding
9:17	nether	lower, bottom
9:23	wrought	were doing
10:1,7	fame	report, reputation
10:1	prove him	challenge, test, see what he's made of
	hard questions	difficult, tricky, puzzles, complicated
10:2	train	retinue, following, attendants
	in her heart	on her mind, desire
10:3	told her	answered, expounded
10:5	meat	food
10:11	great plenty	very many, a lot
10:12	psalteries	lyres
10:13	her desire	she wanted, hoped for
10:16	targets	large shields
10:20	like made	equal, same, uniform
10:21	nothing accounted	not valued, not totaled or added up
10:24	sought to	enquired of, asked
10:26	bestowed	stationed, placed
10:27	vale	lowland
10:29	means	expense, cost
11:1,8	strange	foreign, non-Jewish people
11:4	after	to follow

I KINGS

	perfect with	wholly devoted to, consecrated, dedicated
11:5,6	went	followed
11:5,7	abomination	detestable idol, immoral, corrupt
11:7	Chemosh	the destroyer, subduer, or fish-god, the god of the Moabites
	high place	shrines, altars to pagan gods
11:10	kept not	did not observe, rebelled, disobeyed
11:11	covenant	unconditional agreement, contract, promise
11:11,33,34	statutes	law, rule, commands, decrees, directives
11:11,12,13,31	rend	tear, ripped, shred, pull apart, open
11:14	stirred	raised, agitated, angered
11:14,39	seed	offspring, children, heirs
11:18	appointed	assigned, designated, placed
	victuals	food
11:22	wise	case, anyway, just because
11:25	mischief	evil, wickedness, harm
	abhorred	was hostile to, mean, hated
11:26	lifted up his hand	rebelled, fought against
11:28	charge	burden, labor force
11:30	rent	tear, ripped, shred, pull apart, open
11:38	hearken	listen, pay attention, heed
	sure	enduring, lasting, solid
11:39	afflict	humble, be sorry
12:4	grievous	harsh, hard
12:8	stood before	served, attended,
12:9,13,14	counsel	guidance, wisdom, instruction, teaching, advice
12:11	lade	load, pile up, pack on
12:11,14	chastised	lashed, punished
12:13	roughly	harshly, severe, cruel
	forsook	rejected, left
12:15,16,24	hearkened	listen, pay attention, heed
12:18	tribute	forced labor, money, gifts
12:19	house	family, estate, clan
12:31	house of	temple, altar, sanctuary
12:31,32	high places	shrines, altars to pagan gods
12:32,33	ordained	instituted, commissioned, set up
13:1	by the word of	directed by, commanded
13:2	in the word	by the direction, under inspiration

	offer	sacrifice, dedicate, offer
13:2	high places	altar, shrine, an outdoor place of worship
13:3,5	rent	split away, tear
13:5	Entreat	intercede with, plead, beg
13:9	charged	commanded, ordered
13:15,17,22,23	bread	some food
13:18	angel	messenger, supernatural being
13:21	mouth	word, orders, directions
13:22,31	sepulcher	tomb, grave, crypt
13:26	word	command
13:26,28	torn	mauled, law, prophecies
13:32	cried	declared, spoke aloud
14:3	cracknels	hard biscuits or cakes
	cruse	jar, container, small bottle
14:4	set	dim, weak, faint
14:5	feign	pretend, fake, to put on an act, deceive
14:6	feign	pretend, make believe, trick
	heavy	harsh, badly, hard
14:8	rent	tore, ripped, maul, kill
14:9	cast	thrown, tossed, put down
14:15	smite	attacked, strike, hit, punish
	groves	(Heb:Asherah) either a living tree or a tree-like pole, set up as an object of worship, being symbolical of the female or productive principle in nature. Every Phoenician had an asherah near them. Both the "May Pole" and "Christmas Tree" (Jer.10:3-5) originate with this Asherah. The word is often translated "green trees" or "grove." This "nature worship" became associated with sexual immorality.
14:23	high places	shrines, altars to pagan gods
14:24	sodomites	homosexual male cult prostitutes
	abominations	detestable practices, filthy, immoral
14:28	bore	carried, hauled
	chamber	room, hall
15:12	sodomites	homosexual male cult prostitutes
15:13	grove	a group of trees, an orchard
15:27	not suffer	prevent, hold back, allow

I KINGS

15:19	league	treaty, alliance, group, gang
15:20	hearkened	listen, pay attention, heed
15:22	exempted	left out, not required
15:24	slept	died & buried
15:27	smote	attacked, strike, hit, punish
16:2	Forasmuch	Because
	exalted	lifted, elevated, revered
16:6	slept	died & buried
16:10	smote	attacked, strike, hit, punish
16:13	vanities	worthless idols
16:31	light thing	no big deal, small matter, unimportant
16:32	reared up	erected, built, set up, established
16:33	groves	(Heb:Asherah) either a living tree or a tree-like pole, set up as an object of worship, being symbolical of the female or productive principle in nature. Every Phoenician had an asherah near them. Both the "May Pole" and "Christmas Tree" (Jer.10:3-5) originate with this Asherah. The word is often translated "green trees" or "grove." This "nature worship" became associated with sexual immorality.
16:34	set up the gates	established, started, built a kingdom
17:1	Tish'bite	a person form the Tish tribe – a group of people known for their weaving skills
17:5	dwelled	stayed, lived, established
17:9	sustain	provide for, care
17:10	took an oath	promised, swore, gave his word
17:12,16	cruse	jar, container, small bottle
17:12	dress	prepare, outfit
17:13	blaspheme	speak evil about God or holy things
17:16	wasted not	was not exhausted, not tired or worn out
17:17	sore	bad, extensive, completely
17:19	abode	dwell, live, stay, make a home, settled
17:20	sojourn	temporarily stay, visit, live
17:23	chamber	room, hall
	delivered	gave, provided
18:2	sore	severe, bad, extensive
18:3,12	feared	revered, respected, trembled, dread

I KINGS

18:4	was so	came about, happened
	cut off	destroyed, finished, ended
18:7	fell on his face	bowed, worshipped
18:13	slew	killed, slayed
18:15	show	present, bring to
18:21	halt	limping, hesitate, not decide
18:23,25,26	dress	prepare, clean
18:29	regarded	noticed, heeded, observed, attended to
18:46	girded up loins	tighten belt, tie up, prepare for action
19:1	withal	all about, entire
19:3	went	ran, left to go
19:6	cruse	jar, containier, small bottle
19:7	angel	messenger, supernatural being
19:8	meat	food
19:10,14	covenant	unconditional agreement, contract, promise
19:11	rent	tear, ripped, shred, pull apart, open
19:13	wrapped	covered, placed around
19:16	room	place, hall, space
19:19	mantle	robe, cloak
19:21	instruments	implements, equipment
20:3	goodliest	most beautiful, best, lovely
20:6	pleasant	desirable, attractive
20:7,22	mark	notice, point out, observe, identify
20:7	seeks mischief	is looking for trouble
20:8	hearken	listen, pay attention, heed
20:11	harness	armor, battle dress
20:21	smote	attacked, strike, hit, punish
20:24	rooms	places, hall, space
20:25	number	assemble, gather, count
20:30	chamber	room, hall, space
20:34	covenant	unconditional agreement, contract, promise
20:35	smite	attacked, strike, hit, punish
20:38	ashes	bandages
20:39	keep	guard, protect, watch over
20:43	displeased	angry, grieved, angry, frustrated
21:1	hard	close to, near, by
21:3+	Lord	Jehovah; God in relationship to mankind
21:4	heavy	unhappy, grieved, sad

I KINGS

21:4,5	bread	food
21:10,13	sons of Be'li-al	followers of, or actually *the* fallen angel/demon "Bel." Be'li-al is translated "lawlessness"— and follows a rabbinical tradition which interpreted it as "beli 'ol" the one who has thrown off the yoke of heaven. Belial was accordingly considered the opponent of the rule of God; that is, Satan, or the antagonist of God.
21:13	blaspheme	dishonor, act disgracefully, ruin the name or reputation
21:21	urinates	pisses, takes a piss, take a leak, go to bathroom
21:25	work	do, perform, accomplish
	stirred up	incited, agitated, angered
21:26	abominably	behaved in a very vile, detestable manner
21:27	rent	tear, ripped, shred, pull apart, open
	softly	gently, easily
22:5	at	for
22:6,15	forbear	refrain, hold back, resist
22:10	a void	an opening, blank spot
22:24	smote	attacked, strike, hit, punish
22:25	chamber	room, hall, space
22:28	hearken	listen, pay attention, heed
22:31	save	except, other than, besides
22:34	a venture	random, skirmish
	harness	armor, battle gear
22:34,36	host	army, large group of soldiers
22:35	stayed	propped, held up, supported
	midst	bottom, lower parts
22:40,50	slept	died & buried
22:43	high places	shrines, altars to pagan gods

II KINGS

1:3,15	angel	messenger, supernatural being
1:5	turned back	returned
1:7	manner	kind, type
1:10,12	consume	vanish, waste away, dried up, spent, used up
1:13	besought	humbled, pleaded, begged
2:2	Tarry	wait, stay, remain
2:3,5	your head	boss, being your leader
2:7	afar off	from a distance
2:9	double portion	twice as much, much more than
2:11	chariot	a wagon or cart pulled by horses
2:12	rent	tear, ripped, shred, pull apart, open
	smitten	struck, hit, punished
2:17	sought	searched, looked for
2:20	cruse	jar, container, small jar
2:24	she	female
3:2	wrought	did, performed
	image	sacred pillar, statue, pagan idol
3:6	numbered	mobilized, mustered, counted
3:9	compass, circle of	surround, enclose, go all around
	seven days	one week; also symbolic of "completion"
3:11	poured water on the hands	was the personal servant
3:15	minstrel	musician, instrument player, performer
3:18	light	an easy, simple
3:19	smite	attacked, strike, hit, punish
	fenced	fortified, walled, defensed
3:20	meat	meal
	offered	sacrificed, gave, presented
3:21	gathered	assembled, brought together
	upward	older
3:23,24,25	smote	attacked, strike, hit, punish
3:25	beat down	destroyed, crushed
3:26	sore	fierce, ferocious, heated
3:27	indignation	anger, temper, destructive rage verging on madness
4:1	did fear	revered, scared, troubled

II KINGS

	bondmen	slaves, servants
4:3	not a few	many
4:6	stayed	stopped flowing, ceased
4:8,11	it fell on	there came, occurred. happened
4:8	bread	food
4:13	been careful	showed care, cautious, concern
4;14	verily	surely, truly, honestly, yes, correct
4:16	time of life	nine months of pregnancy
4:18	reapers	those that harvest crops, workers in the fields
4:23	Wherefore	who
4:24	slack	slow, idle, let off, relax
4:27	caught…feet	humbled herself, kneel before, begged
4:29	salute	greet, say hello, ackowledge
4:31	hearing	response, answer
4:34	waxed	became, grew, increased
	lay	hugged tightly, cuddled
	put…his mouth eyes hands…child	like mouth to mouth resuscitation
4:35	sneezed seven times	when God gave life to Adam, He breathed into his nose – when this child came to life, he first breathed out the death by sneezing, then came alive
4:38	dearth	drought, no rain, famine, lack or water/food
	seethe pottage	cook stew
4:41	harm	evil thing, danger, poison
4:42	corn	grain
4:42	husk	outside covering, skin of grain (like the skin on a peanut)
4:43	servitor	assistant, servant
4:44	thereof	some, a little, remains
5:1	honorable	highly regarded, respected
5:2	maid	girl
	waited on	served, attended
5:3	recover	cure, heal, make well
5:5	Go to	come now
	raiment	clothing, garment
5:6,7	recover	make well, cure

II KINGS

5:7,8	rent	tear, ripped, shred, pull apart, open
5:8	know	understand
5:9	stood	stopped, pulled up
5:10,14	clean	made well, healed, cured
5:11	strike	wave
5:15	blessing	present, gift, offering, present
5:17	two…earth	what two mules/donkeys could carry on their backs (to be used to build an altar/shrine)
5:20	somewhat	something, a little
5:21	lighted	came quickly, hurried, sped up
5:24	tower	stronghold, hill
5:24	bestowed	put, places
5:26	went not my heart	was not my spirit, feelings, desire
5:27	seed	offspring, children, heirs
6:1	dwell	stay, live
	strait	narrow, small
6:2	beam	a piece of wood, lumber, house-building material
6:6	swim	float
6;10	saved	guarded, protected
	not once nor twice	several times
6:11	sore troubled	enraged, angered, furious
6:12	None	no one
	your bedchamber	privacy, confidential
6:14,15	compassed	go about, surround, encamp, encircle
6:18,21,22	smite	attacked, strike, hit, punish
6:23	great provision	a great feast
6:25	cab	approximately one quart (1/3 gallonlon)
	dung	waste, poop, crap
6:28	ails	in the matter with
6:30	rent	tear, ripped, shred, pull apart, open
	within	beneath, under
7:1	shekel	the term for Jewish money, like our "dollar"
7:2	windows in heaven	God himself would bless, prosper, provide
7:4	fall	surrender, give up, quit
7:5,8	uttermost part	outskirts, borders
7:10,11	porter	gatekeepers, guards, butlers
7:12	hide themselves in	

II KINGS

	the field	set up an ambush
7:13	consumed	doomed, dying, sick
7:16	spoiled	plunder, booty, stolen goods
7:17,20	trode	walk, trampled, stepped on, beaten, defeated
7:17,18,19	man	prophet, fore-teller
7:20	fell out	happened, occurred, was fulfilled
8:1	sojourn	temporarily stay, visit, live
8:3	cry to	plead with, cry out, plead
8:11	settled his countenance	stared at him, looked at, gawked
	steadfastly	kept staring without stopping
	shewed	showed, revealed, let him know
8:12	dash	smash, break apart, tear up
8:20	revolted	fought against, protested, mutiny, rebelled
8:14	recover	get well, healed, be cured
8:21	compassed him about	go about, surround, encamp, encircle
8:25,26	reign	rule, govern
8:29	sick	wounded, ill, injured
9:1	Gird	bind, fasten, prepare
	loins	waist, hips
9:2	look	search, view, observe
	chamber	room, hall, space
9:3	box/flask	bottle, container to hold liquid or other item
9:3	tarry	wait, delay, put off
9:5	host	army, gathering of many soldiers
9:5	errand	message or matter for
9:7,27	smite	attacked, strike, hit, punish
9:8	urinates	pisses, takes a piss, take a leak, go to bathroom
9:11	communication	talk, discuss, dialogue
9:12	false	a lie, deceptive, incorrect
9:14	conspired	plotted, made a plan, schemed
9:18	turn you	fall in, get behind
9:21	met	found, engaged, confronted
9:23	treachery	treason, disloyalty, backstabbed
9:22	whoredoms	illegallon sex outside of marriage, immoral, prostitution or worse; also describes unfaithfulness to God/His rules (sin)
9:25	laid burden upon	responsibility, path in life, difficult job
9:28	sepulcher	tomb, grave, crypt

II KINGS

9:30	face	eyes, put on make-up
	tired	adorned, fixed, applied
9:32	eunuchs	either a castrated man (no testicles/balls) or, in ancient terms, any man who is impotent with women. They worked as household servants, religious specialists, government officials, and guardians of women
9:33	trode…feet	stepped all over, trampled, walked on
9:36,37	portion	land parcel, plot, piece
10:2	fenced	fortified, walled, well defended
10:3	Look even out	choose, select, inspect
	meetest	most worthy, best, finest
10:4	stood not before	could not resist
10:6	mine	on my side
10:8	entering	entrance
10:9	righteous	just, fair, having integrity
10:11	kinsfolk	close friends, relatives, family
10:13,15	salute	greet, say hello
10:14	pit…shearing house	a place where sheep got their fur cut off
10:15	lighted	saw, recognized, spotted
10:19	wanting	missing, lacking, without
10:22	vestry	wardrobe, clothes, garment
10:23	look	see, inspect
10:25,32	smote	attacked, strike, hit, punish
10:26	images	sacred pillars, statues, pagan idols
10:27	draught house	latrine, toilet, bathroom
10:32	cut Israel short	reduce the size of Israel
10:32	coasts	territory, boundary, border
10:35	slept with…fathers	died and was buried
11:1	seed royal	royal off-spring, children, heirs
11:2	stole	took, removed, kidnapped
11:4,17	covenant	unconditional agreement, contract, promise
11:5,7,9	sabbath	rest day, day off work
	keepers of the watch	guards, protectors, gatekeepers
11:7	parts	companies, units
11:8	compass	go about, surround, encamp, encircle
	ranges	ranks, units of soldiers
11:12	God save	long live

II KINGS

11:15	Have her forth outside the ranges	bring her outside the ranks
11:16	way	road, path, trail
11:18	images	idols, statues
11:20	sword…king's house	killed him with the sword near the king's palace/castle
12:4	dedicated	sacred, set apart, consecrated
	set at	assessed, measured
	that comes into any man's heart	given willingly, freely
12:5,6,7,8	breaches, breach	broken place, crumbled walls, holes, gap
12:10	scribe	secretary, writer, recorder
	put up	tied it, bound
12:10,11	told	counted, added, calculated
12:11	wrought	worked, performed, did
12:12	hewers	stonecutters, masons
	hewed	cut, hacked
	masons	builder, architect, stone worker (ancient brick layer)
12:15	reckoned not with	did not require an accounting from
12:16	trespass money sin money	restitution, repayment, money paid as a penalty or punishment for sin
12:17	to go up to	to fight against, attack
12:18	away	withdrew, left, depart
12:21	smote	attacked, strike, hit, punish
13:1	reigned	ruled, governed
13:3	delivered	gave, brought, provided
13:4	hearkened	listen, pay attention, heed
13:6	groves	(Heb:Asherah) either a living tree or a tree-like pole, set up as an object of worship, being symbolical of the female or productive principle in nature. Every Phoenician had an asherah near them. Both the "May Pole" and "Christmas Tree" (Jer.10:3-5) originate with this Asherah. The word is often translated "green trees" or "grove." This "nature worship" became associated with sexual immorality.

II KINGS

13:7	footmen	a foot soldier, an infantryman
13:9,13	slept	died & buried
13:11	therein	in them
13:12	chronicles	diary, history, journal, narrative
13:14	his face	him
13:17,18,19	smite	attacked, strike, hit, punish
13:18	stayed	stopped, hold, halted
13:19	smitten	struck, hit, punished, attack
13:21	sepulcher	tomb, grave, crypt
13:23	respect	paid attention, heed, listened to
	covenant	unconditional agreement, contract, promise
14:5	confirmed	firmly, established, under control
	slew	killed, murdered
14:9	trods	stepped all over, trampled, walked on
	thistle	thorn, sticker, weeds
14:10	meddle	interfere, interrupt, get in the middle of
14:12	put to the worse	routedbeaten badly, conquered
14:15	might	achievements, success
14:6,22,29	slept	died & buried
14:19	conspiracy	plot against, scheme, to plan together against
14:25	coast	territory, boundary, border
14:26	affliction	suffering, illness, disease, problem
	shut up, nor any left	slave nor free
14:28	warred	fought, battled
14:29	slept…fathers	died and was buried
15:4	Save that	Only, just, barely
15:5	several	separate, others
15:6,11	chronicles	annals, records, historical documents
15:7,22,38	slept	died & buried
15:7	stead	in place of, substitute, replace
15:10	before the people	publicly, openly
15:14,16	smote	attacked, strike, hit, punish
15:19	confirm	strengthen, establish, under control
15:20	exacted	took, required payment
15:25,32,33,38	reigned	ruled, controlled, governed
15:25	room	place, hall
15:35	high places	altar, shrine, an outdoor place of worship
16:1,20	reign	rule, control, govern

II KINGS

16:3	abominations	detestable ways, filthy, immoral
	heathen	non-Jewish people/nations, did not serve the one true God
16:5	overcome	overpower, defeat, conquer
16:6	save	deliver, rescue, defend
16:9	hearkened	listen, pay attention, heed
	took	captured, possessed
16:10	fashion	model, mold, make, shape
16:11	against	before
16:13,15	meat	grain
16:14,15	brazen	the metal brass (symbolically used to identify judgment)
16:15	inquire by	seek guidance, ask, question, consult
16:18	covert	covered corridor, hidden, secret
	sabbath	rest day, day off work
	turned	removed, left, fled
16:20	slept	died & buried
	stead	place
17:3,4	presents	tribute, taxes, money
17:7+	feared	revered, respected, trembled, dread
17:8	statutes…heathen	laws/rules of non-Jewish people/nations
17:9	fenced	fortified, walled
17:10	images	sacred pillars, statues, pagan idols
		groves (Heb:Asherah) either a living tree or a tree-like pole, set up as an object of worship, being symbolical of the female or productive principle in nature. Every Phoenician had an asherah near them. Both the "May Pole" and "Christmas Tree" (Jer.10:3-5) originate with this Asherah. The word is often translated "green trees" or "grove." This "nature worship" became associated with sexual immorality.
17:11	wrought	performed, did
17:14	Notwithstanding	However
	hardened their necks	became stubborn, unyielding, proud
17:15,19,34,37	statutes	law, rule, commands, decrees, directives
17:15,35,38	covenant	unconditional agreement, contract, promise

II KINGS

17:16	all the host of heaven	sun, moon, and stars
17:17	divination and enchantments	fortune telling
17:19	made	crafted, built, formed
17:20	seed	offspring, children, heirs
17:21	rent	tear, ripped, shred, pull apart, open
17:26,27,33,34	manner(s),	custom(s), behavior, principle, traditions
17:29	high places	altar, shrine, an outdoor place of worship
17:32	of the lowest	from the common people
17:37	ordinances	law, rule, commands, decrees, directives
17:40	hearken	listen, pay attention, heed
18:1,2	reign	rule, govern
18:4	images	sacred pillars, statues, pagan idols
	groves	(Heb:Asherah) either a living tree or a tree-like pole, set up as an object of worship, being symbolical of the female or productive principle in nature. Every Phoenician had an asherah near them. Both the "May Pole" and "Christmas Tree" (Jer.10:3-5) originate with this Asherah. The word is often translated "green trees" or "grove." This "nature worship" became associated with sexual immorality.
	Ne-hus'tan	A thing of bronze
18:7	prospered	became rich, successful, grew strong
18:13	fenced	fortified, walled, defensed
18:14	offended	done wrong, sinned, trespass
18:16	cut	strip, shred
18:17	conduit	gutter, water pipeline, aquaduct, channel
18:18	scribe	secretary, writer, recorder
18:20	vain	empty, pointless, without value
18:21	bruised reed	partially broken stick, splintered walking stick
18:22	high places	altar, shrine, an outdoor place of worship
18:23	give	make, provided
18:26	ears	hearing, listening
18:29	deceive	mislead, trick, con, scam
18:31,32	hearken	listen, pay attention, heed
18:31	an agreement	your peace, treaty, alliance

II KINGS

18:32	persuades	misleads, deceives, influences
18:36	held their peace	remained silent, didn't respond
18:37,19:1	rent	tear, ripped, shred, pull apart, open
19:3	blasphemy	disgrace, dishonor, impure, vile
19:4	reprove	rebuke, correct, chasten, punish, warn
	remnant	leftover, remains, survivors
19:7	blast upon	spirit in or wind upon
19:8	warring	fighting, battling, making war
19:11	utterly	completely, fully, totally
	delivered	spared, saved, rescued
19:16,22,23	reproach	insult, insulted, shame, humiliate
19:19	beseech	beg, plead, ask
19:21	scorn	mocked, disrespect, made fun of
19:25	fenced	fortified, walled, defensed
19:26	power	strength, might, force
	corn	grain
	confounded	confused, put to shame, rattled
19:28	tumult	brawl, fight, riot, commotion
19:32	bank	siege mound, fortified defensive perimeter
19:35	angel	messenger, supernatural being
20:3	beseech	beg, plead, ask
	sore	bitterly, badly, terribly
20:9	degrees	a degree is equal to about 4 minutes on a sundial (10 degrees = 40 minutes)
20:10	light thing	easy, no difficulty
20:13	hearkened	listen, pay attention, heed
20:20	conduit	gutter, water pipeline, aquaduct, channel
20:21	slept	died & buried
20:25	ruinous	disastrous, destructive, harmful
20:26	confounded	confused, put to shame, rattled
21:1,19	reign	rule, govern
21:2,11	abominations	disgusting, sick, forbidden, offensive practices
21:6	pass through the fire	pagan ritual
	familiar spirits	witchcraft
	wizards	spiritists, magicians
	wrought	did, performed
21:9	hearkened	listen, pay attention, heed
	seduced	pressured, tricked, decieved

II KINGS

21:12	shall tingle	he will be utterly astonished
21:14	inheritance	people who belong to me
	a spoil	plunder, booty, stolen goods
21:16	innocent	guilt-free, honest, decent, clean
21:18	slept	died & buried
21:26	sepulcher	tomb, grave, crypt
22:1	reign	rule, govern
22:4	sum	count, add
22:5	breaches	broken place, crumbled walls, holes, gap
22:6	hewn	cut, hacked, chopped
	mason	builder, architect, stone worker (ancient brick layer)
22:7	reckoning	to be counted, judgment, answer for behavior
22:8	scribe	secretary, writer, recorder
22:11,19	rent	tear, ripped, shred, pull apart, open
22:13	inquire	seek, ask, plead, question
	hearkened	listen, pay attention, heed
22:14	college	second quarter or district
	communed	spoke, talked, discussed
22:18	as touching	concerning, relating to, in reference
22:19	tender	responsive, gentle, humble, compliant
23:2,3,21	covenant	unconditional agreement, contract, promise
23:3	statutes	law, rule, commands, decrees, directives
	idolatrous	heathen, a non-Jew, person that worshipped idols or any god other than the One God (Jehovah)
23:5	put down	destroyed or dismissed, sacked
23:5,13,20	high places	shrines, altars, pagan churches
23:6,7,14,15	groves	(Heb:Asherah) either a living tree or a tree-like pole, set up as an object of worship, being symbolical of the female or productive principle in nature. Every Phoenician had an asherah near them. Both the "May Pole" and "Christmas Tree" (Jer.10:3-5) originate with this Asherah. The word is often translated "green trees" or "grove." This "nature worship" became associated with sexual immorality.
23:7	sodomites	homosexual male cult prostitutes

II KINGS

23:8,9,13	defiled	broke down the shrines, desecrated, desecrate
23:11	entering	entrance
	chamberlain	official, politician
23:12	beat	break, pull apart
23:13,24	abomination	detestable, disgusting, forbidden
23:16,17,30	sepulcher	tomb, grave, crypt
23:17	title	monument, landmark, memorial
23:19	houses	temples, sacred buildings
23:24	with familiar spirits	mediums, spiritualists, witch
	wizards	magicians
	images	household goods, idols, pagan statues
23:34	room	place, hall, area
	turned	changed, replaced, renamed
24:2	bands	raiders, robbers, gangs, thieves
24:6	slept	died & buried reigned ruled, governed
24:14,15	carried	led, caused, forced
24:16	apt	fit, appropriate, proper
25:1	reign	rule, governed
	pitched	camped, set up, established
25:7	fetters	chains, hand-cuffs, restraints
25:12	vinedressers and husbandmen	farmers, landowners, gardeners
25:17	chapiter	capital
	wreathen	decorated, ornate
	pomegranates	large fruit with many seeds and juicy red pulp in a tough brownish-red skin
	cubit	a type of Jewish measurement (like inches/meters), from the elbow to the tip of the longest finger. a cubit equaled 18" (inches)
25:25	seed royal	royal family
	smote	attacked, strike, hit, punish
25:27	lift up the head of	release, let go, freed
25:29	did eat bread continually before	had his meals with
	prison garment	rags to riches, treated Judah (Israel as a nation) very well, blessed

I CHRONICLES

1:1+	stead	place, position, replaced
2:1	Israel	Jacob
2:7	transgressed	misdeeds, sinned, wrong-doing, violate
	thing accursed	contraband, not supposed to have, illegallon
2:19	took to him	married, offspring, heir
2:30	children	sons
2:48	concubine	a sexual partner that is not a wife nor a prostitute
4:9	honorable	famous, respectable, admired
4:21	wrought	work, labor, build, produce
4:23	potters	person that hand-makes pottery (dishes, cups, bowls)
4:33, 7:7	genealogy	family history, family tree, your relatives
4:33	habitations	settlements, towns, viullages
4:38	princes	leaders, chiefs, rulers, influential men, governors
4:39	fat	rich, fertile, healthy
4:41,43	smote	attacked, strike, hit, punish
4:41	rooms	places, hall, living rooms
5:1	defiled	did evil on, corrupted, sexual sin
	reckoned	known, counted, a part of
	geneology	family history, family tree, your relatives
5:1,2	birthright	the special privileges and advantages belonging to the first-born son; became the leader of the family (financial, spiritual)
5:9	multiplied	increased, prospered
5:18	buckler	shield, used for protection
5:20	was entreated of	answered, responded, helped
5:22	steads	places, homes, buildings
5:25	went a whoring	played the harlot, unfaithful to beliefs
6:32,33	waited on, waited	served, helped, attended
6:32	order	position, title, job
6:49	atonement	a sacrifice, gift offered to forgive sins (sin separated man from God, the gift forgave the sin and united them: at-one-ment, to become one again)
6:54	castles	large camps, settlements, complex
6:54,66	coasts	territory, boundary, border

I CHRONICLES

6:55+	suburbs	pasture land
6:57	namely	specifically, precisely, particularly
6:65	gave by lot	allotted, drawing, lottery
6:66	residue	balance, boundaries, outer territories
7:21	take away	steal, rob, ripoff, jack
7:24	nether	lower, bottom
7:40	apt	likely, fitting, skillful, proper, suitable
8:6,7	removed	exiled, shifted, transplanted
9:1	reckoned by	known, counted, a part of
9:2	Nethinims	temple slaves assigned to the Levites and priests for service in the sanctuary
9:9	chief…fathers	leaders, rulers
9:17+	porter(s)	gatekeepers, guards, butlers
9:19	over	in charge of, responsible, accountable
9:19,22	gates	Jehovah; God in relationship to mankind
9:22	ordained	appointed, commissioned, tasked
9:22,26	set office	office of trust, responsibilities, duties
9:23	by wards	as guards, keepers
9:26	chambers	rooms, halls
9:27,28	charge	responsibility, calling, job, duty
9:28	tale	count, tally, amount, sum
	ministering vessels	dishes, cups etc. used in religious service
9:29	frankincense	spice, incense, perfume
9:32	shewbread	ceremonial bread used in religious service
	sabbath	rest day, day off work
10:1	fell down slain	died, were killed, victims, casualties
10:3,4	sore	fierce, terrible, bad, greatly
10:4	abuse	torture, treat badly
10:5	armor bearer	a soldier's assistant, someone that helped carry heavy weapons & armor (helmet, shield, body armor, swords, etc.)
10:7	forsook	forsake, abandon, dump, reject
10:8,9	strip, stripped	rob, rip off, jack
10:13	one that had a familiar spirit	a fortune teller, demon
11:1	bone and flesh	family, relative, people, blood
11:3	covenant	unconditional agreement, contract, promise
	anointed	consecrated, set apart

I CHRONICLES

11:5,7	castle	stronghold, defensed area, fortress
	city of David	Jerusalem
11:6	smites	strikes down, defeats, kills
11:9	waxed	became, grew, increased
11:12	mighties	strong and brave men, valiant, warrios
11:13	parcel	piece of land, lot, ground, dirt
11:16	hole	stronghold, fort
11:20	name	reputation, fame, notoriety
11:21,25	attained	win, obtain, achieve, accomplish
11:22	valiant	brave, gutsy, fearless, heroic
12:1	close	in hiding
12:2	hurling	throwing, pitch, toss
12:8	themselves	came over, defected, switched sides
	buckler	shield
	roes	gazelles
12:8,16	hold	stronghold, fort, protected area
12:17	knit	tied, united, joined
	wrong	violence, deceit, betrayal
	betray	abandon, leave, betray, walk away
	peaceably	in peace, friendship, not to attack, not enemies
12:19,20	fell	deserted, left
12:19	advisement	consultation, recommendation
12:21	rovers	rogue, drifters, hijackers, wandering group of bandits
12:23	bands	divisions, groups, gangs
12:29	kept the ward	allegiance to, obeyed, followed
12:31	expressed	designated, ordained
12:33	double heart	hypocrite, imposter, poser, fraud, pretender
12:33,37	instruments	weapons
12:38	perfect	sincere, whole, complete
13:8	played	celebrated, rejoiced, partied
	psalteries	lyres
13:8,15:9	cymbals	musical instrument of two pieces of brass, one held in each hand, which were clashed together
13:9	stumbled	nearly upset it, tripped
13:10	smote	attacked, strike, hit, punish
13:11	Pe'rez-uz-za	The Break Through of Uzza
	breach	gap, crack, hole, opening

I CHRONICLES

13:13	city of David	Jerusalem
14:2	lifted up on high	highly exalted, revered
14:8	anointed	consecrated, dedicated
14:11	breaking forth	a flood, massive amount, overrun
14:13	inquired	prayed, asked, petitioned
14:16	smote	attacked, strike, hit, punish
14:17	fear	revered, respected, trembled, dread
15:1	city of David	Jerusalem
15:1	pitched	camped, set up, established
15:5	brethren	relatives, kin, brethren
15:12,14	sanctify	consecrate, dedicate, set aside as holy
15:13	after the due order	according to the ordinance, per policy
15:15	staves	poles, long sticks
15:16,20,28	psalteries	a musical instrument, a harp with twelve strings
15:22	skillful	trained, talented, gifted, having ability
15:27	ephod	priestly garment, robes
15:29	despised…in heart	hated, look down on, feel disgusted
16:1	pitched	camped, set up, established
16:2	made an end of	finished, completed, done
16:3	dealt	distributed, gave, provided
	flagon	bottle, flask, container to hold liquid
16:4	minister	religious servant, worker, caretaker
16:5	psalteries	lyres
16:6,15,16,17	covenant	unconditional agreement, contract, promise
16:12	marvelous	amazing, awesome, wonderful, extraordinary
16:13	seed	offspring, children, heirs
16:18	lot	portion, amount, share
16:21	yea	yes, ok, right
	sakes	behalf, benefit, account
16:25,30	feared	revered, respected, trembled, dread
16:34,41	endures	lasts, hangs in, withstands, persists
16:37	minister	serve, attend, care for
16:38,42	porters	doorkeepers, attendants, butlers
16:39	high place	shrines, altars to pagan gods
16:41	expressed	designated, called, identified
17:1	house of cedars	in Israel's early history God "traveled" and "lived" with them in tents and temporary houses. Once they had become a nation, its kings built

		big, elaborate houses and God still "lived" in a tent – so God asks Davis through Nathan the prophet why God wasn't put first? A "house of cedars" is what wealthy men lived in and cedar was the wood first used to be the Temple in Jerusalem.
17:5	gone	left, moved
17:7	sheepfold	pasture
17:8	cut off	destroyed, defeated, removed
17:8,21	name	reputation, fame, notorious
17:9	ordain	appoint, call, establish
	plant	establish, build, make strong
	waste	oppress, beat, conquer
17:10	subdue	conquer, rule over
17:11	seed	offspring, children, heirs
17:17	estate	lands, plantation, ranch, a large residence
18:1,2,3	smote	attacked, strike, hit, punish
18:4	houghed	hamstrung
18:6,13	garrisons	military outpost/barracks, occupying force
18:8	brazen sea	brass bowl for water
18:14	reigned	ruled, governed
	executed	administered, carried out policy
18:17	about the king	at the king's side, near, close
19:4	hard	close, near
19:5	served	treated, cared for, attended
19:6	odious	a stench, strong smell
19:7	pitched	camped, set up, established
19:9	array	military formation, display, show of strength
19:13	valiantly	courageously, heroic, bravely
19:16,19	put to the worse	being defeated, sacked, beaten, crushed
19:17	put the battle in array	formed his battle lines, prepared to fight
20:1	wasted	destroyed, defeated, sacked
	tarried	stayed, waited, delayed
20:2	spoil	plunder, booty, stolen goods
	precious stone	gems, e.g. diamonds, rubies, emeralds, pearls
	talent	unit of measurement in currency (like dollars), a talent was about the average weight of a man

I CHRONICLES

20:3	harrows	sharp, cutting farm instrument, plow, hoe
20:6	abominable	horrible, lousy, nasty, rotten, stinking
20:7	defied	taunted, mocked, made fun of
21:1	stood	rose, came against, attacked
	provoked	incited, spurred, agitated
21:1,2	number	take a census, count, add up
21:3	trespass	guilt, violation, wrong-doing, sin
21:7	smote	attacked, strike, hit, punish
21:8	beseech	beg, plead, ask
	do	take
21:12,27,30	angel	messenger, supernatural being
21:12	coasts	territory, boundary, border
	pestilence	disease, fungus, mildew, disaster, crop failure
21:13	great strait	deep distress, conflict, dilemna
21:15	repented	regretted, felt sorry
	threshing floor	work area where the shells/skin were beaten/broken off wheat, barley grain
21:22	Grant	give, provide
	plague	epidemic, disease, judgement
21:24	verily	surely, truly, honestly, yes, correct
22:2	hew wrought	chop out, chisel
22:3	without weight	beyond measure, priceless
22:5	magnificent	amazing, awe-inspiring, powerful
22:6	charged	commanded, ordered, required
22:9	rest	quietness, peace
22:12	keep	obey, follow, do, practice
22:14	without weight	too much to count or measure, excess, abundant
22:15	cunning	inventive, inwrought, skillful, expert craftsman
22:18	into my hand	over to me
	subdued	conquered, defeated, beat
23:4	set forward	to supervise, govern, oversee
23:5	porters	gatekeepers, butlers, servants
23:6	courses	divisions, groups
23:11	reckoning	count, summary, grouping
23:24	polls	census, count the people
23:28	office	responsibility, job, duty
	chambers	side rooms, halls
23:31	sabbath	rest days, days without work

I CHRONICLES

23:31	new moons	at the time of the appearance of the first visible crescent (light) of the Moon
23:32	keep the charge of	
	charge	be responsible for, accountable, duty
24:3	distributed	assigned, employed, commissioned, put in place
24:19	ordering	appointed order, hierarchy, chain of command
24:29	showbread	ceremonial bread used in religious service
24:31	cast lots	predictions; like flipping a coin; paper, rock, scissors, throw dice
25:1	separated	set apart, consecrated, dedicated, purified
	psalteries	lyres
25:2	prophesied	spoke, fore-told, tell in advance
25:6	psalteries	lyres
25:8	ward against ward	guards, officers, keepers
26:1,12,19	porters	gatekeepers, guards, butlers
26:12,16	ward	guards, officers, keepers
26:16,18	causeway	ramp
26:20	dedicated	holy, consecrated, pure
26:27	spoils	plunder, booty, stolen goods
	maintain	repair, fix, upkeep
27:1+	course	division, group
27:5	host	fighting force, large number of soldiers
27:24	put	included, added
27:26	tillage	farming, gardening, growing plants/crops
27:31	substance	property, possessions, belongings, stuff
27:32	scribe	secretary, writer, recorder
28:1,21,24	courses	divisions, groups
28:1	substance	property, possessions, belongings, stuff
	officers	officials, governors, politicians
	stewards	managers, personal assistants
28:7	constant	faithful, consistant, loyal
28:11	pattern	plan, blueprint
	parlors	halls, rooms
28:17	fleshhooks	forks
	basins	bowl
28:18	covenant	unconditional agreement, contract, promise
	refined	purified, all impurities removed by heating in a fire

I CHRONICLES

29:1	tender	inexperienced, young, rookie
29:1,19	palace	temple
29:2	glistering	antimony, shiny, false gold
	divers	various, different, many
29:3	proper good	personal treasure, estate, personal wealth
29:5	artificers	craftsmen, skilled workers
29:6,9,17	offered	gave, provided, supplied
29:7	dram	historically both an inexpensive coin and a small weight (1/8th ounce)
29:9	perfect	a whole, complete, finished
29:12	reign	rule, govern, oversee
29:15	sojourners	temporarily stay, visit, live
	none abiding	no hope remaining
29:17	try	test, proove
29:18	prepare	direct, ready, condition
29:21	morrow	day, next, after
29:25	exceedingly	a lot, having plenty, excess, abundant
	bestowed	give, share, let have, provide
29:28	stead	place, area

II CHRONICLES

1:3,13	high place	shrines, altars to pagan gods
1:4	pitched	camped, set up, established
1:5	brazen	the metal brass (symbolically used to identify judgment)
1:8	reign	rule, govern, judge, control
1:10,11	judge	rule, oversee, facilitate
1:15	vale	lowlands
	plenteous	a lot, extra, a whole bunch
1:17	their means	same, equal, by ability to pay
2:2	hew	cut, hack, chop
	oversee	supervise, watch over, have authority
2:4	sabbaths	rest days, days off work
2:4	solemn	serious, no joke, sincere
	showbread	ceremonial bread used in religious service
	ordinance	law, rule, commands, decrees, directives
2:7,13,14	cunning	inventive, inwrought, skillful, expert craftsman
2:7	skill	know how, talented, having ability
2:10,18	hewers	woodsmen, loggers, carpenters
2:10	beaten	crushed, processed
	baths	bath, about 6 gallons.
2:12,13	endued	endowed, supplied, given
2:12	prudence	carefulness, good judgment, common sense
2:13	endued	given, supplied, awarded
2:14	find out every device	discover a plan, execute any design
2:14	engraving	carve, etch; make skillful, decorative marks
2:18	bearers	forced labor; unskilled, manual laborers
3:5	ceiled	wainscoted, overlaid with wood
3:6	garnished	adorned, decorated, dressed up
3:7	graved	carved, carved, etched
3:10	image	sculptured, crafted, carved
3:15	chapiter	capital
3:16	oracle	inner sanctuary
3:17	reared	erected, set up, built, constructed
4:2	molten sea	in the holy temple, there was a large wash

II CHRONICLES

		basin/sink made of brass, the "sea" was for the priest to wash in before they performed their jobs
4:2,3	compassed it round about	went/traveled all the way around, circled
4:3	similitude	likeness, appearance
4:3,4,10,15	sea	large basin
4:4	hinder parts	hindquarters
4:5	handbreadth	3 inches
	baths	about 6 gallons.
4:6,14	lavers	washbasins
4:7	candlesticks	lampstands
4:8,11,22	basins	bowls
4:9	furthermore	additionally, also, besides, as well as
4:12,13	pommels	bowls
	chapiters	capitals
4:14	lavers	it was a "basin" (pot) for boiling in, a "pan" for cooking, a "fire-pan" for baking or roasting, and the sacred wash-bowl used by priests in religious work
4:16	fleshhooks	forks
4:16,5:1	instruments	utensils, equipment
4:18	not…found out	too much to count or measure, excess, abundant
4:20	oracle	inner sanctuary
4:22	censers	firepans
5:2,7,10	covenant	unconditional agreement, contract, promise
5:6	told	counted, added, totaled
5:7,9	oracle	inner sanctuary
5:8,9	staves	poles, long sticls
5:10	save	except, other than, beside
5:12	psalteries	lyres
5:13	as one	in unison
5:14	stand to minister	perform the service
6:11,14	covenant	unconditional agreement, contract, promise
6:13	scaffold	table, altar, bench, platform
	cubits	a type of Jewish measurement (like I inches/meters), from the elbow to the tip of the longest finger. a cubit equaled 18"

II CHRONICLES

		(inches)
6:16	keep	continue, fulfill, honor
6:19,21,29,35,39	supplications	prayer, appeal, plea, beg, ask, petition
6:18	in very deed	indeed, in fact, truly, he will do it
6:20	toward	in
6:21	make	pray, perform, send
6:22	swear	promise, vow, pledge
6:23	requiting	punishing, avenging, pay back
	recompensing	pay back, payment, reward or punishment
6:28	dearth	famine, pestilence, hard times
	pestilence	plague, disease, illness
	blasting	blight, fungus
6:31,33	fear	revered, respected, trembled, dread
6:32	stranger	foreigner, visitor, guest
6:33,34,38	house	temple, hall, area
6:35,39	maintain	uphold, keep, continue
6:37	bethink	repent, change mind, remorse
	amiss	wrong, sin badly
6:40	beseech	beg, plead, request
	attent	focused, alert, wide awake
6:42	turn not away	do not reject, hide from, forsake
7:7	hallowed	respected, revered, sacred, holy
7:8	entering in	entrance
7:11	prosperously	successful, doing well, wealthy
7:15	attent	focused, alert, wide awake
7:17,19	statutes	law, rule, commands, decrees, directives
7:17	judgments	ordinances, laws, policies, decisions
7:18	covenanted	unconditional agreement, contract, promise
7:19	commandments	words, rules, orders
7:20,21	house	temple, sacred building, place of worship
7:20	I pluck them up	shock, horror, can't believe eyes
	byword	made an example of; become ancient history, has been, like a fairy tale or story
	sanctified	consecrated, purified, made holy
	byword	made an example of; become ancient history, has been, like a fairy tale or story
7:21	high	exalted, lifted up, honored
8:1	house	temple, hall, area

II CHRONICLES

8:2	restored	given
8:4,6	store	storage
8:5	nether	lower, bottom
	fenced	fortified, defensed, protected
8:8	pay tribute	serve as laborers, give gifts
8:9	servants	slaves, purchased/forced labor
	chief	commanders, rulers, bosses
8:13	sabbaths	rest days, days with no work allowed
	unleavened	yeast-free
8:14	charges	duties, chores, job
	porters	gatekeepers, guards, butlers
8:16	to	from
9:1	prove	tried, tested, searched, examined, known
	bore	carried, transported, hauled around
	communed	spoke, talked with, discussed
9:2	told	answered, responded
9:4	meat	food
	ascent	stairway
	cupbearers	the attendant/servant (usually an officer of a nobleman's household) whose job is was fill and serve cups of wine (like a restaurant waiter)
9:5	your acts	your words, deeds, behavior
9:11	algum	a type of tree, sandalwood
	terraces	steps
	house	temple, place of worship, religious building
	psalteries	lyres
9:14	chapmen	traders, peddlers, salesmen
9:15	target	large shields
9:18	stays	arms
9:20	accounted of	considered valuable
9:24	raiment	garments, clothes, threads
9:29	against	concerning
9:30	reigned	ruled, governed, controlled
	slept	died & was buried
10:4	grievous	grief, sad, painful, hurtful
	servitude	slavery, forced labor, made to work
10:6,13	took counsel	guidance, wisdom, instruction, teaching, advice
10:10	loins	waist

II CHRONICLES

10:11,14	scorpions	whips with painful metal tips
10:14	chastised	disciplined, punished, rebuked, scolded
	I will…scorpions	an even worse punishment, painful
10:15,16	hearkened	listen, pay attention, heed
10:15	the cause	turn of events
10:16	to your	return home
	tents	homes
10:18	tribute	forced labor, servitude, gifts of people
	made speed	hurried, sped up, rushed
11:1	gathered	assembled, get together, crowd
11:4	done of	from
11:10,23	fenced	fortified, walled, protected
11:11,23	victual	food
11:13	resorted to	stood with, joined, united
	coasts	territory, boundary, border
11:14	executing	serving, performing, doing
11:15	ordained	authorized, chose, selected, purposed
	for the devils	male goats used in sacrifices to heathen gods
11:16	after them	there followed them
11:17	strengthened	lifted up by, made strong, held up, supported
11:23	dispersed	scattered, spread out, divided
12:4	fenced	fortified, walled, protected
12:7	some	some measure of, a little
12:8	know	respect, understand, appreciate
12:15	genealogies	family history, family tree, your relatives
12:16	slept	died & buried
13:5	covenant of salt	agreement of preservation, contract, oath
13:6	is risen up	become a leader, established
13:7	vain men	criminals, punks, gangsters
	Be'li-al	followers of, or actually *the* fallen angel/demon "Bel." Be'li-al is translated "lawlessness"— and follows a rabbinical tradition which interpreted it as "beli 'ol" the one who has thrown off the yoke of heaven. Belial was accordingly considered the opponent of the rule of God; that is, Satan, or the antagonist of God.
13:11	shewbread	ceremonial bread used in religious service
	pure	clean, holy

II CHRONICLES

	keep the charge	observe the requirements, do, perform
13:13	caused	set up, set up
	ambushment	area to be trapped, mugged, intercepted
13:15	smote	defeated, attacked, strike, hit, punish
13:17	chosen men	elite, the best, special, not ordinary
13:18	brought under	subdued, conquered, defeated
13:20	waxed mighty	grew in strength, became
14:1	slept	died & buried
14:3	altars	foreign/pagan shrine
14:3,5	high places	shrines, altars to pagan gods
	images	idols, statues of heathen gods
14:6	fenced	fortified, walled, well-protected
14:6	rest	peace, no wars
14:8	targets	shields
14:11	power	strength, skill, ability, force
	prevail	win, succeed
14:13,14	spoil	plunder, booty, stolen goods
14:14,15	smote	destroyed, attacked, strike, hit, punish
14:14	fear	revered, respected, trembled, dread
14:15	tents of cattle	herdsmen
15:3	long season	a long time, it had been awhile
15:5,6	vexations	disturbances, worries, troubles
15:6	destroyed	crushed, defeated, sacked, thrashed
15:7	let not your hands be weak	do not lose courage, frightened
15:8	abominable	detestable, sick, polluted, unholy
	mount	the hill country
	renewed	restored, recovered, energized
15:9	tell	defected, joined, came
15:11	the same time	that day
	spoil	plunder, booty, stolen goods
15:12	covenant	unconditional agreement, contract, promise
15:14	swore	pledged, vowed, promised, gave an oath
15:15	rest	peace, no wars
16:12	sought not to	did not seek, look
16:14	sepulchers	tomb, grave, crypt
16:14	made	cut out
16:14	divers kinds	different, unalike, dissimilar, various

II CHRONICLES

	apothecaries	medicines, potions, remedies
17:2	forces	troops, soldiers, military
17:2,19	fenced	fortified, walled, well-protected
17:3	first ways	example
	to	help from
17:6	high places	shrines, altars to pagan gods
	groves	(Heb:Asherah) either a living tree or a tree-like pole, set up as an object of worship, being symbolical of the female or productive principle in nature. Every Phoenician had an asherah near them. Both the "May Pole" and "Christmas Tree" (Jer.10:3-5) originate with this Asherah. The word is often translated "green trees" or "grove." This "nature worship" became associated with sexual immorality.
17:10	fear	revered, respected, trembled, dread
17:12	waxed	grew, increased
	castles	fortresses, well-fortified area
17:19	waited	served, attended
18:1	joined affinity	allied himself by marriage
18:9	either	each, opposite, beside
	a void	an open, exclusive, set apart
18:10	horns of iron	influence, power, force that is hard and cruel
18:12	assent	voice, agreement, united
18:14	forbear	refrain, hold back, wait
18:15	adjure	command, order, demand
18:19	entice	temp, tease, lure, draw away
18:19	fall	be killed, be defeated
18:20	Wherewith	how
18:19,20	entice	temp, tease, lure, draw away
18:21	prevail	win, champs, be strong, defeat, overcome
18:23	smote	attacked, strike, hit, punish
18:26	of affliction	pain, torment, suffering
18:27	Hearken	listen, pay attention, heed
18:30	save	except, other than, beside
18:31	compassed about	go about, surround, encamp, encircle
18:32	perceived	saw, observed, looked on
18:33	a venture	random, luck, chance

II CHRONICLES

19:3	groves	(Heb:Asherah) either a living tree or a tree-like pole, set up as an object of worship, being symbolical of the female or productive principle in nature. Every Phoenician had an asherah near them. Both the "May Pole" and "Christmas Tree" (Jer.10:3-5) originate with this Asherah. The word is often translated "green trees" or "grove." This "nature worship" became associated with sexual immorality.
19:4	through	among
19:5	fenced	fortified, walled
19:6	in the	when you render
19:7	fear	revered, respected, trembled, dread
19:8	chief	heads, bosses, leaders
19:8	controversies	arguments, differences, disputes
19:9	charged	commanded, ordered, told
19:11	Deal	act, behave, perform
20:3,29	feared, fear	revered, respected, trembled, dread
	set himself	turned
20:6+	God	El, Elohim; self-existing, Almighty
20:15	Hearken	listen, pay attention, heed
20:20	established	safely kept, proposed, built up
20:22	smitten	routed, defeated, beaten
20:23	made an end	finished with, completed, halted
20:24	watchtower	a tower or tall building in which a person is placed to watch for enemies, or any type of danger
20:27	forefront	out in front, leader, leading position
20:28	psalteries	lyres
20:31	reigned	ruled, governed
20:33	high places	shrines, altars to pagan gods
21:1	slept with	died & buried
21:3	fenced	fortified, walled, well-protected
21:4	was risen up	took over, ascended, elevated
	strengthened	secured, various, different
	divers	some, various, different
21:5	wrought	did, performed, accomplished
21:7	covenant	unconditional agreement, contract, promise

II CHRONICLES

21:8	dominion	rule, domain, central
21:9	compassed	go about, surround, encamp, encircle
21:11	high places	shrines, altars to pagan gods
	compelled	led, influenced
	fornication	illegallon sex outside of marriage, immoral, dirty; also describes a union or relationship to something other than God/His rules
21:13	whoring	unfaithful, untrue to beliefs
21:15	disease of bowels	intestinal disease; possibly Chron's, irritable bowel syndrome or Dysentery (diarrhea)
21:17	substance	property, possessions, belongings, stuff
	never	no
21:19	of sore diseases	in great pain from sickness, illness
	no burning for him	no fire in his honor, no memorial ceremony
	fell out	diarrhea, runs or a cancer of the intestines
21:20	being desired	loved, respected, admired
	sepulchers	tomb, grave, crypt
22:3	counselor	advisor, teacher
22:7	by coming	because he went
	was	had
	cut off	destroy, defeat, end
22:9	keep still	retain control of, rule
22:10	seed royal	children of rich, wealthy, royalty, blue-bloods
22:14	counselors	those that gave advice, opinions, guidance, or instructions
23:1,3,16	covenant	unconditional agreement, contract, promise
23:4	sabbath	rest day, days off from work
23:4, 19	porters of the doors	gatekeepers, guards, butlers
23:6	watch	command, responsibility
23:8	courses	divisions, military grouping
23:9	buckler's	small shields
23:11	save	long live
23:13	entering in	entrance, start, beginning
	rent	tear, ripped, shred, pull apart, open
23:13	treason	unfaithful, disloyal, double-cross, betray
23:14	Have	bring
	of	from
	ranges	ranks,battle lines

II CHRONICLES

23:17	images	idols, statues, carvings
23:18	appointed	assigned, set up, established
	distributed	placed, set, put
23:20	high	upper, top
24:4	minded	reminded, thought about, memory jogged, idea
24:5	hasten	quickly do, hurry, speed up
24:6	collection	levy, tax
24:7	broken up	damaged, smashed, wrecked
	bestow	give, share
24:7	Baalim	principal male god of the Babylonians, sun god
24:11	emptied	transferred, relocated, moved
24:12,13,14	house	temple, place of worship, religious building
24:12,13	wrought	worked with, formed, built
24:14	vessels	utensils, equipment
24:15	waxed	grew, increased, became
24:17	made obeisance	bowed down
	hearkened	listen, pay attention, heed
24:23	spoil	plunder, booty, stolen goods
24:25	sepulchers	tombs, graves, crypts
24:25	conspired	plot against, scheme, plan together
25:2	perfect	whole, complete, 100%
25:11	strengthened	took courage
	valley of salt	Dead Sea area
	smote	attacked, strike, hit, punish
25:13	spoil	plunder, booty, stolen goods
25:16	forbear	refrain, hold back, resist
	determined	planned, decided
	counsel	guidance, wisdom, instruction, teaching, advice
25:17	one another in the face	"meet me face to face", confidential
25:18	thistle	thorn, sticker, weeds
25:19	lifts you up to	has become proud in
	boast	boasting, bragging
	meddle	ask for trouble, involve, butt-in
25:22	put to the worse	defeated, conquered, beat
25:24	hostages	prisoners, captured people, slaves
26:1	room	place, hall
26:10	wells	cisterns, man-made water resevior

II CHRONICLES

	husbandmen	plowmen, farmers, land owners
	husbandry	the soil, farm, plow, cultivate
26:14	habergeons	body armor
26:15	cunning	inventive, inwrought, skillful, expert craftsman
	bulwarks	defenses, fortifications, walls, barriers
	marvelously	awesome, wonderfully, extraordinary
26:17	valiant	mighty, famous, battle-decorated, warrior
26:18	appertains not to you	doesn't involve or relate, not about you
26:20	hasted	hurried, sped up, rushed
	smitten	afflicted, struck, attacked
26:21	several	separate, others, beside
27:2	did yet	continued to act
27:4	mountains	hill country
	castles	fortresses, defensed, built-up
27:5	prevailed against	defeated, conquered, beat
27:6	prepared his ways	walked steadfastly, lived righteously
28:2	molten images	cast idols, statues made of metal
	Ba'al-im	several, many idols
28:3	abominations	detestable things, filthy, unacceptable, impure
28:4,25	high places	shrines, altars to pagan gods
28:5,23	smote	attacked, strike, hit, punish
28:6	valiant	mighty, famous, battle-decorated, warrior
28:7	next	second in command, assistant
28:8,14,15	spoil	plunder, booty, stolen goods
28:10	keep under	subdue, hold under, control
	bondmen and bondwomen	slaves, forced servitude
28:15	expressed	designated, appointed, assigned
28:15	shod	put shoes on, footwear
28:17	smitten	attacked, beat, conquered
28:19	sore	much, badly, aweful, painful
28:20	distressed him	afflicted, bothered, troubled
	but strengthened him not	would not help him
28:21	portion	share, allowance, portion, cut
28:24	vessels	utensils, equipment
28:25	every several	every

II CHRONICLES

28:27	slept with	died & buried
	sepulchers	tombs, graves, crypts
	stead	place, position
	reigned	ruled, controlled, commanded, was the boss
29:4	street	square, area
29:5,15,17,19,34	sanctified	consecrated, set apart, holy
29:5	filthiness	defilement, impurity, sin
29:6	trespassed	been unfaithful, unlawful
	habitation	dwelling place, home
29:8	to hissing	disgrace, shame
29:10	covenant	unconditional agreement, contract, promise
29:11	negligent	careless, slack, not paying attention
29:16	uncleanness	defilement, dirty, polluted, impure
29:18,19	vessels	utensils, equipment
29:19	did cast away	discarded, throw away, toss, abandon
29:23	forth	near, close
29:24	reconciliation	sin offering, united with God
29:34	flay	to take the skin off the body
30:6	remnant	leftover, remains, survivors
30:7	trespassed	were unfaithful, broke law, sinned
30:8	stiffnecked	stubborn, hard headed, proud
30:8,15,17	sanctified	consecrated, set apart, holy
30:10	posts	couriers, informers, spies
30:11	laughed to scorn	mocked, disrespected, made fun of
	divers	some people, different, various
30:12	one	unity, together, in agreement
30:16	manner	custom, ways, protocol
30:20	hearkened	listen, pay attention, heed
30:21	unleavened	yeast-free
30:22	comfortably	encouragingly, supportingly
31:1	groves	(Heb:Asherah) either a living tree or a tree-like pole, set up as an object of worship, being symbolical of the female or productive principle in nature. Every Phoenician had an asherah near them. Both the "May Pole" and "Christmas Tree" (Jer.10:3-5) originate with this Asherah. The word is often translated "green trees" or

II CHRONICLES

		"grove." This "nature worship" became associated with sexual immorality.
	high places	shrines, altars to pagan gods
31:3,4,16	portion	share, amount, cut, take
31:3	substance	property, possessions, belongings, stuff
31:5	corn	grain
31:7	heaps	ruins, piles, rubble, wreckage
31:11	chambers	rooms, halls
31:14	porter toward the east	keeper of the east gate
	oblations	offerings, sacrifices
31:15	set	assigned, appointed, ordered
31:15,16,17	courses	divisions, military units
31:17	charges	responsibilities, offices
31:18	sanctified	dedicated, prepared, purified
	holiness	moral integrity or purity; avoidance of sin dedicated to God,
31:19	suburbs	pasture lands
31:20	wrought	did, performed, acted
32:1	fenced	fortified, walled
32:2	was purposed	intended, planned, designed
32:5	city of David	Jerusalem
	darts	weapons, thrown projectiles
32:6	street	square, area
	comfortably	encouraging, supportive
32:8	rested themselves	relied, trusted, had confidence
32:12	high places	shrines, altars to pagan gods
32:17	rail on	insult, abuse, yell at
32:18	trouble	terrify, scare, frighten
	holiness	moral integrity or purity; avoidance of sin dedicated to God
32:25	rendered	give up, go back, backslide, surrender (to evil)
32:27	pleasant jewels	gems, e.g. diamonds, rubies, emeralds, pearls
32:29	substance	wealth, property, resources, riches
32:30	watercourse	small river, stream, creek
33:3	reared up	built, set up, erected, constructed
33:6	fire in…valley	children were sacrificed by fire to Moloch, and other pagan gods familiar spirit spirit guide, a devil/demon that influenced certain behavior

II CHRONICLES

		common or "familiar" to individuals (anger, drinking, lying etc)
33:9	err	make mistakes, sin, act badly
	worse…heathen	exaggerated, over the top – i.e. if the Ammonites sacrificed ten children to Moloch, the backslidden Jews would kill 100, etc.
33:10	hearken	listen, pay attention, heed
33:11	among the thorns	punished, treated dably/harshly
33:12	affliction	distress, troubles, sickness
	besought	asked, pleaded, begged
33:13	intreated of him	moved by his plea, softened
	supplication	prayer, appeal, plea, beg, ask, petition
	overseers	bosses, head men, top authorities
33:14	city of David	a.k.a. Jerusalem
	compassed	go about, surround, encamp, encircle
	fenced	fortified, walled
33:17	high places	shrines, altars to pagan gods
33:18,19	seers	prophets, fore-tellers, men that had visions
33:19	groves	(Heb:Asherah) either a living tree or a tree-like pole, set up as an object of worship, being symbolical of the female or productive principle in nature. Every Phoenician had an asherah near them. Both the "May Pole" and "Christmas Tree" (Jer.10:3-5) originate with this Asherah. The word is often translated "green trees" or "grove." This "nature worship" became associated with sexual immorality.
	sayings	history, reports, chronicles, folklore
33:20	slept	died & buried
33:23	trespassed	increased his guilt, sinned, broke law/rules
34:2	declined	turned aside, left, departed
34:3,8	purge	cleanse, wash, empty
34:3	high places	shrines, altars to pagan gods
34:3,4,7	groves	(Heb:Asherah) either a living tree or a tree-like pole, set up as an object of worship, being symbolical of the female or productive principle in nature. Every Phoenician had an asherah near them. Both the "May Pole" and "Christmas

II CHRONICLES

		Tree" (Jer.10:3-5) originate with this Asherah. The word is often translated "green trees" or "grove." This "nature worship" became associated with sexual immorality.
	images	idols, statues, carvings, icons
34:6	mattocks	stone cutting tools
34:10	wrought	worked, performed, did
	amend	restore, fix, repair
34:11	artificers	carpenters, craftsman
	hewn	quarried, cut, chisel
34:11	couplings	fasteners, devices that hold joints together
	floor…houses	repaired the wood floor(s)
34:12	could skill of instruments	were skillful with, talented, artistic
34:13	porters	gatekeepers, guards, butlers
34:17	gathered together	emptied out, collected, picked up
34:19,27	rent	tear, ripped, shred, pull apart, open
34:22	college	second quarter, area
34:25	quenched	extinguished, smothered, put out, discourage
34:31,32	covenant	unconditional agreement, contract, promise
34:33	abominations	detestable, immoral, dirty, unclean, unholy
35:2	charges	offices, responsibilities, positions
35:3	burden	carried, hauled, lifted
35:4,21	houses	families, estates
35:6	kill…Passover	kill the lamb used for the sacrifice during a ceremony; in remembrance of an event where God's angel of death did "Passover" any person or house that was marked by blood
	prepare…brethren	get them ready, tell them what to do
	sanctify	consecrate, dedicate, make pure
35:7	substance	property, possessions, belongings, stuff
35:10	courses	divisions, military units
35:11	flayed	skinned, peeled
35:13	sod	boiled, cooked
	cauldrons	cooking pot, large bowl
35:14	busied	occupied, doing many things
35:15	place	station, post
	porters	gatekeepers, guards, butlers

II CHRONICLES

35:17	unleavened	yeast-free
35:21	ambassadors	representative, agent, politician
	meddling	nosy, interfering, pushy
	forbear	hold back, not go forward, withold
35:22	hearkened	listen, pay attention, heed
35:23	Have	take
	sore	badly, aweful, terrible, alot
35:25	lamented	cried, was sad about, mourned, depressed
36:1	stead	place, area
36:3	put him down	disposed him, defeated, replaced
	condemned	despised, mocked, ridiculed, judged, curse
36:4	turned	changed, switched
36:6	fetters	chains, shackles, restraints
36:13	swear	pledged, vowed, promised, gave an oath
36:14	abominations	detestable, immoral, dirty, unclean, unholy
	hallowed	made holy, sanctify, revere
36:15	betimes	early, before things got really bad, sooner rather than later
36:16	despised	scoffed at, mock, ridicule, hate
36:18	vessels	articles, equipment
36:21	sabbaths	rest days, days off from work
	threescore and ten years	70
36:22	stirred up the spirit	moved the heart, inspired

EZRA

1:1	proclamation	announcement, broadcast, public notice
1:2	charged	appointed, ordained, commanded
1:6	strengthened	encouraged, supplied, filled
1:6,10,11	vessels	articles, containers (cups, bowls)
1:7	house	temple, sacred building
1:8	numbered	counted, added, tallied
1:9	chargers	dishes
2:1	province	community, settlement, block, neighborhood
2:42,70	porters	gatekeepers, guards, butlers
2:59	seed	offspring, children, heirs
2:62	polluted	unclean, mixed bloodline, impure
	put	excluded, cast out, disallowed
2:63	U'rim and with Thum'min	translated as "lights and perfections" or revelation and truth" — were a divination, medium or process used by ancient Hebrews/Israelites in revealing the will of God on a contested point of view or other problem
2:69	drams	historically both an inexpensive coin and a small weight (1/8th ounce)
3:1	as one man	in unity, together, consensus
3;3	its bases	its foundation
	fear was upon them	they were terrified, scared, frightened
3:4	by	with the required
3:6	temple of the Lord	the Jewish religious building built in Jerusalem, the Jews most holy, sacred building
	not yet laid	before a building van be built, the foundation or support floor must be constructed (laid)
3:7	meat	food, supplies
3:8,9	set forward	oversee, watch
3:9	together	united, consensus, agreed
3:10	set	placed, assigned
3:12	ancient	old, established
4:1	adversaries	enemies, foes, rivals
4:7	tongue	language

EZRA

4:8,9,23	scribe	secretary
4:10	set	settled
4:13	revenue	income, earnings, proceeds, profits, receipts
	tribute	taxes
	endamage	hurt, cause the king's income to go way down
4:14	maintenance	livelihood, support, are taken care of
	meet	fitting
4:15	sedition	mutiny, rebellion, undermine, work against
4:16	certify	promise, are telling you a truth, guarantee
	portion	possession, share, amount, cut, take
4:17	chancellor	judge, legallon official, mayor, political leader
4:19	commanded	issued an order
	insurrection	uprising, mutiny, rebellion, overthrow
4:21	Give You now	
	commandment	now issue an order
5:1	even to them	who was over
5:8+	house	temple, place of worship
5:8	great	huge, large, massive
5:10	certify	inform, notify
6:1,2	rolls	scrolls, historical records, archives
6:3+	house	temple, place of worship
6:3	king's house	royal treasury, bank
6:5	brought again	returned
6:8	hindered	delayed, slowed down, got in the way
6:10	savours	fragrance, incense, odor, perfume
6:11	decree	announcement, declaration, public notice
	timber be pulled	destroy his house, tear the house down
	dunghill	refuse heap, garbage, dump
6:18	courses	orders, military divisions/ranks
6:22	unleavened	yeast-free
7:6	ready	skilled, seasoned, established
7:6,11,12	scribe	someone that wrote the scriptures by hand, secretary, stenographer, transcriber
7:20	bestow	give, donate, distribute, hand out
7:23	realm	country, kingdom, territory, dominion
8:1	geneology	family history, family tree, your relatives
8:21	afflict	humble, fast, suffer
8:25,29,30,33,36	house	temple, place of worship

EZRA

8:27	basins	bowls
	dram	historically both an inexpensive coin and a small weight (1/8th ounce)
8:29	chambers	storerooms, storage area
8:36	commissions	edicts, orders, directives, policies
	on this side	beyond
	river	a.k.a. Euphrates
	furthered	supported, helped, prospered
8:36	lieutenants	assistants, second-in-command, deputies
9:1,11,14	abominations	detestable, immoral, dirty, unclean, unholy
9:2	trespass	treacherous act, sin, wicked deed
9:3	astonished	appalled, stunned, shocked
9:3,5	rent	tear, ripped, shred, pull apart, open
	mantle	robe, cape
9:7	spoil	plunder, booty, stolen goods
	confusion of face	open shame, embarrassment
9:8	a nail in His holy place	place in the promised land, remembrance
9:9	bondmen	slaves, endentured (bought) servant
	house	temple, place of worship, religious building
	desolations	ruins, destruction
9:11	unclean	detestable practices, impure, unholy
9:14	should	shall, will
	join in affinity	intermarry, mixed race
9:14	consumed	destroyed, used up, finished
10:1	very sore	bitterly, bad, terrible
10:2	trespassed against	been unfaithful to, wronged
10:2,10,14,17,18,44	taken strange	married foreign
10:3	covenant	unconditional agreement, contract, promise
	counsel	guidance, wisdom, instruction, teaching, advice
	tremble	are distressed, anxious, worried, scared
10:5	swear, swore	pledged, vowed, promised, gave an oath
10:6,13	transgression	treacherous acts, unfaithfulness
10:8	forfeited	confiscated, gave up, surrendered
10:10,19	trespass	guilt, transgression, sin
	pleasure	will, commands
10:11	strange	foreign, non-Jew
10:14	rulers	leaders, governers

EZRA

10:16	chief	heads, bosses
10:17	make an end	finished, completed, stopped
10:19	gave their hand	pledged, vowed, promised
10:24	porters	gatekeepers, guards, butlers

NEHEMIAH

1:2	captivity	prisoners, hostages, slaves
1:3	affliction	distress, trouble
	reproach	shamed, ruined reputation, humiliation
1:4	mourned	cried, be sad about, depressed
	terrible	awesome, powerful, frightening
	covenant	unconditional agreement, contract, promise
	observe	obey, follow, do, practice
1:6	attentive	aware, alert, watchful
1:8,11	beseech	beg, plead, ask
1:9	uttermost	every bit of, the very last
1:11	fear	revered, respected, trembled, dread
	cupbearer	the attendant/servant (usually an officer of a nobleman's household) whose job is was fill and serve cups of wine (like a restaurant waiter)
2:2	sore	much, a lot, badly
2:3,5	sepulchers	tombs, graves, crypts
2:7	river	Euphrates
	convey me over	allow me to pass, transport
2:8	appertained	concerning, relates to, in reference to
2:13	dung port	rubbish gate, area to take garbage to
	consumed	vanish, waste away, dried up, spent, used up
2:13,15	viewed	inspected, looked at, observed
2:17	waste	desolate, ruined, torn down
	burned	destroyed, torched
	reproach	disgrace, shame, embarrassment
2:18	strengthened their hands for	began, prepared, readied
2:19	scorn	mocked, disrespect, made fun of
3:5	lord	supervisor, governor, boss
3:6,14	thereof	of it
3:8	apothecaries	perfumers, ointment makers
	fortified	built up, strengthened
3:11,19,20,24,27,30	piece	section, part, portion
3:13	dung gate	the gate in the city authorized to take trash, dung/poop, and the dead out of

NEHEMIAH

3:16	sepulchers	tombs, graves, crypts
3:19	armory	arsenal, headquarters, storehouse, military base
3:22	plain	valley, open area
3:26,27	lies	projection, sticks out, extends
3:30	chamber	cell, room
3:31	merchants	traffickers, businessmen, dealers
4:1	indignation	anger, temper, destructive rage verging on madness
4:2	feeble	weak, not strong, lame, grown old
	make an end	finish, complete, conclude
	revive	bring to life, awaken
4:3	fox	jackal
4:7	made up	being repaired, fixed
	breaches	gaps, broken areas, collapsed
4:10	decayed	failing, broke down
4;13	after	according to, behind
	terrible	awesome, fearful, dangerous
4:16,17	wrought in	carried on, labored, participated
4:16	habergeons	breastplates, body armor
4:17	laded	loaded, burden, piled on
4:20	resort you there to us	rally, gather, form up
4:21	labored	work, put effort into, struggle with
4:23	saving	except, other than, besides
	put them off for washing	took his weapon to the water
5:2,3,10,11	corn	grain
5:3	mortgaged	credit for personal or household use is now money owed, in debt
5:3	dearth	famine, crop failure
5:5,18	bondage	slavery, paid/forced labor
5:7	set	held
	assembly	meeting
5:7	rebuked	corrected, criticized, yelled at
	usury	loan money with interest (like payday loans), loan shark
5:9	ought	should, need, obligation
5:9,15	fear	revered, respected, trembled, dread

NEHEMIAH

5:9	reproach	criticism, mockery, discredit
5:10	might exact	are lending
	usury	money owed on loan with high interest
5:14	bread	food allowance, provisions, store
6:1	breach	gap, hole, broken area
6:6	heathen	nations, non-Jew, pagan
6:8	feign	are inventing, pretend, faking
6:10	shut up	confined, sick, handicapped, bedridden
	house	temple, place of worship, religious building
6:13	reproach	criticism, mockery, discredit
6:14	put me in fear	frightened me, scared, worried
6:14	prophetess	someone that speaks for God, represents God – either predictions of the future or warnings
6:16	wrought	accomplished, performed, did
6:17	sworn	pledged, vowed, promised, gave an oath
7:1,45,73	porters	gatekeepers, guards, butlers
7:2	charge	command, order
	feared	revered, respected, trembled, dread
7:3	by	on guard
	watches	guards, observers, spies
7:4	great	spacious, large, huge
7:61	house	family, estate, properties
	seed	offspring, children, heirs
7:64	genealogy	family history, family tree, your relatives
7:65	U'rim and Thum'min	translated as "lights and perfections" or "revelation and truth" — were a divination, medium or process used by ancient Hebrews/Israelites in revealing the will of God on a contested point of view or other problem
7:70	chief	heads, governors, bosses
7:71	drams	historically both an inexpensive coin and a small weight (1/8th ounce)
7:73	Neth'i-nims	temple servants
8:1,3	street	square, road
8:3	therein	from it
	attentive	concentrating, alert, wide awake, watchful
8:4	scribe	secretary, writer, recorder

NEHEMIAH

	pulpit of wood	platform, stage
8:5	sight	publically, open
8:11	grieved	in pain, sad
8:12	mirth	laughter, joy, glad
8:14,16,17	booths	lean-tos, huts
8:15	myrtle	an evergreen shrub or tree with dark green shiny leaves and usually blue-violet flowers; the flowers, leaves, and berries are used in perfumery and as a condiment to eat.
8:16	house	temple, place of worship, religious building
9:2	seed	offspring, children, heirs
9:4	stairs	ascent, platform, raised area
9:6	preserve	sustain, keep alive
9:8,32,38	covenant	unconditional agreement, contract, promise
9:9	affliction	suffering, agony, pain
9:10,16,29	dealt proudly	acted arrogantly, big shots
9:14	sabbath	rest day, days without being able to work
	statutes	law, rule, commands, decrees, directives
9:14	precepts	rules, doctrines, instructions
9:18,26	wrought	committed, performed, did
9:19,27	manifold	great, many, multiplied
9:21	sustain	refresh, revive, give energy
	waxed	grew, increased, became
9:22	divide	allot, appoint, give
	corners	quarters, sections
9:25,35	wells	tunnels to draw water from
9:25	gallonlows	a platform where people where killed by hanging from the neck
9:26	cast	put, placed, dumped
	provocations	testing, challenges, confronted with choices
9:26,34	testified against	admonished, indicted, accused
9:27	vexed	terrify, trouble, plague, confuse, dismayed
9:29	withdrew	turned away, pulled back, shunned
	hardened their neck	were stubborn, hard-headed
9:31	enjoined	cautioned, warned, urged, instructed
9:32	terrible	awesome, powerful, amazing
9:37	increase	harvest, prosperity, gain, profit
10:28,39	porters	gatekeepers, guards, butlers

NEHEMIAH

10:31	wares	merchandise, goods, consumer items
	victuals	food
	leave	forego, do without, exclude
	exaction	high interest rates (payday money lenders)
10:31,33	sabbath	rest day, days without work
10:32	ordinances	laws, rules, policies
10:32+	house	temple, place of worship, religious building
10:33	showbread	ceremonial bread used in religious service
10:37	chambers	storerooms
	cities	rural towns, large population areas
	tillage	farming, gardening, growing plants/crops
10:39	corn	grain
11:11,12,16,22	house	temple, place of worship, religious building
11:16	chief	leaders, rulers, bosses
	had the oversight	were in charge, ruled
	outward	outside, edges, boundary
11:17	principal	leader, in charge, boss
11:18	porters	gatekeepers, guards, butlers
11:22	business	service, work, duty, responsibility
11:24	was at the king's hand	represented the king
12:9	watches	service divisions, rotations
12:22	to	in
12:24	ward opposite ward	crew shift, detail change, change of guard
12:25,45,47	porters	gatekeepers, guards, butlers
12:25,45	ward	watch, duty, shift
12:25	thresholds	storehouses, bank
12:27	keep	obey, follow, do, practice
	psalteries	lyres
12:31	dung	waste, trash, poop
12:36	scribe	secretary, writer, recorder
12:40	house	temple, place of worship, religious building
12:44	chambers	storerooms
	that waited	who served, attended, hosted
12:47	sanctified	consecrated, dedicated, made pure
13:4,7,9,11,14	house	temple, place of worship, religious building
13:5	great chamber	large room, main area
13:5,12	corn	grain

NEHEMIAH

13:6	leave	permission to go, discharge, travel orders
13:7,8,9	chambers	rooms
13:8	sore	much, badly
13:9	vessels	utensil, equipment
13:11	contended	fought against, undermined, work against
13:12,13	treasuries	storehouses, bank
13:13,14	offices	job, duties, positions
13:15+	Sabbath	rest day, days without work
13:16,20	ware	merchandise, stuff, consumer goods
13:17	contended with	rebuked, fought, argued
	profane	violate, pollute, disrespect
13:21	testified against	warned, accused, spoke against, charged
13:25	cursed	reviled, spoke harshly, condemned
	smote	attacked, strike, hit, punish
13:27	hearken	listen, pay attention, heed
13:29	priesthood	a priest, minister, religious leader
	covenant	unconditional agreement, contract, promise
13:30	strangers	foreign, non-Jewish people
	wards of	duties for, responsibilitie

JOB

1:1,8	eschewed	shunned, hated, avoided
1:1,8	perfect	blameless, righteous, moral
1:1,8,9	feared, fears	revered, respected, trembled, dread
1:3,10	substance	property, possessions, belongings, stuff
1:5	sanctified	consecrated, dedicated, holy
1:10	hedge	barrier, protection, force field1:16 consumed
them	vanish, waste away, dried up, spent, used up	
1:17,19	fell	made a raid, attacked, hijacked
1:19	smote	attacked, strike, hit, punish
1:20	mantle	robe, cloak
1:22	charged	blamed, accused, faulted
2:1	sons of God	angels, heavenly beings
2:3	perfect	blameless, righteous, moral, holy
	fears	revered, respected, trembled, dread
	eschew	shuns, avoids, hates
2:7	sore	severe, bad, terrible
2:8	potsherd	piece of broken pottery
2:9	curse	renounce, bad mouth, disrespect
2:12	knew	recognized, comprehended
	rent	tear, ripped, shred, pull apart, open
	mantle	robe, coat, cloak
	sprinkled	to scatter, toss, throw
3:7	solitary	single, unique, one of a kind
3:12	prevent	stop, hinder, blocked, got in the way
	suck	nurse, breast feed
3:14	desolate	destroyed, ruined, empty
3:16	untimely birth	miscarriage, still born
3:23	hedged in	surrounded, fenced in, blocked on all sides
3:24	roarings	groans, grumblings
4:2	assay	attempt, try
	commune	spoke, talked with, discussed
4:4	upheld	helped, supported, benefitted
4:6,14	fear	revered, respected, trembled, dread
4:9	breath of His nostrils	blast of His anger, fury, wrath

JOB

4:11	whelps	cub, baby lion, young, small prince
4:15	voice	supernatural, other-worldly voice
4:18	angels	messenger, supernatural being
5:5	substance	wealth, property, possessions, belongings, stuff
5:12	devices	plotting, schemes, scams
	enterprise	intentions, business, plan
5:13	froward	twisted, pervert, cheater
	carried headlong	quickly stopped, thwarted
5:14	grope in noonday	fall on its/their face; trip, stumble, blind
5:17	Almighty	Shaddai, strength-giver, nourisher
5:18	makes sore	inflicts pain, suffer badly, revenge
5:21	scourge	plague, curse, pestilence, punishment
5:25	seed	offspring, children, heirs
5:26	shock of corn	stack of grain
6:1	throughly	actually, fully, completely
6:2	calamity	disaster, bad luck, catastrophe, accident
6:5	bray	the cry or noise made by an ass (donkey)
	lows	the calling sound of cows; to moo
6:6	unsavory	tasteless, unseasoned, bland
6:14	fear	revered, respected, trembled, dread
6:16	blackish	dark, hidden
6:17	wax	grow, become, increase
6:20	confounded	distressed, confused, mixed up
6:25,26	reprove	tried, tested, searched, examined, known
6:28	as wind	not solid or stable, nothing to hold on to
6:29	Return	turn back, repent, stop
	iniquity	sins, crime, evildoing, immorality
7:1,2	hireling	hired worker, employee
7:2	earnestly desire the shadow	longs for shade, rest, break
7:8	not	no more
7:12	whale	sea monster, large ocean animal
	watch	guard, observe
7:16	days are vanity	pointless, meaningless, futile
7:19	spittle	spit, slobber
7:21	sleep in the dust	be dead in the grave
8:3,5	Almighty	Shaddai, strength-giver, nourisher
8:3	pervert	twist, distort, change

JOB

8:5	betimes	diligently, earnestly, right away
8:6	awake	rouse Himself, stir, respond
8:8	inquire	ask, research, find out
8:11	rush	papyrus, water plant
	flag	reeds
8:14	trust…spider's web	false confidence, misguided, delusion
8:20	cast away	reject, turn down, abandon
	perfect	blameless, righteous, moral
8:22	hate	abhor, despise, loathe, detest, ridicule
9:3	contend	dispute, argue, find fault
	answer 1 in a 1000	poor odds, doesn't stand a chance
9:9	chambers	constellations, star patterns
9:16	hearkened	listen, pay attention, heed
9:17	tempest	storm, upheaval, disturbance, violence
9:18	allow…take breath	suicide
9:19	judgment	do justice, punish, revenge, sentance
9:20	perverse	crooked, twisted, corrupted
9:25	post	runner, courier, special delivery
9:27	heaviness	sad countenance, depressed, down
9:30	wash with snow	make clean, pure, remove dirt/sin
9:33	daysman	arbitrator, judge, mediator
9:34	rod	chastisement, correction, punishment
9:35	fear	revered, respected, trembled, dread
10:9	beseech	beg, plead, ask, cry out
10:10	curdled	repulsive, disgusting, hated, despised
10:11	fenced	hedged, barrier, supported
	sinews	muscles and tendons
10:14	acquit	forgive, find not guilty, set free
10:15	woe	trouble, danger, look out! – a warning
10:21	land of darkness	the place thought to go to right after death, and before heaven or hell; limbo, purgatory
11:3	hold their peace	silent, shut up, speechless
11:4	doctrine	teaching, belief
11:6	iniquity	evil, crimes, sin, vice, wickedness
11:14	tabernacles	tent, dwelling place, sacred building
11:15	fear	revered, respected, trembled, dread
11:19	make suit to you	seek you out, look for, hunt
12:5	slip with his feet	about to fall, in danger, not safe

JOB

	lamp despised	cocky, arrogant, foolish
12:6	tabernacles	tent, dwelling place, sacred building
12:10	soul	inner person, emotion, life force
12:11	try	test, assess, judge, evaluate
12:12	length of days	long life, health
12:25	grope	fumble with, feel for blindly, struggle
13:4	forgers	speakers, creators, developers, spreaders
13:7	wickedly	unjustly, unfairly, unwisely
13:8	contend	fight against, undermine, work against
13:10	reprove	rebuke, correct, chasten, punish, warn
	secretly accept	favoritism, discrimination, injustice, prejudice
13:14	flesh in my teeth	to bite your lip, reality check
13:24	Wherefore	why, what's the reason
13:25	stubble	dust, small pieces of grass or pollen
13:27	narrowly	closely, scrutinize
	print	carving, map, tattoo
	heels	rule, direction, power
14:1	of few days	short lived
14:5	determined	decreed, appointed, decided
14:6	rest	have peace, relax, take it esy
	hireling	hired worker, laborer, employee
14:8	wax	grow, increase, become
14:10	gives up the ghost	expires, dies, quits living
15:2	the east wind	emptiness, hot air
15:3	unprofitable	useless, worn out, worthless, not helpful
15:4	fear	revered, respected, trembled, dread
	restrain	hinder, hold back, reserve
15:5	tongue of crafty	deceptive, crafty, half-truths
15:11	consolations	repayment, punishment, judgments not matter,
	small with thee	frighten or deter
15:16	abominable	detestable, vile, filthy, impure
15:20	travails	writhes, suffers, in agony
15:21	destroyer	Satan
15:22	waited for of	kept watch over by, spied on by
15:23	abroad	all over, different locations
15:24	strengthens	vaunts, resists, defies
15:26	bosses of his bucklers	masses of his shields
15:27	collops	bulges or folds (of fatty flesh)

JOB

	flanks	hips and thighs
15:29	substance	wealth, property, possessions, belongings, stuff
	perfection	its prosperity, usefulness
15:31	recompence	reward, pay back
15:34	hypocrites	godless, disloyal, dishonest. two-faced
	bribery	the use of money, gifts to influence
16:3	vain	empty, pointless, meaningless
16:5	strengthen	encourage, support, help
16:5,6	assuage	lessen, soften, lighten, make easier
16:8	wrinkles	folds of skin left after weight loss
6:10	gaped	stare, gawk, eyeball
	reproachfully	disapprovingly, shamefully, with contempt/hate
16:12	broken me asunder	shattered me, tore up, devistated
	mark	notice, point out, observe, identify
16:13	compass	go about, surround, encamp, encircle
	reigns	ability to reason, think, make dicisions
	asunder	cuts in half, splits, divides, tears open
	gallonl	exposes shame, rips my insides out, bitterness
16:15	sackcloth	rough clothing, burlap material, rags - humility
	horn	symbol of strength, power, authority
16:16	foul	bitter, nasty, mean, ugly
16:18	cover not my blood	don't forget, hide; remember
16:21	neighbor	friend, buddy
17:1	breath	spirit, life-force, energy
17:2	continue	gaze on, look at, behold
17:3	strike hands	shake hands, agree with, act as a friend
17:7	members…shadow	weak, no longer strong, not what they used to be
17:14	corruption	death, sickness, decay
	worm	skin worm, maggot
17:16	rest	burial & grave
18:3	reputed	believed to be, considered, regarded as
18:6,14,15	tabernacle	tent, dwelling place, sacred building
	candle	lamp, spirit, life force
18:7	steps…straitened	wobbly, crooked, messed up
18:8	upon a snare	into its mesh, netting of a trap
18:9	gin	snare, trap
	robber	thief, crook, thug, gangster
18:12	hungerbitten	bitten with hunger, famished, starved

JOB

18:13	firstborn of death	Lucifer, Satan, the Devil
	devour	eat up, consume, destroy
18:15	brimstone	God's judgment/anger, sulphur (on the tip of a matchstick)
18:17	street	large roads, highway (for horses, carts, chariots)
18:20	day	day of judgment (fate)
	frightened	seized with terror, scared
19:2	vex my soul	terrify, trouble, plague, confuse, dismayed
19:3	verily	truly, absolutely, for sure, for real, beyond doubt
19:3,5	reproached, reproach	insulted, humiliation
19:3,17	strange	foreign, non-Jew
19:6	compassed	go about, surround, encamp, encircle
19:7	wrong	violence, injustice, unfairness
	judgment	do justice, punish, revenge, sentance
19:8	fenced	walled, fortified, protected
19:12	tabernacle	tent, dwelling place, sacred building
19:14	familiar	intimate, close, long time
	kinsfolk	family, direct relative, blood
19:16	entreated	pleaded, begged, sincerely requested
19:19	inward friends	close associates, best friends
	abhorred	hate, disgusted by, dislike
19:20	skin of my teeth	a near miss, avoided some disaster, a close call
19:24	graven	engraved, scratched, enscribed
	lead	set or covered in lead
19:27	reins	thoughts, emotions, affections, self-control
20:3	check of my reproach	criticism, self-evaluation
20:5	triumphing	victory, success, celebration
	hypocrite	imposter, poser, fraud, pretender, two-faced
20:10	please	favor, repay, make up with
20:14,21	meat	food
20:14	turned	changed, soured, spoiled
	gallonl	venom, poison, hatred
20:16	asps	small, aggressive poisonous snakes
20:17	brooks	flowing water, river, creek, stream
	honey and butter	honey was scarce, and used to sweeten (like sugar), butter took a lot of time and was also considered a treat – so for it to "flow" means the land would be full of good things/prosperity

JOB

20:18	restitution	repayment, money paid as a penalty or punishment for sin
20:20	quietness	calm, peaceful, without worries
20:22	straits	distress, confusion, difficulties
20:26	tabernacle	tent, dwelling place, sacred building
	fire not blown	not fanned, whipped up, raging
20:29	appointed	decreed, established, ordained
	heritage	estate, inheritance, earthly possessions, assets
21:5	mark	notice, point out, observe, identify
21:8	seed	offspring, children, heirs
21:9	fear	revered, respected, trembled, dread
21:10	genders	mates, breeds, offspring
	casts not here	does not miscarry
21:18	chaff	the shells/skin that were beaten/broken off wheat, barley grain and then thrown away
21:24	breast	pails, buckets, containers
21:27	devices	plans, schemes
21:29	tokens	indications, signs, evidence
21:30	day of wrath	judgment, apocalypse, hellfire, punishment
21:33,38:38	clods	a piece of earth, dirt, chunk of dirt
	sweet	fertile, rich, full of life
22:4	reprove	correct, scold, show the error of
	fear	revered, respected, trembled, dread
22:6	for nothing	without cause
	stripped naked	shamed, humiliated, acted cruelly
22:10	snares	trapped, caught, imprisoned, tripped up, lure
22:15,28:8	trodden	trampled, crushed or broken, stepped upon
22:16	overflowed	washed away, flooded
22:18	counsel	guidance, wisdom, instruction, teaching, advice
22:20	substance	wealth, property, possessions, belongings, stuff
	consumes	vanish, waste away, dried up, spent, used up
22:23	built up	restored, repaid, reestabish
23:2	my stoke is heavier groaning	compared to his pain and suffering, he feels that his complaints are small and he whines little
24:3	widow's ox pledge	the ox was used to perform much of the work around a farm, without the ox a single woman would not survive – so to take the ox because of debt was cruel and heartless

JOB

24:6,24	corn	grain
24:9	of	against
24:10	sheaf	sheaves, i.e. wheat
24:17	shadow of death	wicked men (burglars, house robbers) worked at night and slept in the day – their identities could also be better hid at night, another reason to avoid the day
24:20	broken as a tree	ended, over, stopped, cut down
24:21	evil entreats	curses, bad-mouth, mocks, reviles
24:24	exalted	prosperous, famous, celebrity
25:2	fear	revered, respected, trembled, dread
25:4	how…clean	moral integrity or purity; avoid sin, be dedicated to God
	born of woman	born, alive, once a child and now grown
25:6	worm	lowly, unimportant, worthless
26:13	garnished	decorated, dressed up, designed
26:8	rent	tear, ripped, shred, pull apart, open
26:10	compassed	go about, surround, encamp, encircle
26:11	astonished	aghast, stunned, blown away
27:2	vexed	troubled, disturbed, upset, shocked
27:5	remove	put away, get rid of, forsake
27:8	hypocrite	godless, dishonest, two-faced
27:16	raiment	garments, clothes
27:22	fain	surely try to, pretend, poor attempt
28:1	vein	mine, channel, deposit
28:8	trodden	walk, trampled, stepped on, beaten, defeated
29:4	tabernacle	tent, dwelling place, sacred building
29:6	steps with butter rivers of oil	better times, prospered, blessings were upon
29:14	diadem	turban, headdress, crown
29:18	nest	own house, apartment, place to live
29:20	fresh	new, vital, fresh
29:24	they cast not down	was precious to them, valuable, precious
30:1	disdained	refuse, looked down on, despised
	derision	insulted, disrespect, laughing stock, mocked
30:4	mallows	plant used for herbs and food; grew near water
30:5	meat	food

JOB

30:7	brayed	cried out, made noise, called out
30:8	base	nameless, poor, low-life, scum
30:10	spare	refrain, give a break to, refuse
30:11	cord	bowstring, restraint, protection
	bridle	restraint, control, decency
30:12	ways of destruction	rebellion, mutiny, attempt to overthrow
30:13	mar	ruin, scar, mark up, disfigure
30:14	breaking in	flood, torrent
30:17	sinews	muscles and tendons
30:18	changed	distorted, dirtied
30:22	dissolve my substance	take away success, i.e. destroy my property
30:27	bowels boiled	cramps, inside churned
	prevented	hindered, bothered, consumed
30:29	brother to dragons	
	companion to owls	lived alone out in the wilderness, desert
30:30	black	deeply tanned
31:1	covenant	unconditional agreement, contract, promise
	maid	virgin, sexy woman
31:9	deceived	enticed, seduced, aroused
31:10	grind to	have sex with, intercourse
31:11	heinous	monstrous, revolting, shocking, evil
31:23	highness	splendor, grandeur, greatness
31:29	hated	despised, abhorred, disliked greatly
31:34	fear	revered, respected, trembled, dread
31:35	adversary had	
	written a book	prosecutor, enemy, judge, accuser
31:40	cockle	weeds
32:10	Hearken	listen, pay attention, heed
32:11	searched out	pondered, , considered, thought about
32:18	constrains	hold back, hold down, restrain, bind
32:19	wine…no vent	tense, upset, shaken up (e.g. a soda shook up)
32:19	bottles	wineskins, containers made of animal skins
33:1	speeches	arguments, debates
33:1,31,33	hearken	listen, pay attention, heed
33:8	my hearing	my ears, presence, publically
33:13	strive against	complain to, fight, argue
33:15	slumberings	deep sleep
33:17	purpose	pursuit, deed, plan, intent

JOB

33:20	dainty	delicious, well-cooked and beautifully prepared
33:24	ransom	payment, atonement
34:3	tries	hears, tests, weighs, judges
	meat	food
34:6	transgression	faults of my own, sin, wrong-doing
34:7	scorning	derision, mocking, criticism
34:10,15,34	hearken	listen, pay attention, heed
34:12	Almighty	Shaddai, strength giver, nourisher
34:12,23	judgment	do justice, punish, revenge, sentance
34:17	hates	abhor, despise, loathe, detest
34:24	number	measure, count, untold
	stead	place, position, certain spot
34:28	afflicted	needy, suffering, hurt
34:30	hypocrite	godless, two-faced, unreliable
	ensnare	trapped, fall, tripped up, ruined
34:31	meet	fitting, appropriate, right
34:31	borne chastisement	took it, suffered it, endured, hung in there
34:36	constrains	holds back, keeps
34:36	for	like
35:15	extremity	foolishness, stupidity, arrogance
36:3	ascribe	credit to, attribute to, assign
36:8	cords	bonds, ropes, restraints
36:10	discipline	correction, counsel, learning
36:13	hypocrites	godless, two-faced, unreliable
36:16	strait	difficulty, confusion
36:23	enjoined	appointed, set up, united, established
	wrought iniquity	sins, crime, evildoing, immorality
36:26	know	understand, comprehend
36:31	meat	food
37:4	stay	stop, hold back, prevent
37:9	whirlwird	hurricane, tornado, dust devil, trouble
37:10	straitened	stopped, held back, hindered
37:11	wearies	burdens, makes the clouds heavy with water
37:16	balancings	patterns, arrangement in the sky
37:18	molten looking	liquid mirror, fluid, flowing
37:19	darkness	lack of understanding, ignorance
37:22	terrible	awesome, unbelievable, amazing
37:24	fear	revered, respected, trembled, dread

JOB

38:9	swaddling	wrapping, baby blanket
38:12	dayspring	dawn, morning star, daybreak (Venus)
38:15	high arm broken	authority, influence, powers-to-be are ended
38:29	hoary	white, old age
	gendered	given at birth, fathered, birthed
38:31	sweet influences	pull, desire, passion, urgings
38:32	Maz'za-roth	the constellations, star signs
38:37	stay	stop, hold back, control
	bottles	water jars
38:41	meat	food
39:1	hinds	deer
39:3	sorrows	labor pains, birth pains, contractions
39:4	corn	grain
39:9,10	unicorn	wild ox
39:9	crib	food holder, silo, grain barn
39:10	furrow	ditch, channel, rut, trench
	harrow	plow, dig long rows, cultivate
39:12	seed	grain
39:16	fear	concern, care, revered, respected, trembled
39:18	scorns	laughs at, mocks, makes fun of
39:20	nostrils	nose holes
39:21	paweth	digs at the ground, scratches
39:28	crag	ridge, overhanging rock wall, cliff
39:29	seeks the prey	spies out food
40:7	demand	ask, question, cross-examine
40:8	disannul	cancel, remove, revoke, end
40:11	abase him	bring him low, embarrass, humiliate
40:15	behemoth	huge animal, like an extinct dinosaur
40:17	stones	scrotum (balls), inner thighs
40:21	fens	marshes, swamps
40:22	compass	go about, surround, encamp, encircle
40:23	trusts	is confident, believes
40:24	snares	barbs, hooks, traps
41:1	leviathan	very large sea creature, like an extinct dinosaur
41:4	covenant	unconditional agreement, contract, promise
41:5	bind him	tie him up, put on a lease, make a pet
41:9	in vain	false, pointless, dumb, empty
41:11	prevented	stopped, held back, denied

JOB

41:13	discover the face	strip off the outside
41:14	doors of his face	mouth, jaws
41:17	sundered	separated, split, pulled apart
41:20	seething	boiling, cooking
41:23	flakes	folds, scales, leathery reptilian skin
41:24	nether	lower, bottom
41:25	breakings	crashing, crushing
41:26	habergeon	body armor (perhaps a javelin, lance)
41:28	slingstones	stones hurled by a slingshot
40:30	mire	muck, mud, slime, swamp
41:32	hoary	grey haired, ancient, respected, old
42:4	beseech	beg, plead, ask, beg, petition
42:6	abhor	despise, hate, loathe
42:11	bemoaned	consoled, supported, wept for/with

PSALMS

1:1	Blessed	happy, fortunate, special, unique, favored
1:2,3	his, he	man, person
1:4	chaff	the shells/skin that were beaten/broken off wheat, barley grain and then thrown away
2:1,8	heathen	nations, non-Jew, pagan
2:2	Anointed	called, chosen, sanctioned (e.g. prophet, king)
2:3	cast	throw, toss, pitch, remove
2:5	vex	terrify, trouble, plague, confuse
	sore displeasure	fury, wrath, plague
2:6	set	installed, enthroned, establish
2:11	fear	revered, respected, trembled, dread
2:12	kiss the son	a formal greeting, to kiss on the back of the neck (Europeans kiss both cheeks, Americans shake) hands, Orientals bow, etc.)
	wrath	anger, fury, punishment
	Blessed	happy, fortunate, special, unique, favored
3:2	soul	inner person, emotion, life-force, being, life
3:5	sustained	refreshed, revived, gave energy
4:1	enlarged	relieved, strengthened, supported
4:2	leasing	falsehood, lies, deception
4:7	corn	grain
5:1	meditation	musing, ponder, contemplate, daydream
5:2	Hearken	listen, pay attention, heed
5:5	hate	despise, loathe, detest
5:6	leasing	falsehood, lies, deception
5:7	fear	revered, respected, trembled, dread
5:9	sepulcher	tombs, graves, crypts
5:12	compass	go about, surround, encamp, encircle
6:2,3,10	vexed	terrify, trouble, plague, confuse, dismayed
6:6	groaning	moan, cry, sigh, turmoil
6:7	consumed	waste away, dried up, spent, used up
	waxes	has become
7:2	rending	tear, ripped, shred, pull apart, open
7:9	reins	emotions, feelings, thoughts/control
7:10	upright in heart	honorable, decent, having good character

PSALMS

7:12	whet	sharpen, prepare for battle
7:13	ordains	directs, sends, dispatches
7:14	travails	labor, struggles, work, difficulties
	iniquity	sins, crime, evildoing, immorality
7:16	pate	head (often 'bald'), skull
8:2	sucklings	nursing babies
8:4	visit	pay attention to, concern self with, befriend
9:1	show forth	tell, testify, publish
9:5,15,19	heathen	nations, non-Jewish people
9:12	inquisition	request, asks about, investigates
9:14	in the gates of the daughter of Zion	openly, publicly, before all
9:16	snared	trapped, caught, imprisoned, tripped up
10:3	boasts	arrogant, brag, talk big, act tough
	covetous	envious, greedy, wants what others have, lust
10:5	puffs	snorts, considers unimportant, laughs at
10:6	adversity	trouble, danger, opposition
10:8	secret	hidden, private
10:13	contemn	revile, mock, judge
	require	call me to account, judge
10:16	heathen	nations, non-Jew, pagan
11:3	foundations	supports, basic truth, convictions, beliefs
11:5	hates	abhor, despise, loathe, detest
11:6	tempest	wind, storm, trouble, adversary
	snares	trapped, caught, imprisoned, tripped up
12:2	double heart	hypocrite, imposter, poser, fraud, pretender
	vanity	falsehood, deceit, foolishness
12:5	sighing	groaning, sadness, despair, emotional pain
	puffs	snorts, considers unimportant, laughs at
12:6	tried	refined, cleansed, impurities removed
12:7	them	the godly, righteous, believers
13:2	shall I take counsel in my soul	wrestle with my thoughts, internal debate
14:1	abominable	detestable, unlawful, evil, filthy
14:5	fear	revered, respected, trembled, dread
15:1	abide	dwell, live, stay, make a home
15:3	backbites	spreads rumors, liar, gossip, false witness
	nor takes up a reproach	slander, gossip, falsehood, casts no slur

PSALMS

15:4	condemned	despised, mocked, ridiculed, judged, curse
15:5	usury	loan money with interest (like payday loans), loan shark
16:3	saints	holy ones, purified, believers, true followers
16:7	counsel	guidance, wisdom, instruction, teaching, advice
	reins	thoughts, affections, self-control
17:1	feigned	pretend, faked, put on an act, deceived
17:2	sentence	do justice, punish, revenge
17:3	proved	tried, tested, searched, examined, known
	visited	examined, met with, looked at
	nothing	no evil in me, no sin or bad intent
17:4	destroyer	violent, murderer, criminal
17:9,11	compass, compassed	go about, surround, encamp, encircle
17:13	disappoint	confront
18:2,30	buckler	shield
18:2	horn	symbol of strength, power, authority
	high tower	influence, power, force that keeps safe
18:4	compassed	go about, surround, encamp, encircle
18:5	snares	trapped, caught, imprisoned, tripped up
18:8	mouth devoured	ate up, consumed, destroyed
18:9	bowed the heavens	lowered, descended, bridged heaven and earth
18:11	pavilion	tent, temporary dwelling/house
18:14	discomfited	overwhelmed, troubled, hurt
18:18	prevented	confronted, hindered, attacked
	stay	trust, support, strength, comfort
18:20	recompensed	payed back, payment, rewarded
18:22	judgments	ordinances, laws, policies, decisions
	statutes	law, rule, commands, decrees, directives
18:26	froward	twisted, crooked, arrogant
18:27	high looks	proud, arrogant, self-important
18:29	run thru a troop	broke thru enemy lines, crashed thru
18:33	hinds	deer's
18:36	enlarged my steps	prospered, strengthened, made secure
18:39	girded	equipped, armed, prepared to fight/battle
18:40	hate	abhor, despise, loathe, detest
18:43	strivings	fights, struggles, controversy, conspiracies
	heathen	nations, non-Jew, pagan
18:45	close	hidden, secret, privated

PSALMS

18:49	thanks	praise, public testimony, appreciation
18:50	seed	offspring, children, heirs
19:1	declare	tell of, talk about, report
	firmament	expanse, heavens, constellation
19:2,3	day uttereth speech night…knowledge	the day & night, all things seen, "talk" and express an intelligent design and/of God
19:6	His	the sun
19:8	statutes	law, rule, commands, decrees, directives
20:3	Se'lah	music term for pause
20:4	counsel	guidance, wisdom, instruction, teaching, advice
20:7	trust	boast, confidence, faith
21:1	salvation	Heb. Jeshua; redeem, rescue, ransom, keep safe
21:2	Se'lah	pause
21:3	prevent	support, strengthen, uphold
21:6	countenance	presence, influence, power
21:7	moved	shaken, deterred, troubled
21:8	hate	abhor, despise, loathe, detest
21:9	fiery oven	burn up, consume, destroy
21:10	seed	offspring, children, heirs
22:1	forsaken	to be abandoned, left, betrayed, walk away from
	roaring	groaning, pleading, begging, crying
22:2	night seasons	at night, during the time set for sleep, bedtime
22:5	confounded	disappointed, let down, confused
22:7	shoot out the lip	hurl insults, mock, ridicule, make fun of
22:9	upon mother's breasts	chest, breast (for purpose of breastfeeding)
22:10	mother's belly	within the womb, upon conception
22:12,16	compassed	go about, surround, encamp, encircle
	beset me round	encircled me, surround, attacked
22:14	in the midst of my bowels	within me, inside
22:15	potshard	piece of broken pottery
22:16	dogs	wicked, cruel, gangsters, immoral
22:17	tell	count, see, observe
22:18	upon my vesture	for my clothing, garments, what you wear
	cast lots	gambled (threw dice)
22:21	unicorns	wild bulls
22:23,25	fear	revered, respected, trembled, dread
22:23	seed	offspring, children, heirs

PSALMS

22:26	meek	shy, gentle, peaceful, easy to get along with
22:29	fat	prosperous, successful , rich
24:1	fulness thereof	all it contains, entire, sum, everything
24:2	floods	rivers, streams
24:3	ascend into	climb, go up, proceed forward
24:4	vanity	worthlessness, emptiness, meaningless
24:6	Se'lah	pause
25:1,20	soul	inner person, emotion, life-force, being, life
25:9	meek	humble, afflicted
25:10	keep	obey, follow, do, practice
	covenant	unconditional agreement, contract, promise
25:12,14	fears	revered, respected, trembled, dread
25:13	seed	offspring, children, heirs
25:14	covenant	unconditional agreement, contract, promise
25:21	wait	look eagerly for, trust, have confidence, patience
26:1	slide	slip, waver, fall away
26:2	reins	thoughts, emotions, affections, self-control
26:4	dissemblers	pretenders, complainers, trouble-makers
26:5	hated	abhor, despise, loathe, detest
26:6	compass	go about, surround, encamp, encircle
26:7	publish	proclaim, report, tell, testify
27:6	lifted up	exalted, victorious, recognized
27:14	wait	look eagerly for, trust, have confidence, patience
28:2	holy oracle	inner sanctuary, sacred area
28:3	mischief	injury, harm, deception, evil
28:4	endeavors	attempts, best efforts, good try
28:5	regard	noticed, heeded, observed, attended to
29:9	hinds	deer
29:10	sits	rules, reigns, dominates, in control
30:1	extol	praise, brag, boast, talk about
30:3	soul	inner person, emotion, life-force, being
30:3,9	pit	hell, hades, torment, punishment, death to body
30:8	supplication	prayer, appeal, plea, beg, ask, petition
30:11	sackcloth	coarsely woven fabric, sign of mourning, submission and humility
	girded	dressed, put on, covered
31:4	pull	free, release, cut loose
31:6	hated	abhor, despise, loathe, detest

PSALMS

	lying vanities	falsehoods, deceit, retense, hypocrisy
31:9	belly	body, emotions, feelings
31:11,13,19	fear	revered, respected, trembled, dread
31:11	reproach	shamed, ruined reputation, humiliated
31:17	the grave	hell, death
31:18	contemptuously	disapprovingly, shamefully, with contempt/hate
31:20	pavilion	shelter, secure place
31:22	supplications	prayer, appeal, plea, beg, ask, petition
32:1,2	Blessed	happy, fortunate, special, unique, favored
32:2,5	iniquity	sins, crime, evildoing, immorality
32:2	guile	deceit, hypocrisy, maliciousness
32:3	waxed	grew, increased, became
	roaring	groaning, pleading, begging, crying
32:4,5,7	Se'lah	music term for pause
32:7,10	compass	go about, surround, encamp, encircle
33:2	psaltery	lyre
33:5	judgment	do justice, punish, revenge, sentance
	goodness	unfailing love, mercing, blessing
33:7	depth	deep sea, ocean, abyss
	storehouses	containers, the oceans themselves – coast to coast
33:8,18	fear	revered, respected, trembled, dread
33:10	heathen	nations, non-Jew, pagan
	devices	plans, schemes, tricks
33:12	Blessed	happy, fortunate, special, unique, favored
33:17	a vain thing	false hope, uncertain
34:8	blessed	happy, fortunate, special, unique, favored
34:9,11	fear	revered, respected, trembled, dread
34:11	hearken	listen, pay attention, heed
34:13	guile	deceit, hypocrisy, maliciousness
34:17	delivers	rescues, saves
34:18	contrite	sorry, remorseful, apologetic, humbled
35:2	shield and buckler	large shield and small shield
35:3	the way	the path, road, course, trail
35:4	confounded	ashamed, confused, unsettled
35:5,6	angel	messenger, supernatural being
35:12	spoiling	bereavement, grieving, upset
35:13	sackcloth	rough clothing, burlap material, rags - humility

PSALMS

35:15	adversity	stumbling, limping
	abjects	outcasts, losers, troublemakers
35:16	gnashed	grit/grind teeth, grumble, threaten
35:17	darling	precious life, soul
35:19	hate	abhor, despise, loathe, detest
35:26	confusion	humiliation, uncertainty, shame
36:1	fear	revered, respected, trembled, dread
36:2,3	iniquity	sins, crime, evildoing, immorality
36:7	lovingkindness	goodness, kindness, mercy, care, concern
36:8	fatness	richness, blessing, prosperity
36:12;37:1	workers of iniquity	sinful people, evil doers, criminals
37:7,8	fret	anger, worry, stress out
37:11	meek	shy, gentle, peaceful, easy to get along with
37:21	shows mercy	gracious, kindness, forgiveness
37:26,28	seed	offspring, children, heirs
37:28	judgment	do justice, punish, revenge, sentance
37:34	keep	obey, follow, do, practice
37:35	green	luxuriant, lush
37:36	lo	behold, because, therefore
38:2	stick fast	pierce, sink in deep, plunge
38:2,11	sore	harsh, rough, badly, painfully
38:3	soundness	strength, health, energy
38:5	foolishness	stupidity, bad judgment, craziness
	wounds	stripes, lashes from a whip, injuries
38:8	sore broken	badly crushed, smashed
	restlessness	groaning, growling, unease
38:10	heart pants	beats, pulses, is in need of
38:12	snares	trapped, caught, imprisoned, tripped up
38:14	reproofs	arguments, correction, warnings, scoldings
38:17	halt	stumble, trip, tumble over, falter
38:19	wrongfully	unjustly, unfairly, falsely
	lively	vigorous, enthusiastic, hyped, psyched
39:2,9	dumb	mute, cannot speak
39:3	musing	musing, ponder, contemplate, daydream
	my heart	mind, thought
39:5	verily	surely, truly, honestly, yes, correct
39:5,11	altogether vanity	completely worthless, pointless, illogical
39:6, 43:5	disquieted	troubled, bugged, perplexed, anxious

PSALMS

39:10	stroke	plague, wound
39:11	iniquity	sin, evil, wrong-doing, break the law
39:12	sojourner	temporarily stay, visit, live
40:2	miry	mucky, muddy, slimy, swampy
40:4	Blessed	happy, fortunate, special, unique, favored
40:9	refrained	held back, deterred, restrained, stopped
40:12	innumerable	many, a lot, countless, too many to count
	compassed	go about, surround, encamp, encircle
	iniquities	sins, crime, evildoing, immorality
41:1,11,13	Blessed	happy, fortunate, special, unique, favored
41:3	languishing	sickness, suffering, mourning
41:6	vanity	wickedly, foolish, boastful, arrogant, proud
41:7	hate	abhor, despise, loathe, detest
41:8	clings fast	is poured on to, sticks to, attaches, anoints
42:1	hart	deer
42:3	meat	food
42:4	house	temple, place of worship, religious building
	holy day	festival, religious holiday, festival
42:7	billows	big waves, ocean swells, flood waters
43:5	disquieted	troubled, vexed, bothered, upset
44:2,11,14	heathen	nations, non-Jew, pagan
44:7,10	hated	abhor, despise, loathe, detest
44:11	appointed for meat	seasonal food, grain to be eaten - destroyed
	countenance	"face" - influence, personal attention, blessings
44:13	derision	joke, laughing-stock, ridiculed
44:17	covenant	unconditional agreement, contract, promise
44:18	declined	deviated, gone back, quit following
44:19	sorebroken	crushed, defeated, beaten
	dragons	dinosaurs, large reptile-like creatures
45:1	indicting	composing, thinking about, working through
	touching	for, pertaining to, related
45:3	Gird your sword upon your thigh	prepare for war, ready for battle-to fight
45:4	terrible	awesome, fearful, dangerous
45:6	right	true, honest, proper
45:7	hate	abhor, despise, loathe, detest
45:8	cassia	a spice used in perfume, religious anointing oil

PSALMS

45:9	gold of Ophir	a region known for high quality gold
45:10	Hearken	listen, pay attention, heed
	incline your ear	turns to listen, obey, consider
45:13	of wrought	interwoven with, mingled, blended
45:14	raiment of needlework	embroidered clothing, sewing, needlework
45:16	instead of your fathers…your children	a promise to King David that the generations after him will remember his name and have influence and power in the world
46:3,7,11	Se'lah	musical term "pause"
46:6	heathen	nations, non-Jew, pagan
46:8	behold	see, observe, watch
46:9	sunder	cuts in half, splits, divides, tears open
47:2	terrible	awesome, fearful, dangerous
47:4	Se'lah	musical term, praise
47:7	heathen	nations, non-Jew, pagan
47:9	shield of the earth	defenses, ability to protect
	princes	leaders, chiefs, rulers, influential men
48:1	city	i.e. Jerusalem
48:6	Fear	revered, respected, trembled, dread
	travail	labor, pain, work hard, toil, difficulty
48:8	Se'lah	musical term, praise
48:11	daughters	offspring of a nation, citizens
48:12	tell	count, add up, measure
48:13	bulwarks	defenses, fortifications, walls, barriers
	mark	notice, point out, observe, identify
49:4	open my dark saying upon the harp	perform a song that explains his feelings
	incline	listen, attend, consider
	dark saying	mystery, parable
49:5	iniquity of my heels	those on my heels, betrayers, double-cross
	compass	go about, surround, encamp, encircle
49:7	None of them	no man, no one
49:8	precious	costly, expensive, valuable, highly prized
49:9	corruption	decay, death, bad
49:10	brutish	wild, animal-like, barbaric, cruel
49:11	houses	family, estate, properties
49:12	abides	endures, dwell, live, stay, make a home

PSALMS

49:13	folly	silly, foolish, stupid, idiotic
49:13,15	Se'lah	musical term, praise
49:18	though	for
	blessed his soul	congratulated himself, pride, boastful
50:3	tempestuous	emotional, hysterical, wild, stormy
	devour	destroy, consume, defeat
50:5	saints	holy ones, purified, believers, true followers
50:5,16	covenant	unconditional agreement, contract, promise
50:6	Se'lah	musical note, pause
50:8,21	reprove	rebuke, correct, chasten, punish, warn
50:16	declare my statutes	tell of my decrees, publish, inform
50:17	hate	abhor, despise, loathe, detest
50:19	frames	speaks, pronounces
50:21	order	detail, arrange, setup
50:23	conversation	way, behavior, actions
51:4	clear	blameless, free, unhinderd
51:7	purge	clean, wash, purify
	hyssop	a common plant (Oregano?), used like a brush to apply blood for forgiveness of sins
51:12	free	willing, unhindered, not obligated
51:14	bloodguiltiness	guilt from murder, violence against others
52:2	devises	plots, plans, schemes
52:3,5	Se'lah	musical note, pause
52:9	saints	holy ones, purified, believers, true followers
53:3	filthy	corrupt, dirty, unclean, defiled
54:3	Se'lah	musical note, pause
54:5	cut them off	destroy, defeat, confuse
54:7	desire	want, hunger, intent on
55:1	supplication	prayer, appeal, plea, beg, ask, petition
55:3,12	hate, hated	abhor, despise, loathe, detest
55:4	sore pained	anguish, suffering, ache, hurt
55:7,19	Se'lah	musical note, pause
55:8	tempest	storm, hurricane, upheaval, disturbance
55:9	divided their tongues	bring confusion, breakdown of communication
55:10	mischief	wickedness, deceit, trouble
55:11	guile	dishonesty, falsehood, fraud, deceit, baloney
55:13	house	temple, place of worship, religious building
55:14	company	the throng, mob, crowd, gang

55:15	quick	alive, energetic, active, powerful
	hell	the grave, death, place of punishment, torment
55:19	abides of old	God – ancient, everlasting, eternal
	fear	revered, respected, trembled, dread
55:20	covenant	unconditional agreement, contract, promise
55:21	drawn swords	prepared to fight, weapons ready
56:3	what time	when
56:6	mark	notice, point out, observe, identify
56:12	vows	promises, oath, contracts
57:1	the shadow of wings	protection, safety, defense
57:3	swallow me up	trample upon me, defeat, destroy
57:3,6	Se'lah	musical note, pause
57:4	soul is among lions	under attack, in danger
57:8	psaltery	lyre
	weigh	mete out, measure, count, consider
58:3	estranged	an outcast, alienated, abandoned
58:5	hearken	listen, pay attention, heed
58:6	break out the great teeth…young lions	a curse; if teeth are broken, a lion will die of starvation
58:7,8	melt	flow, run, go away
58:8	untimely birth	miscarriage
58:11	Verily	surely, truly, honestly, yes, correct
59:2	bloody men	cutthroats, murderers, robbers, gangsters
59:5,8	heathen	nations, non-Jew, pagan
59:6,14	make a noise	growl, howl
59:8	derision	disrespected, laughing stock, mocked
59:15	grudge	grumble, complain
60:3	wine of astonishment	confused, dazed, surprised, afraid
60:4	banner	flag, symbol, logo, gang colors
	fear	revered, respected, trembled, dread
60:8	washpot	something to be used and discarded
	I cast out my shoe	a sign of disrespect
60:11	vain	worthless, empty, pointless, waste
60:12	do valiantly	gain the victory, mightily, heroic
61:4	covert	shelter, protection, defense
61:5	fear	revered, respected, trembled, dread
61:7	preserve	protect, keep safe, guard

PSALMS

61:8	vows	promises, contract, oath
62:2	defense	stronghold, protection, safety
62:3	bowing	leaning, crumbling, unstable
	tottering	falling down, weak, damaged
62:4,8	Se'lah	musical note, pause
62:9	vanity	worthless, empty, pointless, waste
	render	reward, repay, give back
63:5	marrow and fatness	the richest of foods, nutritional, healthy
63:7	shadow	protection, shelter, defense
	wings	presence, strength, watchfulness
63:8	follows hard after	clings to, pursues, runs after, chases
63:10	portion	possession, share, amount, cut, take
64:2	secret counsel	conspiracy, plot, plan, scam
	insurrection	uprising, mutiny, rebellion, to attempt an overthrow
64:3	whet	sharpen, prepare
64:5	commune	spoke, talked with, discussed
64:8	their own tongue	plan, plot, curse
64:9	fear	revered, respected, trembled, dread
65:1	vow	promise, oath, pledge
65:4	Blessed	happy, fortunate, special, unique, favored
65:6	terrible things	awesome, fearful, dangerous deeds
65:7	tumult	uproar, chaos, free-for-all
	stills	quiets, calms, makes peaceful
65:8	tokens	sign, pledge, testimony
65:9	visit	care for, attend, watch over
65:9,13	corn	grain
65:10	furrows	ditches, channels, ruts, trenches
65:11	paths drop fatness	riches, wealth, prosperity
66:1	lands	people, nations, countries
66:3,5	terrible	awesome, fearful, dangerous
66:6	flood	river, overlow, wash out
66:9	soul	inner person, emotion, life-force, being, life
66:12	wealthy	abundant, prosperous, fruitful, rich
66:15	incense of rams	smell of burning meat, like a BBQ
66:17	extolled	praised, worship, spoke highly of
66:18	iniquity	sins, crime, evildoing, immorality
66:19	verily	surely, truly, honestly, yes, correct

PSALMS

67:2	saving health	salvation, prosperity
67:7	fear	revered, respected, trembled, dread
68:1	hate	abhor, despise, loathe, detest
68:4	JAH	Jehovah, ie. God is great
	extol	praise, worship, speak highly of
68:6	solitary	lone, single, individual
68:8	dropped	rain
68:12	apace	at a rapid pace, quickly, in a hurry
68:13	lain among the pots	poverty, homeless – rags to riches
68:16	why leap you	excited, overjoyed, jazzed
68:21	hairy scalp	wild, unruly, uncivilized type of person
68:24	goings	procession, results, works
68:25	among	in the midst of, with, joining
	damsels	maidens, young women, virgins
	timbrels	tambourines
68:34	clouds	skies, heavens
68:35	terrible	awesome, fearful, dangerous
69:1	waters…into my soul	shipwrecked, overwhelmed
69:9	zeal	excited, ambitious, energetic, hyper
69:10	chastened	disciplined, punished, rebuked, scolded
69:11	proverb	story, tale, fable, lesson for application
69:21	gallonl	venom, bitterness, poison
	meat	food
69:22	snare	trapped, caught, imprisoned, tripped up, lure
69:23	loins …shake	frightened, shake in boots, panic attack
69:27	iniquity to their iniquity	charge them with many sins
69:29	salvation	Heb. Jeshua; redeem, rescue, ransom, keep safe
69:31	hoofs	divided hoofs
69:36	seed	offspring, children, heirs
70:2	my soul	inner person, emotion, life-force, being
70:3	aha, aha	mock, laugh at, make fun
70:5	tarrying	hesitation, delay, put off
	poor	afflicted, powerless, helpless
71:6	help up	sustained, protercted, nourished
	bowels	insides, womb
71:7	wonder	marvel, curiosity, peculiar
71:10	lay wait	watch, set a trap, ambush

PSALMS

	take counsel	conspire, plot, plan, scam
71:20	sore	severe, bad, aweful, painful
71:22	psaltery	lyre
71:24	confounded	confused, mixed up
72:5	fear	revered, respected, trembled, dread
72:10	isles	distant lands, maritime nations, coastland
72:16	handful	abundance, plenty, alot
	corn	grain
72:17	endure	last, hang in, withstand, persist
73:2	steps…near slipped	almost fallen, collapsed, knocked out
73:6	compasses	go about, surround, encamp, encircle
73:7	eyes stand…fatness	a very fat person's facial features are not distinguishable, except the eyes
73:8	loftily	boastful, arrogant, proud, know-it-all
73:10	wrung	drained, choked, strangled
73:13	verily	surely, truly, honestly, yes, correct
73:14	plagued	stricken, troubled, bothered
	chastened	punished, corrected
73:16	painful	oppressive, hurtful, unpleasant
73:17	end	final destiny, results
73:21	pricked in my reigns	stomach-ache, troubled
73:27	go a whoring from	are unfaithful to, decietful
73:28	Lord God	Jehovah Eiohim, the self-existing God now interacting with mankind
74:1	smoke against…sheep	angry with His people, mad at his kids
74:2	rod	tribe, family, offspring
74:4	ensigns	banner, flag, family crest, gang colors
	roar	threaten, commotion, noisy
74:7	sanctuary	temple, religious building, holy site
74:8	synagogues	churches, religious buildings
74:10,18	reproach, reproached	revile, mocked
74:11	pluck it out…bosom	withholding his help, keeping his hands in pocket
74:13	dragons	dinosaurs, reptile-like creature
74:14	leviathan	sea creature
	meat	food
74:18	blasphemed	spurned, spoke badly about, put down
74:19	turtledove	beloved, precious, love

PSALMS

74:20	covenant	unconditional agreement, contract, promise
75:4	lift not up the horn	the horn is a symbol of power, like a sword or gun; this means "don't challenge me to a dual or smackdown
75:5,10	horn	symbol of strength, power, authority
	a stiff neck	insolent pride, arrogant, big-headed
75:8	dregs	leftovers, like used coffee grounds
76:1	gave ear	listened, pay attention, considered
76:4	mountains of prey	piles of loot, plunder, spoils, stolen treasure
76:5	stouthearted	brave, gutsy, fearless, heroic
76:9	selah	a technical, musical term for "pause or interrupt
77:4	hold my eyes waking	eyes wide open, frightened, can't sleep
77:6	commune	talk with, reason, daydream
77:13	sanctuary	temple, religious building, holy site
78:1	incline your ears	listen, pay attention, consider
78:2	dark sayings	parable, story, riddle/puzzle
78:3	known	understood, comprehended, realize
78:8	set not	did not prepare, correct, establish
78:10,37	covenant	unconditional agreement, contract, promise
78:18,25,30	meat	food
78:20,66	smote	attacked, strike, hit, punish
78:27	flesh	meat
78:30	estranged	separated, cutoff, divorced
	lust	desire, hunger, crave, want badly
78:35	redeemer	savior, buy/win back something lost (like pawn shop), pay ransom, purchased
78:37	steadfast	faithful, reliable, trustworthy
78:40	provoke	rebel against, anger, aggravate, annoy
78:43	wrought	performed, made, accomplished
78:44	floods	streams, rivers
78:45	divers	various, different, many
78:46	increase	fruit, produce, crops
78:49	evil angels	evil/bad messenger, supernatural being
78:55	heathen	nations, non-Jew, pagan
78:56	tempted	tested, tried, enticed, challenged
78:57	deceitful bow	crooked or unaligned bow, the arrows wouldn't shoot straight
78:58	high places	shrines, altars to pagan gods

	images	idols, statues of false gods, carvings
78:64	lamentations	crying, mourning, agonizing, distress
78:66	hinder	restrict, hold back
78:67	tabernacle	tent, dwelling place, sacred building
78:71	ewes	sheep
79:1	on heaps	in ruins, wrecked, broken down
79:6,10	heathen	nations, non-Jew, pagan
79:7	devoured	destroyed, attacked, consumed
79:8	prevent	hold, keep, maintain
79:11	sighing of the prisoner	show mercy, don't forget/forsake
	power	arm, strength
	preserve	save
79:12	render	return
80:3	cause…face to shine	"face" - influence, personal attention, blessings
80:5	with the bread of tears	in sorrow, painfully, without joy
80:6	strife	controversy, disagreement, dispute, fight
80:7,19	turn	restore, bring back, change the heart
80:8	vine	Isreal, the people of God, chosen
	heathen	nations, non-Jew, pagan
80:10	goodly	mighty, strong, impressive
	boughs	tree branches, limbs, long twigs
80:12	pluck her	attack, ruin, terrorize, rob
80:14	beseech	beg, plead, cry out, ask
81:2	psalm	song, poem, praise, melody
	psaltery	lyre
81:4	statute	law, rule, commands, decrees, directives
81:7	secret place of thunder	heaven, where God lives
81:8,11,13	hearken	listen, pay attention, heed
81:15	haters	despisers, rebels, self-willed
81:16	honey out of the rock	honey was scarce, and used to sweeten (like sugar), so for it to come "out of the rock" means good things, blessings would be everywhere
82:2	se'lah	a technical, musical term for "pause or interrupt
82:4	rid	deliver, remove, take away
82:5	out of course	are shaken, crooked, twisted
83:2	make a tumult	rage, uprising, protest
	hate	abhor, despise, loathe, detest
	lifted up the head	exalted themselves

PSALMS

83:5	confederate	fought against, back-stabbed, mutinied, rebelled
	consent	mind, agreement, accord, alliance
83:6	tabernacle	tent, dwelling place, sacred building
83:10	dung	refuse, waste, poop
83:18	JE-HO'VAH	Adonai –Supreme being
84:1	amiable	friendly, pleasant, cozy
84:7	strength	company, army, military might/numbers
85:5	draw out	extend, prolong, carryover
85:8	folly	stupidity, foolishness, sin
85:9	fear	revered, respected, trembled, dread
85:12	increase	harvest, prosperity, abundance
86:2	holy	godly, clean-living, pure, honest
86:11	fear	revered, respected, trembled, dread
86:13	hell	the grave, death, place of punishment, torment
86:15	long suffering	patient, merciful, generous
86:16	have mercy upon	be gracious to, forgive, be kind
86:17	token	sign, pledge, testimony
	Hate	abhor, despise, loathe, detest
87:5	born in her	came from, their hometown was
87:6	count	record, number, tally
87:7	my springs…in you	spring water; David is proud of, bragging about living in Zion and is basically saying "we have the best"
88:2	incline your ear	listen, pay attention, focus
88:3	grave	hell, death, place of punishment, torment
88:4	the pit	hell, hades, torment, punishment, death to body
88:5	free	forsaken, cut off, loosed
88:7	hard	heavy, painful, brutal
88:8	abomination	detestable, immoral, dirty, unclean, unholy
88:13	prevent	come before, interrupt, hinder
88:17	about together	completely, fully, entirely
89:3,28,34,39	covenant	unconditional agreement, contract, promise
89:4,29,36	seed	offspring, children, heirs
89:7	feared	revered, respected, trembled, dread
89:10	Re'hab	Egypt
89:14	go before your face	lead, forerun, prepare the way before
	Habitation	foundation, principles, heart & soul
89:15	countenance	presence. Power, influence

PSALMS

89:17,24	horn	symbol of strength, power, authority
89:23	hate	abhor, despise, loathe, detest
89:25	hand also in the sea	
	right hand in the rivers	power, military control of the oceans and rivers
89:26	rock	strength, protection, confidence, safety
89:27	make…my firstborn	give him the special privileges and advantages belonging to the first-born son; power, money
89:31	statutes	law, rule, commands, decrees, directives
89:32	stripes	lashes; marks caused by being whipped/beaten
	Visit	punished, avenged, judgement
89:33	utterly	completely, fully, totally
89:34	thing	word, plan, promise, intent
89:35	I will not lie to David	keep his word, fulfill promises
89:39	void	break, cancel, end
89:40	hedges	walls, barriers, boundries, defenses
89:41	spoil	plunder, booty, stolen goods
89:42	adversaries	enemies, foes, opponents, competitors
89:49	swore	pledged, vowed, promised, gave an oath
89:50	bosom	chest, breast, heart
89:52	Amen	so be it, let it be, yes
90:7	consumed	waste away, dried up, spent, used up
90:8	countenance	presence, power, influence
90:10	we soon fly away	die, life is over
	Three score years	
	And ten	70
	Fourscore years	80
	Strength	results, work, ability
90:11	fear	revered, respected, trembled, dread
90:13	repent	grieve, sad, change your mind
91:1	secret place	private room, VIP seating
91:3	snare of the fowler	traps of the bird catcher
	Noisome	deadly, aweful, terrible
91:4	buckler	arm-shield
91:6	pestilence	sickness, disease, trouble, catastrophe
	Wastes	destroys, ruins, wrecks
91:11	angels	messenger, supernatural being
91:12	dash your foot	trip, stumble, stub toe
	Bear	lift, carry, support

PSALMS

91:13	adder	poisonous snake, viper
91:14	set him on high	exalt him, worship, praise
92:2	show forth	declare, talk about, declare, publish
92: 3	lyre	ten stringed instrument
	solemn sound	reverent, sacred, holy i.e. deep tone
92:6	brutish	wild, animal-like, barbaric, cruel
92:8	most high	exalted, supreme, absolute
92:10	horn	symbol of strength, power, authority
92:12	cedar	strong, tall, straight-growing trees
	Flourish	prosper, benefit, grow, do well
93:1	moved	shaken, knocked out of place, changed
93:3	floods have lifted up their voice	the sound of the crashing waves was very loud
93:5	becomes	adorns, is appropriate, fits
94:8	brutish	senseless, dense, slow-witted, idiots
94:9	He that planted	God knows what you do and the ear, shall he not the condition of your heart/life hear? He that formed the eye, shall he not see?
94:10,12	chastises	punishes, corrects, disciplines
	Heathen	nations, non-Jew, pagan
94:13	rest	relief, peace
94:20	have fellowship	be allied, commune, friendship
95:9	tempted	tested, enticed, given challenges
	Proved	tried, tested, searched, examined, known
95:11	enter into my rest	literally the Promised Land, symbolic of the "rest" promised to Christians that are born-again, ultimately heaven
96:3,10	heathen	nations, non-Jew, pagan
96:4,9	feared	revered, respected, trembled, dread
	Isles	distant lands, maritime nations, coastland
97:2	habitation	foundation, basic beliefs, what matters
97:4	enlightened	lit up, brightened, illuminated
97:7	images	idols,representation of false gods
97:10	hate	abhor, despise, loathe, detest
	Preserves	guards, watches over, keeps safe
	Saints	holy ones, purified, believers, true followers
98:2	heathen	nations, non-Jew, pagan
98:9	equity	fairness, decency, justice

PSALMS

99:3	terrible	awesome, fearful, dangerous
99:4	judgment	do justice, punish, revenge, sentance
	Establish equity	make fairness the rule
99:7	ordinance	law, rule, commands, decrees, directives
99:8	inventions	deeds, plans, schemes, plots
100:1	you lands	the earth (nations)
101:3	hate	abhor, despise, loathe, detest
101:4	forward	perverted, corrupt, proud, arrogant
101:6	perfect	blameless, clean, law abiding
101:7	tarry	dwell, hang around, be near
102:3	hearth	fireplace, an open oven e.g. like a pizza oven
102:14	her stones	streets, buildings, walls
102:15	heathen	nations, non-Jew, pagan
102:17	destitute	poor, broke, without money, ghetto
102:26	wax old	wear out, fade, ruin
	Vesture	clothing, garments
102:28	seed	offspring, children, heirs
103:9	chide	contend, strive, fight
103:11,17	fear	revered, respected, trembled, dread
103:14	frame	body, physical ability
103:18	covenant	unconditional agreement, contract, promise
103:20	angels	messenger, supernatural being
103:22	soul	inner person, emotion, life-force, being
104:1	soul	inner person, emotion, life-force, being
104:4	angels	messenger, supernatural being
	Ministers	servants, ministers/priests
104:6	deep	ocean
104:17	fir	a fast-growing type of evergreen tree
104:18	conies	rabbits, bunnies
104:21,27	meat	food
104:24	manifold	many, a lot, extra
104:25	innumerable	many, a lot, countless, too many to count
104:26	leviathan	sea creature, large ships/boats
104:32	trembles	is shaken, quakes, moves
104:35	be consumed	vanish, waste away, dried up, spent, used up
105:8,9	covenant	unconditional agreement, contract, promise
105:14	reproved	rebuke, correct, chasten, punish, warn
105:18	fetters	

PSALMS

	he was laid in iron	chains, hand-cuffs, restraints
105:19	tried	tested, proved, corrected
105:20	loosed	set free, let go, discharged
105:21	substance	wealth, property, possessions, belongings, stuff
105:22	senators	elders, older people, wise
105:23	sojourned	temporarily stay, visit, live
105:25	subtly	tricky, deceitfully, crafty, outwit
	Hate	abhor, despise, loathe, detest
105:27	wonders	miracles, amazing deeds/actions
105:30	chambers	rooms, halls
105:32	hail for rain	
	fire in their land	hailstones; like a meteor shower
105:33	coasts	territory, boundary, border
106:3	judgment	do justice, punish, revenge, sentance
106:10,41	hated	abhor, despise, loathe, detest
106:15	leanness into their soul	unhappy, unsatisfied, empty inside
106:16	saint	holy ones, purified, believers, true followers
106:20	similitude	similarity, likeness, image, copy
106:25	murmured…tents	complained, whined in private
	Hearkened	listen, pay attention, heed
106:27	seed	offspring, children, heirs
106:28	sacrifices of the dead	pagan feasts, food sacrificed to false gods
106:29	inventions	deeds, acts
106: 30	plague was stayed	ended, stopped, halted
106:33	unadvisedly	foolishly, hastily, without thought/plan
106:36	snare	trapped, caught, imprisoned, tripped up, lure
106:39	defiled	unclean, dirty, impure
	Whoring	unfaithfulness, dishonest, disloyal
106:41,47	heathen	nations, non-Jew, pagan
106:44	regarded	noticed, heeded, observed, attended to
106:45	covenant	unconditional agreement, contract, promise
	Repented	regretted, changed mind, felt sorry
107:5	soul fainted	became tired, weary, discouraged
107:10	bound	prisoners, captive
107: 11	contemned	spurned, despises, ignored
107:14,16	sunder	cuts in half, splits, divides, tears open
107:22	rejoicing	joyful singing, praise, worship
107:24	deep	ocean

PSALMS

107:27	they reel to and fro	wobble, stagger
107:34	barrenness	empty, unfruitful, unfertile, desolate
107:42	stop her mouth	shut up, silenced, humbled
108:2	awake and harp	become lively, start the music
	Psaltery	lyre
108:7	mete	measure out, assign, ration
109:3	compassed	go about, surround, encamp, encircle
109:8	office	leadership
109:10	vagabond	wanders
109: 11	extortioner catch	creditor seize
109:13	posterity	children, future generations, offspring
109:16	broken	despondent, sad, discouraged, depressed
109:17	loved cursing	wishing evil/bad luck on someone
109:18	clothed himself	did something often, alot
	bowels like water	dysentery, constant diarrhea
	oil into his bones	weak, brittle, soft
109:25	reproach	object of scorn, laughing stock
109:29	mantle	cape, cloak, long coat with a hood
109:30	condemn	despised, mocked, ridiculed, judged, curse
109: 45	precepts	rules, doctrines, instructions
110:3	womb of the morning	beginning, start of the day
	dew of your youth	innocence, youthful strength, beauty
110:5	strike through	shatter, defeat, kill
110:6	heathen	nations, non-Jew, pagan
	Wound the heads	shatter the leaders
111:5	Covenant	unconditional agreement, contract, promise
111:5,10	fear	revered, respected, trembled, dread
111:6	heritage	inheritance, family treasure
	Heathen	nations, non-Jew, pagan
111:7	verity	truth, honesty, correct
	Judgment	do justice, punish, revenge, sentance
111:9	reverend	respected, held in awe, worshipped
112:1	fears	revered, respected, trembled, dread
112:2	seed	offspring, children, heirs
112:5	lends	has enough extra money to lend/loan
	discretion	wisdom, good sense, judgment
112:6	moved	shaken, overthrown, defeated
112:8	his heart is established	stable, strong, confident

PSALMS

112:9	dispersed	scattered, spread out, divided
	Horn	symbol of strength, power, authority
113:7	out of the dunghill	rags-to-riches, honored, prospered
113:9	barren…keep house	have children, be a mother
114:8	turned	changed, made, caused
115:11,13	fear	revered, respected, trembled, dread
115:17	go down into silence	die, dead, go into the grave
116:2	inclined	turned, interested
116:3	compassed	entangled, surrounded, flooded
116: 7	bountifully	successful, doing well, wealthy
116:12	render	return, give back, pay back
116:16	loosed	set free, let go, discharged
118:4	fear	revered, respected, trembled, dread
118:7	hate	abhor, despise, loathe, detest
118:9	princes	leaders, chiefs, rulers, influential men
118:10,11,12	compassed	go about, surround, encamp, encircle
118:12	quenched…thorns	thorns burn hot and fast, but their fire goes out very suddenly when its fuel ends (unlike hardwoods)
118:13	thrust sore	stabbed at, swung crazily at (with a sword)
118:21	salvation	Heb. Jeshua; redeem, rescue, ransom, keep safe
118:25	beseech	beg, plead, implore, ask
119:1,2	Blessed	happy, fortunate, special, unique, favored
119:1	undefiled	blameless, clean, pure, holy
119:2,17,60,129,145	keep	obey, follow, do, practice
119:3	iniquity	sins, crime, evildoing, immorality
119:4	diligently	faithfully, carefully, with effort, hard work
119:4+	precepts	rules, doctrines, instructions
119:5+	statutes	law, rule, commands, decrees, directives
119:9	where withal	how, with what means
119:13,43	judgments	ordinances, laws, policies, decisions
119:15	Respect	noticed, heeded, observed, attended to
119:21	do err	made a mistake, messed up, sinned
119:25+	quicken	alive, energetic, active, powerful
119:28	melts	weeps, breaks up, hurts
	Heaviness	sorrow, sadness, depression
119:31	have stuck	cling, kept true, been faithful
119:38	establish	confirm, keep, bring to pass

PSALMS

119:38,63,74,79	fear	revered, respected, trembled, dread
119:50	affliction	sickness, disease, problem
119:51	derision	insulted, disrespect, laughing stock, mocked
119:54	pilgrimage	travels, journey, road trip
119:61	bands	companies, groups, units, gangs
119:69	forged	fabricated, made, built
119:70	heart…fat as grease	unhealthy, sick, heart problems
119:77	tender mercies	compassion, kindness, care
119:80	sound	healthy, solid, strong, well
119:83	bottle in the smoke	animal skins (bottles) dry up in the heat; David's spirit/emotions were dried up and exhausted
119:96	broad	big, hard to complete or fulfill
119:104,113,128,163	hate	abhor, despise, loathe, detest
119:108	beseech	beg, plead, ask, pray
119:110	snare	trapped, caught, imprisoned, tripped up, lure
119:118	trodden down	beat down, stepped on, kicked around
119:119	dross	waste, all impurities removed from metal by heating in a fire
119:122	surety	guarantee, pledge, down payment
119:130	order	establish, set up, plan well
119:139	zeal	excited, ambitious, energetic, hyper
119:152	I have known of old	long time, since he was young
119:157	decline	turn aside, leave, fall away
119:158	trangressors	sinners, wrong-doers, criminals, gangsters
119:161	princes	leaders, chiefs, rulers, influential men
120:3	false tongue	deceiver, lier
120:4	juniper	a type of bush/plant
120:5	woe	trouble, danger, look out! – a warning
120:6	hates	abhor, despise, loathe, detest
122:1,9	house	temple, place of worship, religious building
123:2	wait upon	look to, trust, hope
123:4	scorning	mockery, disrespect, hatred
124:5	proud	raging, arrogant, unthinking
124:7	fowlers	a wild bird hunter, trapper
126:1	them that dream	couldn't believe, amazed, beyond imagination
126:2	heathen	nations, non-Jew, pagan
126:4	turn again	restore, fix, repair
126:6	sheaves	bundle, stack, group of wheat plants

PSALMS

127:5	quiver	shoulder-held arrow holder, a lot of kids at home
128:4	fears	revered, respected, trembled, dread
129:1,2	afflicted	oppressed, tormented, punished, hurt
129:3	plowed upon my back furrows	rows, channels made upon his back by being beaten, whipped
129:4	cords of the wicked	ropes, bindings that tied hands & feet
129:5	hate	abhor, despise, loathe, detest
129:7	mower	unsuccessful reaper, bad harvest
130:4	feared	revered, respected, trembled, dread
130:7	redemption	Heb. Jeshua; redeem, rescue, ransom, keep safe
130:8	iniquities	sins, crime, evildoing, immorality
130:16	fashioned	made, shaped, molded
131:1	haughty/ lofty	proud, arrogant, boastful
132:4	slumber to eyelids	won't rest, take a break, fall asleep
132:12	covenant	unconditional agreement, contract, promise
132:16	saints	holy ones, purified, believers, true followers
132:17	horn	symbol of strength, power, authority
135:4	peculiar treasure	priceless possession, special
135:14	repent himself concerning	have compassion on, merciful, caring
135:15	heathen	nations, non-Jew, pagan
137:2	harps upon…willows	gave up, quit playing music
137:3	mirth	comedy, joking around, laughter
	Wasted	harmed, ruined, destroyed
137:5	hand forget…cunning	lose skill, strength
137:6	tongue cling	tongue-tied, speechless
137:7	raze	destroy, tear down, level
139:2	downsitting	sit down, rest, relax
139:3	compass	are familiar with, circled, surrounded
139:5	beset	hemmed in, surrounded
	wings of the morning	daybreak, dawn, sunrise
139:13	reins	thoughts, emotions, affections, self-control
139:16	continuance	period of time, without stop
139:21,22	hate	abhor, despise, loathe, detest
139:22	perfect	complete, finished
140:2	which imagine	who devise, scheme, make plans
140:5	gins	lures, traps
	Snare	trapped, caught, imprisoned, tripped up, lure

PSALMS

140:7	covered my head	overwhelmed, beaten, defeated
141:4	dainties	delicacies, fancy foods
141:5	calamities	bad luck, accidents, troubles
141:6	stony places	mountains, tall hills, secure places
	Judges	rulers, governors, bosses
141:8	destitute	poor, broke, without money, ghetto
141: 9	gins	lures, traps
	Snares	trapped, caught, imprisoned, tripped up, lure
142:3	secretly	craftily, privately, deceptively
	Snare	trapped, caught, imprisoned, tripped up, lure
142:6	attend	listen, pay attention, observe
142:7	bountifully	successful, doing well, wealthy
	Compass	go about, surround, encamp, encircle
143:3	smitten	struck, hit, beaten, attack
143:5	muse on	meditate upon, ponder, think about
143:11	quicken	alive, energetic, active, powerful
144:2	goodness	loving kindness, purity, decency
	Deliverer	liberator
144:4	dainties	expensive, exotic foods, fancy foods
144:7	strange children	foreigners, non-Jew
144:9	psaltery	lyre
144:10	salvation	deliverance, victory, help
144:11	rid me	get rid of, lose
	Vanity	wickedly, foolish, boastful, arrogant, proud
144:12	similitude	similarity, likeness, resemblance, image
144:13	garners	granary, storage shed, grain barn, silo
145:1	discretion	wisdom, good sense, judgment
	extol	praise, acclaim, boast, brag about
145:6	terrible	awesome, fearful, dangerous
145: 7	abundantly	a lot, plentiful, extra, eagerly
145:10	saints	holy ones, purified, believers, true followers
145:15	wait upon	look to, be patient, trust
	Meat	food
145:17	holy	faithful, pure, righteous
145:19	fear	revered, respected, trembled, dread
146:4	his breath goes forth	dies, quits breathing
147:16	hoarfrost	white frost, frozen moisture, morning dew

PSALMS

148:2	angels	messenger, supernatural being
148:14	horn	symbol of strength, power, authority
149:4	meek	humble, quiet, simple
150:1	firmament	heavens, sky, the kingdom above the earth
150:5	cymbals	musical instrument of two pieces of brass, one held in each hand, which were clashed together

THE PROVERBS

1:3	equity	fairness, decency, justice
1:4	subtilty	logic, wisdom, street smarts
1:6	interpretation	meaning, the point
1:6	discretion	wisdom, good sense, judgment
1:7,26,27,29	fear	revered, respected, trembled, dread
1:10	entice	tempt, tease, lure, draw away
1:11	lurk secretly	stalk, be hidden from sight
1:12	pit	hell, hades, torment, punishment, death to body
1:14	purse	bag to hold money, common money fund
1:20	without	outside
1:21	concourse	trade, buy or sell
1:23	reproof	correction, scold, punish
1:29	hated	abhor, despise, loathe, detest
1:32	turning away	waywardness, backslidden, leave
1:33	hearkens	listen, pay attention, heed
2:5	fear	revered, respected, trembled, dread
2:7	buckler	shield
2:9	equity	fairness, decency, justice
2:12,14	froward	perverse, wicked, unfair, deceitful
2:17	covenant	unconditional agreement, contract, promise
2:22	rooted	uprooted, pulled up, destroyed
3:3	table of your heart	memory, conscience, thoughts
3:6	acknowledge	accept, recognize, give credit
3:8	health	healing, well
	navel	stomach, abdomen, loins
	marrow	refreshment, health, life
3:10	presses	wine vats
3:15,18	She	Wisdom
3:17	pleasantness	sweet, lovely, appealing
3:18	tree of life	healthy, healing, life-giving
3:22	grace to your neck	adornment, expensive jewelry
3:25	fear	disaster, revered, respected, trembled, dread
3:31	oppressor	tormentor, bully, slave master
3:32	froward	perverse, wicked, unfair, deceitful
	abomination	detestable, immoral, dirty, unclean, unholy

PROVERBS

4:2	doctrine	teaching, concepts, truths
4:5	decline	turn away, backslide, fall away. leave
4:9	crown of glory	a crown is a symbol of power, success
4:12	straitened	hindered, confused, distracted
4:23	diligence	care, effort, hard work
4:24	froward	perverse, wicked, unfair, deceitful
	perverse	devious, wicked, tricky, wrong
4:26	ponder	think about, reason, daydream
5:5	hell	the grave, death, place of punishment, torment
5:6	ponder	reflect on, think about, consider, meditate
	moveable	wandering, travel, nomad
5:10	stranger(s)	alien(s), guests, visitors
5:12	hated	abhor, despise, loathe, detest
5:15	cistern	have sex with your wife, lovemaking
5:19	hind	deer
5:19,20	ravished	intoxicated, captivated
6:1	surety	guarantee, promise, pledge, downpayment
	stricken your hand	promise, vow, made a pledge
6:5	roe	small, graceful male deer
6:6	ant	busy, hard-working, focused
	sluggard	lazy, slow, worthless, slacker
6:8	meat	food
6:12,14	froward	perverse, wicked, unfair, deceitful
6:14	devises	schemes, plots, thinks up
	discord	friction, fuss, hassle, hostility
6:18	imaginations	plans, schemes, vain ideas
6:23	reproofs	corrections, punishment
6:24	strange	foreign, non-Jew
6:26	whorish woman	cheap, slutty, prostitute
	to a piece of bread	poverty, destroy his life
6:32	is own soul	sex, (adultery) with another, not your wife, destroys your soul (soul your inner person)
6:35	regard	noticed, heeded, observed, attended to
7:2	apple of your eye	best, favorite, top choice
7:5	strange woman	adulteress, immoral
7:6	casement	shutters, outside window coverings
7:13	impudent	brazen, rude, smart mouth
7:18	solace	enjoy, comfort

	loves	caress, touch, pet
7:19	goodman	husband
7:23	a dart strikes his liver	shot with an arrow, stabbed with small
7:24	hearken	listen, pay attention, heed
7:25	astray	wander, get lost, leave path
7:27	hell	the grave, death, place of punishment, torment
8:7	an abomination	detestable, immoral, dirty, unclean, unholy
8:12	prudence	carefulness, good judgment, common
8:13	fear	revered, respected, trembled, dread
	forward	perverse, wicked, unfair, deceitful
8:13,36	hate	abhor, despise, loathe, detest
8:21	substance	wealth, property, possessions, belongings, stuff
8:27	set a compass	inscribed a circle
8:32	hearken	listen, pay attention, heed
8:32,34	blessed	happy, fortunate, special, unique, favored
9:1	hewn	hacked, chopped, cut, chiseled, sculpted
9:2	mingled	mixed, blended, joined
9:4	wants	lacks, missing
9:7,8	reproves	rebuke, correct, chasten, punish, warn
	scorner	mocker, makes fun of, clown
9:7	blot	blemish, stain, imperefection
9:8	hate	abhor, despise, loathe, detest
9:10	fear	revered, respected, trembled, dread
9:13	clamorous	uproar, make a racket, noisy
9:15	passengers	those passing
9:17	stolen waters are sweet	a feeling you get when you think you have gotten away with something, tricked someone
9:18	hell	the grave, death, place of punishment, torment
10:8,10	prating	babbling, gossip, talks nonsense
10:9	surely	securely, safe
10:10	winks with the eye	trickery, deception, enticements
10:16	fruit	results, after effects, consequences
10:18	hatred	anger, hostility, resentment
10:19	refrains	hold back, resist, stop from doing
10:24,27	fear	revered, respected, trembled, dread
10:26	as vinegar to the teeth	like drinking coca-cola in the morning, makes you shudder
10:27	prolongs	adds, puts off, delays

PROVERBS

10:31,32	froward	perverse, wicked, unfair, deceitful
11:1,20	abomination	detestable, immoral, dirty, unclean, unholy
11:13	tailbearer	gossip, lier, false witness
11:14	counsel	guidance, wisdom, instruction, teaching, advice
11:15	surety	guarantee, down payment, pledge, bond
	hates	abhor, despise, loathe, detest
	sure	safe, certain
11:20	froward	perverse, wicked, unfair, deceitful
11:22	discretion	wisdom, good sense, judgment
11:23	wicked is wrath	the results of a wicked life are punishment
11:25	fat	prosperous, wealthy, rich, successful
	liberal	excess, plenty, generous
11:26	corn	grain
11:29	shall inherit the wind	end up with nothing, no guarantees
11:30	wins souls is wise	smart, cunning – people live in a deceived state/condition and it takes wisdom to be able to gently, yet clearly show a person their sins and need for God
11:31	recompensed	rewarded, payed well, cared for
12:1	hates	abhor, despise, loathe, detest
	brutish	stupid, slow, dim-witted
12:2	devices	plans, schemes
12:5	counsels	guidance, wisdom, instruction, teaching, advice
12:8	heart	mind, thoughts, emotions
12:9	honors himself	arrogant, stuck-up, boastful, brags
12:10,13:10	contention	fight against, disputes, opposes
12:11	void	devoid, empty, pointless, meaningless
12:13	snared	trapped, caught, imprisoned, tripped up, lure
12:14	recompense	pay back, payment, reward or punish
12:15	hearkens	listen, pay attention, heed
12:21	mischief	trouble, danger
12:22	abomination	detestable, immoral, dirty, unclean, unholy
12:23	prudent	careful, good judgment, common sense, wise
12:24	slothful	lazy, slow, worthless, slacker
12:27	substance	wealth, property, possessions, belongings, stuff
13:1	rebuke	correct, criticize, yell at, scold
13:3	keeps his mouth	shuts up, doesn't blab, is patient
13:4	fat	prosperous, wealthy, rich, successful

PROVERBS

13:5,24	hates	abhor, despise, loathe, detest
	loathsome	disgusting, ugly, nasty
13:10	contention	fighting, disagreeing
13:11	vanity	fraud, foolish, boastful, arrogant, proud
13:12	deferred	put off, delay, wait, postpone
13:13	fears	revered, respected, trembled, dread
13:14	snares	trapped, caught, imprisoned, tripped up, lure
	fountain of life	a well for water or natural spring is how people survived in the desert, without water death was swift and certain
13:16	lays open	exposes, uncovers
13:19	abomination	detestable, immoral, dirty, unclean, unholy
13:24	betimes	diligently
14:2,16,26,27	fears	revered, respected, trembled, dread
14:7	lips	words, sayings, speech
14:10	intermeddle with	share, involve, participate
14:14	back slider in heart	to drift or fall away slowly/gradually from God in your thoughts; you may not do wrong things, you begin to want to do them
14:15	looks well	gives thought, prepares, wise
14:20	hated	abhor, despise, loathe, detest
14:22	devise	plan, do
14:23	penury	poverty, being broke, no money
14:29	folly	silly, foolish, stupid, idiotic
14:30	sound heart	healthy, solid, strong, well
14:31	Maker	the Creator God – Jesus
15:4	wholesome	soothing, decent, healthy
	perverseness	crookedness, corrupt
15:5	despises	spurns, turns down, ignores
15:5,10,31	reproof	correction, punishment, chastise
15:6	revenues	income, earnings, proceeds, profits, receipts
15:8,9,26	abomination	detestable, immoral, dirty, unclean, unholy
15:10	correction	stern discipline, punish
15:10,27	hates	abhor, despise, loathe, detest
15:16,33	fear	revered, respected, trembled, dread
15:17	stalled	fattened, well-fed, plump
	hatred	enmity, dislike, fury
15:18	wrathful	hot-tempered, vengeful, anger

PROVERBS

15:19	slothful	sluggard, lazy, worthless
15:27	gifts	bribes
15:30	light of the eyes	youth, health
15:32	hears	heeds, listens, obeys
16:1	preparations	plans, inclinations
16:5,12	an abomination	detestable, immoral, dirty, unclean, unholy
16:6	purged	atoned for
	fear	revered, respected, trembled, dread
16:9	devises	plans, schemes
16:10	sentence	decision, judgement, punishment
16:11	work	business, job
16:14	pacify	calm, make peace, chill out
16:18	haughty	arrogant, stuck up, know-it-all
16:22	wellspring	fountain, source of life
16:28,30	froward	perverse, wicked, unfair, deceitful
16:29	entices	tempts, teases, lures, draws away
16:31	hoary	gray hair, old, wise, experienced
17:3	fining	refining, purifying, cleansing
17:7	lest	less than, useless, worthless
17:10	reproof	correction, chasten, punish
17:12	whelps	cubs, baby lions, young
17:15	abomination	detestable, immoral, dirty, unclean, unholy
17:18	void	empty, pointless, no power
	strikes hands	pledges, gives word
	surety	security, bond, down payment
17:20	froward	perverse, wicked, unfair, deceitful
	perverse	deceitful, dishonest, fake
17:25	grief	sorrow, regret
18:1	meddles	involved, gets wrapped up
18:3	ignominy	shame, disgrace, humiliation
18:6	strokes	blows, punches, whippings
18:6	contention	fight against, disputes, opposes
	calls for strokes	demands punishment, vengeance
18:8	talebearer	liar, gossip, false witness
	innermost parts	heart, guts, feelings/intuition
18:9	waster	slacker, goof-off, lazy
18:14	infirmity	sickness, illness, disease
18:15	prudent	careful, good judgment, common sense, wise

PROVERBS

18:17	searches	questions, investigates, explores
18:23	entreaties	pleadings, begging, sincere requests
19:1	perverse	deceitful, wicked, corrupt, twisted
	lips	speech, dialogue, conversation
19:2	hastens with his feet	hurries, runs, moves quickly
19:3	perverts	ruins, corrupts, changes
19:7	hate	abhor, despise, loathe, detest
19:10	seemly	fitting, proper, right
19:11	discretion	wisdom, good sense/judgement
19:13	calamity	disaster, big mess, destruction
	contentions	fights against, disputes, opposition
19:15	slothfulness	slacking off, goofing around, lazy
	idle	lazy, slow, worthless, slacker
19:18	soul spare for his crying	don't let his tears effect your decision to punish
19:21	devices	plans, schemes, ideas
	counsel	purpose, plan, idea
19:23	fear	revered, respected, trembled, dread
19:24	slothful	lazy, worthless, slacker
	bosom	jacket pockets, inside robe
19:25	beware	learn, heed, pay attention
20:2	fear	terror, frightened, worry
20:4	plow by reason of the cold	because its cold outside, an excuse to be lazy
20:8	scatters	disperse, spread
20:10,23	Divers	differing, various, many kinds
	abomination	detestable, immoral, dirty, unclean, unholy
20:14	nothing	worthless, no good
20:15	lips	speech, dialogue, conversation
20:20	obscure	darkest, middle of the night
20:25	snare	trapped, caught, imprisoned, tripped up, lure
20:30	blueness	a new bruise, fresh injury
21:2	ponders	knows, comprehends, considers
21:8	froward	perverse, wicked, unfair, deceitful
21:9	brawling	argumentative, bad-tempered, crabby
21:14	pacifies	soothes, calms, settles down
	bosom	hidden, inside robes, under shirt/coat
21:19	contentions	fights against, disputes, opposition

PROVERBS

21:22	scales	climbs, goes up, ascends
21:27	abomination	detestable, immoral, dirty, unclean, unholy
22:4	fear	revered, respected, trembled, dread
22:5,25	snares	trapped, caught, imprisoned, tripped up, lure
22:5	froward	perverse, wicked, unfair, deceitful
22:7	lender	someone that has enough money to loan
22:10,24:9	scorner	mocker, disrespectful, makes fun of
22:13	slothful	lazy, worthless, slacker
	without	outside
22:14	abhorred	despise, loathe, detest
22:18	withal	likewise, at the same time
22:19	even	especially
22:24	furious	hot-tempered, anger, wrath
22:25	soul	inner person, emotion, life-force, being
22:26	strike hands	give pledges, vow, oath
	sureties	guarantees, downpayment, bond
22:28	landmark	boundary marker
23:2,3	desirous	hopeful, eager, wishful
	knife to your throat	kill yourself and get it over with
23:3,6	meat	delicacies
23:16	reins	thoughts, emotions, affections, self-control
23:17	fear	revered, respected, trembled, dread
23:20	wine bibbers	drunks, partiers
	riotous	reckless, hard partiers, club-goers
23:22	hearken	listen, pay attention, heed
23:27	whore	prostitute, hooker, paid sex
23:27,33	strange	adulterous, unfaithful woman
23:29	woe	trouble, problems, danger, wrath
23:33	heart	mind, thoughts
24:1	envious	jealous, greedy, wanting
24:3	lips	speech, dialogue, conversation
24:9	an abomination	detestable, immoral, dirty, unclean, unholy
24:9	scorner	mocker, disrespectful, makes fun of
24:21	fear	revered, respected, trembled, dread
24:22	fret	upset, worry, fret, bothered with/by
24:26	kiss	praise
24:28	witness against your neighbor without cause	false witness, lie, make trouble

PROVERBS

24:30	void	devoid, empty
	fields of the slothful	overgrown with weeds, ruined
24:31	nettles	stickers, thorns, weeds
24:33	folding of the hands	laziness, procrastinate, put off, delay
25:1	copied out	made copies of, duplicated
25:4	finer	refiner, metal purifier
25;5	put not forth	do not exalt
25:10	infamy	bad news, notorious, famous for bad reasons
25:11	apples of gold	appropriate, good fit, elegant
	pitcher of silver	
25:14	boasts of a false gift	empty promise, vain, boast
25:15	long forbearing	patience
	soft tongue	deceptive, flatterer, smooth talker
25:17	hate	abhor, despise, loathe, detest
	foot from your neighbors house	don't wear out welcome, short visit
25:18	maul	club, beat down
25:20	niter	a fizzing cleaner; "soda", properly "natron," a substance so called because, rising from the bottom of the Lake Natron in Egypt, it becomes dry and hard in the sun, and is the soda which effervesces when vinegar is poured on it.
25:23,25	backbiting	lying, gossiping, false witness
25:24	brawling	argumentative, bad-tempered, crabby
25:28	walls	protection, defense
26:3	bridle	restrain, control, hold back
26:6	fool cuts off feet	the message won't arrive intact; it will be changed, twisted
26:9	parable	story, myth, riddle/puzzle
26:13,14,15	slothful	lazy, slacker, worthless
26:13	lion in the way	
	lion in the streets	it's dangerous out there, safe in here
26:16	sluggard	lazy, worthless, slacker
26:18	firebrands	anything on fire that is thrown in the air
26:19	in sport	joking, kidding, teasing
26:20	talebearer	gossip, false witness, lier, rumor spreader
26:21	contentious	fights against, disputes, opposes
26:23	potsherd	earthen vessel, pottery

PROVERBS

26:26	hatred	anger towards, malice
27:7	loathes	despises, hates, detests
27:13	surety	guarantee, promise, pledge
27:16	hides	treasures up or stores up
27:18	keeps	tends, saves, holds on to
27:22	mortar	stone bowl used to hold items needing to be crushed
	pestle	stone tool used for crushing or grinding
28:7	riotous	glutton, pigs, partying
28:14	fears	revered, respected, trembled, dread
28:16	wants	lacks, needs
		hates abhor, despise, loathe, detest
	covetousness	envious, greedy, wants what others have, lust
28:17	to the pit	hell, hades, torment, punishment, death to body
	stay	support, strength, comfort
28:18	perverse	crooked, dishonest, corrupt, twisted
28:19	tills	works the ground, plow, farmer
28:20	abound	become rich, successful, grow strong
28:22	evil eye	bad judgment, greedy, short-sighted
28:24	destroyer	Satan
28:25	fat	prosperous, healthy, wealthy, rich
29:1,15	reproved	rebuke, correct, chasten, punish, warn
29:1	hardened his neck	in charge, boss, rules over
29:5	spreads a net	sets him up, tries to trick or deceive
29:6,8,25	snare	trapped, caught, imprisoned, tripped up, lure
29:10,24	hate(s)	abhor, despise, loathe, detest
29:10	soul	inner person, emotion, life-force, being
29:13	deceitful	dishonest, false, fraud, cheat
29:21	delicately brings up	pampers, babys
29:25	fear	revered, respected, trembled, dread
29:27	abomination	detestable, immoral, dirty, unclean, unholy
30:2	brutish	ignorant, slow, dim-witted, dull
30:4	wind in his fists	controls the wind, in charge of nature
30:10	accuse	slander, false witness, blame
30:12	filthiness	dirty, disgusting, evil, nasty, sickening
30:15	horseleech	leech, blood-sucking insect/bug
30:22,25	meat	food
30:22	odious	unloved, hated, dispised

PROVERBS

30:23	odious	bad, vile, evil, disgusting, offensive
31:5	pervert	alter, cheat, corrupt, twist
	afflicted	oppressed, put down, tormented
31:6	heavy	anguished, sad, discouraged, burdened
31:15	gives meat	provides food
31:17	girds	equips, fastens, puts on, gets dressed up
31: 19	spindle	parts of a loom, used to make/weave clothes
	distaff	the staff of a spinning-wheel
31:21	scarlet	the best, finest, expensive
31:24	girdles	waistbands
31:29	virtuously	honorably, decently, honestly
31:30	fears	revered, respected, trembled, dread

ECCLESIASTES

1:1,2,12	Preacher	Solomon
1:3	takes	does, performs, accomplishes
1:5	hastes	hurries, rushes
1:6	circuits	tunnels, paths, channels
1:8	full of labor	wearisome, work
1:13	sore travail	heavy work, long hours of work
1:14,17	vexation	waste of time, chasing after the wind
1:15	wanting	lacking, missing, needing
2:1	myrth	laughter, joy, gladness, happiness
2:4,5,6,7,8,9,15	me	Solomon
2:9,10,11,15	my	Solomon
2:11,17,26	vexation of spirit	waste of time, chasing after the wind
2:17,18	hated	abhor, despise, loathe, detest
2:17	vanity	take pride, self honor, emptiness
2:21	equity	wrong doing, sin
	portion	possession, share, amount, cut, take
2:22	vexation	waste of time, anxious, striving
2:23	travail	labor, pain, work hard, toil, difficulty
2:24	his soul	inner person, emotion, life-force, being
3:5	cast away stones	in the old days, people would clear a field for planting crops or for animals to live – in both cases, rocks would be picked up and used for building or if not needed they got rid of them
3:14,19	preeminence	in charge, control, seniority, power
3:19	vanity	fraud, foolish, boastful, arrogant, proud
4:4	travail	labor, pain, work hard, toil, difficulty
	right work	skill, talent, expertise
4:4,6,16	vexation of spirit	stress, chasing after the wind
4:5	fool folds his hands	lazy, won't work
	eats his own flesh	meaning: because he won't work & make money, there is nothing real to eat
4:7,8,16	vanity	pointless, waste of time, emptiness
4:8	sore travail	labor, pain, work hard, toil, difficulty
	bereave	sad, mourn

ECCLESIASTES

4:10	woe	trouble, danger, look out! – a warning
4:13	admonished	warned, advised, yelled at, threatened
5:1	keep your foot	protect, keep safe
5:5	vow a vow	promise, pledge, give your word
5:7	fear	revered, respected, trembled, dread
5:14	travail	labor, pain, work hard, toil, difficulty
5:16	sore	great, really bad, aweful
5:18	comely	proper, right, fit, correct
6:1	evil	wrong doing, sin, wickedness
6:2	soul	inner person, emotion, life-force, being
6:2,9,11	vanity	fraud, foolish, boastful, arrogant, proud
6:3	untimely birth	miscarriage, still born
6:6	one place	heaven or hell
6:9	vexation of spirit	anxiety, boredom, empty feeling inside
7:6,15	vanity	fraud, foolish, boastful, arrogant, proud
7:12	defense	stronghold, protection, safety
	excellency	advantage
7:14	against	opposite
7:18	fears	revered, respected, trembled, dread
7:21	heed	attention, listen, do
7:25	applied my heart	directed my mind
7:26	snares	trapped, caught, imprisoned, tripped up, lure
	bands	chains, restraints, handcuffs
7:29	found upright	honest, decent, trustworthy
	Inventions	schemes, well-designed plans
8:3	stand	join, participate, support
8:8	marvel	stunned, amazed, shocked
8:9	hurt	harm, injury
8:10,14	vanity	pointless, emptiness, no satisfaction
8:12	fear	revered, respected, trembled, dread
9:9	vanity	fraud, foolish, boastful, arrogant, proud
9:10	device	planning, sceme
9:12	snare	trapped, caught, imprisoned, tripped up, lure
9:14	besieged	surround, attack over and over, blockade
	bulwarks	defenses, fortifications, walls, barriers
9:17	cry	shouting, yelling, scream
10:1	apothecary	perfumer
	savor	odor, good smell, scent

ECCLESIASTES

10:2	wise man…right	
	fools…left	the right hand was a symbol of power, strength
10:5	proceeds	goes forth, continues
10:6	great dignity	exalted places
10:10	whet	sharpen
10:11	babbler	talks nonsense, liar, gossip, false witness
10:16	woe	trouble, danger, look out! – a warning
	eat	feast, banquet, chow
10:17	blessed	happy, fortunate, special, unique, favored
10:18	slothfulness	laziness, slacker
10:20	bedchamber	bedroom, sleeping area
11:4	regards	noticed, heeded, observed, attended to
11:5	spirit	wind
11:8	vanity	fraud, foolish, boastful, arrogant, proud

** Chapter 12 describes a time(s) of great trouble, being under attack. It could possibly be prophetic and identify the time of the great tribulation period. So each word there will be a literal and a figurative meaning or definition.

12:3	keepers	servant, housekeeper
	house	estate, farm, ranch
	strong men	healthy, fit, athletic
	grinders	those that ground grains for flour
	windows	in times of trouble people would put out the lights to hide themselves in the dark
12:4	doors	gates
	grinding is low	quiet, slowed down
	brought low	stopped, not allowed to play music
12:5	which is high	powerful, in charge, authority
	fears…in the way	anxiety, phobias will paralyze action
	almond tree..	
	grasshopper	in a time of a full crop, the grasshoppers will take over and eat the almonds
	desire	the will, the drive, energy
	long home	death, heaven
12:6	silver chord	
	golden bowl	
	pitcher	all these symbols represent death e.g. grim

ECCLESIASTES

	wheel broken	reaper
12:7	dust	a term for humans, what our bodies are made of
12:8	vanity	fraud, foolish, boastful, arrogant, proud
12:9	order	understandable
12:11	goads	challenges
	one shepherd	someone that watches over, keeps safe, i.e. Jesus
12:12	by these	words of truth
12:13	Fear God	revered, respected, trembled, dread
	keep	obey, follow, do, practice

THE SONG OF SOLOMON

** The whole book of Song of Solomon is said to be a symbolic, figurative, prophetic account of the love story between God and his people. It is also a very real love story that Solomon wrote about his life, it could be a single woman or a composite of his many loves. The language is sensual, imaginative and sexy, this story is about passion and romance. Trees, gardens, fruit all are used to describe people, the bodies anatomy, actions, aromas, taste, etc.

1:2,3	your	groom, i.e. Jesus
1:3	savor	fragrance, smell
	ointments	perfumes
	virgins	maidens, young women
1:4	you	Solomon (symbolic of Jesus)
	draw me	call, tease, entice
1:6	black	sun burned, deep tan
1:10	rows of jewels	coins and jewels were attached to a veil, which women covered their head and faces
1:12	spikenard	expensive plant from the Himalayas (India) used to make perfume
1:13	myrrh	fragrant resin
	well beloved	dearly loved
1:14	camphor	an aromatic, smelly resin used in perfumes and as an insect repellant (moth balls)
1:16	bed	couch
	green	luxuriant, full of life
1:17	rafters fir	a type of wood used to build the roof of a house, this tree grew quickly, tall and straight
2:3	his fruit	kisses, body
2:4	flagons	raisin cakes
2:7	roes	gazelles
	hinds	does
2:9	hart	stag, male deer, antelope
	lattice	grate, grill, mesh, a woven pattern
2:12	turtle	turtle dove
2:14	countenance	"face" - influence, personal attention, blessings
	clefts	cracks, openings, empty spaces

THE SONG OF SOLOMON

2:15	foxes	(thought to be) symbolic i.e. sin – little thoughts/actions
2:16,17	beloved	symbolic of marriage
2:16	feeds among…lilies	either has a picnic or daily works/eats out among the lily flowers that are colorful, love the sun and can grow over six feet tall
2:17	roe	gazelle
	hart	stag
3:5	roes	gazelles
	hinds	does
3:6	myrrh	perfume
	frankincense	fragrant resin
	powders	spices
3:8	fear	terrors, revered, respected, trembled, dread
3:11	espousals	engagement & wedding celebrations/parties
4:2	shorn	after a sheep is shorn (all its wool cut off), the base of its roots is very white and the color even
4:4	bucklers	arm shields
4:6,14	myrrh	perfume
4:6,14	frankincense	fragrant resin
4:6	mountain of myrrh hills of frankincense	this is poetic language describing her body, specifically her breasts that have been perfumed
4:7	spot	blemish
4:10	smell	fragrance, smell, scent
	ointments	perfumes
4:13	spikenard	an expensive plant from the Himalayas (India) used to make perfume
4:14	saffron	an exotic plant used for a food spice and clothing dye (yellow)
	calamus	an exotic water plant/reed used for perfume
5:4	bowels	emotions, feelings
5:5,13	myrrh	fragrant, type of perfume, scent
5:8	sick of love	lovesick
5:10	chiefest	outstanding, best, finest
	ruddy	healthy glow, tan
5:13	sweet	fragrant, delicious smelling
6:4,10	terrible	awesome, fearful, dangerous
6:6	barren	childless, not fertile

THE SONG OF SOLOMON

6:8	threescore	60
	fourscore	80
	virgins	maidens, young women
6:9	she	the bride, the woman he is attracted to
	undefiled	pure, untouched, virgin
7:5	held	captive, cuddled
7:13	mandrakes	an aphrodisiac, love potion, a substance believed to increase sexual desire and performance, induce euphoria, an ancient form of Viagra
8:10	favor	peace, kindness
8:14	roe	a small type of deer, gazelle
	hart	stag

ISAIAH

1:3	crib	manger, simple baby bed
1:4	iniquity	sins, crime, evildoing, immorality
	seed	offspring, children, heirs
	gone away backward	turned from Him
1:6	putrefying	rotten, decayed, puss-filled
	mollified	soothe, calm down, cool off
1:7	devour	vanish, waste away, dried up, spent, used up
1:8	besieged	surround, attack over and over, blockade
	cottage	shelter, simple home
1:8,27	Zi'on	Israel
1:9	Lord of Hosts	commander of Heaven's army
1:12	tread	trample, stomp, walk all over
1:13	oblations	donations, offerings, gifts
	an abomination	detestable, immoral, dirty, unclean, unholy
	iniquity	sins, crime, evildoing, immorality
	Sabbaths	rest, holy day
1:14	hates	abhor, despise, loathe, detest
1:17	oppressed	abused, controlled, beat down, crushed
1:20	devoured	vanish, waste away, dried up, spent, used up
1:21,26	the faithful cry	Jerusalem
1:22,25	dross	impurities
1:23	gifts	bribes, special favors for unfair influence
1:24	ease me	be relieved, get rid off, lose
	Lord of hosts	Commander of Heaven's armies
1:25	purely purge	completely clean, wash, purify
1:26	faithful cry	the people of Jerusalem pray
1:27	converts	new believers, change of belief/faith
1:28	consumed	vanish, waste away, dried up, spent, used up
1:29	oaks	mighty trees, i.e. pagan shrines
	confounded	disgraced, embarrassed, confused
1:30	you	i.e. Israel
	oak	dying oak tree
1:31	tow	a strand of flax, straw
	the maker of it	his work, farmer, grower
2:3	Zi'on	Israel

ISAIAH

2:4	plowshares	plow, a tool used to dig long rows, cultivate
	pruning hook	a long-handled edge tool with a curved blade at the end and sometimes a clipper; used to prune small trees
2:5	light	ways, illumination, knowledge, revelation
2:6	house	family, heritage, estate
	soothsayers	fortune tellers, predictors, seers
2:9	mean	common, ghetto, cheap, poor
2:9,11,17	bows down	is humble, apologizes, is sorry
2:10,19,21	fear	revered, respected, trembled, dread
2:11	haughtiness	proud, arrogant, boastful, stuck-up
2:11,17	lofty	proud, lifted up, dreamer
2:12	day of the lord of hosts	revenge, retaliation, punishment, reckoning
2:15	fenced	fortified, enclosed, protected, defended
2:19	terribly	thunder
2:20	cast	throw away
2:22	cease	stop
3:1	staff	guidance, control, leadership
	stay	support, strength, comfort
3:2	prudent	careful, good judgment, common sense, wise
3:2,5,14	ancient	aged, old, experienced, wise
3:3	artificer	craftsman, artist, worker
	orator	public speaker, politician
3:5	base	inferior, lowlife, ghetto, criminal
3:7	swear	protest, complain, state
	healer	helper, doctor
3:8	tongue	talk, speech, communication
3:9,11	woe	trouble, danger, look out! – a warning
3:9	soul	inner person, emotion, life-force, being
3:14	eaten up	consumed, ruined, destroyed
3:15	Lord GOD	Jehovah Elohim, the self-existing God now interacting with mankind
3:16,17	daughters of Zi'on	offspring of a nation, citizens
3:16	wanton	seductive, flirtatious, sexy, trampish
	mincing	wiggle, a sexy walk/strut
3:18	cauls	scarf, head band, hood, head covering
	tinkling ornaments	ankle bracelets

	round tires like the moon	the word is derived from "tiara;" a "turban" or an ornament for the head (headband)
3:19	chains	pendants, ornaments, necklaces, "bling"
	mufflers	veils, scarfs
3:20	headbands	sashes, scarfs, bows, ribbons
3:22	wimples	cloaks, cape, shawl
	crisping pins	money purses, handbags
	apparel	clothing, garments, outer wear
3:23	glasses	hand mirrors
	hoods	turbans, head coverings
3:24	rent	rope, cheap string to hold up pants
	stomacher	rich robe
	sackcloth	coarsely woven fabric, sign of mourning, submission and humility
3:26	desolate	deserted, left alone, abandoned, rejected
4:2	branch	God is the "root" or source of life, when he comes again, it will be a growth or "branch"
4:3,4	Zi'on	Israel
4:5	upon	over
	defense	canopy, stronghold, protection, safety
4:6	convert	the place of shelter or protection
5:1	fruitful	fertile, healthy, well-nourashed
5:2	fenced	dug it up, cultivated
	Looked	expected, counted on
5:5	go to	listen, obey, do
5:6	briers	stickers, thorns, weeds
5:8,11,18,20,21,22	woe	trouble, danger, look out! – a warning
5:11	follow	pursue, chase, go after
5:12	viol	a stringed instrument played with a bow, like a violin
5:14	hell	the grave, death, place of punishment, torment
	pomp	big show, flashy, showy
5:18	Vanity	fraud, foolish, boastful, arrogant, proud
5:21	eyes	self opinion, conceit
5:23	reward	bribes, payoff
5:24	chaff	the shells/skin that were beaten/broken off wheat, barley grain and then thrown away

ISAIAH

5:26	ensign	banner, flag, family crest, gang colors
	Hiss	whistle, signal
5:27	latchet	leather thong or strap used to fasten a shoe or sandal on the foot
5:30	that day	judgment, day of Lord, 1000 year period
6:2	seraphims	special type of angel, "the fiery ones", archangels
6:5	woe	trouble, danger, look out! – a warning
6:7	iniquity	sins, crime, evildoing, immorality, depravity
	Purged	atoned for, forgiven
6:10	make…ears heavy	unable to understand, dense, stupid
6:11	houses	families, estates
6:13	teil	a type of citrus tree, lime tree
7:2	confederate	allied, joined, united
7:3	conduit	gutter, water pipeline, aquaduct, channel
7:4	firebrands	torches, anything on fire that is thrown in the air
	Heed	care, pay attention, listen
	Two tails of these	
	Smoking fire brands	two big, important leaders
7:6	vex	terrify, trouble, plague, confuse, dismayed
7:8,9	head	rulers, leaders
7:11	Height above	heaven
7:12	tempt	test, try, prove, entice
7:13	teil	a type of citrus tree, lime tree
7:14	Im-man'u-el	God with us
7:16	abhor	despise, loathe, detest
7:17	house	family, estate
7:18	fly uttermost	remotest, far away, edges of empire
	river	Nile
7:20	consume	vanish, waste away, dried up, spent, used up
7:21	nourish	keep alive, strengthen
7:23	silver linings	money, small coins/pieces of silver
7:25	lesser cattle	sheep
8:3	went	married
8:4	shall have knowledge	know how, wisdom, skill, cunning
8:7	river	Euphrates
8:8	Im-man'u-el	God with us
8:9	gird yourselves	tighten belt, equip, prepare for action/battle

ISAIAH

8:11	a strong hand	mighty power
8:12	a confederacy	conspiracy, treason
8:13	sanctify	purify, make clean, holy
	Fear	revered, respected, trembled, dread
8:14	sanctuary	refuge, safe place
	offense	stumbling, trip-up, offend
8:14,15	Snare	trapped, caught, imprisoned, tripped up, lure
8:16	bind up	protest, complain
	testimony	records, verbal account, story
8:19	family spirits	spirits, demons
	wizards	mediums, magicians
	peep	chirp, enchant with words i.e. whisper
8:21	hardly bestead	deeply troubled, bothered
9:1	vexation	anguish, pain, sorrow
9:4	broken	shattered, crushed, demorilized
9:7	zeal	excited, ambitious, energetic, hyper
9:9	stoutness	arrogance, pride, over-confident
9:10	hewn	cut, hacked, chiseled
9:13	smite	attacked, strike, hit, punish
9:14	rush	bulrush, water plant
9:15	ancient	aged, old, experienced, wise
9:18	briers	stickers, thorns, weeds
9:20	snatch	slice off, take, remove
	flesh of his own arm	cannibalism, eat human flesh
10:1	woe	trouble, conflict, pity me, feel sorry for me
10:3	desolation	destruction, ruin, emptiness
10:4	bow down under	be frightened, fearful
10:6	mire	dust, dirt, trash in the street a person walks on
	Hypocritical	godless, two-faced, deceiver, false
10:8	altogether	all, as one, united
10:11	idols	images, likeness of false gods
10:12	performed	finished, accomplished, completed
	high looks	haughtiness, proud, arrogant
10:13	I am prudent	careful, good judgment, common sense, wise
	valiant	mighty, famous, battle-decorated, warrior
10:15	hews	chops, cuts, hacks, chisels
10:18	standard bearer	a person that holds/carries the tribe or nations banner, flag, family crest, gang colors

ISAIAH

10:20	remnant	survivors, small group
	Stay	support, strength, comfort
	Smote	attacked, strike, hit, punish
10:21	Mighty God	El Gibbor
10:22	consumption	destruction, annihilation, wiped out, slaughter
10:26	scourge	plague, curse, pestilence, punishment
10:27	yoke	control, lead
10:28	carriages	baggage, luggage
10:33	lop the bough	cut off the tree branch, limb, long twig
	High ones	tall, powerful, important
10:34	iron	an iron ax
11:2,3	fear	revered, respected, trembled, dread
11:4	reprove	rebuke, correct, chasten, punish, warn
11:5	girdle	sash, belt, support, upholding
	loins	strength, life
	reins	thoughts, emotions, affections, self-control
11:8	cockatrice	poisonous snake, viper
	weaned	grown up, no longer breast-fed
11:10	root of jes'se	offspring (prophetically i.e. Jesus)
11:10,12	ensign	rallying flag, banner, gang colors
11:13	vex	terrify, trouble, plague, confuse, dismayed
11:!4	spoil	plunder, booty, stolen goods
11:15	dryshod	"feet dry" - dry river bed, dry wash
12:6	Zi'on	Israel
13:2	exalt	honored, celebrated, make famous
13:3	sanctified	consecrated, dedicated
	highness	triumph, might, power, authority
13:4	tumultous	commotion, excitement, preparation for battle
13:6	howl	wail, cry, moan
13:11	arrogancy	foolishness, stupidity, pride
13:12	precious	scarce, rare
13:21	doleful	gloomy, dreary, sad
	satyrs	male goat, sacrificial animal, mythological half man-goat
13:22	dragons	sea creature, crocodile, dinosaur
	prolonged	continual, non-stop, on-and-on
14:3	fear	turmoil, revered, respected, trembled, dread
	hard bondage	harsh slavery, labor, work

ISAIAH

14:4	proverb	story, tale, fable, lesson for application
14:8	feller	tree cutter, trimmer, pruner
14:9	chief ones	leaders, bosses
14:11	viols	a stringed instrument played with a bow, like a violin
	pomps	big show, flashy, showy
14:12	Lu'ci-fer	"light bearer" used one of the king of Babylon and/or Satan
14:18	house	tomb, grave, crypt
14:19	abominable	detestable, polluted, filthy, unclean
	raiment	clothing, garment, apparel
14:20	seed	offspring, children, heirs
	renowned	honored, respected, famous
14:21	iniquity	sins, crime, evildoing, immorality
14:23	bittern	porcupine, hedgehog
	besom	broom
14:25	depart	be removed, leave, be taken away
14:27	disannul	break, void, make an end, cancel
14:29	cockatrice	viper, adder or other poisonous snake
14:30,32	poor	helpless, powerless, without money
14:32	trust	find refuge, be safe, have confidence
15:1	brought to silence	ruined, destroyed, unpopulated
15:4	grievous	a misery, painful, unbearable
16:4	covert	shelter, covering, hiding place
16:5	hasting	prompting
16:8	heathen	nations, non-Jew, pagan
16:11	bowels	innards, guts, feelings
16:12	prevail	have power, overcome, victorious
16:14	hireling	servant, paid laborer, worker
	Contemned	disgraced, dishonored
17:4	wax	become, grow, increase
17:8	images	idols, statues, pagan gods
17:10	Rock	foundation, support, strength
17:12	woe	trouble, danger, look out! – a warning
17:14	nor	no more
18:1	woe	trouble, danger, look out! – a warning
	land shadowing with wings	Ethiopia

ISAIAH

18:2	meted	measured, divided, cut up
	trodden	walk, trampled, stepped on, beaten, defeated
	spoiled	cut through, infected, damaged, tainted
18.3	ensign	rallying flag, banner, gang colors
18:4	take my rest	be silent, stop, not work
	consider	think about, look over
18:5	sprigs	twig, small branches, shoots
19:3	destroy	confound, cut off, end, finish
	Familiar spirits	mediums, demons, spirit-guides
	Wizards	magicians, conjurers
19:7	paper reeds	bulrushes, water pkants
	mouth	edge, bank, shoreline
19:7,8	brooks	Nile canals
19:8	languish	weaken, depressed, sad, burn out
	angle	hooks
19:9	networks	linen clothes, clothing, garments
	confounded	dejected, confused, frustrated
19:10	sluices	lagoon, pond, fish farm
	broken	defeated, crushed, destroyed
19:11	brutish	stupid, dense, low intelligence, thug
19:12	purposed upon	planned against, plotted, conspired
19:14	perverse	distorted, twisted
21:1	burden	message, prophecy, God's will
21:2,24:16	treacherous	deceitfully, dishonestly, fraud, tricky
	spoiler	robbers, thieves, vandals
	spoils	destroy, pollute, wreck, change for the worse
21:4	fear	revered, respected, trembled, dread
21:7	hearkened	listen, pay attention, heed
21:8	ward	guard, protect
21:14	prevented	blocked, cut-off, stopped
21:17	residue	remainder, left-over
22:2	stirs	trouble, small uprisings, commotion
22:4	look	turn from, leave, ignore
	spoiling	destruction, ruin, wreck
22:5	perplexity	confusion, uncertainty
22:7	gate	entrance, door
22:9	breaches	broken place, crumbled walls, holes, gap
22:11	ditch	reservoir, pond

ISAIAH

22:16	sepulcher	tombs, graves, crypts
22:24	flagons	bottle, flask, container to hold liquid
23:2	replenished	enriched, fill-up, strengthen
23:3	mart	market, store – a place where other nations come
23:6	isle	coast, island
23:7	sojourn	temporarily stay, visit, live
23:8	traffickers	traders, salesmen, businessmen, dealers
23:10	pass through	overflow, flood, run over
	Strength	restraint, power, defense
23:13	razed	stripped, sacked, demolished
23:14	laid waste	destroyed, leveled, ruined, defeated
23:17,18	hire	employment, work, service
23:17	fornication	illegallon sex outside of marriage, immoral, dirty; also describes a union or relationship to something other than God/His rules
24:2	usury	interest, payday loan
24:3	spoiled	plundered, sacked, looted
24:5	covenant	agreement, promise, contract
24:6	desolate	guilt, sad, depressed
24:8	tabrets	tambourine, a small hand-drum
24:15	isles	distant lands, maritime nations, coastland
24:16	treacherous	dishonest, crafty, sly
	uttermost part	ends, boundary
	my leanness	I waste away, "suck up", lose a lot of weight
	woe	trouble, danger, warning
24:17	pit	hell, hades, torment, punishment, death to body
24:17,18	fear	revered, respected, trembled, dread
	snare	trapped, caught, imprisoned, tripped up, lure
24:18	noise	report, gossip
24:20	reel	stagger, wobble (like a drunk walking)
24:21	punish	judge, pay back
	Host	multitude, army, many, group
	High ones	rulers, powerful leaders
24:22	pit	hell, hades, torment, punishment, death to body
	visited	punished, avenged, judgement
24:23	ancients	elders, wise people, experienced
25:2	defensed	stronghold, protection, safety, guarded
25:3,5	terrible	ruthless, cruel, aweful

ISAIAH

25:5	branch	pruning, trim, cut
	Brought low	stilled, shut up, humbled
25:6	lees	dregs (bitter wine),like used coffee grounds
dregs		
25:10	trodden	walk, trampled, stepped on, beaten, defeated
25:11	spoils	plunder, sack, loot
26:2	keeps the truth	remains faithful, obedient
26:5	brings down	humbles, broken, humiliates
26:6	tread it down	trample it, stomp on
26:7	weigh	prepare, plan, think through
26:10	behold	perceive, consider, watch
26:11	at the people	against God's people
26:12	ordain	establish, set up
26:14	visited	punished, avenged, judgement
26:18	wrought	worked, accomplish, have done
26:21	behold	look, see
27:1	leviathan, dragon	monsters, cruel animals, devils
27:2	vineyard	a.k.a. Israel
27:3	keep	watch over
	It	Israel
27:4	who	Israel's enemies
	go through them	march against, defeat
	them	unbelievers, heathens
27:5	take hold	grip, grasp, hold on to
27:7	him	i.e. Israel
	those	enemies
27:9	sunder	cut in pieces, divide
	groves	(Heb:Asherah) either a living tree or a tree-like pole, set up as an object of worship, being symbolical of the female or productive principle in nature. Every Phoenician had an asherah near them. Both the "May Pole" and "Christmas Tree" (Jer.10:3-5) originate with this Asherah. The word is often translated "green trees" or "grove." This "nature worship" became associated with sexual immorality.
	Images	idols, statues
27:10	defensed	stronghold, protection, safety, guarded

ISAIAH

27:12	beat off	thresh, defeat, punish
27:13	they	i.e. Israel
28:1	woe	trouble, danger, warning
28:4	fat	fertile, healthy
28:5	diadem	a crown - a symbol of power, success, control
28:7	have erred	sinned, made mistakes; lost, left the right path
28:9	doctrine	tidings, message, beliefs, teachings
28:10,13	precept	command, rule, principles
28:11	tongue	language, speech
28:11,32:4	stammering	stutter, mumble, speak unclearly
28:13	snared	trapped, caught, imprisoned, tripped up, lure
28:15,18	covenant	agreement, plan, contract
28:17	plummet	straight, level, correct, perfect
	Judgment	do justice, punish, revenge, sentance
28:18	disannulled	break, voided, make an end to, cancelled
	scourge	plague, curse, pestilence, punishment
	trodden	walk, trampled, stepped on, beaten, defeated
28:19	vexation	sheer terror, trouble, fear, anxiety
	report	what it means, news
28:21	strange	extraordinary, odd, peculiar
28:22	mockers	scoffers, disrespectful
	bands	fetters, hand-cuffs, restraints
	consumption	destruction, spoiled, wrecked
28:23	cummin	a fragrant spice
	hearken	listen, pay attention, heed
	plowman	farmer
28:25	cast abroad	sow, throw seeds
28:25,27	fitches	dill, a type of spice/seasoning
28:28	corn	grain
	bruise	grind
29:1,15	woe	trouble, danger, warning
29:1,2,7	A'ri-el	i.e. Jerusalem
29:3	mount siege	war equipment used to break walls down
29:5	strangers	enemies, non-Jew
	terrible	ruthless, cruel, hateful
29:7	munition	fortress, stronghold, weapons, military defenses
29:8	Zi'on	Israel
29:9	wonder	be amazed, stunned, shocked

ISAIAH

29:13	fear	revered, respected, trembled, dread
29:13,23	precept	rule, law, principle
29:15	council	plans, group decisions
29:19	meek	humble, gentle, obedient
29:20	terrible	ruthless, cruel, hateful
	iniquity	sins, crime, evildoing, immorality
29:21	snare	trapped, caught, imprisoned, tripped up, lure
29:22	wax	grow, increase, more
29:24	murmured	complained, whined
	Learn doctrine	accept instructions
30:1	woe	trouble, danger, warning
	cover with a covering	make an alliance, secret agreement
30:2	asked at my mouth	consulted me, asked me
30:4	Ha'nes an	Egyptian City
30:8	table	tablet, something used to write on in old days
30:9	hear	listen to, obey, understand
30:10	smooth	flattering, agreeable, nice
30:12	oppression	extortion, cruel leadership
	stay	trust, support, strength, comfort
30:14	shard	fragment, broken pieces, splinter
30:17	ensign	a rallying flag, banner, gang colors
30:22	menstruous	like a sanitary napkin, tampon used for a woman's blood during her period, menstrual cycle
	graven images	idols & carvings, statues of pagan gods
30:24	clean provender	good fodder, clean hay/straw
	winnowed	the process of throwing the parts of wheat in the air to separate the grain from the husk/skin
30:28	sieve	screen, filter, sifter
	vanity	fraud, foolish, boastful, arrogant, proud
30:31	smote	attacked, strike, hit, punish
30:32	with it	them
31:1	woe	trouble, pain, sorrow
	stay	trust, support, strength, comfort
31:2	help	support, assistance, aid
31:8	discomfited	forced labor, slavery, pain
31:9	fear	revered, respected, trembled, dread

ISAIAH

	ensign	battle standard, flag, gang colors
32:2	convert	shelter, house, refuge
32:3	dim	blind, lose sight
	hearken	listen, pay attention, heed
32:4	rash	hasty, without thought
32:5,6	vile	foolish, vain, immoral, punk
32:5,7	liberal	gentleman, noble, well-born, dignified
	churl	peasant, creep, bum, punk, thug
32.6	villainy	folly, treachery, deception
	hypocrisy	ungodliness, unfaithful
33:1	woe	trouble, danger, warning
	spoiled	destroyed, ruined
33:5	Zi'on	Israel
33:6	fear	revered, respected, trembled, dread
33:7	valiant	brave, noble, courageous
	without	outside
33:8	covenant	unconditional agreement, contract, promise
33:9	hewn	cut, chop, chisel
33:11	chaff	the shells/skin that were beaten/broken off wheat, barley grain and then thrown away
33:14	fearfulness	trembling, terror, frightened
	surprised	shocked, stunned, seized
	hypocrites	godless ones, heathen, unfaithful
33:15	gain of oppressions	unjust gains, rip-offs, criminal activity
	blood	violence, murder
33:18	meditate	think about former, ponder, consider
33:19	stammering	foreign languages, other dialects
33:21	gallonlant	noble, powerful, important
	gallonley	boat
34:1	hearken	listen, pay attention, heed
34:6	fat	rich, successful, prosperous
34:9	pitch	tar, asphalt
34:10	pass	cross, go past
34:11	cormorant	long legged, long necked bird, like the pelican
	Bittern	hedgehog
34:13	dragons	serpents, dinosaurs
	nettles	stickers, thorns, weeds
	brambles	thorn bush, hedge

ISAIAH

34:14	wild beasts	hyenas
	Satyr	male goat, mythological half man
34:16	want	lack, missing, needing somethng
35:6	hart	deer
35:8	wayfaring	traveler, wanderer, nomadic
35:9	redeemed	saved, bought back, rescue, save
36:5	vain	empty, pointless, waste of time/effort
36:11	ears	hearing, listening, obeying
36:16	cistern	water tank, barrel, container, well
	hearken	listen, pay attention, heed
36:17	corn	grain
36:21	held their peace	were silent, didn't speak
36:22	rent	tear, ripped, shred, pull apart, open
37:3	blasphemy	cursing; saying/behaving badly against God
37:4	reprove	rebuke, correct, chasten, punish, warn
37:7	fall	killed, die, destroyed
37:9	say	report, state, mention
37:18	countries	lands, nations
37:24	multitude	masses, large number of people
37:25	besieged	surround, attack over and over, blockade
37:27	corn blasted	burnt, consumed, destroyed by sun & heat
37:31	remnant	small group, extra, what is left
	escaped	got away, survived, spared
37:33	cast a bank	build a siege ramp
37:36	angel	messenger, supernatural being
38:3	beseech	beg, plead, ask
	sore	bitterly, bad, painful
38:5	days	life, amount of time to live
38:12	pining	anxious, depressed, unmotivated
38:13	reckoned	counted off, waited patiently
38:16	recover	restore, bring back, take possession
38:18	truth	faithfulness, honesty
38:20	house	temple, place of worship, religious building
39:2	things	treasures, possessions, belongings
40:2	comfortably	kindly, friendly, peafeful
40:7	withers	dry up, shrink, slowly die
40:9	Zi'on	Israel
40:10	strong hand	mighty, powerful, supernatural

ISAIAH

40:12	meted out	marked off, counted, measured
40:14	judgment	justice, wisdom, punishment, penalty
40:15	takes	lifts, carries, removes
	Isles	distant lands, maritime nations, coastland
40:20	impoverished	poor, broke, without money, ghetto
	oblation	offering, gift, present
	cunning	inventive, inwrought, skillful, expert craftsman
40:22	circle	round, globe, the Earth
40:31	wait upon	look eagerly for, trust, have confidence, patience
41:5	isles	distant lands, maritime nations, coastland
41:6	good courage	brave, fealess, heroic
41:7	soldering	joining together of different metal pieces, weld
41:8	seed	offspring, children, heirs
41:12	nought	non-existent, nothing, zero
41:15	chaff	the shells/skin that were beaten/broken off wheat, barley grain and then thrown away
41:19	shittah tree	a type of tree grown in the desert, used to build the tabernacle (church building) in the wilderness
41:21	cause	argument, problem, issue
41:24,29	nothing	no amount, worthless, nothing
	abomination	detestable, immoral, dirty, unclean, unholy
41:28	answer a word	give an answer, respond
41:29	vanity	empty, worthless, pointless
42:1	elect	chosen, special, singled out
42:3	truth	faithfully, honest, reliable
42:6	covenant	agreement, promise, contract
42:8,17	graven images	idols & carvings, statues of pagan gods
42:14	devour	consume, eat up, destroy
42:15	islands	coastlands
42:22,24	spoiled	plundered, sacked, robbed, looted
	snared	trapped, caught, imprisoned, tripped up, lure
42:23	hearken	listen, pay attention, heed
43:5	seed	offspring, children, heirs
43:17	tow	straw, hay, dry weeds
43:20	dragons	serpents, dinosaurs
42:23	small cattle	sheep
43:24	serve	labor, work, obey

ISAIAH

43:27	first	Adam – the first man
44:3	Seed	descendents, offspring, children
44:5	subscribe with	write on
44:9	delectable	delicious, yummy, tasty, choice
44:10	image	idol, statue
	profitable	good, successful, beneficial
44:14	hews	cuts, hacks, chisels
	strengthen	secures, possesses, helps
44:15,17,20	image	idols, statue
44:19	an abomination	detestable, immoral, dirty, unclean, unholy
44:25	diviners	various, many different
44:26	decayed places	ruins, wreckage
45:1	leaved	paneled, door
45: 4	surnamed	title, family/given name, honored name (e.g. Sir, Reverend)
45:9	potsherd	clay pot fragment, broken dishes
45:10	woe	trouble, danger, warning
45:18,19	in vain	purposeless, pointless
45:24	incensed	angered, destructive rage verging on madness
46:3,12	hearken	listen, pay attention, heed
46:4	hoar	grey, old, experienced
46:8	show yourselves	act like men, don't be cowards
46:11	executes	performs, does
46:13	astrologers	forecasters, predictors; guess the future by analyzing the stars and constellations
	prognosticators	fortune tellers, prophets, predictors
	tarry	be delayed, hold back, keep from
47:6	ancient	aged, old, experience, wise
47:13	prognosticators	fortune tellers, prophets, predictors
	councils	advice
47:15	quarter	region, zone, district, neighborhood
48:4	obstinate	stubborn, hard-headed
48:5	image	idol, statue
48:9	defer	delay, put off
48:10	with	as
48:12	hearken	listen, pay attention, heed
48:13	spanned	spread, went across
48:19	seed	offspring, children, descendents

ISAIAH

49:1	isles	distant lands, maritime nations, coastland
49:8	covenant	agreement, promise, contract
49:13	afflicted	oppressed ones, suffering
49:19	waste	empty, ruin, destroyed
49:20	straight	narrow, confining
49:21	removing to and fro	a wanderer, nomad, regular traveler
	Gen'tiles	nations other than Israel
	standard	rallying flag, banner, gang colors
49:26	sweet	new, tender, early harvest
50:1	iniquities	sins, crime, evildoing, immorality
	transgressions	wrongdoings
50:9	wax old	wear out
50:10	fears	revered, respected, trembled, dread
	stay	trust, support, strength, comfort
50:11	compass	go about, surround, encamp, encircle
51:1,4,7	hearken	listen, pay attention, heed
51:1	follow	pursue, chase, go after
51:3	Zi'on	Israel
51:5	isles	distant lands, maritime nations, coastland
51:6	wax old	wear out, ruined, broken down
51:6,8	salvation	in Hebrew Jeshua means "God who saves" – rescues, etc.
51:10	ransomed	redeemed, buy/win back something lost (like pawn shop), once held prisoner, purchased
51:11	redeemed	saved, rescued, forgiven
51:16	plant	established, start, begin
51:20	fury	wrath, intense anger
52:1	uncircumcised	non-Jew, unbelieving, heathens
52:4	sojourn	temporarily stay, visit, live
52:7,8	Zi'on	Israel
52:10	make bare	revealed, make clear, explain
52:15	sprinkle	rain, spatter, put water on, influence
53:1	report	message, news, facts
53:3	esteemed Him not	disrespect, ignored
53:4	sorrows	pains, troubles, sadness
53:5	stripes	whip-lashes, beatings
	chastisement	punishment, penalty
53:6	iniquity	sins, crime, evildoing, immorality

ISAIAH

53:10	seed	posterity, offspring, children
53:11	travail	labor, pain, work hard, toil, difficulty
54:1	barren	Jersualem will be empty, destroyed
54:3	seed	offspring, children, heirs
	Inherit	possesses, ownership, control
	Gen'tiles	nations other than Israel, non-Jew
54:4	confounded	humiliated, ashamed, confused
54:8	wrath	judgment, anger, hellfire, punishment
54:10	covenant	agreement, promise, contract
54:11	windows	battlements, strong windows
54:14	fear	revered, respected, trembled, dread
54:16	waster	Satan, destroyer
55:1	waters	a.k.a. the Spirit
	wine	a.k.a. joy
	milk	a.k.a. nourishment
55:2	hearken	listen, pay attention, heed
55:3	covenant	agreement, promise, contract
55:11	void	without result, no luck, not done
56:1+	Lord	Jehovah; God in relationship to mankind
56:2,6	sabbath	rest day, day without work
56:4	take hold	hold firmly to agreement, grab, keep
	Covenant	unconditional agreement, contract, promise
56:10	dumb dogs	stupid, worthless, sub-human
56:11	dogs	men for hire (evil deeds i.e. prostitutes)
	his	every
57:1	merciful	faithful, devout, kind, generous
58:5	afflict his soul	humble himself, feel sorry for behavior, humble
58:7	deal	divide, seperate
	cast out	wandering, rejected, outcast
58:8	rearward	rear guard
58:9	vanity	fraud, foolish, boastful, arrogant, proud
58:10	afflicted	oppressed, tortured, punished
58:11	make fat	give strength to, health, prosper
58:12	old waste places	ancient ruins, collapsed buildings
58:13	sabbath	rest day, day without work
59:1	iniquities	sins, crime, evildoing, immorality
59:3	blood	murder, violence
	perverseness	wickedness, evil, immorality

ISAIAH

59:5	cockatrice	adders, poisonous snakes
59:15	prey	victim
	judgement	justice, punishment, sentance
59:18	island	coastlands
59:19	fear	revered, respected, trembled, dread
59:21	covenant	agreement, promise, contract
	Seed	offspring, children, heirs
	Seed's seed	descendents, grandchildren
60:3,5,11,16	Gen'tiles	nations, non-Jew
60:6	dromedaries	camels
60:9	isles	distant lands, maritime nations, coastland
60:10	smote	attacked, strike, hit, punish
60:11	forces	strength, military power
60:14	Zi'on	Israel
60:15	hated	abhor, despise, loathe, detest
60:22	hasten	cause, make happen, speed up, hurry
61:3	appoint	proclaim, announce, declare
61:6,9	Gen'tiles	nations, non-Jew
61:6	glory	wealth, power, influence
61:8	hate	abhor, despise, loathe, detest
	covenant	agreement, promise, contract
61:9	seed	offspring, descendents, children
62:1,11	Zi'on	Israel
62:1	hold	keep, hang on to, preserve
62:2	Gen'tiles	nations, non-Jew
	new name	names represented major changes and/or when a woman got married she took her husbands "name"
62:8	corn	grain
	meat	food
62:10	standard	rallying flag, banner, gang colors
63:3	raiment	garments, clothes
63:6	fury	wrath, intense anger
63:10	vexed	terrify, trouble, plague, confuse, dismayed
63:15	the surroundings of your bowels	compassion, deep feelings that surface
63:17	fear	revered, respected, trembled, dread
64:1	rend	tear, ripped, shred, pull apart, open

ISAIAH

64:9	very sore	beyond measure, a lot
	Beseech	beg, plead, ask
64:10	Zi'on	Israel
64:11	laid waste	in ruins, destroyed
64:12	hold	keep, save, preserve
	afflict	punish, trouble, attack, torment
	very sore	beyond measure, a lot, badly
65:3	gardens	pagan shrines
	alters of brick	pagan altars
65:4	abominable	detestable, nasty, offensive
65:7	iniquities	sins, crime, evildoing, immorality
	measure	pay back, repay
65:9, 23	seed	offspring, children, heirs
	Elect	chosen, special few, the faithful ones
65:11	troop	groups, military units
65:14	howl for vexation of spirit	moan, cry out with a heavy heart
65:25	meat	food
66:3	abominations	detestable ways, gross/nasty behavior
66:4	fears	revered, respected, trembled, dread
66:5	hated	abhor, despise, loathe, detest
66:7	travailed	labor, pain, work hard, toil, difficulty
66:8	Zi'on	Israel
66:9	cause to bring forth	give delivery, birth
66:11	consolations	comforts, soothes, concern
66:17	sanctify	consecrate, wash, make clean/pure
	abominations	detestable things, nasty, gross
66:19	isles	distant lands, maritime nations, coastland
66:20	nations	peoples, groups
66:22	seed	offspring, children, heirs
66:23	sabbath	rest day, day without work
66:24	worm	maggot, gnawing/painful memories
	quenched	put out, extinguished, ended
	abhorring	loathsome, disgusted, hate

JEREMIAH

1:1	in the beginning	God, forever
1:5	sanctified	consecrated, dedicated, made pure/holy
1:11	rod	staff, walking stick, branch
1:13	seething	boiling, cooking
1:16	touching	concerning, relating to
1:17	confound	dismay, confuse, trouble
2:2	espousals	betrothals, engagement plans
	went	followed, pursued, chased
2:3	offend	be guilty, hurt
2:7	an abomination	detestable, immoral, dirty, unclean, unholy
2:8	prophesied	foretell, make a prediction, speak for God
2:10	pass over	cross over to, go across
	isles	distant lands, maritime nations, coastland
2:12	very desolate	in despair, depressed, sad
	astonished	confused, dazed, surprised, afraid
2:13	hewed	cut, hacked, chiseled
	cisterns	water tanks, barrels, containers, wells
2:14	home born	born a slave
2:21	degenerate	unhealthy, decaying, dying
2:22	iniquity	sins, crime, evildoing, immorality
	niter	strong soap, cleanser, detergent
2:27	stock	wooden idol, statue
2:33	trim	prepare, cut
2:36	gad	wander, move about restlessly or roam idly
3:1	greatly polluted	completely unclean, filthy
3:2	have polluted	made unclean, dirtied
3:6	harlot	hooker, prostitute, call girl
3:8,14	backsliding	turn away, stop doing what is right, lose enthusiasm
3:10	feignedly	pretense, false, putting on an act, deception
3:20	treacherously	dishonestly, falsely, fraud, cheat
4:1	abominations	disgusting, sick, forbidden, offensive
4:21	standard	the tribe or nations banner, flag, family crest, gang colors
4:22	sottish	silly, foolish, stupid, idiotic

LAMENTATIONS OF JEREMIAH

4:30	despise	detest, hate, reject, disgust
4:31	bewails	cries, weeps, moans
5:6	transgressions	misdeed, sin, wrong-doing, violation
	backsliding	turn away, stop doing what is right, lose enthusiasm
5:10	battlements	defenses, wall, fortress, barrier, blockade
5:11	treacherously	dishonestly, falsely, fraud, cheat
5:12	belied	deny, disagreed, twisted the truth
5:17	impoverish	poor, broke, without money, ghetto
6:6	hew	cut, hack, chisel
	cast a mount	build fortifications, set up defenses
6:7	grief	suffering, sadness, anguish
6:9	thoroughly glean	pick clean
6:13	covetousness	envious, greedy, wants what others have, lust
6:15	abomination	detestable, immoral, dirty, unclean, unholy
6:17,19	hearken	listen, pay attention, heed
6:18	know	realize, awareness, insight
6:22	sides	uttermost parts, far corners, from all over
6:23	daughter	offspring, children of/followers or devotees of something or someone
6:24	wax	grow, get stronger, become
6:26	spoiler	destroyer, wrecker, vandal
6:28	founder	metal worker, iron smith
6:30	reprobate	rejected, unbeliever, quitter
7:5	judgment	justice, punished. thoroughly execute
7:9	swear	promise, vow, give word
7:10,30	abominations	detestable, immoral, dirty, unclean, unholy
7:15	whole seed	posterity, descendents, children
7:16	intercession	mediate, go-between, plead/pray on behalf of
7:18	queen of heaven	probably Astarte, the moon-goddess
	knead	squeeze bread dough
7:24	hearkened	listened, pay attention, inclined their ear
7:26	Me	God, Almighty
7:29	lamentation	cry, be sad about, agonize, mourn
7:30	house	temple, place of worship, religious building
7:31	high places	shrines, altars to pagan gods
7:33	carcasses	corpses, dead bodies
	fray	frighten, scare

LAMENTATIONS OF JEREMIAH

8:3	residue	what is left, remnant, handful
8:6	hearkened	listen, pay attention, heed
	repented	grieve, regret, feel sorry/ashamed
8:7	turtle	turtledove, small/gentle bird
	judgment	do justice, punish, revenge, sentance
8:8	in vain	deceitful, pointless, waste
8:11,19	daughter	offspring, children of/followers or devotees of something or someone
8:13	water of gallonl	poisoned water, bitterness
8:17	cockatrices	adders, poisonous snakes
8:21	black	weathered, suntanned skin
8:22	recovered	restored, bought back, saved
	balm	medicinal cream, lotion
9:2	adulterers	fornicators, sexually unfaithful
	treacherous	deceitful, liar, dishonest
	way faring men	travelers, wanderers, nomads, gypsies
9:4	supplant	replace by deceit, steal a job or position
	with slanders	craftily, lies, false gossip
9:5	commit iniquity	sins, crime, evildoing, immorality
9:7	melt	refine (by fire)
	try	test, examine, prove, challenge
9:10	habitations	pastures, fields, land
	burned up	desolate, empty, destroyed
9:11	heaps	ruins, piles, rubble, wreckage
	dragons	monsters, dinosaurs
9:14	imagination	fraud, foolish, boastful, arrogant, proud
9:17	cunning	skilled (at mourning), trained/paid mourners
9:22	carcasses	corpses, dead bodies
	harvestman	harvester, reaper, soul collector
9:24	judgment	do justice, punish, revenge, sentance
9:25	circumcised	medical surgery that cuts off skin that covers the tip or head of the penis; a religious act
9:25,26	uncircumcised	heathen, pagans, unbelievers, non-Jew
10:3	vain	a delusion, empty dream
10:5	borne	carried, supported, took care of
	go	go by their own power
10:7	fear	revered, respected, trembled, dread
	appertain	concerning, relates to, in reference to

LAMENTATIONS OF JEREMIAH

10:8,14,21	brutish	stupid, dense, like an animal
10:9,14	founder	goldsmith
	cunning	inventive, inwrought, skillful, expert craftsman
10:10	everlasting	eternal, forever, very long time
10:14	graven image	idol, statue of pagan gods
	molten image	metal, molded
10:15	errors	mockery, delusions
10:16	rod	tribe, family, heritage
10:19	woe	trouble, danger, warning
	my wound is grievous	painful, hurtful, diseased, infected
10:21	pastors	shepherds, caretakers
10:22	noise	sound, a report
	dragons	snakes, monsters, dinosaurs
11:2,6,8,10	covenant	agreement, promise, contract
11:5	perform	fulfill, complete, accomplish
11:8	imaginations	false pride, vanity
11:10	iniquities	sins, crime, evildoing, immorality
11:15	beloved	chosen, favorite, special
	wrought lewdness	done evil, nasty, dirty things
11:20	reins	thoughts, emotions, affections, self-control
	heart	mind, thoughts
11:23	visitation	punished, avenged, judgement
12:2	reins	thoughts, emotions, affections, self-control
12:4	how long shall the land mourn	not produce, be barren, remain empty
12:8	hated	despise, detest, reject, disgust
12:10	pastors	shepherds, caretakers
12:12	spoilers	destroyers, robbers
12:13	revenues	harvest, crops, in-kind money
12:14,15,17	pluck	uproot, tear up, take, remove
12:16	swear	promised, vow, give word
13:1+	Lord	Jehovah; God in relationship to mankind
13:2,4,6,7,11	girdle	waistband, waistcloth
13:7,9	marred, mar	destroyed, ruin, damage, disfigure
13:10	imagination	false pride, vanity, foolish ideas
13:18	principalities	dominion, chief place
13:21	woman in travail	labor, pain in child birth, struggled
13:22,26	discovered	uncovered, saw naked/nude

LAMENTATIONS OF JEREMIAH

13:23	accustomed	conditioned, used to, in the habit of
13:25	falsehood	dishonesty, lies, fraud, deceit, baloney
13:2	abominations	detestable, immoral, dirty, unclean, unholy
13:27	lewdness	evil, nasty, dirty things
14:1	dearth	drought, no rain
14:2	languish	weaken, depressed, sad, burn out
14:4	chapped	dried up, cracked, broken
14:5	hind	doe
14:6	dragons	serpents, i.e. Satan
	did fail	became weak, faltered, not successful
14:8	stranger	temporary resident, visitor
14:9	are called by	bear, endure, put up with
14:10	refrained	restrained, held back, stopped
14:13	assured	true, honest, promised
14:14	lies	falsehood, deception
	divination	witchcraft, insights, spiritualism
14:16	pour	give, share, open up
14:17	virgin	unwed, never had sex
	breach	breaking, open up
	grievous blow	hit hard, punched, beat up
14:19	loathed	despised, disgust, hated
14:21	covenant	agreement, promise, contract
14:22	vanities	worthless things, pointless
15:1	toward	with, alongside
15:5	bemoan	show grief, cry over, feel sorry/pit
15:6	repenting	grieving, guilt, feel sorry/ashamed
15:7	bereave	sorrow, be sad, mourn
15:8	spoiler	destroyer, criminal, vandal
15:9	languishes	rests, sits back, relaxes
15:10	woe	trouble, danger, warning
	usury	interest, money lender, loan shark
15:11	verily	surely, truly, honestly, yes, correct
15:12	steel	bronze, hard metal
15:13	spoil	plunder, booty, stolen goods
15:14	pass	cross, intersect, run into
15:15	visit	take notice of, pay attention
	persecutors	attackers, hasslers, bullies, trouble makers
15:17	mockers	irreverent, disrespectful, skeptics, unbelievers

LAMENTATIONS OF JEREMIAH

	indignation	anger, temper, destructive rage verging on madness
15:18	incurable	no cure, hopeless, terminal illness
15:20	fenced	fortified, protected
16:4	dung	refuse, waste, poop
16:6	shall men lament	cry, be sad about, agonize, mourn
16:9	mirth	laughter, joy, gladness, happiness
16:10,17	iniquity	sins, crime, evildoing, immorality
16:12	hearken	listen, pay attention, heed
16:16	holes	crevices, hiding places, pits
16:18	carcasses	corpses, dead bodies
	detestable	unclean, despised, hated, rejected, disgusting
17:2	altars	shrines, altar
17:3	the spoil	plunder, loot, stolen money/goods
17:4	discontinue	loose, stop, end
17:6	heath	bush, shrub
17:10	try the reins	know/search the heart, emotions
	give	repay, provide again
17:16	pastor	shepherd, caretaker, religious worker
17:17	hope	refuge, safety, confidence
17:22,24,27	sabbath	rest day, day without work
17:23	inclined their ear	listened, pay attention, thought about
	made their neck stiff	were rebellious, stubborn, hard-headed
17:24,27	hearken	listen, pay attention, heed
17:27	hallow	make holy, revere, respect
	quenched	put out, ended, finished
18:3	wrought	made, created, performed
18:4	marred	destroyed, ruined, broke
18:8,10	repent	grieve, regret, feel sorry/ashamed
18:11	frame	fashion, make
18:12	devices	plans, ideas, schemes, tricks
	imagination	false pride, vanity
18:13	virgin	untouched, never had sex
18:15	burned incense	worshiped, praised
18:16	perpetual	long, long time; forever
18:17	calamity	disaster, misfortune, accident, bad luck
18:18	devise	conspire together, plan
18:21	pour out their blood	bring death, kill, murder

LAMENTATIONS OF JEREMIAH

	bereaved	sorrowful, troubled, mournful
18:22	snare	trapped, caught, imprisoned, tripped up, lure
18:23	inclined their ear	considered, listened, paid attention, thought about
19:1	get	buy, purchase, obtain
	earthen bottle	clay jar/pot
	ancients	aged, old, experience, wise
19:4	estranged	alienated, an outcast, abandoned, left out
19:5	high place	shrines, altars to pagan gods
19:7	void	empty, worthless, nothing
	meat	food
19:8	hissing	object of scorn, laughing at, mock
	hiss	scoff, mock, laugh at
19:9	straitness	hardship, difficulties, shock
	straiten	oppress, rule over
19:13	burned incense	worshiped, made offerings
19:14;20:1	house	temple, place of worship, religious building
20:2	smote	attacked, strike, hit, punish
20:2,3	the stocks	prison, hands & head stuck through holes
20:3	Ma'gor-mis'sa-bib	i.e. terror on every side
20:5	strength	wealth, power, authority
	spoil	plunder, loot, stolen money/goods
20:7,8	deceived	tricked, fooled, scammed, fraud
	derision	insulted, disrespected, laughed at, mocked
20:10	familiars	trusted friends, close family
	halting	stumbling, mistakes, difficulty
	defaming	making fun of, mocking, laughing at, disrespecting
	enticed	tempted, teased, lured, drawn away
20:11	terrible	awe-inspiring, awesome, fearful, dangerous
20:12	reins	thoughts, emotions, affections, self-control
20:13	soul	inner person, emotion, life-force, being
20:16	repented	regretted, felt sorry, changed old ways
	besiege	surround, attack over and over, blockade
21:5	wrath	indignation, anger, fury
21:6	pestilence	disease, fungus, mildew, disaster, crop failure
21:9	falls	surrenders
	prey	plunder, steal

LAMENTATIONS OF JEREMIAH

21:12	spoiled	plunder, booty, stolen goods
22:3	Execute you judgment	do justice, punish, revenge, sentance
	spoiled	robbed, ripped off, jacked
	oppressor	tormentor, bully, slave master
22:5	swear	pledged, vowed, promised, gave an oath
	desolation	destruction, ruin, emptiness
22:7	choice cedars	best, finest of these strong, tall, straight-growing trees
22:9	covenant	agreement, promise, contract
22:10	sore	bitterly, bad
22:13	woe	trouble, danger, warning
22:14	vermilion	colored or dyed red, ruby, crimson, scarlet
	ceiled	roof, ceiling, the covering over their head
22:17	oppression	extortion, cruelty, unfair treatment
	covetousness	envious, greedy, wants what others have, lust
22:23	pangs	cramps, spasms, convulsions, struggles
22:24	signet	sealing ring, seal of authorization
22:35	fear	revered, respected, trembled, dread
22:28,30	seed	descendents, offspring, children
23:1	woe	trouble, pain, punish, problems
	pastors	shepherds, caretakers
	visit	allow, bring upon, give
23:3,13	repent	grieve, regret, feel sorry/ashamed
23:4	shepherds	caring leaders
23:8	seed	descendents, offspring, children
	house	family, clan, estate
23:9,10,12	house	temple, place of worship, religious building
23:10,13	adulterers	unfaithfulness, cheaters
	swearing	pledged, vowed, promised, gave an oath
23:14	meet	proper, correct, decent
23:15	wormwood	bitterness, dissatisfaction
	gallonl	poison
	profaneness	godlessness, irreverence, extreme disrespect
23:19	fear	revered, respected, trembled, dread
	repented	grieve, regret, feel sorry/ashamed
	grievously	bad, ugly, nasty
23:20	consider	understood, thought about

LAMENTATIONS OF JEREMIAH

23:22	stood in My counsel	understood my mind
23:27	cause	make, force
23:28	chaff	the shells/skin that were beaten/broken off wheat, barley grain and then thrown away
23:32	lightness	reckless, extravagance, frivolity
23,33,34,36,38	burden	message, report, prophecy
23:40	perpetual	long, long time; forever
24:2	naughty	bad, nasty, wicked
24:5	acknowledge	regard, recognize, admit
24:8	evil	bad, wicked, vile
24:10	consumed	vanish, waste away, dried up, spent, used up
25:3,7	hearkened	listen, pay attention, heed
25:9,17	hissing	object of scorn, laughing at, mock, despise
25:9	prophesied	foretell, make a prediction, speak for God
25:11	desolation	lonely wasteland, destruction, ruin
25:15	fury	violent anger, wrath
25:16	be moved	stagger, rocked, shock
25:23	utmost	remote, far away, distant, high
25:24	mingled	mixed, blended, joined
25:29	evil	misfortune, calamity
25:31	controversy	conflict, argument, debate, dispute
25:33	lamented	cried, was sad about, agonized, mourned
25:34	pleasant	valuable, important, choice
	wallow	roll around, slosh, splash
25:35,36	principal	master, chief, boss
25:36	howling	wailing, crying
	spoiled	destroyed, ruined
25:38	covert	hiding place, secret, den, fortified
	oppressor	cruel person, dictator
26:2	diminish	take away, omit, lessen in importance
26:3,4,5	hearken	listen, pay attention, heed
26:13	pronounced	declared, decreed, testified
27:5	meet	proper, correct, decent
27:8	yoke of the king	submit, surrender, serve
27:9	hearken	listen, pay attention, heed
	diviners	soothsayers, fortune tellers
	enchanters	magicians, spell casters
	sorcerers	wizards, witches

LAMENTATIONS OF JEREMIAH

27:11,12	bring	place, put
27:11	till	plow, dig long rows in the ground, cultivate
27:18	intercession	mediate, go-between, plead/pray on behalf of
27:20	nobles	rich, wealthy, royalty, blue-bloods
28:2	broken the yoke	ended, destroyed the power, rebelled
28:16	rebellion	uprising, mutiny, fight against, attempt an overthrow
29:1	residue	what is left, remnant, handful
29:2	eunuchs	court officials, men unable to have children
29:8	diviners	soothsayers, fortune tellers
	hearken	listen, pay attention, heed
29:11	expected	hopeful, planned
29:17	vile	spoiled, nasty, dirty
	evil	bad, wicked, cruel
29:18	a hissing	object of scorn, laughing at, mock, despise
	astonishment	shock, horror, disbelief, amazement
29:19	hearkened	listen, pay attention, heed
29:32	seed	posterity, descendents, children
30:5	fear	fright, dread, worry
30:6	does travail with child	about to give birth, in labor, able to perform
30:15	incurable	no cure, hopeless, terminal illness
30:16	yoke…off your neck	power over you, control
	devoured	ate up, consumed, destroyed
30:18	heap	ruins, piles, rubble, wreckage
30:23	whirlwind	tempest; strong, violent wind
	fury	violent anger, wrath
31:4	tabrets	tambourines
	satiate	satisfied, enough, content
31:8	coasts	territory, boundary, border i.e. distant lands
31:9	supplication	prayer, request, petition, plea
31:10	isles	distant lands, maritime nations, coastland
31:11	ransomed	redeemed, buy/win back something lost (like pawn shop), once held prisoner, purchased
31:14	satiate	satisfied, enough, content
	fatness	abundance, health, prosperity
31:15	weeping	crying, moaning, wailing
	incurable	no cure, hopeless, terminal illness
31:18	unaccustomed	not used to, strange, awkward

LAMENTATIONS OF JEREMIAH

31:19	smote upon	remorse, regret, was angry with self
31:20	bowels	emotions, feelings
31:21	waymarks	roadmarks, signs
	high heaps	guide posts, surveyor markings, boundries
	virgin	pure, unblemished, sexually inexperienced
31:22	daughter	offspring, children of/followers or devotees of something or someone
	compass	go about, surround, encamp, encircle
	backsliding	turn away, stop doing what is right, lose enthusiasm
31:24	husbandmen	cattle, sheep caretakers
31:25	satiated	satisfied, content, full
31:28	afflict	punish, torment, trouble, give difficulties to
31:31,32,33	covenant	agreement, promise, contract
31:31,37	seed	posterity, descendents, children
31:36	ordinances	rules, laws
32:8	prison	jail, a locked building to keep/punish people
32:9,11,12,14,16	evidence	dead
32:24	pestilence	disease, fungus, mildew, disaster, crop failure
32:29	offered incense	sacrificed, worshipped God
32:31	provocation	testing, challenge, confronted with a choice
32:33	hearkened	listen, pay attention, heed
32:34	abominations	detestable, immoral, dirty, unclean, unholy
32:39,40	fear	revered, respected, trembled, dread
32:41	assuredly	in truth, definitely, guarenteed
32:44	subscribe evidence	sign deeds, complete paperwork
33:4	mounts	ladders that were placed on the city walls, then the enemy climbed over and attacked/defeated
33:8	iniquity(s)	sins, crime, evildoing, immorality
33:9	fear	revered, respected, trembled, dread
33:11	bridegroom	the man that is getting married
33:12	desolate	destruction, ruin, emptiness
33:15	Branch	descendent, son, direct family blood line
33:17,18	want	lack, missing something, need
	kindle meat	burn grain, start a fire
33:20,21,25	covenant	agreement, promise, contract
33:2,26	seed	posterity, descendents, children
34:3	mouth to mouth	face to face, directly

LAMENTATIONS OF JEREMIAH

37:7	defensed	stronghold, protection, safety, guarded
34:8,10,13,15,18	covenant	agreement, promise, contract
34:11	subjection	under control, a servant, obedience
	handmaids	a female servant, personal assistant
34:14,17	hearkened	listen, pay attention, heed
34:14	been sold	sold as a slave; purchased, bought
34:18	transgressed	violated, broken rules
34:19	eunuchs	court officials, men unable to have children
34:22	desolation	destruction, ruin, emptiness
35:2,3	house	temple, place of worship, religious building
35:4	chamber	room, hall
35:11	fear	revered, respected, trembled, dread
35:13,14,15,16	hearken	listen, pay attention, heed
35:18	precepts	rules, laws, instructions
36:2+	roll	scroll, paper document
36:5	shut up	restricted, closed, confined
36:5, 8	house	temple, place of worship, religious building
36:10,12,20,21	chamber	room, hall
36:23	pen knife	small knife
36:25	intercession	mediate, go-between, plead/pray on behalf of
36:31	seed	posterity, descendents, children
	iniquity	sins, crime, evildoing, immorality
36:31, 37:2	hearkened	listen, pay attention, heed
37:11	fear	revered, respected, trembled, dread
37:12	separate himself	receive a portion there
37:13	ward	guard, patrol, security
	fall away	deserting, leave, abandon
37:14	fall not away	are not deserting, faithful, loyal
	hearkened	listen, pay attention, heed
38:4,20	beseech	beg, plead, ask, cry out
38:4	men of war	soldiers, warriors, troops
	welfare	good, care, concern
38:6	cords	ropes
	mire	muck, mud, slime
38:11,12	cast clouts	ragged cloths, worn out clothes
38:11,12	rotten	worn out, ruined, threadbare
38:12	under the cords	put the hand-made ropes under your armpits
38:17,18,21	go forth	surrender, give up

LAMENTATIONS OF JEREMIAH

38:19	fallen	captured, given up, surrendered
	mock	abuse, make fun of, harass
38:27	left off	stopped, quit, became silent
	perceived	overheard, recognize
39:4	men of war	soldiers, warriors, troops
39:5	gave judgment	do justice, punish, revenge, sentance
39:9	fell away	deserted, gave up, surrendered
39:11	charge	command, order, direct
40:4	forbear	never mind, give in, yield
40:5	reward	gift, bonus, present
	victuals	food, snacks, meals, grub, chow
40:15	remnant	leftover, remains, survivors
41:1	seed royal	royal family
41:3	men of war	soldiers, warriors, troops
41:8	forbore	restrained himself, held back
41:9	for fear	on account, because of
41:10	residue	what is left, remnant, handful
41:16	eunchs	court officials, men unable to have children
42:2	beseech	beg, plead, ask, cry out
42:10	repent	grieve, regret, feel sorry/ashamed
	abide	dwell, live, stay, make a home, settled
42:15,17,22	sojourn	temporarily stay, visit, live
42:15,17	wholly set your faces	completely, fully persuaded, mind is made up
42:18	execration	a swear word, a curse, remembered for evil
42:19	admonished	warned, threatened
42:20	dissembled	used deceit, lie, gossip
43:5	remnant	leftover, remains, survivors
43:9	hide	bury, cover
	kiln	oven that baked brinks to harden the mortar
44:2,6	desolation	in ruins, destroyed, complete wreck
44:3,8,15,17,18	burn incense	sacrifice, worship
44:4	abominable	detestable things, nasty, gross
	hate	despise, detest, reject, disgust
44:5	listened	listen, pay attention, heed
44:8	reproach	embarrassment, laughing stock
44:10	feared	revered, respected, trembled, dread
	statutes	law, rule, commands, decrees, directives
44:11	set My face	determined, decided, purposed to do

LAMENTATIONS OF JEREMIAH

44:12,14	sojourn	temporarily stay, visit, live
44:12	execration	a swear word, a curse, remembered for evil
44:16	hearken	listen, pay attention, heed
44:17,18,25	queen of heaven	female deity idol, a.k.a. Ashtarte
44:18	wanted	lacked, need, missing
44:22	abominations	detestable, immoral, dirty, unclean, unholy
44:25	vowed	promised, pledge, given oath
44:28	sojourn	reside, live, visit
45:3	woe	trouble, pain, punish, problems
46:1	against	concerning, regarding, about
	Gen'tiles	non-Jewish nations
46:3	order	prepare, plan, set in order
	buckler	small shield
46:4,19	furbish	polish, shine, clean
46:4	brigandines	armor
46:5	beaten down	defeated, tired, discouraged
	fear	revered, respected, trembled, dread
	apace	at a rapid pace, quickly, gone ahead
	dismayed	confused, puzzled, shaken up
46:10	satiate	satisfied, content, filled up
46:21	calamity	disaster, misfortune, accident, bad luck
46:23	innumerable	many, a lot, countless, too many to count
46:27	seed	posterity, descendents, children
47:2	howl	cry out, moan, wail
47:3	rumbling	sound; loud noise, roar, hum
	feebleness	weak, without strength, powerless
47:4	spoil	destroy, ruin, wreck
	Caph'tor	a.k.a. Crete
48:1,46	woe	trouble, pain, punish, problems
48:2	cut down	silenced, stopped, defeated
48:6	heath	shrub, small bush
48:8,18,32	spoiler	destroy, ruin, wreck
48:9	desolate	destroyed, ruined, empty
48:11	less	dregs, strong wine
48:19	espy	watch, observe closely
48:25	horn	symbol of strength, power, authority
48:27	since	each time
	skipped	jumped, lept

LAMENTATIONS OF JEREMIAH

48:29	haughtiness	proud, arrogant, boastful, stuck-up
48:35	high places	shrines, altars to pagan gods
	burns incense	sacrifices, worship
48:38	lamentation	mourning, crying, sad
48:43	fear	revered, respected, trembled, dread
	snare	trapped, caught, imprisoned, tripped up, lure
48:43,44	pit	hell, hades, torment, punishment, death to body
48:45	tumultuous	commotion, excitement, ready for battle/riot
48:47	captivity	bondage, slavery, prisoner
49:1	inherit	take possession of, control, new ownership
49:2	desolate heap	ruins, piles, rubble, wreckage
49:5	fear	revered, respected, trembled, dread
49:10	seed	posterity, descendents, children
	spoiled	destroyed, vandalized, wrecked, sacked
49:16	terribleness	horror, aweful, frightening
49:17	hiss	object of scorn, laughing at, mock, despise
49:23	faint hearted	disheartened, broken, despair
	sorrow	anxiety, sadness, discouragement
49:24	waxed	grown, increase, become
	fear	dread, terror, panic
	travail	childbirth, pain, labor
49:28,32	spoil	plunder, booty, stolen goods
49:29	fear	dread, terror, panic
49:30	taken council	devised a plan, plot
49:32	calamity	disaster, misfortune, accident, bad luck
49:35	bow	power, strength, ability to fight
49:37	dismayed	shattered, broken, confused, powerless
49:38	set	lift, place, put in order
50:2	set	lift, place, put in order
50:3	desolate	destroyed, ruined, empty
50:5	covenant	agreement, promise, contract
50:6	resting place	dwelling place, home
50:10	spoil	plunder, booty, stolen goods
50:12	sore	greatly, badly, aweful
	hindermost	rear, back of
50:13	hiss	object of scorn, laughing at, mock, despise
50:16	for fear	because
	sower	a person that spreads/scatters plant

		& vegetable seeds
	sickle	sharp, cutting farm instrument used for harvest
50:20	reserve	leave behind, keep, account for
50:21	waste	lay waste, destroy, ruin, sack
50:23	asunder	cut/tear in two, half
50:24	snare	trapped, caught, imprisoned, tripped up, lure
50:26	utmost	farthest, borders
50:27	woe	trouble, pain, punish, problems
50:36	dote	become fools, worry, fret
50:38	graven images	idols & carvings, statues of pagan gods
	upon	over
50:42	array	military formation, display, show of strength
50:43	waxed	grew, increased, become
50:44	swelling	flooding, surrounding
	appoint	decide, choose, elect
51:2	fanners	counter-revolution forces, instigators, agitators
	fan	winnow, blow, increase, trouble
51:3	brigandine	armor
51:8	howl	lament, weep, scream
51:11	bright	sharp, polished, cleaned up
	device	purpose, plan, plot
51:12,27	standard	nations banner, flag, family crest, gang colors
51:12	ambushes	defenses, secret tactics, covert operations
51:13	covetousness	unjust gain, greedy
51:14,27	caterpillars	young locust (early age)
51:17	brutish	stupid, dense, like an animal
51:18	errors	delusions, mistakes, poor judgement
	visitation	punished, avenged, judgement
51:19	rod	descendents, heir, offspring, direct line
51:25	mountain	power, strength, stability
	burnt	burning, ruined, destroyed (a volcano?)
51:26,29	desolate	destruction, ruin, emptiness, waste place
51:29	land shall tremble and sorrow	the people in the land will be afraid and sad
51:31	post	runner, messenger, herald
	at one end	from one end to end
51:32	stopped	seized, blocked, cut off
51:36	sea	ocean, large body of water

LAMENTATIONS OF JEREMIAH

51:37	heaps	ruins, piles, rubble, wreckage
	dragons	snakes, monsters, dinosaurs, i.e. Satan
	astonishment	object of horror, terror
	hissing	object of scorn, laughing at, mock, despise
51:42	sea	flooded Euphrates
51:46	fear	revered, respected, trembled, dread
51:47,52	graven images	idols & carvings, statues of pagan gods
51:48,53,56	spoilers	destroyers, vandals, criminals
51:51	sanctuaries	holy place, sacred part of temple
	house	temple, place of worship, religious building
	confounded	confused, put to shame, rattled
	heard reproach	they are mocked, laughed at, ridiculed
51:55	spoiled	destroyed, ruined, wrecked
51:56	recompences	pay back, repayment, reward or punish
51:58	folk	nations for, people, natives
51:62	desolate	uninhabited, empty, barren
52:4	pitched	camped, set up, established
52:6	sore	severe, bad, aweful
52:7	up	into, apart
52:13	house	temple, place of worship, religious building
52:15	residue	what is left, remnant, handful
	fell away	died, were killed, left, departed
52:16	vine dresser	someone that took care of agriculture (plants, trees, vines, etc.), gardening, landscaping
52:17	brazen sea	in the holy temple, there was a large wash basin/sink made of brass, the brazen "sea" was for the priest to wash in before they performed their jobs
52:18	caldrons	cooking pots, large bowls
52:19	fire pans	used for roasting, grilling, baking in an oven
52:20	without	beyond, past
52:21	did compass	go about, surround, encamp, encircle
	fillet	joint, attachment, hook
52:22	chapiter	capital
52:23	pomegranates	large fruit having many seeds with juicy red pulp in a tough brownish-red skin
52:25	eunuch	court officials, men unable to have children
52:27	smote	attacked, strike, hit, punish

LAMENTATIONS OF JEREMIAH

52:31	lifted up the head of	showed favor to, helped, befriended
52:34	diet	food allowance, meat
52:4	pitched	camped, set up, established
52:6	sore	severe, bad, aweful
52:7	up	into, apart
52:13	house	temple, place of worship, religious building
52:15	residue	what is left, remnant, handful
	fell away	died, were killed, left, departed
52:16	vine dresser	someone that took care of agriculture (plants, trees, vines, etc.), gardening, landscaping
52:17	brazen sea	in the holy temple, there was a large wash basin/sink made of brass, the brazen "sea" was for the priest to wash in before they performed their jobs
52:18	caldrons	cooking pots, large bowls
52:19	fire pans	used for roasting, grilling, baking in an oven
52:20	without	beyond, past
52:21	did compass	go about, surround, encamp, encircle
	fillet	joint, attachment, hook
52:22	chapiter	capital
52:23	pomegranates	large fruit having many seeds with juicy red pulp in a tough brownish-red skin
52:25	eunuch	court officials, men unable to have children
52:27	smote	attacked, strike, hit, punish
52:31	lifted up the head of	showed favor to, helped, befriended
52:34	diet	food allowance, meat

LAMENTATIONS OF JEREMIAH

1:1	solitary	empty, alone, desolate
	tributary	a gang or body of forced laborers
1:2	sore	bitterly, badly, sadly
1:3	straights	narrow, confined places or passages
1:4,6	Zi'on	Israel
	is in bitterness	suffers bitterly, mourns, depressed
1:6	harts	bucks, male deer
1:7	sabbaths	rest days, day without work
1:9	shirts	clothes, garments
1:10	heathen	nations, non-Jew, pagan
1:11	vile	worthless, disgraceful
1:15	trodden under foot	rejected, imposed on, humiliated
1:15	Lord has trodden the virgin, the daughter of Ju'dah, as in a winepress.	smashed, squeezed, punished
1:16	comforter	support, Spirit of God
1:17	Zi'on	the elect of Israel
1:20	bowels	feelings, emotions
1:21	called	proclaimed, chosen
2:1,6+	Lord	Jehovah; God in relationship to mankind
2:1,10	daughter of Zi'on	offspring of a nation, citizens
2:2,5	swallowed up	destroyed, wasted, consumed
2:2	habitations	dwellings, houses
	daughter of Ju'dah	offspring of a nation, citizens
2:3	horn	symbol of strength, power, authority
2:6	tabernacle	booth, pavilion
2:7	cast off	rejected, hated, forsaken
	given up	delivered, surrendered, sacrifice
2:8	purposed	determined, decided, chosen
2:9	Gen'tiles	nations, heathen, non-Jew
2:11,12	swoon, swooned	faint, dizzy, confused, disoriented
2:12	their soul was poured out	expired, broken, cried out
2:15,16	hiss	whistle, mock, laugh at
2:16	gnash	grind, sneer, be angry at

LAMENTATIONS OF JEREMIAH

	swallowed	destroyed, wrecked
2:18	wall of the daughter	strength, defense
2:20	fruit	offspring, children, results
2:22	swaddled	lovingly cared for, wrapped
3:5	compassed	go about, surround, encamp, encircle
3:5,19	gallonl	bitterness, sorrow
3:11	made me desolate	left me without help, helpless, ruined
3:13	reins	thoughts, emotions, affections, self-control
3:15,19	wormwood	bitterness, poison, sorrow
3:22+	Lord	Jehovah; God in relationship to mankind
3:25	soul	inner person, emotion, life-force, being
3:29	puts his mouth in the dust	speaks humbly, quiet, broken
3:35,38	Most High	Almighty God, Supreme Deity
3:39	wherefore	why, for what reason
3:40	search	examine, ponder, consider
3:45	offscouring	scum, filth, lowlife
3:46	fear	panic, dread, fright
	snare	pitfall, trapped, imprisoned, tripped up, lure
3:52	sore	badly, awful, terrible
3:59	judge You my cause	decide, determine
3:63	music	mocking song, joke, ridicule
3:64	recompence	payment, reward, pay back
4:3	sea monsters	large mammals (whales?)
	give suck	nurse, breast feed
4:4	sucking	nursing, breast feeding
4:5	dunghills	piles of refuse or manure
4:6	stayed on	turned toward, held, kept
4:7	ruddy	red, healthy
4:8	visage	appearance, form, looks
4:10	sodden	boiled, cooked
	meat	food
4:15	unclean	unfit, dirty, impure
	sojourn	dwell, live, visit
4:21	yourself naked	open to, exposed, vulnerable
4:22	visit	punished, avenged, judgement
	iniquity	depravity, sins, crime, evildoing, immorality
	discover	expose, make plain, understand

LAMENTATIONS OF JEREMIAH

5:1+	Lord	Jehovah; God in relationship to mankind
5:2	aliens	foreigners, visiters
5:5	our necks *are* under	suffer, in bondage, captivity
5:7	are not	has died, dead, no more
5:10	terrible	fever, heat up, burning up
5:20	wherefore	why, for what reason

EZEKIEL

1:1	captives	exiles, prisoners of war
1:4	infolding itself	looping, clasping, twisting

** Read this explanation for verses 4-21

Ezekiel had a vision of four living creatures, each of which had four faces. Chapter 1 verse 10 reads: 'Their faces looked like this: Each of the four had the face of a man, and on the right side each had the face of a lion, and on the left the face of an ox; each also had the face of an eagle.' John had a similar vision in Revelation 4: 6,7: 'In the centre, around the throne, were four living creatures, and they were covered with eyes, in front and behind. The first living creature was like a lion, the second was like an ox, the third had a face like a man, the fourth was like a flying eagle.' What does all this mean?

God chose four men to write about the life of Jesus, corresponding to these four creatures. Matthew sees Jesus as the lion or king. (The lion is associated with the royal tribe of Judah to which King David and his descendants belonged.) Accordingly Matthew begins his gospel with the words 'A record of the genealogy of Jesus Christ the son of David, the son of Abraham', and continues by tracing his lineage all the way down. What could be more fitting for a king?

Mark sees Jesus as the exact opposite, an ox or servant, a sacrificial animal. There is no genealogy, nor even any kind of birth story. It wouldn't be appropriate for a servant. Neither is there much teaching recorded. Mark is all about action. Jesus is serving his father. Appropriately his gospel is the shortest.

Luke sees Jesus as the man. He gives us all the details about his birth, and then traces his ancestry right the way back up to Adam (whose name means man). It is Luke who gives us the more personal details of Jesus' life. Only he tells us how Jesus was thrown out of his own city of Nazareth and sweated drops of blood in Gethsemane.

John sees Jesus as the flying eagle that soars up in the heavenly realms. This represents the prophetic aspect of God. A prophet sees what man does not, and understands the true interpretation of the Word. In John the birth story is very different from what Matthew and Luke give. Simply, 'In the beginning was the

Word'. We are seeing not man, but God. John is the gospel of ***'I am'.*** I am the bread of life, the light of the world, the door, the good shepherd, the resurrection, and the life, the way, the truth and the life, the true vine. Who but God can say such things?

These four living creatures moved together in all directions in perfect unison. The secret of this was, 'Wherever the spirit would go, they would go' (v20). They were all perfectly led by the Spirit of God.

The Holy Spirit in us gives us kingly power and authority. The Holy Spirit gives us the humble attitude of servants, and the power to serve. By the Holy Spirit we will be fully integrated humans and also manifest the nature of God. And by the Holy Spirit giving the same inward witness to each one of us we will move in perfect unity with each other member of the body of Christ.

1:5	four living creatures	powerful beings, higher and greater than even the archangels
	Likeness of man	having the features of a human body (standing upright with legs, torso, arms)
1:6	four faces four wings	like a cube or square, each side a different face
1:7	burnished	polished, shined up (reddish-orange)
1:8	hands of a man on their four sides	they had arms and human hands
	they four had their faces their wings	simply, they had four faces and four wings
1:9	everyone straight forward	as each "face" represented a certain "nature" or personality (eagle, lion, etc.), whenever that living creature "acted" like an eagle it went in that direction – not acting as two creatures at the same time.
1:11	wings …stretched upward joined…another two covered their bodies	a double set of wings; one with wing tips up and the other set crossed or folded in front of their bodies
1:12	spirit was to go they went turned not when they went	these creatures are visible representatives of four key personalities of God; they serve and obey God or the "spirit", which is God's life force or power. i.e I am one man, yet I am

EZEKIEL

		a father, a husband, a boss etc. – I act or "go" a certain direction depending upon which character (face) I want or need to be.
1:13	likeness… living creatures	they looked like
	Coals of fire	charcoal, glowing red-hot, sparking
	Appearance of lamps	glowing, radiating light
1:14	creatures ran… returned	back and forth, to and fro
	Flash of lightning	very quickly, flash
1:15-	one wheel upon the earth by The living creatures	some say that the wheels were symbols of swift travel and a vehicle that needed to be driven and guided – not self-propelled; others say that the wheels were literal and were connected together like a gyroscope, each wheel interconnected and finely balanced
1:16-21	the spirit was to go there was their Spirit to go the wheels were lifted up opposite of them the spirit of the living creature was in the wheels	(see above explanations in verse 12 & 15)

** Some say that these living creatures were either the "angels" that guarded the tree of life in the midst of the garden of Eden or were at least patterned after the ones in heaven. It is also believed that the four living creatures are depicted in the symbols of the zodiac and positioned at 12, 9, 6 and 3 o'clock; the lion being Leo, the ox as Taurus, the man as Aquarius and the eagle is Aquila flying above Ophiucus (the serpant holder) that is above Scorpio.
Psalms 19:1 "the heaven's declare the glory of God." Romans 1:20 "For the invisible things of him since the creation of the world are clearly seen, being perceived through the things that are made."

1:22	likeness of the	a roof, ceiling above their heads that looked

	firmament upon the heads of the living creature the color of the terrible crystal, stretched forth over their heads above	like frost or frozen water that sparkles
1:23	terrible wings straight every one had two which covered on this side which covered Side, their bodies	if you were to look at these creatures, they would be facing eachother, two pairs – say the eagle facing the ox and the lion facing the man. Their wings would be semi-stretched out slightly forward of their bodies, so one pair would cover the front and the other pair the back, each overlapping or interlocked with the creature next to itself.
1:24	noise of great Waters	waterfall, waves crashes on the beach
	As the voice of the Almighty host	a large crowd in a sports arena, cheering/screaming
	When they stood, They let down Their wings	
1:26	firmament likeness of the throne appearance of a man above upon it	if you could imagine looking up throught the floor of a frozen pond, or a glass floor – the creatures were below the floor and above the floor was a throne or large chair where God was sitting above everything
1:27	appearance of fire	amber today is different than described here - this amber was a brass-like metal, this passage describes the color of metal that has been heated in fire and is starting to cool
	Appearance of His Loins even upward His loins even Downward	loins, means the waist and hips
1:28	appearance of the Bow	the combination of the fire and the water/crystal created a rainbow effect that

EZEKIEL

	is in the cloud on the day of rain likeness of the color of the Lord	circled around the throne
2:2	Spirit	God's spirit/force, Holy Spirit
2:3	He	Holy Spirit
	Son of man	prophet
	Rebellious nation That has rebelled Against Me	Israel
2:4	impudent	obstinate, arrogant, rebellious
	Stiffhearted	stubborn, proud, resistent
2:5	they	Israel, unbelieving
	Forbear	stop, let go, not hear
	Prophet among Them	Ezekiel
2:6,8	son of a man	prophet
2:6	briers	a thorny bush or shrub
	dismayed	confused, puzzled, shaken up
2:7	forbear	stop, let go, not hear
2:9	sent	extended, called for
	Roll	scroll, paper document
	Book	scroll, paper document
2:10	inside and outside	on both sides
	Woe	trouble, pain, punish, problems
3:1	he	God
3:1,4,5	house	leadership, authority
3:1,2,3	roll	scroll, paper document
3:5,6	strange	foreign, other nationalities/dialects
3:6,7	hearkened	listen, pay attention, heed
3:8	strong against	harsh, rough, hard as
3:9	adamant	a sharp stone, hard rock
	rebellious	stubborn, disobedient, disagreeable
3:10	son of man	prophet
3:12	rushing	wind blowing, breeze
3:13	over against	opposite to, against
3:14	heat	rage, anger, fury
	strong upon me	forceful, persuasive, in control

EZEKIEL

3:17	watchman	caretaker, guard, observer, sentry
	House	family, nation, kingdom
3:18,20	iniquity	sins, crime, evildoing, immorality
3:20	stumbling block	means or occasion of stumbling
3:25	bands	ropes, restraints i.e. handcuffs
3:26	dumb	mute, voiceless
4:3	moreover	also, additionally
4:4,5,6	iniquity	sins, crime, evildoing, immorality
4:7	set	turn, direct attention
4:8	lay bands	put ropes on, tie up, restrain
4:9	millet	a small grain used for breads, usually mixed
	lentils	a small bean-like food, boiled in soups/stews
	fitches	commonly known as spelt, a type a grain used in breads
4:14	abominable flesh	forbidden meat, religiously prohibited
4:16	by weight	counted, measured out to them
	care	anxiety, concern
	astonishment	terror, shock, horror
4:17	want	lack, miss, need
	astonished	terror, shock, horror
	consume	vanish, waste away, dried up, spent, used up
	iniquity	sins, crime, evildoing, immorality
5:2	knife	small bladed sword
	smite	hurt, punch, hit, strike
5:6,7	statutes	law, rule, commands, decrees, directives
5:7	multiplied more	increased trouble, made worse
5:9,11	abominations	detestable, immoral, dirty, unclean, unholy
5:10,12	scatter	disperse, send
5:11	sanctuary	temple, religious building, holy site
	detestable things	idols, hated, despised, unlawful
5:12	pestilence	disease, fungus, mildew, disaster, crop failure
5:13	fury	anger, violence, actions
	zeal	enthusiasm, excitement, passion
5:15	reproach	shame, disgrace, dishonor
6:5	carcasses	dead bodies
6:6	high places	shrines, altars to pagan gods
	Images	idols, statues of pagan gods

EZEKIEL

	Desolate	destroyed, ruined, empty
6:9	whorish	adulterous, unfaithful, cheating
6:9,11	abominations	detestable, immoral, dirty, unclean, unholy
7:3,4,8,9	recompense	repay, reward, revenge
	Abominations	detestable, immoral, dirty, unclean, unholy
7:7	mountains	leaders, countries
7:9	smites	strike, hit, destroys
7:10	budded	come alive, grown, starting to be seen
7:13,16,19	iniquity	sins, crime, evildoing, immorality, depravity
7:15	without	outside, against, attacking
7:19	bowels	emotions, inner feelings, stomachs
	stumbling block	something to trip over (a rock, a tree stump) be offended by
7:20	images of their abominations	detestable, immoral, dirty, unclean, unholy
	set it far from	made it abhorrent
7:21	strangers for a prey	foreigners for plunder, spoils, loot
7:24	holy places	sacred places, holy sites
7:26,11	ancients	aged, old, experience, wise
8:5	entry	entrance, front door, lobby
8:6	sanctuary	temple, religious building, holy site
8:6,8,10,15,17	abominations	detestable, immoral, dirty, unclean, unholy
8:10	Portrayed	were carved
9:2	inkhorn	a jar or bowl that a feather or metal tool was dipped in to write on skins, parchment etc.
	abominations	detestable, immoral, dirty, unclean, unholy
9:5	smite	hurt, punch, hit, strike
9:6	utterly	completely, fully, all
	ancient men	aged, old, experience, wise
9:8	residue	the whole remnant
9:9	iniquity	sins, crime, evildoing, immorality
	perverseness	sick, warped, twisted, injustice
9:11	inkhorn	a jar or bowl that a feather or metal tool was dipped in to write on skins, parchment etc.
10:5	Almighty God	El Shaddai
10:7	cherubims	angels, heavenly beings, guardians
10:10	wheel	(see notes form Chapter 1 verse 15 above)
11:2	devise	plan, make

EZEKIEL

11:3,7	caldron	a big cooking pot or kettle
11:8	feared	avoided, were afraid, worried
11:10,11	border	country, boundaries
11:12,20	statutes	law, rule, commands, decrees, directives
11:21	abominations	detestable, immoral, dirty, unclean, unholy
11:24	went up from me	disappeared, vanished, went away
12:3,4,7	stuff for removing	goods/belongings for exile, banishment
12:10	burden	message, prophecy, warning
12:13	snare	trapped, caught, imprisoned, tripped up, lure
12:14	bands	troops, military units
12:15	disperse	scattered, spread out, move all over the place
12:18	quaking	trembling, shaking, fear, terror
12:18,19	carefulness	anxiety, worry, concern
12:19	astonishment	horror, terror, shock
12:23	effect	fulfillment
12:24	divination	prediction, prophecy
12:25,28	prolonged	extended, dragged out, lingering
13:4	in the desert	among ruins, wilderness
13:5	gaps	breaks, holes, ruins
	made up the hedge	did you build up the wall
13:6,9	vanity	fraud, foolish, boastful, arrogant, proud
13:6,7	divination	predictions, foretell
13:7	albeit	although, yet, but
13:10,11,12	daubed	cover, plastered
14,15	untempered mortar	whitewash, dry-wall covering
13:13	rend	tear, ripped, shred, pull apart, open
13:14,18,19,20	souls	lives, persons
13:17	daughters	offspring, children of/followers or devotees of something or someone
13:18	souls	lives, persons
	kerchiefs	a covering for the head of a woman; scarf/shawl; women caught for immorality (adultery, prostitutes) had their hair cut off and would wear a scarf to hide their shame
14:3	idols in their heart	hidden evil, lust, greed
14:3,4,7,10	iniquity	sins, crime, evildoing, immorality
14:6	abominations	detestable, immoral, dirty, unclean, unholy

EZEKIEL

14:7	sojourns	dwells temporarily, visitor
14:11	house	family, people, tribe
	polluted	defiled, dirty, corrupt
14:15	noisome	bad, evil, vicious
14:21	sore	severe, harsh, cruel
15:4,5	meet	proper, correct, decent
16:3	nativity	place of birth, hometown
16:4	salted	rubbed with salt, cleaned
	waddle	wrapped in cloths, bundle
	supple	moisten, wash, clean
16:5	loathing	abhorrence, hate, detest
16:6	polluted	dirtied, messy, filthy, corrupted
16:7	waxen	grown, increased, became
	excellent ornaments	the most beautiful of jewels
16:8	spread my skirt over	took you as my wife, married, cared for
16:8+	covenant	agreement, contract, promise
16:9	badger's skin	leather
16:12	jewel on your forehead	headband/frontlet made of jewels
16:13	raiment	clothing, garments
	broidered	hand stitched, like knitting or crochet
16:14,15	renown	fame, well known, notorious
16:14	comeliness	beauty, attractiveness, good looks
16:16+	high places	shrines, altars to pagan gods
16:19	meat	food
16:20	to be devoured	food sacrificed to idols
16:20+	whoredoms	faithlessness, dishonesty, wickedness
16:22+	abominations	detestable things/ idols, nasty, gross
16:24,39;17:22	eminent	important, exalted, a place built on a hill or in an attractive location to worship
16:25	abhorred	despised, hate, resent
16:27,37	hate	abhor, despise, loathe, detest
	daughters	offspring, children of/followers or devotees of something or someone
	lewd	nasty, dirty, sexy, immoral
16:28	whore	prostitute, a provider of sex for money
	insatiable	unsatisfied, can't get enough
16:30	imperious	brazen, sarcastic, having an attitude

EZEKIEL

16:36	discovered idols of your	uncovered, see clearly, expose
16:38	wedlock	married, united
16:43	fretted	enraged, obsessed, worried, troubled
	recompense	repay, punish, reward
16:53,57	daughters	offspring, children of/followers or devotees of something or someone
16:55	estate	status, condition, position
16:58	lewdness	nasty, dirty, sexy, immoral
16:60	everlasting covenant	never ending, perpetual
17:2,3,9,16	house	people, nation, leadership
17:3	divers	many, various, different
17:4	traffic	traders, salesmen
17:6	sprigs	shoots, twigs, branches
	spreading vine	fast growing, strong, extensive coverage
17:8	soil	field, dirt, ground
17:13,14,15	seed	offspring, children, heirs
18,19	covenant	agreement, promise, contract
17:18	had given his hand	pledged his allegiance, gave his word
17:20	snare	trapped, caught, imprisoned, tripped up, lure
17:21	bands	troops, military units, gangs
17:22	eminent	important, exalted, a place built on a hill or in an attractive location to worship
18:4,20,27	soul	inner person, emotion, life-force, being, life
18:6	menstrusous woman	woman during her period, menstrual cycle
18:7,16	spoiled	robbed, ruined, wrecked
18:8,17	usury	interest, loan
18:8+	iniquity	sins, crime, evildoing, immorality
18:9,17,19,21	statutes	law, rule, commands, decrees, directives
18:10	shedder	spill, shed blood; murderer, killer
18:12,13,24	has given forth upon usury	has lent on interest, loan shark, payday loans
18:15	upon the mountains	at the mountain shrines, heathen altars
18:25	equal	just, fair, right, balanced
	house	family, nation, leadership
19:1	prince	leaders, chiefs, rulers, influential men
19:2,3,5	whelps	cubs, offspring, immature
19:4	nations	tribes, groups

EZEKIEL

19:10	mother	family, heritage
19:11	scepters	a symbol of the king's power, authority; it looked like a club or band-leaders baton
19:14	lamentation	crying, mourning, agonizing, distress
20:1,3	inquire	ask for guidance, seek information
20:4,7,30	abominations	detestable things/ idols, nasty, gross
20:5+	lifted up My hand	took a vow, swore an oath, promised
20:5	seed	offspring, children, heirs
20:6	espied	selected, chose, picked
20:8,39	hearken	listen, pay attention, heed
20:9,+	polluted	profaned, dirtied, corrupted
20:9,41	heathen	nations, non-Jew, pagan
20:10+	statutes	law, rule, commands, decrees, directives
20:12+	sabbaths	rest days, days without working
20:13,39	house	people, leadership, tribe
20:14,22	wrought	acted, performed, have done
20:27	have blasphemed	reviled, spoken evil, profaned
20:29	high place	shrines, altars to pagan gods
20:30	whoredom	immorality, impurity, unfaithfulness
20:38	sojourn	travels, visit, stay away from home
20:40	first-fruits	choice, best, finest
	oblations	gifts, offerings, sacrifices
20:41	sanctified	holy, clean, pure
	parables	story, myth, riddle/puzzle
20:43	loathe	despise, hate
20:44	wrought	dealt, accomplished, have done
20:46; 21:2	drop…word	speak, prophesy, deliver & leave
20:47	quenched	put out, stopped, ended
20:49	parables	story, myth, riddle/puzzle
21:5	sheath	holder, scabbard; a holster for a knife or sword
21:6	the breaking of your loins	broken heart, grief
	bitterness sigh	bitter grief, sad
21:9,10,11	abominations	detestable things/acts, nasty, gross
21:10	sore	great, bad, awful
21:10,13	contempt	despised, rejects, scorn
21:12	shall be upon	against, oppose

EZEKIEL

21:14	privy	private, secret, hidden, personal
21:15	wrapped	prepared, ready for
	defensed	stronghold, protection, safety, guarded
21:21	looked in the liver	fortune tellers would cut open an animal and look at its internal organs (guts) for "signs" based on size, color, shape, markings etc.
21:26	diadem	a crown - a symbol of power, success, control
21:28	furbished	polished, shined, prepared
	glittering	shine, sparkle
21:30	nativity	birthplace, hometown
21:31	brutish	beast-like, brutal, stupid
	indignation	anger, temper, destructive rage verging on madness
22:2	bloody	murderous, sinful
22:2,11	abominations	detestable things/acts, nasty, gross
22:4	mocking	make fun of, laughing stock
22:5,7	much vexed	terrify, trouble, plague, confuse, dismayed
22:7	oppression	extortion, cruel/mean
22:8	profaned	violated, polluted, disrespected
22:8,26	sabbaths	rest days, days without working
22:9,11	lewdness	immoral, nasty, slutty behavior
22:10	discovered	uncovered, made plain, revealed
22:12	usury	high rate of interest, loan shark
	greedily	unjustly, unfair
22:15	consume	put an end to, stop
	disperse	scattered, spread out, move all over the place
22:18	house	people, leadership
22:25,27	souls	persons, lives
22:26	profane	violate, pollute, disrespect
22:27	ravening	tearing, ripping, vicious
22:28	daubed	smeared, coated, plastered
	untempered mortar	whitewash
23:3+	whoredoms	harlotries, unfaithfulness, disloyal
23:5	much vexed	angry, annoyed, harassed, frustrated
23:5,9	doted	lusted after, followed, desired strongly
23:10,29	discovered	uncovered, made plain, found out

EZEKIEL

23:10	famous	a byword, celebrity, notorious
23:11	inordinate	colored or dyed red, ruby, crimson, scarlet
23:22	alienated	estranged, an outcast, abandoned, left out
23:15	girdles	belts, waistband
23:16,19	doted upon	lusted after, followed, desired strongly
23:17,18	alienated from	estranged, an outcast, abandoned, left out
23:20	paramours	lovers, sexual partners
23:21+	lewdness	nasty, dirty, sexy, immoral
23:22	alienated	estranged, an outcast, abandoned, left out
23:25	residue	survivors, remnant
23:29	hatefully	despitefully, cruel, vicious
23:34	shards (sherds)	broken pieces of plates/dishes
23:36	abominations	detestable things/ acts, nasty, gross
23:37	adultery	unfaithfulness, immorality
23:38	sabbaths	rest days, days without working
23:39	profane	violate, pollute, disrespect
23:42	common sort	multitude of mankind, different ethnic groups
	Sabeans	drunks; a tribe known for their excessive drinking
23:43	adulteries	unfaithfulness, immoral
23:44	lewd	nasty, dirty, sexy, immoral
23:45	adulteresses	unfaithful, cheating, disloyal
23:46	spoiled	plundered, robbed, jacked
23:47	daughters	offspring, children of/followers or devotees of something or someone
23:49	recompense	repay, punish, revenge
24:5	seethe	boil, heat up, cook
24:6	scum	leftovers, dregs, crumbs, filth, trash
24:9	woe	trouble, pain, punish, problems
24:10,11	consume	vanish, waste away, dried up, spent, used up
24:13	lewdness	nasty, dirty, sexy, immoral
24:14	repent	grieve, change of heart, apologize
24:16	desire	delight, long for, lust
24:17	forbear to cry	stop, let go, not hear, groan silently
24:17, 23	tire	turban, headdress
24:21	house	people, nation, tribe
	Soul	inner person, emotion, life-force, being, life
	dainties	delights, rich/exotic foods

EZEKIEL

24:23	iniquity	sins, crime, evildoing, immorality
25:3,8	house	people, leadership, tribe
25:3	desolate	destroyed, ruined, empty
25:5	couching	resting, bending down, squat
25:6	despise	scorn, mock, ridicule, hate
25:7	spoil	plunder, loot, stolen goods
25:7,8	heathen	nations, non-Jew, pagan
25:15	spiteful	malicious, hateful, cruel
	hatred	enmity, despises
26:2	replenished	filled, supplied, strengthened
26:5	spoil	plunder, loot, stolen goods
26:8	buckler	shield, military armor
26:11	garrisons	military units, troupes, ranks of soldiers
26:14	shall be a place	thoroughly destroyed, ruined and unable to be saved
26:15,18	isles	coastlands
26:17	seafaring	sailors, traveling with boats or ships
	haunt it	supposedly ghosts/demons that live there after its destruction (real or imagined)
26:20	low parts	supposedly inside the earth
	down the pit	hell, hades, torment, punishment, death to body
26:21	you shall be no more	dead, gone
	yet shall you never be found again	no recovery, destroyed, no rememberance
27:6,7,15,35	isles	coastlands
27:6	Chit'tim	distant land
27:9,27	caulkers	workers that used a substance, as a puttylike sealant, glue or tar, used to stop up cracks/leaks in a boat.
27:10	comeliness	beauty, attractiveness, good looks
27:16	the wares	your goods, belongings, possessions
27:19	occupied in your fairs	bartered your wares, sales, business
	market	merchandise, goods, stuff
27:20	precious cloths	saddle blanket, clothes, pad
27:21,22,27	occupied	traded, dealt, business
27:26	rowers	oarsmen, crew on a boat/ship
27:28	suburbs	pasture lands
27:35	sore	horribly, bad, awful

EZEKIEL

28:2,5	lifted up	full of pride, arrogant
28:5	traffic	trade, business, commerce
28:7	terrible	ruthless, awful, evil, cruel
28:12	seal up the sum	the best, greatest, "all that"
28:13	tabrets	tambourines
28:15,18	iniquity	sins, crime, evildoing, immorality
28:16	multitude of your merchandise	abundance of your trade, business
28:18	the iniquity of your traffic	dishonest trade, illegallon business
28:22	be sanctified	manifest holiness, cleansed, purified
28:23	pestilence	disease, fungus, mildew, disaster, crop failure
	the sword	war, violence, aggression
28:24	pricking	painful, hurtful
	house	people, nation, tribe
	brier	stickers, thorns, weeds
28:25	sanctified	set apart, cleaned, prepared
29:3	dragon	evil beast, Satan, serpent
29:5	meat	food
29:6	staff of reed	weak support, unsteady help
29:12	river	a.k.a. Nile
29:14,15	habitation	origin, where a person lives, home
	base	lowly, poor, ghetto
29:18	wages	reward, payment, salary, money
29:20	labor	work, activity
29:21	horn	symbol of strength, power, authority
30:2	woe	trouble, pain, punish, problems
30:4	pain	anguish, hurt, torment
30:9	careless	complacent, lazy, innattentive
	lo	look; see; behold; observe
30:13	fear	fright, worry, scared
	Noph	another name for 'Memphis' the capital city of Egypt
30:14	desolate	empty, destroyed, ruined
30:14,15,16	No	Thebes, the ancient capital of Egypt
30:15	cut off	destroy, end, finish
30:16	rent asunder	tear, ripped, shred, pull apart, open

EZEKIEL

	Noph	Memphis, the ancient city in Egypt
30:18,33:28	captivity	bondage, slavery, prisoner
	pomp	big show, flashy, showy
30:23	nations	people, groups, tribes
	countries	regions of the world
31:3	him	Babylon
	shroud	covering, canopy, thick set of branches & leaves
31:5	when he shot fourth	spread them out, scattered
31:10	height	stature, size
	lifted up	haughty, pride, arrogant
31:12	strangers	foreigners, non-native, non-Jew
	terrible	tyrants, dictators, evil leaders
31:14,16,18	nether	lower, bottom
31:16	comforted	consoled, cared for
32:9	vex	terrify, trouble, plague, confuse, dismayed
32:12	spoil the pomp	shatter the pride, humble
32:15	destitute	poor, broke, without money, ghetto
32:16	lamentation	cry, be sad about, agonize
32:18	daughters	offspring, children of/followers or devotees of something or someone
32:19,29	uncircumcised	ungodly, heathen, non-Jew
32:24	borne	took it, suffered it, endured, hung in there
32:25	multitude	group, crowd, gathering, horde
32:29	pit	hell, hades, torment, punishment, death to body
33:5	deliver	save, rescue, heal
	soul	inner person, emotion, life-force, being, life
33:6+	iniquity	sins, crime, evildoing, immorality
33:10	pine	rot, grow weak, fade away
33:15	statutes	law, rule, commands, decrees, directives
33:26	work abomination	detestable things/acts, nasty, gross
33:27	wastes	ruins, wilderness
33:30	still are talking against	rumor, talk about, run down, gossip
33:32,33	lo	behold, look
34:1+	Lord	Jehovah; God in relationship to mankind
34:2	prophesy	preach, predict
34:2	woe	trouble, pain, punish, problems

EZEKIEL

34:4	cruelty	severity, evil, mean
34:5,8	meat	food
34:7+	shepherds	leaders, caretakers
34:12	sheep	believers, followers
34:14,16	fat	rich, prosperous, wealthy
34:18	residue	the rest, left over, remnant
34:21	scattered them abroad	driven them away, spread
34:24	renown	famous, well-known, celebrity
34:25	covenant	agreement, promise, contract
34:27	yield	give, provide, bear fruit
34:29	renown	fame, reputation, well-known, celebrity
35:3	desolate	empty, barren, waste, stripped
35:5	perpetual hatred	everlasting enmity, despise
	calamity	disaster, misfortune, accident, bad luck
35:11	hatred	enmity, strong dislike
35:12	blasphemies	irreverence, disrespect, slander, evil speaking
35:12,14,15	desolate	waste, ruin, empty
35:15	house	people, leadership, tribe
36:2	ancient high places	shrines, altars to pagan gods
36:3	infamy	bad news, notorious, famous for bad reasons
36:3,4,5	residue	the rest, left over, remnant
36:3+	heathen	nations, pagans, non-Jew
36:4	derision	insulted, disrespect, laughing stock, mocked
36:5	spiteful	malicious, cruel, vengeful, mean
36:9	tilled	plowed, dug long rows in the ground, cultivated
36:13,14	bereaved	sorrowful, troubled, mournful
36:17	removed	impure, filthy, menstruous, set apart (till period over)
36:22	house	family, estate, tribe, leadership
36:23	sanctify	set apart, make clean, prepare
36:24	own land	country, territory, nation
36:26	new spirit	a spirit or powerful influence to behave properly
36:27	My spirit	God's Spirit
36:29	corn	grain
36:31	loathe	despise, hate, detest
	abominations	detestable things/acts, nasty, gross

EZEKIEL

36:31,33	iniquities	sins, crime, evildoing, immorality
36:34,35,36	desolate	forsaken, empty, barren
36:35	fenced	fortified, defended, protected
36:38	solemn	serious, no joke, sincere
37:1,5,7	bones	symbol of descendents of Israel
37:4,9,10,12	prophesy	preach, predict, foretell
37:4	dry bones	without life, no spirit
	You	Israel
37:6	sinews	muscles and tendons
37:8	lo	behold, look
37:10	army	many people, military units
37:12	bring	return, carry
37:22	nation	united people, no longer Judah or Israel
37:23	detestable	despised, hated, rejected, disgusting
37:24	statutes	law, rule, commands, decrees, directives
37:26	covenant	agreement, promise, contract
37:27	tabernacle	dwelling place, church, religious building
37:28	sanctify	make Israel holy, purify, prepare
38:4	army	warriors, soldiers, military
38:8	latter	future, later on, last
38:11	unwalled	in the open, suburbs, outside the protected city
38:12,13	spoil	plunder, loot, stolen goods
38:13	lions	future leaders
38:14	Gog	a large region or land area (most say the Soviet Union
38:16	heathen	nations, non-Jew, pagan
38:23	nations	peoples, groups, tribes
39:6	carelessly	safely, without care/concern
	Isles	coastlands
39:7	pollute	profane, dirty, unclean
39:9	bucklers	small shields, defensive armor
	handstaves	war clubs
39:10	spoil	plunder, rob, vandalize
39:13	renown the day	memorable day, special
39:14	sever out	set apart, separate, divide
39:14,15	passengers	travelers, visitors
39:15	sign	marker, sign post
39:17,19	drink blood	kill, pillage & plunder, enjoy spoils of war

EZEKIEL

39:18	drink the blood of	revenge, conquer, destroy
39:21,23	heathen	nations, non-Jew, pagan
39:22,23,25	house	people, leadership, tribe
39:23	iniquity	sins, crime, evildoing, immorality
39:25	bring…the captivity	slavery, captivity, servitude, bondage
39:27	people	Israel re-gathered
	sanctified in	show myself holy through…
40:3	flax	a type of plant, after beaten, would be used for fine clothes (linen, gauze)
40:4	set your heart	give attention to, listen & obey
	House	people, leadership, tribe
40:5	breadth	width, length, distance across
40:6	threshold	doorstep, doorway, entrance
40:7+	chamber	alcoves, small rooms
40:16	round about inward	facing in, as seen from the inside
40:17	ephah	a measurement for dry items (flour etc.)
40:19	forefront	beginning, at the front, start, leading
40:42	hewn	cut, dressed, hacked, chisel
40:44,45,46	prospect	view, sight, survey
40:46	charge	rule, duty, job, responsibility
41:1	broad	wide, big, hard to complete or fulfill
41:3	inward	inside
41:5+	chamber	room, hall
41:12	place	area, space
41:16	ceiled	paneled
41:18	cheribums	angels, archangels, heavenly beings, guardians
42:1+	chamber	room, hall
42:6	building was straitened	upper rooms were set back
42:10,13	separate place	opposite of the temple courtyard
42:20	profane	treat as common, cheap, ordinary
43:7,9	whoredom	unfaithfulness, dishonesty
43:8	abominations	detestable things/acts, nasty, gross
43:10	house	people, leadership, tribe
43:11,18	ordinances	regulations, rules, laws
43:13	breadth	width, length, distance across
43:14,17,20	settle	porch, ledge, enclosure
43:19	seed	offspring, descendants, children

EZEKIEL

43:22	kid of the goats	male baby goat
43:22,23,25	blemish	defect, spot, stain
43:23	bullock	young male cow, steer, bull
43:26	purge	make atonement for, cleanse
	consecrate	dedicate, prepare, make sacred
44:1	outward	outer gate of the
44:5	mark well	give attention, focus on
	ordinances	regulations, rules, laws
44:5,6	house	temple, place of worship, religious building
44:6,7,13	abominations	detestable things/acts, nasty, gross
44:7,9	flesh	body, skin
44:8,14,15,16	charge	custody, responsibility, duty
44:9	stranger	heathen, ungodly, non-Jew
44:10,12	iniquity	sins, crime, evildoing, immorality
44:16	sanctuary	temple, religious building, holy site
44:18	gird	wear, fasten, put on, get dressed up in
44:19	holy chambers	sacred rooms
	sanctify	consecrate, prepare, make ready
44:20	poll	trim, cut
44:22	put away	divorced
	seed	offspring, children, heirs
	maidens	virgins, unmarried women
44:23	profane	common
	discern	know, recognize, understand, comprehend
44:24	statutes	law, rule, commands, decrees, directives
	sabbaths	rest days, days without working
44:27	inner court	the courtyard, front yard of a sacred building/holy site
44:29	dedicated thing	offerings, gifts, sacrifices
44:30	first	best, finest
44:30	oblation	offering, gift
45:2	suburbs	open place, pasture lands
45:4	holy	separated, clean, purified
45:5	chambers	rooms, halls
45:9	spoil	destruction, waste, ruin
	exactions	dispossessing, kick out, evict
	suffice	enough, satisfied, adequate, good enough
45:10	just	fair, honest, responsible

EZEKIEL

45:12	maneh	fixed weight
	shekel	the term for Jewish money, like our "dollar"
45:13	homer	a heap full; the largest measurement of dry goods
45:14	cor	6.25 bushels or 58 gallonlons
45:15,24	meat	grain
45:17	sabbaths	rest days, days without working
	solemnities	reverent, sacred, holy occasions/events
45:18,23	blemish	defect, spot, impurity
45:19	settle	porch, ledge, enclosure
45:21	unleavened	yeast-free
46:3,4,12	sabbaths	rest days, days without working
46:7	hand attain to	handful, hold in the hand, grab
	ephah	a measurement for dry items (flour etc.)
46:9	forth opposite	go out a different door, the opposite door (i.e. go in front door, come out back door)
46:12	looks	faces, expressions
46:19	chambers	rooms, halls
46:22	one measure	the same size, equal
	broad	wide, big, hard to complete or fulfill
46:23	boiling places	place for fire, cook/camp area
46:24	places	cooking houses, kitchen
47:1	threshold	doorway, entrance, opening
47:3	ankles	ankle deep, above soles of feet and below calf
47:5	waters	enough water, deep, flowing
	passed over	crossed, walked, waded
47:11	miry places	swamps, muddy
47:12	meat	food
47:14	lifted My hand	took a vow, swore an oath, promised
47:19,20	great	a.k.a. Mediterranean
47:23	sojourns	travels, visit, stay away from home
48:9+	oblations	allotment, sacrifices, gifts
48:9+	Lord	Jehovah; God in relationship to mankind
48:11	kept my charge	served me, obeyed, followed orders
48:15,17	suburbs	backyard, i.e. pasture, Garden land
48:21	residue	balance, left over
48:28	great sea	a.k.a. Mediterranean

DANIEL

1:3	kings seed	royal family, children, offspring
1:4	blemish	defect, impurity, fault
	favored	handsome, beloved, respected
	tongue	language, dialect
1:4,5	stand	serve, attend, wait on
1:5,8,10,13,15,16	meat	food
1:8	portion	possession, share, amount, cut, take
1:8,9,10	eunuchs	court officials, men unable to have children
1:10	worse liking	looking more haggard, tired
	sort	age
1:12,14	prove	tried, tested, searched, examined, known
	beseech	beg, plead, ask, cry out
	pulse	fresh squeezed fruit (juice and fruit), smoothy
1:12,16	pulse	vegetables
1:15	fatter in flesh	better nourished, healthy
1:19	communed	spoke, talked with, discussed
	stood	serve, attend, wait on
1:20	astrologers	forecasters, predictors; guess the future by analyzing the stars and constellations
2:1	broke	was gone, left
2:2,27	astrologers	conjurers, horoscope readers
2:3,30	know	understand, comprehend
2:6,16,24,27	show	declare, point out
2:8	thing	i.e. dream
2:11	rare	difficult, hard, unusual
2:15	hasty	hurried, speedy, fast, quickly, last minute
2:15,25	made the thing know	explained the matter, described
2:23	desired	sought, wanted, hoped for
2:24	ordained	appointed, elected, ordained
2:31,35	image	idol, statue
2:31	excellent	pre-eminent, dazzling
	terrible	awesome, fearful, dangerous
2:35,45	stone	rock, power; a symbol of Jesus (who would fulfil this prophecy in the future)
2:38	head	i.e. kingdom of Babylon
2:39	another kingdom	i.e. Medo-Persia

	third kingdom	i.e. Greece
2:40	fourth kingdom	i.e. Roman
2:41	feet and toes	i.e. individual nations resulting from Roman empire – (EEC?)
2:43	seed	descendents, children, offspring
	cleave	cling, hold on to
2:45	hereafter	in the future
2:46	oblation	offering, gift
2:59	gate	gate, door, i.e. court
3:1	threescore	60
	cubits	about 18"
3:2+	image	idol, statue
3:5,7,10,15	sackbut	a Syrian stringed instrument resembling a harp
	dulcimer	an instrument composed of a series of pipes, a bag-pipe
	psaltery	lyre, stringed instrument
3:12	regarded	noticed, heeded, observed, attended to
3:16	careful	full of care or needing, concerned
3:19	wont it be	customarily, usually
	visage	appearance; "face" - influence, personal attention (his facial expressions changed to anger)
3:21	hosen	undergarments, underwear, boxer shorts
3:22	slew	killed, murdered
3:26	of	i.e. out of
3:28	changed	violated, disrespected, altered
3:29	amiss	offensive, wrong
	dunghill	garbage dump
4:7	astrologer	conjurers, horoscope readers
	soothsayers	fortune tellers
4:10	saw	was looking, observed
4:11,20	sight	view, visibility
4:14,23	hew	cut, hack, chisel
4:16,23,25,32	times	periods of time, seasons
4:17	basest of men	no honor, punks, thugs, wicked, lowdown, vile
4:19	hate	abhor, despise, loathe, detest
4:21	meat	food
4:26	sure	assured, confident, positive

DANIEL

4:17	iniquities	sins, crime, evildoing, immorality
4:27	lengthening	extend, continue, increase
4:31	departed	removed, left, taken away
4:35	reputed	believed to be, considered, regarded as
	stay	stop, hold back, fight
5:2	concubines	a sexual partner that is not a wife nor a prostitute
5:7,15	astrologers	conjurers, horoscope readers
5:7	show	declare to, publish, reveal
	third ruler	co-ruler below the King; like a vice-president
5:7,11	soothsayers	fortune tellers, spiritualists
5:7	third ruler	third in command, prime minister
5:9,10	countenance	face, influence, appearance, expression
5:9	astonished	perplexed, shocked, stunned
5:11	soothsayers	psychics, fortune tellers, prophets, predictors
5:11,13,18	father	i.e. grandfather
5:16,29	make	give, provide
	third ruler	i.e. (1) Nabonidues, (2) Belshazzar, (3) Daniel
5:19	slew	kill, murder
5:20	disposed	removed, replaced, kicked out
6:2	give account	be accountable, responsible, explain
	damage	loss, ruin, waste
6:7,15	statute	law, rule, commands, decrees, directives
6:7	save	except, besides, other than
6:10	chamber	room, hall
6:14	sore	very, harsh, painful
	heart	mind, thoughts
	labored	made every effort, worked
6:17	signet	sealing ring, stamp, like a notary public
6:20	lamentable	pained, sad, sorrowful
6:22	angel	messenger, supernatural being
6:26	fear	revered, respected, trembled, dread
7:1	told the sum of	summarized, explained
7:3	diverse	different, unalike, varied
7:4	first	i.e. Babylon
	heart	mind, thoughts, desires
	plucked	pulled off, broken off, taken off

DANIEL

7:5	second	i.e. Medo-Persia (v.20)
7:6	another	i.e. Greece
	heads	i.e. officers under
	Alexander	Supreme Commander of Greece & ruler of the known world in his day
7:7,19,23	fourth	i.e. Rome
7:7	terrible	terrifying, awful, cruel
	strong exceedingly	very strong, powerful
7:7,8,20,21,24	horns	Nations from Roman empire
7:9,13,22	Ancient of days	i.e. God (Father)
7:12	season	period of time
7:13	one	i.e. Jesus Christ
7:15	midst of my body	within me, inside
7:18,25	saints	holy ones, purified, believers, true followers
7:18+	Most High	Almighty God, Supreme Deity
7:19,24	diverse	different, various, many
7:21,27	saints	holy ones, purified, believers, true followers
7:24	ten horns	rulers, powers
	another	ruler (antichrist)
7:26	judgment	do justice, punish, revenge, sentance
7:28	cogitations	thoughts, ideas
	countenance	complexion grew pale
8:3,4,6,7	ram	Medo-Persia
8:3,6,7	two horns	i.e. Cyrus & Darius
8:5	he goat	i.e. Alexander of Greece
	touched not the ground	i.e moved fast, flew
	notable	conspicuous, obvious, significant
8:7	choler	enraged and bitter, angry
8:7,10	stamped upon	defeated, crushed, beaten
8:8	he goat	i.e. Alexander
	great horn was broken	Alexander, died age 33
	our notable ones	officers under Alexander
8:8,9	waxed	grew, increased, became stronger
8:9	little horn	little ruler, lesser
8:11	prince of the host	leader of the army
8:13	saint	holy ones, purified, believers, true followers

DANIEL

	give	allow, permit
8:14	cleansed	put right, purified, prepared for God's use
8:18	set me upright	made me stand, strengthened
8:19	end shall be	end of time, Rapture, resurrection new heaven
8:23	are come to the full	have run their course, finished
	a king	evil ruler
8:25	peace	prosperity, calm, rest from wars
	Prince of princes	Jesus Christ
8:26	shut you up	keep to yourself, seal up, hide
9:1	seed	offspring, children, heirs
9:2	desolations	ruin, waste, destroy
9:4	dreadful	fearsome, evil, aweful
9:4,27	covenant	agreement, promise, contract
9:5	committed iniquity	sins, crime, evildoing, immorality
	precepts	commands, laws, rules
9:7,8	confusion	shame, humiliation, embarrassment
9:7	You have driven them	scattered, run off, defeated
9:9	Him	God, i.e. Jesus
9:13	iniquities	sins, crime, evildoing, immorality
9:15	gotten You renown	made a name for Yourself
9:17	cause Your face to shine	look with favor, be merciful, bless
9:21	to fly	come, hurry over
9:21,27	oblation	offering, sacrifice
9:24,25,27	weeks	units of seven
9:25,26	threescore and two	62
9:26	cut off	killed, end rule/life
9:27	he	antichrist, religious/political leader, (Pope?)
	midst	middle, half way
	abominations	detestable things, nasty, wicked
10:1	thing	message, prophecy, plan
	long	great, far away, many years away
10:3	pleasant bread	tasty food, sweets, treat
10:5	fine	pure, clean
10:6	beryl	gemstone
10:8	comeliness	splendor, beauty, health

DANIEL

	corruption	deathly pale, sickness, weakness
10:11,12,18	He	angel, heavenly messenger
10:13	prince	Satan's representative, evil leader
	Mi'chael	archangel/prince of God
10:15	set	turned, faced
10:16	similitude	similarity, likeness, image, copy
	sons of men	human being, offspring
10:20	wherefore	why
11:4	posterity	descendents, children, heir
11:10	be stirred up	mobilize, energized, fired up
11:11	moved with choler	enraged, furious, angry
11:14	establish	fulfill, set up, strengthen
11:15	fenced	fortified, well defended, protected
	arms	forces, military strength
	withstand	stand their ground, defend, protect
11:16	glorious land	Judah, Israel
11:16	consumed	vanish, waste away, dried up, spent, used up
11:20,21	estate	place, house, home
11:21	vile	despicable, evil, nasty
	flatteries	vanities, lies, deceit
11:22,31	arms	forces, military strength
11:22,28,32	covenant	agreement, promise, contract
11:23	league	treaty, agreement, accord
11:24	fattest	richest, strongest, very prosperous
11:24,25	forecast his devices	devise his schemes, deception
11:25	stir	call, enlist, recruit
	be stirred up	excited, motivated, challenged
	stand	win, survive, vivtorious
11:26	meat	food, supplies
11:31	abomination	detestable things, nasty, evil
11:32	corrupt by flatteries	turn to godlessness, deception
11:34	flatteries	vanities, deception, lies, scemes
11:38	pleasant things	treasures, wealth
11:41	glorious land	Judah, land of Israel
11:42	stretch forth his hand	extend his power, attack, fight
11:44	utterly to take away	exterminate, destroy, annihilate
12:1	the book	sacred texts, Old Testament records
12:3	be wise	have insights, understanding

DANIEL

12:7	time, times, and a half	3 1/2 years
12:11	abomination	detestable things, vile, evil

HOSEA

1:2	whoredoms	prostitution, fornication, adultery
1:4	avenge	punish, pay back
1:5,7	bow	strength, military power
1:11	head	leader, boss, king, ruler
2:2,4	whoredoms	prostitution, fornication, wrong spiritual unions
2:6	walls	obstruction, defense, fortification
2:8,9,22	corn	grain
2:10	discover	expose, reveal, show
	lewdness	immodesty, private parts, immorality
2:11	mirth	laughter, happiness, joy
	Sabbaths	rests, day without working
2:13	Days of Ba'al-im	ceremony involving human sacrifice, by burning, to Syrian-Phoenician deity/god
2:16	Ish'I	my husband, man
	Ba'al-I	my lord
2:18	covenant	agreement, promise, contract
2:22	hear	respond, answer, listen to
3:4	image	idol, statue
	ephod	priestly robe, garments
	teraphim	household/personal idols
4:1+	God	El, Elohim; self-existing, Almighty
4:3	languish	waste away, faint, weaken
4:7	iniquity	sins, crime, evildoing, immorality
4:9	reward	repay, punish
4:12	stocks	wooden idols, decorated trees? (Jer10:1-5)
	staff	diviner's wand, magic wand
4:16	backsliding	stubborn, wayward, fallen
5:1	snare	trapped, caught, imprisoned, tripped up, lure
5:2	profound	determined, persuade, committed to
5:3,4	whoredom	illicit intercourse, prostitution, unfaithfulness
5:5	iniquity	sins, crime, evildoing, immorality
5:7	devour	destroy, ruin, wreck
	portions	land parcels, tracks, acreage
5:15	early	earnestly, right away, without delay
6:4	goodness	faithfulness, decent, trustworthy
6:5	hewed	chiseled, moulded, crafted

HOSEA

6:7	covenant	agreement, promise, contract
6:8	iniquity	sins, crime, evildoing, immorality
	polluted	evil, corrupt, stained, dirtied
6:9	lewdness	nasty, dirty, sexy, immoral
6:11	returned the captivity	restored the fortunes
7:1	iniquity	sins, crime, evildoing, immorality
	spoils	plunders, raids, rips off
7:4	leavened	rises
7:5	bottles	wineskins, vessels, container for liquid
	scorners	scoffers, irreverent, disrespectful
7:7,9	devoured	ruined, destroyed, wasted
7:10	pride	arrogance, bad attitude
7:13	woe	trouble, pain, punish, problems
7:14	corn	grain
7:15	bound	disciplined, trained, prepared
8:1	covenant	agreement, promise, contract
8:4	knew	acknowledged, consented
	cut off	destroyed, ended, finished
8:5,6	calf	an image, statue that represented a pagan god
8:8	Gen'tiles	Nations, non-Jews
8:12	strange	alien, foreign
8:13	iniquity	sins, crime, evildoing, immorality
8:14	fenced	fortified, walled, protected, fortified
9:1	gone a whoring	committed prostitution, adultery
	loved a reward	prostitute, hooker, call girl every corn floor
9:1	corn	grain
9:2	floors' winepress	
	shall not feed them	not enough, not satisfied, famine/drought
9:4	polluted	defiled, dirtied, corrupted, impure
9:5	nettles	thorns, stickers
9:6	thorns shall be in	
	their tabernacles	stickers, sharp objects on the floor of their tents
9:7	visitation	punished, avenged, judgement
	recompense	retribution, revenge
9:7,8,15	hatred	hostility, anger
9:7,9	iniquity	sins, crime, evildoing, immorality
9:8	snare	trapped, caught, imprisoned, tripped up, lure
9:10	separated	devoted, set apart, chosen, called

HOSEA

	abominations	detestable ways, vile, evil ways
9:12	woe	trouble, pain, punish, problems
	bereave	sorrowful, troubled, mournful
9:15	princes	leaders, chiefs, rulers, influential men
	revolters	rebels, conspirators, disobedient
10:1,2	images	statues, idols, hand-made pagan statues
10:2	spoil	break down, destroy, ruin
10:3	feared	revered, respected, trembled, dread
10:4	covenant	agreement, promise, contract
10:5	calves	an image, statue that represented a pagan god
10:7	cut off	destroyed, ruin, end
	foam upon...water	foam or froth is separated from the actual water it sits on top or is cast to the side/banks
10:9,13	iniquity	sins, crime, evildoing, immorality
10:11	corn	grain
	to ride	to be harnessed, hooked up
10:13	plowed wickedness	has a pattern of doing bad things, and the bad will come back on him; like karma
	fruit of lies	results, outcome
11:1	child	lad, youth, immature
11:2	graven images	idols & carvings, statues of pagan gods
11:4	take	lift, remove
	laid meat to	fed
	cords of a man	human emotions, feelings, devices
	bands of love	feelings of love, desire, longing, passion yoke
11:7	bent	determined, chosen, decided
	exalt	praise, worship
11:8	repenting	compassions, humility, change of heart
	kindled	aroused, get started
11:11	place	settle, put, set up
11:12	compasses	go about, surround, encamp, encircle
	saints	holy ones, purified, believers, true followers
12:1	desolation	violence, destruction, hurt
	covenant	agreement, promise, contract
	feeds on wind	vanity, futility, wasted effort; when one swallows the wind, he fills his mouth, and his throat, and his chest, and his whole stomach; but there is nothing but air, no nourishment

HOSEA

12:2	controversy	dispute, argument, fight
12:3	power	contended, fought
12:3,4	power	strength, authority, rights/priviledges
12:7	balances of deceit	a dealer of lies, dishonesty, cheating
12:8,11	iniquity	sins, crime, evildoing, immorality
12:10	similitudes	illustrations, figures of speech
13:2	images	statues, idols
	kiss the calves	i.e. worship the calf idols
13:3	morning cloud	clouds in the desert were a good thing; they at least brought shade from the hot sun, possibly brought rain
	whirlwind out	blown away, cleared away of the floor
13:7	observe	lie in wait for, ambush
13:8	rend the caul	tear the enclosure, rip the veil
13:11	king	a.k.a. Saul
	wrath	anger, fury, punishment
13:12	iniquity	sins, crime, evildoing, immorality
	hidden	stored up, secret, unknown
13:13	too long breaking forth of children	instead of being delivered or born anew, Israel refused to repent/change and therefore by delaying they risked spiritual death/punishment – like a stillborn child
13:14	grave	Hell, death, place of punishment, torment
	plagues	pestilence, diseases
	repentance	grieving, change of mind/heart
13:15	wind	breath (Holy Spirit), power, force
	spoil	plunder, rob, rip-off
	pleasant	precious, expensive, beautiful, valuable
14:1,2	iniquity	sins, crime, evildoing, immorality
14:2	calves	an image, statue that represented a pagan god
14:5	grow	blossom, improve, strengthen
	cast forth his	grow, spread, send out
14:6	smell	fragrance, perfume, aroma
14:7	revive as the corn	come back to life; from drought wilted corn to
	upright	scent fragrance, perfume, aroma

JOEL

** the insects mentioned in Chapter 1:4 are the same insects, in different stages (like a caterpillar and then a butterfly)

1:4	palmerworm	caterpillar stage of the locust, it ate leaves
	locust	the flying, swarming stage that continued to eat
	cankerworm	the larva stage of the locust, it ate the bark
	caterpillar	the full circle of the insect, ate into the sap
1:5,11	howl	wail, yell, scream
	cut off	kept from, held back
1:6	nation	people, groups by tribe, by selection
	cheek teeth	molars, premolars (back teeth)
1:7	barked	cut off the bark from
	clean	completely, fully
1:10	wasted	destroyed, ruined, wrecked
	corn	grain
1:10,12	languishes	fails, runs out, used up
1:12	withered	dried out, shrunk, dying
1:13	sackcloth	coarsely woven fabric, sign of mourning, submission and humility
1:13,16	meat	food
1:14	sanctify	consecrate, dedicate, purify
1:17	clods	pieces of earth, dirt, chunks of dirt
	garners	granary, storehouse for grain
	corn	grain
1:18	perplexed	disturbed, confused, uncertain i.e. milling about
2:1,15	Zi'on	Israel
2:1	tremble	shake, fear, worry
2:1+	Lord	Jehovah; God in relationship to mankind
2:5	battle array	in battle formation
2:6	faces…blackness	trouble, punished; dirty, smoky, sooty from smoke
2:8	fall upon the sword	injured, hurt, wounded (self-inflicted?)
2:11	day of the Lord	reference to end times, 1000 year reign
	terrible	awesome, fearful, dangerous
2:13	rend your heart	soften, open, repent, be sorry for sins/behavior
2:13,14	repents	change mind, feel soorow/guilty

JOEL

2:15,16	sanctify	consecrate, dedicate, purify
	solemn assembly	reverent, sacred, holy occasions/events
2:16	bride…closet	come out of her room (smaller than the bridegrooms) and present herself to the wedding party
2:17	ministers	leaders, religious workers
2;17,19	heathen	nations, non-Jew, pagan
2:19	corn	grain
2:20	hinder	back, rear
	utmost	i.e. Mediterranean
	ill savor	foul smell, stink
2:23	former	spring rain (during planting season)
	latter	fail rain (during harvest season)
2:28	flesh	i.e. people
2:31	terrible	awesome, fearful, dangerous
2:32	delivered	saved, rescued, spared
	deliverance	redeem, rescue, ransom, keep safe
3:2	nations	people, groups, by tribe
3:4,7	recompense	reward, payment
3:5	pleasant	precious, valuable, expensive
3:6,7	sold	traded to, turned into slaves
3:9	Gen'tiles	nations, non-Jew, pagan
3:10	pruning hooks	a long-handled edge tool with a curved blade at the end and sometimes a clipper; used to prune small trees
3:11	heathen	nations, non-Jew, pagan
3:14	multitudes	many people, crowds, gatherings
	valley	time of deciding (literal, figurative, prophetic)
	decision	judgment, i.e. God's verdict
3:16,17,21	Zi'on	Israel
3:16+	Lord	Jehovah; God in relationship to mankind
3:17	holy mountain	area set apart and consecrated
	holy	set apart, purified, dedicated
3:18	fountain	life, God's spirit, blessing, health
	house	temple, place of worship, religious building
3:20	Ju'dah	Southern Kingdom, i.e. Judah Benjamin

AMOS

1:2	Zi'on	Israel
1:3	threshed	worked to beat/brake the shells/skin off wheat, barley grain
1:4,7	devour	consume, use up, lay waste
1:5,8	holds the scepter	rules, has the power, in charge
1:5	bar	gates, fences, metal doors
1:6	whole	all, everyone
1:7, 2:2	devour	destroy, consume, use up, lay waste
1:8	remnant	leftover, remains, survivors
1:9	covenant	agreement, promise, contract
1:11	wrath	anger, fury, punishment
2:1+	Lord	Jehovah; God in relationship to mankind
2:1	burned the bones of king of Edom into lime	dishonored, desecrated, had no respect for burial rites
2:2	tumult	commotion, excitement, outcry, pandemonium
2:7	meek	humble, modest, gentle
	maid	young woman, virgin
	profane	defile, pollute, disrespect
	pant after the dust	long for, want the poor man as a slave laborer
2:8	condemned	despised, mocked, ridiculed, judged, curse
2:11	Naz'a-rites	dedicated, devoted ones
2;13	sheaves	grain stems
2;14,15	deliver	save, rescue, help, assist
2:16	courageous	bravest, strong, heroic
3:1	whole family	all, nation, people of Israel
3:2	iniquities	sins, crime, evildoing, immorality
3:5	snare	trapped, caught, imprisoned, tripped up, lure
	gin	bait, lure, enticement
3:6	done	caused, allowed, permitted
3:9	publish	declare, announce, broadcast
3:10	robbery	ruin, rob, steal
3:11	spoiled	plundered, looted, sacked
3;14	visit	punished, avenged, judgement
4:1	cattle	cows
4:2	posterity	future family, descendents, heirs
4:4	transgress	commit sin, wrong-doing

AMOS

4:5	leaven	yeast, a symbol of corruption and evil
4:9	blasting	heat, drought, harsh weather conditions
4:11	were as a firebrand	rebel, troublemaker; torch, anything on fire that is thrown in the air
5:2	virgin	pure, faithful, never had sex
5:5	Beth'-el	house of God, a city of refuge for Israel
5:6	devour	destroy, consume, ruin
5:9	spoiled	ruined, destroyed
5:10	hate	abhor, despise, loathe, detest
5:11	hewn	cut, hacked, chiseled
	pleasant	pleasing, lovely, beautiful
5:12	manifold	numerous, many, a lot, excessive
5:13	prudent	careful, good judgment, common sense, wise
5:16	lamentation	crying, mourning, agonizing, distress
5:18,20	day of the Lord	end times, 1000 years
5:21	hate	abhor, despise, loathe, detest
	smell	fragrance (a pleasing aroma) i.e. delight
5:22	meat	grain, food
	fat	rich, wealthy, healthy
5:23	viols	musical instruments
5:23;6:5	viols	a stringed instrument played with a bow, like a violin
5:24	judgment run	justice prevail/prosper
5:36	borne	carried, lifted, hauled around
5:27	God of Hosts	Elohe Tsebaoth
6:1	woe	trouble, pain, punish, problems
	Zi'on	Israel
6:3	cause	encourage, support, push
	you the put far	pretend that judgment is far off, not near away the evil day
6:4	stall	pen, cage, barn where animals lived
6:4,7	stretch	sprawl, spread out
6:6	affliction	ruin, wreck, lay waste
	wine in bowls	in excess, to spare; very big glasses
6:11	breaches	broken place, crumbled walls, holes, gap
	clefts	cracks, crevices, holes
6:12	hemlock	wormwood, i.e. bitterness
	gall	venom, bitterness, poison

AMOS

6:13	horns	symbol of strength, power, authority
7:1	latter growth	the first growth of plants is the stalk, then the bud and finally the fruit or grain – so God would allow them to grow/prosper and believe all was well, then when they thought they were safe, punishment would come
	kings mowings	taxes, firstfruits; the king got the first fruits that were ripe
7:2	beseech	beg, plead, ask, cry out
7:3,6	repented	grieved, felt sorry, change of mind
7:4	contend	to strive, i.e. for judgment
	great deep	deep oceans, seas
7:7	plumbline	a reference line guided by a string or cord weighted at the end with a large weight known as a plumb bob. It is used to create a vertical reference line to build a straight wall.
7:8	plumb	straight, measure, correctly alighend
7:9	high place	shrines, altars to pagan gods
7:10	bear	endure, put up with, tolerate, mercy
7:12	seer	prophet, holy man, teacher
7:13	chapel	sanctuary, religious building
	court	meeting hall, place of judgement
7:14	sycamore fruit	wild figs; an inferior fruit, not very tasty
7:17	polluted	unclean, dirty, corrupted
	harlot	hooker, prostitute, call girl
8:1, 2	summer fruit	overripe, beginning to rot on the inside
8:3	howlings	wailings, mourn, cry out
8:4	swallow… needy	take advantage of, bully, abuse
8:5	corn	grain
	sabbath	rest day, day without working
8:6	buy the poor	make slaves, work for very little
8:8	wholly	all, completely, fully
	flood	water, overflow, flooding
	flood of E'gypt	flooding the river of the Nile
8:14	manner	way, tradition, custom
9:1	lintel	upper door post, crosspiece at the top of the door
	cut them in the head	fall on, collapse on
	cut	break, ruin, destroy

AMOS

9:2	dig into hell	dig dip into the earth trying to hide
9:3	the serpent	mythological sea serpent, dragon
	flood of	flooding of Nile
9:6	stories	stairs, steps
	saving	except, besides, other than
	utterly	completely, fully, totally
9:9	sift	shake, judge, test
	corn is sifted	the grain is shaken
9:10	prevent	go before, confront, stop
9:11	breaches	broken place, crumbled walls, holes, gap
	remnant	leftover, remains, survivors
9:13	plowman shall overtake the reaper	blessings, successful seasons; no interruption in the planting, harvest, plowing cycle

OBADIAH

1:1	vision	message/picture given by God (like a video), divine instructions
	Lord God	Jehovah Elohim, the self-existing God now interacting with mankind
	E'dom	son of
1:1+	Lord	Jehovah; God in relationship to mankind
1:7	a wound under	an ambush for, trap, deception
1:9	mount	mountain, tall hill
	cut off	destroyed, waste, stop
1:11	forces	substance, wealth, army
1:12	looked on	not helped, overlooked, ignored
1:13	calamity	affliction, problem, trial, trouble
	affliction	sickness, disease, trouble, difficulties
1:14	delivered up	imprisoned, captured
1:15	day of the Lord	end time, Jesus returns to rule on earth
1:17	Zi'on	Israel
	deliverance	those who escape, saved, rescued
1:18	flame	destroyed, burned up, punished
	stubble	burnt down, little left, stubs
	devour	destroy, ruin, lay waste
1:20	captivity of Je-ru'sa-lem	when Jews were not in control
1:21	saviors	deliverers, rescuers, helpers

JONAH

1:2	cry	preach, warn, announce
	Tarshish	a city of the Phoenicians in the Mediterranean Sea the prophet Jonah was running away to
1:4	broken	shattered, broken in pieces
1:5	mariners	sailors, those that traveled with boats or ships
	wares	merchandise, products, stuff
1:7	cast lots	predictions; like flipping a coin; paper, rock, scissors, throw dice
1:8	pray	beg, plead, ask
1:9	fear	revered, respected, trembled, dread
1:11,13	wrought	churned, worked, made
	tempestuous	emotional, hysterical, wild, stormy
1:12	tempest	violent storm
1:14	beseech	beg, plead, ask, cry out
1:16	feared	revered, respected, trembled, i.e. were in awe of
	vows	pledges, promises, oath
1:17	prepared	made ready, created
	three days and three nights	type and fhadow of Jesus burial & resurrection
2:3	billows	big waves, ocean swells, flood waters
2:5	compassed	surrounded, enclosed, go all around
	weeds were wrapped about my head	tangled in seaweed (also a prophesy of Jesus wearing a thorn of crowns)
2:6	corruption	near death, disaster
2:8	vanities	falsehoods, illusions, fantasies
2:9	Salvation	Heb. Jeshua; redeem, rescue, ransom, keep safe
3:6	sat in ashes	humbled himself, showed sincere wish to be forgiven
3:9,10	repent	grieve, forgive, change his mind
4:2	repent	grieve, forgive, change his mind
4:3	beseech	beg, plead, ask, cry out
4:5	booth	shelter, tent, temporary shelter
4:6	deliver	save, rescue, help
	grief	discomfort, sadness, sorrow
	gourd	a wild vine-grown fruit that was hollowed out

JONAH

		and used for drinking or eating out of (cup/bowl)
4:7	smote	attacked, strike, hit, punish
	gourd	plant, bottle gourd, castor oil plant
4:8	vehement	harsh, hot, fierce, powerful
4:11	spare	save, forgive, show mercy

MICAH

1:2	hearken	listen, pay attention, heed
1:4	molten	melted
	cleft	cracks, crevices
1:6	pour down the stones	break down the city walls and roll them down into the valley
1:7	hire	earnings, money,pay
	she gathered it of the hire of an harlot	used the money made as a "harlot", money made illegallonly or immorally, dirty money
1:9	wound is incurable	no cure, hopeless, terminal illness
1:10	roll thyself…dust	humble yourselves, show a sincere wish to be forgiven
1:11	naked	unclothed, exposed, revealed, shown
1:13	Zi'on	Israel
1:14	lie	deception, dishonesty, falsehood
1:16	enlarge thy baldness as the eagle	shave your head; shaving the hair off was a sign of shame/disgrace
	poll you	cut your hair
	delicate children	weak, tender, young
2:1	iniquity	sins, crime, evildoing, immorality
2:2	oppress	rob, torment, bully
	covet	envy, greed, lust, wanting what is not yours
2:3	devise	plan, scheme, plot
	not remove…necks	no escape, won't get away
2:4	doleful	gloomy, dreary, sad
	spoiled	destroyed, ruined, wrecked
2:5	thou shalt have none …cast a cord by lot	predictions; like flipping a coin; paper, rock, scissors, throw dice
2:6	prophesy	speak, foretell, warn
2:7	straightened	shortened, confined, limited
2:8	securely	peaceably, safely
2:10	sore	grievous, severe, harsh, cruel
2:11	walking in the spirit and falsehood do lie	under the influence if a lying spirit
2:13	on the head of them	the Lord will be in the lead, up ahead of all
	breaker	destroyer
3:1	judgment	justice, punishment, sentance

MICAH

3:2	hate	despise, detest, scorn
3:3	eat the flesh of my people, and flay their skin from off them	Israel's enemies will kill them, skin them, cut them up in pieces, toss them in a pot and eat them
3:4	ill	evil, badly, improper
3:5	err	do wrong, sin, make mistakes
3:9	heads	rulers, leaders, bosses
	abhor	despise, detest, scorn
	pervert all equity	injustice, unfair, corrupt
3:10	Zi'on	Israel
	blood	bloodshed, murder, violence
3:11	hire	wages, pay, salary
	divine	instruct, inform, intuit
	none	no
3:12	heaps	ruins, piles, rubble, wreckage
4:1	But in the last days	end time, return of Jesus
	exalted	honored, celebrated, made famous
4:2,11,13	Zi'on	Israel
4:3	pruning hooks	farming tools, a long-handled edge tool with a curved blade at the end and sometimes a clipper; used to prune small trees
4:4	Lord of Hosts	Commander of Heaven's armies
4:6	halts	limps, is lame, stumbles
4:7	limped a remnant	rags to riches, reversal of fortunes, take a cripple that limps and make her special, chosen
4:8	tower of the flock	watchtower, guardian, protector
4:8,10,13	daughter of Zi'on	offspring, children, descendants of Israelis
	pangs	cramps, spasms, convulsions, struggles, birth pains
	woman in travail	giving birth, birth pains, labor
4:11	be defiled	shamed, spoiled, abused
4:12	counsel	guidance, wisdom, instruction, teaching, advice
	gather as sheaves into the floor	Israel's enemies were gathered against her, God says He will defeat them easily – like sheaves (plants) brought in from the field and put on the storeroom floor
4:13	horn	symbol of strength, power, authority
	brass	judgment, punishment

MICAH

5:1	smite the judge	struck, hit, punish
5:2	Ruler	Master
	everlasting	eternity, a very long time
5:4	stand	stop, take time
5:5	man	a savior, messiah, king/ruler (Jesus)
	come into	enter, conquer
5:6	waste	ruin, wreck, sack
5:8	remnant	part, a few, survivors
	none	no one
	treads	tramples, stomps, walks on/over
5:9	hand	control, power, might, strength
	adversaries	enemies, foes, rivals
5:9,13	be cut off	killed, destroyed, defeated
5:13	graven images	idols & carvings, statues of pagan gods
	standing images	large idols, statues
5:14	groves	(Heb:Asherah) either a living tree or a tree-like pole, set up as an object of worship, being symbolical of the female or productive principle in nature. Every Phoenician had an asherah near them. Both the "May Pole" and "Christmas Tree" (Jer.10:3-5) originate with this Asherah. The word is often translated "green trees" or "grove." This "nature worship" became associated with sexual immorality.
6:1	contend thou before the mountains	make a public statement, for all to hear; like an ad on TV or web blog
6:2	controversy	dispute, argument, fight
6:7	fruit	offspring, children, descendents, heir
6:9	see	consider, comprehend, understand
6:10	wickedness	wrong doing, evil, sin
	house	tent, home, crib
	treasures…	dirty money, criminal gains
	scant	wealth gotten illegallonly, there was still wickedness in their houses – still a trace, therefore not clean, pure
6:11	deceitful	false, dishonest, cheat
6:16	hissing	derision, mock, laugh at, ridicule
7:1	woe	trouble, problems, pain

MICAH

7:3	wrap it up	put together, join, combine
7:4	perplexity	puzzled, confused, uncertain, anxious
7:10	trodden	trampled, crushed or broken by being stepped upon
	mire of the streets	dust, dirt, trash in the street a person walks on
7:11	decree	law, limit, order, command
7:12	As-syr'I-a	a heathen nation (modern Syria), an enemy of Israel and often used to punish her
7:14	Feed	shepherd, care for, provide
	solitary	alone, by themselves
7:16	their mouth	to stop speaking, silent, shut up
	be deaf	not hear, not understand
7:18	pardons	forgives, is merciful, kind
7:18+	He	the Mighty God
7:19	iniquities	sins, crime, evildoing, immorality

NAHUM

1:1	burden	concern, prophecy, God's thoughts
1:2	jealous	zeal, desire for, protected, pure love
1:3	acquit	forgive, find not guilty, set free
1:4	languishes	weakens, dries up, discouraged
1:6	indignation	anger, temper, destructive rage verging on madness
1:7	strong hold	fortress, defensed area
1:9	utter	complete, full, total
1:10	folded	interwoven, looping, clasping, twisting
1:11	imagines	thinks about, reasons, daydreams
1:12	afflict	sickness, disease, trouble, difficulties
1:13	his	Israel's enemies, devil, evil spirit
	sunder	divide, cut, split, two pieces
1:14	sown	planted seeds, invested, perpetuated
	cut off	destroy, end, finish
	image	idol, statue
2:1	munition	weapons, military defenses
2:2	emptiers	vandals, destroyers, terrorists
	marred	damage, deface, bust up, tag
2:3	red	i.e. bloody
2:4	chariots	wagons, carts, buggy, horse-drawn car
	jostle	bump, bang into, crash; (re: driving a car in busy traffic)
2:5	worthies	gentleman, noble, well-born, dignified
2:6	dissolved	destroyed, finished, ended
2:7	plead	sob for, cry, beg
	taboring	pounding, banging, hitting with fists
2:8	look	turn, watch, gaze upon
2:9	spoil	loot, plunder, spoils, stolen treasure
	pleasant furniture	desirable, favorable, beautiful
2:10	She	Nin'e-vah
	gather	look, crowd around, draw in
	blackness	despair, sad, hopeless
2:12	holes	small bits, storage places
2:12,13	prey	plunder, treasure, wealth
3:1	woe	trouble, danger, look out! – a warning

NAHUM

	prey	plunder, treasure, wealth
	bloody city	violent, dangerous; full of criminals
3:4	multitude	many, crowds, a lot of people
	whoredoms	illegallon sex outside of marriage, immoral, prostitution or worse; also describes unfaithfulness to God/His rules (sin)
	witchcrafts	sorceries, spells, magic
3:5	I will discover thy skirts upon thy face	shame, embarrass, humiliate; God will lift up the front of her skirt and expose her private area
3:6	vile	disgusting, evil, filthy, nasty, sickening
	gazing stock	street show, comedy act, something to laugh at
	abominable filth	horrible, lousy, nasty, rotten, stinking
3:7	waste	desolate, empty, barren
	comforters	supporters, friends, helpers
3:8	better than Populous	an Egyptian god, originally the local god of Thebes, later head of the Egyptian pantheon
	rampart	wall, fortress, barrier, blockade
3:9	infinite	without end, long lasting
3:10	cast lots	predictions; like flipping a coin; paper, rock, scissors, throw dice
3:12	strong holds	fortifications, military defenses
3:13	women	sarcastic expression, put-down i.e. weak, scared
3:14	draw	set aside, store up, make reserve
	go into clay	mud pit, mire, damp dirt
	mortar	cement-like mixture of clay and straw
	kiln	oven that baked brinks to harden the mortar
3:15	cankerworm	a type of locust that ate/chewed
3:16	spoils	strips off, eats hurriedly
3:17	crowned	princes, anointed ones, officers
3:18	slumber	sleep, do nothing, unconcerned
3:19	bruise	wound, injury, hurt
	bruit	report, story, news
	wickedness	evil, crimes, sin, vice, wrong doing

HABAKKUK

1:3	iniquity	evil, crimes, sin, vice, wrong doing
	spoiling	destroy, ruin, waste
1:4	slacked	made feeble, ignored, weakened
	compass	go about, surround, encamp, encircle
	behold you among defeated	consider your position, living among and
	the heathen	nations, non-Jew, pagan
1:8	hastes	hurries, speeds up
	faces sup up as the east wind	appearance, presentation of their armies will be fierce and the results devastating (like the harsh, hot east wind)
1:10	scoff	make fun of, mock, laugh at, disrespect
1:12	established	ordained, designed, planned
1:13	hold Your tongue	be silent, shut up
	creeping things	insects, bugs
	are of purer eyes than to behold evil	God hates evil, therefore how can He watch bad people hurt good people?
1:14	men as the fishes	bad people scam, hurt & cheat good people, treat them as fish to be caught
1:15	angle	hook, fishhook
1:15,16	drag	fishing net
1:16	sacrifice to their net	worship whatever makes them rich or happy
1:17	slay	kill, murder
2:1	He	God
2:3	tarry	delay, put off, wait
2:5	nations	people groups, tribes
2:6,12,15,19	woe	trouble, danger, look out! – a warning
2:6	thick clay	pledges, heavy debt, a lot of bills
2:7	vex	terrify, trouble, plague, confuse, dismayed
	booties	loot, plunder, spoils, stolen treasure
2:8	spoiled	loot, plunder, spoils, stolen treasure
2:9	evil	crimes, sin, vice, wickedness
2:12	establishes	builds, develops, creates
2:13	vanity	nothing, pointless, meaningless, futile
2:15	nakedness	sexual organs, private parts
2:17	violence	war thinking, bloodthirsty, savagery

HABAKKUK

	blood	death
2:18	image	idol, statue
2:19	breath	life
3:2	revive	make alive, resurrect
3;3	Se'lah	musical term, pause
3:4,5	His,Him	the Lord Almighty
3:5	pestilence	disease, fungus, mildew, disaster, crop failure
3:6	bow	collapse, fall down, crumble
3:7	affliction	sickness, disease, trouble, difficulties
3:9	quite naked	without power, arrows; defenseless
	cleave	split, divide, cut in half
	bow was made naked	(bow & arrow) taken out and made ready for war, killing
3:11	habitation	home, crib, city, where they come from
	glittering spear	the metal tips of the spears glittered, shined in the sun
3:13	anointed	chosen, elect, empowered
	discovering	seeing, recognizing, being revealed
3:14	devour	destroy, eat up, consume
3:15	heap	waves, ocean swells
3:16	rottenness	weakness, corruption, poor health
	invade them	attack, strike
3:17	meat	food3:19 hinds deers, mountain sheep/goats

ZEPHANIAH

1:2,3	consume	vanish, waste away, dried up, spent, used up
1:3	cut off	destroy, stop, finish
1:5	swear	pledged, vowed, promised, gave an oath
1:6	back	away, retreat, quit
	inquired	asked, questioned
1:7	bid	invited, asked, requested
1:8	strange	foreign, unique, non-Jewish
1:9	leap on	jump over, attack, invade
1:10	crashing	destruction, ruin, break
1:12	lees	strong wine (vinegar), leftovers, dregs, crumbs, like used coffee grounds
1;13	booty	loot, plunder, spoils, stolen treasure
1:14;2:2	great day of the Lord	"end of time", Lord returns to the Earth judgment; 1000 year rule of Jesus on earth
1:15,18	wrath	anger, fury, judgment
1:16	fenced	fortified, defended, protected
1:18	jealousy	undivided desire, passion, possessive
2:2	bring forth	take effect, deliver
2:3	wrought	work, labor, build, produce
	meekness	shy, gentle, peaceful, easy to get along with
2:5	woe	trouble, danger, look out! – a warning
2:6	folds	pen, covering for sheep
2:8	magnified	made big, enlarged, exalted
	revilings	criticism, bad mouthing, curses, put downs
2:9	breeding of nettles	stickers, thorns, weeds – produce bad things
	salt pits	i.e. pool water where water has evaporated
	spoil	loot, plunder, stolen treasure
2:11	famish	starve, go hungry, dry up, destroy
	isles	distant lands
2:14	cormorant	long legged, long necked bird, like the pelican
	bittern	porcupine, hedgehog
	lintels	upper door post, crosspiece at the top of the door
	uncover	reveal, make plain, expose
3:1	woe	trouble, danger, look out! – a warning
	filthy	vile, disgusting, evil, nasty, sickening
3:4	polluted	profaned, violated, disrespected

ZEPHANIAH

3:5	unjust	unfair, false, unrighteous
3:6	none	not one, zero, empty
3:7	fear	revered, respected, trembled, dread
3:8	fire	anger, fury, consuming, burn up
	jealousy	deeply care about, spiritual concern
3:10	suppliants	worshipper, petitioner, devoted person, pilgrim
	dispersed	scattered, spread out
3:11	haughty	arrogant, stuck up, know-it-all3:12 name
		Jehovah, the Almighty
3:14	daughter	offspring - people, children, redeemed, beloved
3:16	Zi'on	Israel
3:19	halts	limps, is weak, struggles, has difficulties
	get	bring, give
	fame	renown, famous, heroic, popular
3:20	turn back	come back, return, i.e. release

HAGGAI

1:4	ceiled	roof, ceiling, the covering over their head
1:4,9	waste	be desolate, empty, ruined
1:10	stayed	restrained, withheld
1:11	corn	grain
1:12	fear	revered, respected, trembled, dread
2:2	residue	what's left over, excess, surplus
2:3	first glory	splender, might, greatness
2:5	Spirit	Holy Spirit
2:6	shake…earth	shake them, make them tremble or be afraid
2:7,14	nations	people, groups, tribes, selection
2:12	holy…garment	meat sacrificed to God was carried by the priests and the clothes were considered "dirty" if anything else touched them – thus when a person does one "evil" thing, they were considered evil/sinful until they apologized and were forgiven
2:14	this people	nation, fellow-countrymen
2:16	pressfat	winepress, a place where wine was made & sold
2:17	blasting	blight, disease
2:18	upward	forward, from now on
2:23	signet	seal, stamp of approval, authorization

ZECHARIAH

1:2,15	sore	severe, harsh, cruel
1:8	myrtle	an evergreen shrub or tree with dark green shiny leaves and usually blue-violet flowers; the flowers, leaves, and berries are used in perfumery and as a condiment to eat.
1:9,11,12,14,19	angel	messenger, supernatural being
1:12	threescore and ten	70
1:13	comfortable	soothe, calm, support
1:14	cry	get attention, proclaim, announce
1:14,17	Zi'on	Israel
1:15	forward	further, advance, increase, worsen
1:18,19,21	horns	rulers, powers, leaders
1:20	carpenters	craftsmen, skillful, destroyers
2:3	angel	messenger, supernatural being
2:5	wall of fire	defense, protection
2:6	ho, ho	oh no!, help me, woe, help
2:7,10	Zi'on	Israel
2:8	nations (people)	groups by tribe, selection
	spoiled	plundered, sacked, defeated
2:13	flesh	mankind, people, humanity
	habitation	dwelling, where one lives
3:1,3,5,6	angel	messenger, supernatural being
3:1	resist	oppose, resist, accuse
3:2	brand	burning stick, torch, anything on fire that is thrown in the air
3:4	iniquity	sins, crime, evildoing, immorality
	raiment	clothing, garment
3:5	mitre	a turban or long braid wrapped around the head, worn by the High Priest - a symbol of power, authority
3:7	keep	perform, fulfill, honor
	charge	agreement, obligation, service
3:8	BRANCH	an offspring of King Davis, prophesied to save Israel
3:9	seven	i.e. perfect number in Holy Scriptures
	one…seven eyes	the stone was Jesus, the eyes were the "Angels"

		or messengers that could "see" the future/were prophets; these seven were the leaders of the various Christian eras (Revelation chapters 2-3).
4:1,4,5	angel	messenger, supernatural being
4:3,11	olive trees	Moses & Elijah (law & the prophets)
4:7	mountain	authority, symbol, headstone
4:10	plummet	plum line, a mason's tool to build straight walls
	day of small things	slow start, humble beginnings
4:12	olive branches	prophecy of Moses-Elijah during tribulation period
	pipes	spouts, tubes
4:14	anointed ones	dedicate, or consecrate, empowered by God
5:1,2	roll	scroll, text, document
5:5,10	angel	messenger, supernatural being
5:6,7,8,9,10	ephah	a measurement for dry items (flour etc.)
5:6	resemblance	appearance, image
5:7	a talent	100 lbs.
5:8	mouth	opening
5:9	wind…their wings	there was a breeze, the birds were powered by the wind (not flapping in their own strength)
6:1	brass	judgment, wrath
6:3,7	bay/dappled	spotted, freckled, multicolored
6:4	angel	messenger, supernatural being
6:5	spirits	winds
6:7	walked	patrolled, guard
6:8	quieted	appeased, stilled, calmed
7:3	separating	abstaining, avoiding, segregating
7:5	fifth…seventh month	the fast was a memorial, a remembrance, not a true fast of humility and separation from their sins
7:6	eat for yourselves	selfish, put themselves first, not thankful
7:9	execute	dispense, fulfill, accomplish
7:11	stopped	closed, ended, shut
7:12	adamant	stubborn, hard headed, inflexible, tough
7:14	pleasant	precious, valuable, appealing
	desolate	destroyed, ruined, empty
8:2,3	Zi'on	Israel
8:3	Lord	Jehovah; God in relationship to mankind

ZECHARIAH

8:6	marvelous	difficult, extraordinary, amazing
8:10	hire	wages, reward, i.e. work
8:11	residue	what is left, remnant, handful
8:13	heathen	nations, pagans, people other than Jews
8:14	repented	grieved, felt sorry, change of mind
8:16	execute	bring to pass, fulfill
8:17	hate	despise, detest, contempt
	love no false oath	don't love lies or false promises
8:21	speedily	quickly, in a hurry
8:23	nations	people, groups by tribe, selection
9:1	burden	word of correction; prophecy, orders, commands
9:3	mire	dust, dirt, trash in the street a person walks on
9:5	perish	die, cease, end
9:6	illegitimate child	a mixed-breed (Gentile/Jew)
9:7	abominations	disgusting, sick, forbidden, offensive
	his…teeth	God will heal, clean up, make pure – take the bad things out of Israel's mouth
9:7	governor	leader, official, politician, ruler
9:9,13	Zi'on	Israel
9:9	having	endowed with, possessing, owning
9:11	covenant	agreement, promise, contract
9:13	Greece	a nation to North of Israel
9:16,17	His	God, Jehovah
9:17	corn	grain
10:2	idols	statues, pagan gods
	diviners	soothsayers, predictors, spiritualists
10:3	goats	i.e. leaders, chief ones
10:8	hiss	derision, mock, laugh at, ridicule
11:1	devour	feed on, eat up, destroy, consume
11:2	forest of the vintage	the oldest, most beautiful forests are destroyed and stripped of their leaves, cut down
11:3	spoiled	ruined, sacked, destroyed, ended
	pride	reputation, image, status, honor
11:7	staves	rods, i.e. Jewish tribes
	bands	pledged, bound
11:7,10	1 staft	Judah-Benjamin
	2 staft	other 10 tribes
11:8	cut off	destroyed, ended, wasted

ZECHARIAH

	loathed	despised, detest, contempt, make sick
	abhorred	despised, detest, contempt, hated
11:9,16	that	it
11:10	staff	rod, called Beauty i.e. Judah
11:10,14	asunder	in two, divided, split (i.e. Ju'dah-Israel)
11:10	covenant	agreement, promise, contract
11:13	prized at of	valued by, measured
11:14	Bands	i.e. 10 tribes
11:15	foolish	unwise, stupid
11:16	cut off	perishing, ending, finished, kicked out
11:17	woe	trouble, danger, look out! – a warning
	idle	worthless, lazy, selfish
	shepherd	caretaker, helper, religious leader
	the…eye	take away their sight, make them blind (a curse)
12:1,3	burden	trouble, weight, concern, issue
12:2	trembling	fear, concern, worried
12:3	burdensome	weighted, burdened, struggle, difficult
12:4	smite	attacked, strike, hit, punish
12:5,6	governors	leaders, officials, rulers, politicians
12:6	devour	defeat, destroy, beat
12:7	magnify	exalt, praise, make great
12:8	feeble	weak, unhealthy, powerless
	house	family, estate, tribe, nation
	Angel	messenger, supernatural being
12:9	pass	happen, fulfilled
12:10	they	all Israel
	bitterness	sad, heartbroken, mournful
12:12	land	country, Israel-Zion
12:12,13,14	apart	separately, alone,individually
13:3	thrust him through	kill, speared, stabbed
13:4	rough	old, ragged, humble, cheap
	deceive	fool, trick, deceive
13:5	husbandman	farmer, land owner
13:9	day of the Lord	End time, Jesus returns to earth
	spoil	plunder, loot, stolen goods
14:2	rifled	ripped off, looted, plundered, stolen
	ravished	defeated, sacked, spoiled
	residue	what is left, remnant, handful

ZECHARIAH

14:4	cleave	split, divide open by earthquake
	remove	move, slide
	half..south	an earthquake will rip the mountain apart, half will go one way and the other another
14:5	saints	holy ones, purified, believers, true followers
14:8	former	Eastern
	hinder	Western
14:9	one	Lord Jesus Christ; no more false gods or the antichrist taking God's name
14:12,18	plague	disease, sickness, disaster
14:13	tumult	commotion, excitement, outcry, pandemonium
14:14	at	against
14:14,15,18	heathen	non-Jewish people/nations, did not serve the one true God
14:15	these tents	those camps, houses, gathering of people
14:16	King	the Lord Jesus Christ in the Millenium
14:21	seethe	boil, cook

MALACHI

1:1	burden	message, warning, correction, prophecy
1:3	hated	despised, rejected, resented, thought less of
	heritage	inheritance, land, possessions
	laid his mountains	destroyed, wasted, ruined, leveled
1:5	magnified	honored, exalted, praised
1:6	fear	revered, respected, trembled, dread
1:7,12	polluted	profaned, violated, disrespected
	contemptible	cheap, ghetto, not worth anything
1:8	for	as a
1:9	beseech	beg, plead, ask, petition
	means	work, labor, ability
1:11	My name	Jeshua; Jehovah is savior – aka Jesus
	pure	sincere, honest, integrity
1:11,14	heathen	non-Jewish people/nations, did not serve the one true God
1:12	meat	food
1:14	corrupt	blemished, profane, violated, disrespect
2:2	lay it to heart	consider, listen to, pay attention to, think about
2:3	seed	offspring, descendants, children
	dung	refuse, garbage, poop
	spread dung…face	shame you, embarrass, humiliate – smear poop, crap on their faces
2:4,5,8,10,14	covenant	agreement, promise, contract
2:5	fear	revered, respected, trembled, dread
2:6	iniquity	sins, crime, evildoing, immorality
	equity	uprightness, honesty, fairness
2:8	stumble…law	the ministers once were honest and good, and they helped many people – but then they fell away or no longer were good and honest and this caused many followers to lose faith
2:9	base	no honor, punks, thugs, wicked, lowdown, vile
2:10	profaning	violate, pollute, disrespect
2;11	abomination	disgusting, sick, forbidden, offensive
2:12	master	teacher, instructor, professor
	scholar	student, disciple, learner
2:14	wherefore	why, because

MALACHI

	treacherously	dishonestly, falsely, fraud, cheat
2:15	residue of the spirit	God made man and woman as "one" being and then split them into two persons – one a masculine spirit/nature, the other with a feminine spirit/nature – the man was made first and that left the feminine or "residue" of the original spirit that contained both.
2:16	hates	abhor, despise, loathe, detest
3:1	covenant	agreement, promise, contract
	my messenger	God would send a man to announce good news, or a warning, to prepare them for when the savior would come. (like a weather newscaster warns the public before a hurricane)
3:2	refiners	men that used hot fires to melt metals (gold/silver) and purify them, taking out dirt and unwanted metals fuller's soap a strong, harsh soap used to clean clothes
3:3	purge	refine, purify, cleanse, wash
3:4	pleasant	pleasing, lovely, wonderful, good
3:5	false swearers	liars, rumor spreaders, gossips
	hireling	hired man, hourly worker, temp
	fear	revered, respected, trembled, dread
3:7	gone away	turned aside, left, departed
3:10	meat	food
	prove	test, try, examine, find out
	windows of heaven	God himself would bless, prosper, provide
3:11	devourer	enemy, foe, destroyer
3:13	stout	arrogant, proud, self-assured
3:14	mournfully	sorrowfully, sadly, mournfully
3:15	tempt	test, try, examine under pressure
3:16	feared	revered, respected, trembled, dread
3:17	I…Jewels	they will be selected, chosen, special
4:1	root, branch	nothing, that sustains life
4:2	fear	revered, respected, trembled, dread
	calves	animals without knowledge
4:4	statutes	law, rule, commands, decrees, directives
	judgments	ordinances, laws, policies, decisions
4:5	day of the Lord	end time – Judgment seat

MALACHI

4:6	smite	attacked, strike, hit, punish

New Testament

MATTHEW

1:18	Ghost	God's Spirit, supernatural force/ power
1:19	just	righteous, honest, fair
	privily	privately, secretly, hush-hush
1:20	angel	messenger, heavenly being, guardian
	conceive	begotten, conception, starting a baby
	Ghost	Spirit, supernatural force/ power
1:21	Jesus	Savior, the Son of God
1:24	angel	messenger, heavenly being, guardian
	bidden	directed, invited, asked, requested
1:25	knew her not	did not have sex, had no intimate contact with her
2:6	Governor	Ruler, civil authority
2:7	secretly	privately, quietly
	enquired	asked, sought information, interrogated
2:11	frankincense	spice, incense, perfume
2:13	angel	messenger, heavenly being, guardian
2:13,14,20,21	young Child	i.e. Jesus
2:16	mocked	tricked, mocked, deceived
	coasts	territory, boundary, border
3:2	repent	change one's mind & purpose; regret, guilt
3:4	raiment	clothing, garments, apparel
	meat	food
3:5	went out	came, left, departed, visited
3:6	baptized	dipped repeatedly, immersed, submerged – a symbol of washing, cleaning
3:7	Sadducees	a sect/group of the Jewish Elders, they did not believe in a literal, physical resurrection of the body after death
3:8	meet	fitting, appropriate, correct
	repentance	to change one's mind & purpose; regret, guilt
3:11	Ghost	God's Spirit, supernatural force/ power
3:12	purge	cleanse, empty, wash out
	garner	barn, farm building, storage silo
	fan	blower, palm leaf; used to blow away the shells off the wheat
4:1,5,8,11	devil	spirits, devils, demons, i.e. Satan

MATTHEW

4:3	tempter	tester, tormentor, Satan
4:5	pinnacle	the top of the building, the tallest point
4:6	angels	messenger, heavenly being, guardian
4:12	cast	throw, toss, pitch, remove
4:16	is sprung up	arose, came after, blew in
4:17	at hand	near, close, within reach
4:24	divers	different, unalike, dissimilar, various
	devils	spirits, devils, demons
	lunatic	crazy, insane, out of their mind
	torments	pains; illnesses (mental, emotional)
	palsy	physical handicap, paralysis of part(s) of body
5:1	was set	had sat down, got comfortable, settled down
5:3+	Blessed	happy, fortunate, special, unique, favored
5:5	meek	mild, gentle, non-violent
	earth	land, our world
5:8	heart	emotions, thoughts, intents, inner man
5:11	falsely	lying, dishonestly, falsehood, fraud, deceit
5:13	salt	preserve, flavor, seasoning
5:14	You	i.e. Jewish people, Israel
5:15	bushel	i.e. basket
5:18,26	verily	surely, truly, honestly, yes, correct
	jot	both are of the smallest grammatical marks in
	tittle	the Hebrew language (like an accent mark or comma)
5:22	Raca	stupid, senseless, idiot, dummy
5:26	uttermost farthing	every bit of, the very last money owed (a farthing equaled about 1/2 of a penny)
5:29	right eye…pluck	do whatever it takes to live right; no excuses
5:29,30	members	parts, pieces, individuals
	hell	a deep, dark, miserable prison for the dead whom have not believed & served God. A place of never-ending torment i.e. the Lake of Fire, Sheol, Gehenna, grave
5:31	put away	a.k.a. divorce
	writing..divorcement	a paper or certificate from the religious authorities giving permission to divorce
5:32	saving	except, beside, other than
	fornication	illegallon sex outside of marriage, immoral,

		dirty; also describes a union or relationship to something other than God/His rules
5:33	forswear yourself	false promise, not keep your word, break vow
5:36	swear by your head	a serious promise/vow – swearing by something implies that if you don't keep your promise, the thing you swear by is forfeit or lost to the one you promise. So If I swear by my head (literal head, or figurative my boss, master etc.) then I could be killed or my boss would have to pay
5:37	Yea, yea	Yes, yes
	Nay, nay	No, no
5:43,44	hate	abhor, despise, loathe, detest, reject
5:44	spitefully	shamefully, cruelly, unfairly, mean
5:45	rise	i.e. shine, give light & heat, life
5:46,47	publicans	tax collector/gatherers
5:47	salute	a formal greeting, say hello, hi there, recognize
6:1,2,3,4	alms	donation, hand-out, offering, financial gift
6:2,5,16	hypocrites	imposter, poser, fraud, pretender
	Verily	surely, truly, honestly, yes, correct
6:5	synagogues	churches, religious buildings
6:7	vain	empty, worthless, shallow, proud
6:12	debts	what we owe
	debtors	those that owe us money or anything
6:14,15	trespasses	sins, does wrong/bad things
6:18	secret	private, not for show
6:19,20	corrupt	decay, destroy, ruin, spoil
6:22	single	healthy, whole, without injury
6:23	evil	diseased, sick, unhealthy
6:24	hate	abhor, despise, loathe, detest, reject
	mammon	money, wealth, riches, material things
6:25	Take no thought	worrying, anxious, troubled
	meat	food
	raiment	clothing, garments, apparel
6:26	much better	more valuable, important
6:27	taking thought	worrying, anxious, troubled
	stature	height
6:28	take you thought	are you concerned, worrying, anxious, troubled
	raiment	clothing, garments, apparel

MATTHEW

6:29	arrayed	clothed, dressed
6:31	take no thought	worrying, anxious, troubled
	wherewithal	ability, talent, the means to do something
6:34	take no thought for	worrying, anxious, troubled
	morrow	tomorrow, the next day
7:2	judgment	do justice, punish, revenge, sentance
	mete	pay, give, disperse, deal out
7:3,4	mote	speck, splinter, small piece of dust/dirt
	beam	log, big piece of wood
7:5	hypocrite	imposter, poser, fraud, pretender
	beam	log, big piece of wood
	mote	speck, splinter, small piece of dust/dirt
7:6	pearls	words of wisdom, scriptures, insight
	rend you	tear, ripped, shred, pull apart, open
7:13,14	strait	narrow/skinny, bottleneck, channel of water
7:14	narrow	confining, tight
7:15	ravening	hungry, starving, bloodthirsty, violent
7:16	fruits	actions, results, offspring
7:17,18	corrupt	rotten, spoil, pollute, change for the worse
7:22	prophesied	foretell, make a prediction, speak for God
	devils	demons, evil spirit, bad supernatural force
7:23	iniquity	evil, crimes, sin, vice, wickedness
7:24,26	liken	compare, relate, similar to
7:26,28	sayings	words, speech, stories
7:28	doctrine	teaching, rules, instruction
8:5	beseeching	begging, pleed, intensely ask
	centurion	a soldier that was the boss of 100 soldiers
8:6	sick of the palsy	physical handicap, paralysis of part(s) of body
	grievously	terribly, sad, painful, hurtful
8:10	Verily	surely, truly, honestly, yes, correct
	marveled	amazed, blown away, wow!
8:12	gnashing	grit/grind teeth, grumble, threaten
8:17	infirmities	sickness, illness, disease
8:20	not where	no place
8:22	dead	spiritually dead, separated from God i.e. unbelievers
8:24	tempest	storm, upheaval, disturbance, violence

MATTHEW

8:28	devils	demons, evil spirit, bad supernatural force
8:30,31,32	swine	pigs, hogs
8:31	besought	begged, pleaded, asked
8:33	the	the ones
	of the devils	by demons, evil spirit, bad supernatural force
9:2	palsy	physical handicap, paralysis of part(s) of body
9:3	blasphemes	irreverence, disrespect, slander, evil speaking
9:9	receipt of custom	tax office
9:10,11	at meat	eating, dining, have a meal
	publicans	tax collector/gatherers
9:15	bridechamber	wedding party, banquet hall
9:12,21,22	whole	healthy, united, uninjured
9:16	new	unshrunk, never used
	rent	tear, ripped, shred, pull apart, open
9:17	bottles	wineskins, animal skins used to hold liquids
	perish	are destroyed, ruined i.e. break
9:20	diseased	sickness, enhealthy
	issue of blood	period, menstrual cycle
9:23	minstrels	flute players, entertainers
9:24	Give place	make room, backup, get away
9:25	forth	out, went
9:26	hereof	of this thing
9:31	fame	report, publishing, news
	country	land, counties, area
9:32,33	dumb	mute, can't speak
	devil	demons, evil spirit, bad supernatural force
9:34	prince of the devils	i.e. Satan
9:38	forth	out, went
10:3	surname	title, family/given name (Robert vs. nickname "Bo")
10:7	at hand	near, close by
10:8	devils	demons, evil spirit, bad supernatural force
10:10	scrip	A small bag or wallet used to carry money, usually fastened to the belt
	staves	clubs, sticks, poles, bats
	meat	food
10:12	house	estate, household, i.e. family

MATTHEW

	salute	a formal greeting, say hello, hi there, recognize
10:13	house	estate, household, i.e. family
10:15,23,42	verily	surely, truly, honestly, yes, correct
10:16	harmless	innocent, not guilt, without blame
10:18	testimony	witness, talks about, tells, testifies
10:19	take no thought	worrying, anxious, troubled
10:22	hated	abhor, despise, loathe, detest, rejected
	sake	behalf, benefit, account
10:23	gone over	finished, done, traveled to all nations
10:28	soul	inner person, emotion, life-force, being, life
10:29	farthing	small amount of money (a farthing equaled about 1/2 of a penny)
10:31	Fear you not	don't be afraid, don't worry
10:34	send	bring, deliver
10:35	at variance	at odds, disagree, fighting, at war
10:36	household	estate, household, i.e. family
10:40	Me	i.e. Jesus as man
	Him	the Heavenly Father, Creator
11:6	blessed	happy, fortunate, special, unique, favored
11:8	raiment	clothing, garments, apparel
11:11	Verily	surely, truly, honestly, yes, correct
11:17	piped	played music
11:18	devil	demons, evil spirit, bad supernatural force
11:19	winebibber	wine drinker, wino, partier
	publicans	tax collector/gatherers
11:20	unbraid	reproach, defy, taunt, yell at, scold
11:21	Woe	trouble, danger, look out! – a warning
11:21, 23	mighty works	supernatural deeds, actions i.e. miracles
11:25	Lord	master, ruler; deity (Jesus or God)
11:27	save	except, besides, other than
11:28	heavy laden	burdened, beat down, having a hard time
11:29	yoke	power/control over, burden or bondage, serve
	meek	gentle, mild
11:30	yoke	power/control over, burden or bondage, serve
12:1	corn	grain
12:2+	Sabbath	rest day, day off, seventh day of the week
12:4	showbread	ceremonial bread used in religious service
12:5	profane	violated, polluted, disrespected

MATTHEW

12:11	lay	take, get, obtain
12:18	soul	inner person, emotion, life-force, being, life
12:19	strive	fight, struggle, work hard at
12:20	quench	extinguish, smother, put out, discourage
12:21	His name	i.e. the name of the Lord Jesus Christ
12:22	devil	demons, evil spirit, bad supernatural force
	dumb	mute, can't speak
	insomuch	then, so, wherefore
12:24	devils	demons, evil spirit, bad supernatural force
	prince	leaders, chiefs, rulers, influential men
12:24,27	Be'el'ze-bub	Lord of the Flies/Corruption i.e. Satan
12:26	cast	throw, drive, kick out
12:27,28	devils	demons, evil spirit, bad supernatural force
12:29	spoil	plunder, loot, stolen goods, money
12:30	gathers	pulls, draws
12:31	blasphemy	irreverence, disrespect, slander, evil speaking
12:31,32	Ghost	God's Spirit, supernatural force/ power
12:33	corrupt	rotten, spoil, pollute, change for the worse
12:34	generation	modern crowd, group
12:36	idle word	mindless chatter, saying things about something/ someone without knowing the facts or it being true
12:42	queen	Queen of Sheba
12:44	garnished	in order, decorated, dressed up, designed
13:3,10,13,34	parables	story, myth, riddle/puzzle
13:4	fowls	birds
13:11	mysteries	hidden truths, parables, doctrinal uncertainties
13:15	waxed gross	grown dull, lazy, tuned out
13:15,19	heart	soul, one's innermost being
13:17	verily	surely, truly, honestly, yes, correct
13:18+	parable	story, myth, riddle/puzzle
13:19	wicked one	i.e. Satan, the devil
13:20	anon	right away, immediately, instantly
13:25+	tares	stickers, thorns, weeds
13:26	blade	single shoot or stalk of a plant
13:29	nay	no, never, incorrect
13:32	least	smallest, humblest, least important
	greatest	largest, most important

MATTHEW

13:33	leaven	added to bread making it rise, puff up
	leavened	yeast, a symbol of corruption and evil
13:37	Son of Man	a prophet, a chosen person i.e. Jesus
13:39	reapers	those that harvest crops, workers in the fields
13:40	burned in the fire	judged, punished, tortured
13:41	angels	messenger, heavenly being, guardian
	iniquity	evil, crimes, sin, vice, wickedness
13:44	treasure	money, wealth, riches, material things
13:45	goodly pearls	excellent, beautiful
13:49	angels	messenger, heavenly being, guardian
	sever	separate, cut off, divided
13:52	scribe	a state official, writers, ("literate" and able to make letters, words etc.), scripture interpreter
	instructed	taught, tutored, educated
	householder	head of family, landlord, building owner
13:57	save	except, besides, other than
14:1	tetrarch	a governor, co-ruler, small-time prince
14:2	do show forth themselves	demonstrate, display
14:7	oath	promise, pledge, vow
14:8,11	charger	a big plate, a serving dish, platter
14:9	them	i.e. dinner guests
	meat	food
14:11	damsel	girl, young woman
14:20	fragments	leftovers, pieces, small bits
14:21	beside	not counting women and children
14:22	constrained	made, strongly encouraged, forced
14:24	contrary	resisting, opposing, i.e. blowing
14:25	fourth watch	3 A.M. to 6 A.M.
14:26	spirit	God's Spirit, supernatural force/ power
14:27	Be of good cheer	take courage, relax, take it easy
14:30	boisterous	strong, powerful, harsh
14:31	wherefore	why
14:35	had knowledge	recognized, understood
14:36	whole	well, healthy
15:2,3	transgress	misdeed, sin, wrong-doing, break the law
15:6	none	no
15:7	hypocrites	imposter, poser, fraud, pretender

	well	rightly, proper, correct
15:9	doctrines	teaching, rules, instruction
15:11	goes…man	two meanings – the foods most Jews ate was "clean" yet their waste (poop, etc.) was "unclean" and had to be taken outside the city. Secondly, what you may hear or see won't necessarily make you unclean (I hear a curse word), but IF I curse/swear or my actions are bad, that comes "out" of me and makes me "defiled" or wrong
15:13	not planted, shall be rooted up	unfaithful, unbelievers, non-elect
15:15	Declare	explain, make clear, teach
	parable	story, myth, riddle/puzzle
15:17	draught	butt, anus – literally the drain pipe
15:20	defile	dirty, dishonor, disgrace, spoil
15:22	grievously vexed with a devil	miserably, seriously demon possessed
15:24	but	except, only
15:25	worshipped	bowed before, pray, respect, adore
15:26	meet	fitting, proper, expected, the right thing
	children's	i.e. Israel's, Jews
	dogs	wicked, cruel, gangsters, immoral
15:28,31	made whole	well, healthy, strong, renewed
15:30,31	dumb	mute, can't speak
	maimed	permanently injured, handicapped
15:31	glorified	praised, exalted, adored, revered
15:33	fill	satisfy, feed, care for, provide
15:37	meat	food
15:38	beside	not counting, other than
16:1	tempting	testing, tease, lure, draw away
16:2	evening	end of day, i.e. sunset
16:3	lowering	billowy, puffy clouds (rain clouds)
	hypocrites	imposter, poser, fraud, pretender
16:4	adulterous	unfaithful, cheating, disloyal
	sign	miracle, wonder, unusual event
16:6,11,12	leaven	a substance added to bread that made it rise,

MATTHEW

		puff up, i.e. evil teaching
16:9	took up	gathered, collected
16:12	bid them not	asked, urged them not to
	doctrine	teaching, rules, instruction
16:17	Bar-io'na	Son of John
16:18	Peter	little rock (petros)
	rock	mountain; cliff of rock (petra)
	prevail	win, champs, be strong, defeat, overcome
16:20	charge	ordered, warned, commanded
	Christ	Messiah, the Anointed One
16:23	offense	obstruction, violation, trespass
	savor	care about, regard, respect, understand
16:26	soul	inner person, emotion, life-force, being, life
16:27	angels	messenger, heavenly being, guardian
16:28	Verily	surely, truly, honestly, yes, correct
17:2	transfigured	changed, morphed, appeared differently
	raiment	clothing, garments, apparel
17:4	tabernacles	monuments, shrines
17:6	sore	greatly, badly
17:8	save	except, besides, other than
17:9	charged	ordered, warned, commanded
17:12	listed	wanted, willed, desired, wished
17:15	sore vexed	greatly troubled, disturbed, bothered
17:17	perverse	perverted, crooked, wicked; unfair, mean
17:18	devil	demons, evil spirit, bad supernatural force
17:20	verily	surely, truly, honestly, yes, correct
17:22	Son of man	a prophet, a chosen person i.e. Jesus
17:23	sorry	grieved, upset, disturbed
17:24,25	tribute	tax, money owed to the government
17:25	take	collectpick up, gather
17:25,26	strangers	foreigners, non-Jews
17:26	children	sons, i.e. citizens
17:27	lest	unless, or, otherwise
18:3	Verily	surely, truly, honestly, yes, correct
	converted	changed, transformed; The turning of a sinner to God. "Converted" means a person has left their old way of living/believing and has embraced the Christian faith; and in a more special sense

MATTHEW

		men are converted when, by the influence of divine grace in their souls, their whole life is changed.
18:6	offend	cause to stumble, sin, done wrong, hurt someone
18:7	Woe	trouble, danger, look out! – a warning
	offenses	sins, wrongdoings, violations
18:8	halt	lame, crippled, can't walk
	maimed	crippled, permanently injured, handicapped
	everlasting fire	hell, punishment, torment
18:9	offend	cause to stumble, sin, done wrong, hurt someone
18:10	angels	messenger, heavenly being, guardian
18:11	Son of man	a prophet, a chosen person i.e. Jesus
18:12,17	neglect	leave, ignore, go away from
18:13,18	verily	surely, truly, honestly, yes, correct
18:15	trespass	sins, does wrong/bad things
18:16	in the mouth	several people must agree, testify
18:17	heathen man	pagan, Gentile i.e. unbeliever
	publican	tax collector/gatherers
18:18	and…in heaven	what we say (vow/promise or curse/wish evil on someone) is powerful and "heaven" or supernatural forces help to fulfill our sayings
18:22	Until seventy times seven	490 years – the time Israel was in Babylon see Daniel, Jeremiah
18:23	take account	settled accounts with, paid up
18:27	compassion	mercy, pity, sympathy, kindness
	loosed	unbind, untie, set free, let go
18:28	that	what, all, the total
	pence	a Roman coin/money – it was worth one days wages/pay
18:32	desired	entreated, asked, wanted
18:33	compassion	mercy, pity, sympathy, kindness
18:34	delivered	transferred, brought
19:3	tempting	testing, tease, lure, draw away
	every	any
19:3,8,9	put away	divorced
19:11	receive	accept, take
	save	except, besides, other than
19:12	eunuchs of men	castrated; a male's testicles were cut off (the

		logic being that it reduced sex drive and temptation, a man could focus on his service to God, etc.)
	which…sake	behalf, benefit, account
19:15	laid	placed, put, set down
19:17	good	completely good, perfect, without fault
19:20	lack I yet	am still missing, deficit, shortfall, not enough
19:22	great possessions	many estates or properties
	sorrowful	depressed, down, troubled, mournful
19:23,28	Verily	surely, truly, honestly, yes, correct
19:28	regeneration	new creation, new world, after resurrection
19:29	hundredfold	100 more, multiplied by 100
20:3	third hour	9 A.M.
20:4	sixth and ninth hour	12 noon and 3 P.M.
20:6	eleventh hour	5 P.M.
20:8	hire	wages, pay salary
	steward	manager, personal assistant
20:11	murmured	complain, fuss, whine, grumble
	Goodman of the House	landowner, foreman, boss
20:12	wrought	worked, labored, crafted, made
	borne	took it, suffered it, endured, hung in there
20:15	evil	envious, jealous, ungrateful
20:19	mock	taunting, make fun of, laugh at, disrespect
	scourge	whipped, punishment, plague, curse, pestilence
20:20	desiring	requesting, wanting, wishing
20:21	Grant	permit, allow, place
20:25	princes	leaders, chiefs, rulers, influential men
	dominion	authority, command, power over
20:26	minister	servants, caretakers, helpers, preachers
20:31	hold their peace	be quiet, don't speak, remain silent
20:32	will you	are you wanting
	to	for
20:34	compassion	mercy, pity, sympathy, kindness
21:5	foal	young mule, old enough to ride
21:8	way	road, path
21:9,15	Ho-san'na	"Save now!" – a short Jewish prayer

MATTHEW

21:15	sore	very, really, badly
21:18	hungered	was hungry
21:19	presently	immediately, right now
21:21,31	Verily	surely, truly, honestly, yes, correct
21:29	repented	change one's mind & purpose; regret, guilt
21:31,32	publicans	tax collector/gatherers
21:32	repented not	had no remorse, guilt, regret & wouldn't change
21:33	let it out	rented or leased it
	husbandmen	someone that took care of agriculture (plants, trees, vines, etc.), gardening, landscaping
21:34	the time of the fruit	i.e. harvest time
	husbandmen	someone that took care of agriculture (plants, trees, vines, etc.), gardening, landscaping
21:36	likewise	in the same manner, just like
21:37	reverence	worship, pay respect to
21:38,40,41	husbandmen	someone that took care of agriculture (plants, trees, vines, etc.), gardening, landscaping
21:41	render	give, provide
21:42	head of the corner	headstone or cornerstone; a block/large square stone of great importance in binding together the sides of a building (if the corner wasn't straight the walls will go up crooked etc.); the word "corner stone" is sometimes used to denote some person of rank and importance
21:45	perceived	understood, comprehended, "got it"
22:1	parables	story, myth, riddle/puzzle
22:3,4,8	bidden	ask for, called, invitation, request to come
22:4	fatlings	fattened, well-fed animal
22:5	made light of it	paid no attention, dismissed, discounted
22:6	remnant	leftover, remains, survivors
	entreated	plead, beg, to sincerely request
	spitefully	shamefully, cruelly, unfairly, mean
22:10	furnished	filled, provided
22:13	gnashing	grit/grind teeth, grumble, threaten
22:16	person	physical appearance, status, or rank
22:17	lawful	allowed, legallon i.e. permitted in God's Law
	tribute	tax, money owed to the government
22:18	perceived	understood, comprehended, "got it"

	tempt	testing, tease, lure, draw away
	hypocrites	imposter, poser, fraud, pretender
22:19	tribute	tax, money owed to the government
22:20	superscription	signature, writing, engraving
22:21	Render	give, provide
22:22	marveled	wondered, awe, amazed
22:25	deceased	died
	issue	children, seed
22:29	do err	make mistakes, sin, act badly
	knowing	understanding, comprehend, aware
22:31	touching	regarding, concerning, relating to
22:33	doctrine	teaching, rules, instruction
22:35	tempting	testing, tease, lure, draw away
22:38	great	important, valuable
23:3	after their works	deeds, actions, behavior i.e. what they do
23:5	phylacteries	prayers; these were said regularly by the Jews; four specific ones (were also written Ex 13:1-10, 11-16, Deut 6:4-9, 11:18-21) were also written on paper and put in a small tube that was tied on their foreheads
	make broad	made the tubes bigger so people could see them (look at me, I'm religious, holy)
	enlarge…garments	certain prayer shawls were worn inside their clothes and down through their sleeves – so they would make the clothe long or extended so people could see they were wearing the "right" garment – again, "look at me…"
23:6	and….feasts	best seats, box seats, VIP seats
23:12	exalt	praises, applauds, makes important
	abased	humbled, broken, ashamed
23:13+	Woe	trouble, danger, look out! – a warning
23:14	hypocrites	imposter, poser, fraud, pretender
	devour	eat up, consume, destroy, gobble up
	pretence	pretend, fake, to put on an act, deceive
	damnation	judgment, condemnation, punishment, guilty
23:15	hypocrites	imposter, poser, fraud, pretender
	compass	travel all over, go about, surround, encircle
	proselyte	disciple, follower, convert, supporter

MATTHEW

	twofold	twice as much, double
23:16	debtor	obligated, owes
23:20,21	swear	pledge, solemnly promise, vow
23:23,25,27,29	hypocrites	imposter, poser, fraud, pretender
23:23	anise	known as the dill plant, herb, spice
	cumin	another plant, herb, spice (used in curries, gravy)
	omitted	left off, forgotten, abandoned
23:24	blind guides	someone of little help
23:25	extortion	blackmail, loan sharks, money/payday lenders
23:27,29	sepulchers	tombs, graves, crypts
23:28	hypocrisy	insincerity, imposter, fake, fraud, pretend
	iniquity	evil, crimes, sin, vice, wickedness
23:29	garnish	in order, decorated, dressed up, designed
23:30	fathers	ancestors, family, blood-line, kin
	blood	murder, kill, violence
23:32	fathers	ancestors, family, blood-line, kin
23:36	Verily	surely, truly, honestly, yes, correct
23:38	desolate	destroyed, ruined, empty, alone
24:4	heed	listen to, obey, pay attention to
24:2,34,47	verily	surely, truly, honestly, yes, correct
24:7	divers	various, different
24:9,10	hated, hate	abhor, despise, loathe, detest, rejected
24:12	iniquity	evil, crimes, sin, vice, wickedness
	wax	grew, increased, became
24:15	abomination	disgusting, sick, forbidden, offensive
24:19	woe	trouble, danger, look out! – a warning
	give suck	nurse, breast-feed
24:20	sabbath	rest day, day off, seventh day of the week
24:21,29	tribulation	trials, difficult times, hardships, suffering
24:22	elect's	chosen, special, singled out
	days…shortened	the time period won't be long, short duration
24:24	elect	chosen, special, singled out
24:26	secret chambers	inner rooms, private quarters
24:31	angels	messenger, heavenly being, guardian
	elect	chosen, special, singled out
24:36	day and hour	end time prophecy, exact moment of return
	angels	messenger, heavenly being, guardian
24:38	giving in marriage	pledging, engagement, arranged marriages

MATTHEW

24:39	knew	understood, comprehended, "got it"
24:43	up	into
24:45	meat	food
24:46	Blessed	happy, fortunate, special, unique, favored
24:49	smite	beat, strike, hit, punch, slap
24:51	asunder	cut into pieces, half, divide, split
	hypocrites	imposter, poser, fraud, pretender
25:4	vessels	containers, cups, bowls, vase, holder
25:5	tarried	waited, delayed, put off
25:5, 6,10	bridegroom	husband, spiritual symbol of Jesus
25:10	marriage	marriage feast, ceremony
25:12,40,45	Verily	surely, truly, honestly, yes, correct
25:15	several	own, individual, each
25:16	made them	produced, created
25:18	lord's	master, ruler; deity (Jesus or God)
25:19	lord	master, ruler, boss
	reckons	settle accounts, payday, judgment
25:20+	Lord	master, ruler; deity (Jesus or God)
25:24	sow	planted seeds, invested
25:25	hid your talent	did not use ability, underperformed
25:26	slothful	lazy, slow, worthless, slacker
25:27	exchangers	bankers, money-changers
	usury	loan money with interest (like payday loans), loan shark
25:31,32	Son of man	a prophet, a chosen person i.e. Jesus
25:33	sheep	obedient, followers of Jesus i.e. believers
	goats	disobedient, rebellious, self-willed i.e. lukewarm
25:34	King	God, the Almighty
25:45	verily	surely, truly, honestly, yes, correct
26:4	subtilty	logic, wisdom, street smarts
26:7	at meat	eating, dining, snacking
	alabaster	a type of stone material used for perfume bottles
26:8	to….waste?	the men felt that the pouring out of this very expensive money on Jesus feet was a "waste" of money, they could have sold it and spent it on poor people, etc.
26:10	wrought	worked, labored, crafted, made

MATTHEW

26:13,21,23	Verily	surely, truly, honestly, yes, correct
26:15	covenanted	agreed, made a deal, promised
26:17	unleavened	yeast-free
26:22	exceeding	very, a lot, having plenty, excess, abundant
26:24	woe	trouble, danger, look out! – a warning
26:28	new testament	agreement, contract – based upon grace & the life/death/resurrection of Jesus Christ
	remission	forgiveness, removal, taking away
26:31	sheep	obedient, followers of Jesus i.e. believers
26:37	heavy	distressed, pressure
26:47,55	staves	clubs, sticks, poles, bats
26:48	fast	firmly fastened, solid, unmoving
26:50	Wherefore	why
26:53	presently	immediately, right now
	twelve legions	72,000
26:56	forsook	left, abandoned, betrayed, left alone
26:63	held his peace	remained silent, didn't speak
	adjure	plead, beg, to sincerely request
26:65	rent	tear, ripped, shred, pull apart, open
	blasphemy	irreverence, disrespect, slander, evil speaking
26:66,68	smote	struck, hit, smacked, punched
26:68	Prophesy	foretell, make a prediction, speak for God
26:69	damsel	girl, young woman
26:74	cock crew	the noise a rooster (male chicken) makes – cock-a-doodle-doo
27:1	took counsel	conspired, made plans
27:3	repented himself	change one's mind & purpose; regret, guilt
27:5	cast	scatter, threw, tossed
27:6	price of blood	contract, hit, i.e. blood money
27:7	took counsel	conspired, plotted, talked together
	them	i.e. the silver pieces
27:14	marveled greatly	amazed, stunned, shocked
	answered him…	gave no reply, remained quiet never a word
27:15	wont	accustomed, used to, usual
17:16	notable	famous, well-known, celebrity
27:21	Whether	which
27:22,26, 35,38,44	crucified	nailed to a cross; public execution; a common mode of punishment among heathen nations in

		early times. This was regarded as a horrible form of death. This punishment began by subjecting the sufferer to whippings. The condemned person carried his own cross to the place of execution, which was outside the city, in a well-traveled place chosen for the purpose of humiliation and warning to others.
27:24	tumult	commotion, excitement, outcry, pandemonium
27:26	scourged	whipped, punishment, plague, curse, pestilence
27:27	common hall	a large room in a palace, used for meetings/trials
27:29	platted	braided, twisted, tied together
27:30	smote	struck, hit, smacked, punched
27:31	mocked	taunting, make fun of, laugh at, disrespect
	raiment	clothing, garments, apparel
27:34,48	vinegar	sour wine or vinegar & water mixture
27:35	parted	divided, split up
	casting lots	gambled, like flipping a coin; paper, rock, scissors, throw dice
	vesture	clothes, garments, what you wear
27:39	reviled	criticized, bad mouthed, cursed, put downs
27:41	mocking	taunting, make fun of, laugh at, disrespect
27:42,43	He, Him	Jesus
27:44	same	i.e. same insult
	cast…teeth	speak against, criticize, bad mouth
27:45,46	sixth hour	12:00 noon
	ninth hour	3:00 p.m.
27:49	yielded up the ghost	died
27:51	veil of the temple	thick curtain that separated two of the holiest rooms in the temple
	rent	tear, ripped, shred, pull apart, open
27:52	slept	died & buried
27:53	resurrection	rising, raise from the dead
27:54	feared	terrified, scared
27:58	begged	asked for, pleaded
27:60	hewn	cut, hack, chisel, chop
27:60,61,64,66	sepulcher	tombs, graves, crypts
27:63	deceiver	liar, con artist, false witness i.e. imposter
27:64,65,66	sure	secure, positive, definite

MATTHEW

27:65,66	watch	guard, protect, keep safe
27:66	sealing	securing, closing
28:2,5	angel	messenger, heavenly being, guardian
28:3	raiment	clothing, garments, apparel
28:8	sepulcher	tombs, graves, crypts
	fear	revered, respected, trembled, dread
28:9	they….feet	fell at his feet in worship and held them/him
28:11	watch	guard, protect, keep safe
28:12	large	big, huge i.e. a large sum of
28:14	secure	protect, keep safe
28:15	reported	told, rumored, i.e. believed
28:19	teach	tutor, mentor, disciple, instruct

MARK

1:4	remission	forgiveness, removal, taking away
1:6	loins	hips/waist/upper thighs
	wild honey	honey found out in the wilderness, not kept by people
1:7	One	i.e. Jesus
	latchet	leather thong or strap used to fasten a shoe or sandal on the foot
1:8	He	i.e. Jesus
	Ghost	God's Spirit, supernatural force/ power
1:13	tempted	testing, tease, lure, draw away
	ministered	attended, served, cared for
1:15	repent	change one's mind & purpose; regret, guilt
1:16,17	fishers	fishermen
1:18	forsook	left, gave up, walked away from
1:20	after	with, followed, accompanied
1:22,27	doctrine	teaching, rules, instruction
1:23	unclean	impure, dirty, filthy, unacceptable
1:25	rebuked	corrected, criticized, yelled at, warn
1:26	torn	violently shook, convulsed
1:28	fame	news, report, information
1:29	forewith	at once
1:30	anon	right away, immediately, instantly
1:31	she….them	served them, gave them food and drink
	ministered	attended, served, cared for
1:32,34,39	devils	demons, evil spirit, bad supernatural force
1:34	divers	various, different
1:35	solitary	lonely, quiet, private
1:40	beseeching	begging, plead, ask with intensity
1:43	straitly charged	sternly ordered, warned, commanded
1:45	every quarter	everywhere, all parts of the city (Jerusalem)
	to blaze	spread, deliver, take everywhere
2:1	noised	heard, broadcast, published, spoken, rumored
2:4	press	crowd, cram, huddle, puss
2:7	blasphemies	irreverence, disrespect, slander, evil speaking
2:9,11,12	bed	cot, pallet
2:12	we….fashion	like this, done this way

2:14	receipt of custom	place where taxes were collected
2:15	sat at meat	ate, dined, had a meal
2:15,16	publicans	tax collector/gatherers
2:18	used to fast	fasting; not eating all or certain foods
2:19,20	children	attendants, guests, close friends/relatives
	fast	go without, not eating all or certain foods
	bridgegroom	husband, man of honor
2:21	rent	tear, ripped, shred, pull apart, open
2:22	bottles	wineskins
	marred	damage, deface, bust up, tag
2:23	corn	grain
2:24,27,28	sabbath	rest day, day off, seventh day of the week
2:26	house	temple, place of worship, religious building
	showbread	ceremonial bread used in religious service
3:2,4	sabbath	rest day, day off, seventh day of the week
3:4	held their peace	kept silent, didn't speak, said nothing
3:5	restored whole	became completely healed, well
3:9	throng	group, crowd, gathering, horde
3:10	plagues	disease, sickness, disaster, curse, punishment
3:12	straitly	sternly, directly, pulled no punches
3:13	whom He would	i.e. those he wanted
3:14	ordained	authorized, chose, selected, purposed
3:15	power	authority, force, strength
	devils	demons, evil spirit, bad supernatural force
3:21	lay hold on	take possession of, subdue
	beside Himself	crazy, insane, out of his mind
3:22	devils	demons, evil spirit, bad supernatural force
3:26	has an end	i.e. he is finished
3:27	spoil	plunder, loot, stolen goods, money
3:28	Verily	surely, truly, honestly, yes, correct
3:30	unclean	impure, dirty, filthy, unacceptable
4:1,36,37,38	ship	boat
	in the sea	in a boat offshore
4:2	parables	story, myth, riddle/puzzle
	doctrine	teaching, rules, instruction
4:5	earth	soil, dirt, ground
4:10,11,13,33,34	parable	story, myth, riddle/puzzle
4:11	mystery	hidden truth

4:12	converted	changed, transformed; The turning of a sinner to God. "Converted" means a person has left their old way of living/believing and has embraced the Christian faith; and in a more special sense men are converted when, by the influence of divine grace in their souls, their whole life is changed.
4:13	Know	understand, comprehend, "get it"
4:17	for	because of
	offended	cause to stumble, sin, done wrong, hurt someone
4:20	thirtyfold, some sixty and some a hundred	thirty times, 60 (more)
4:22	manifested	displayed, demonstrated, brought out, show
	abroad	to light, be known, revealed
4:24	mete	pay, give, disperse, deal out
4:26,30	kingdom	power, kingship, dominion, rule
4:26	cast	scatter, threw, tossed
4:28	corn	grain
4:32	greater	larger, bigger, stronger
4:34	expounding	explaining, interpreting, clarifying, teaching
4:38	hinder	back, rear, stern
5:4	fetters	shackles, chains, hand-cuffs, restraints
	plucked asunder	torn/cut into pieces, half, divide, split
	tame	subdue, break, control
5:5	cutting…stones	cut himself on his arms and legs with sharp stones (people use knives, razors today)
5:7	adjure	plead, beg, to sincerely request
5:10,23	besought	asked, pleaded, begged
5:11,12,13,14,16	swine	pigs, hogs
5:12,15,16,17	devils	demons, evil spirit, bad supernatural force
5:13	leave	permission, go, depart
	choked	drowned
5:17,18	pray	request, petition, plea; sometimes contemplation, meditation or deep thought; communing/talking with God – this implies that God can/does hear us, talks back to us and can answer our prayers if He chooses to.

MARK

5:21	ship	boat
5:25	issue	period, menstrual cycle
5:26	things	treatments, remedies, medicine
	nothing bettered	didn't help, no improvement
5:27	press	crowd, cram, huddle
5:28	whole	well, healthy
5:29	fountain…her blood	period, menstrual cycle
5:29,34	plague	disease, sickness, disaster, curse, punishment
5:30	virtue	power, force, energy
	press	crowd, cram, huddle
5:38	tumult	commotion, outcry, pandemonium, riot
5:39	was come	entered, arrived
	ado	big deal, noise, commotion, uproar
5:39,40,41,42	damsel	girl, young woman
5:43	straitly	sternly, directly, seriously
6:2	sabbath	rest day, day off, seventh day of the week
6:4	kin	family, direct relative, blood
	house	family
6:7	power	authority, force, strength
6:8	scrip	A small bag or wallet used to carry money, usually fastened to the belt
6:9	shod	put shoes on, footwear
6:10	soever	wherever
6:11	testimony	witness, talks about, tells, testifies
	verily	surely, truly, honestly, yes, correct
6:12	repent	change one's mind & purpose; regret, guilt
6:13	devils	demons, evil spirit, bad supernatural force
6:15	prophet	someone that speaks for God, represents God – either predictions of the future or warnings
6:19	against	with
6:20	observed	watched, kept an eye on
6:22,28	damsel	girl, young woman
6:25,28	charger	a big plate, a serving dish, platter
6:26	reject	refuse, turn down
6:30	gathered themselves	grouped, assembled, crowded together
6:31	apart	aside, separate, alone
	desert	deserted, solitary, lonely, uninhabited
	leisure	extra, free-time, non-work related

MARK

6:32,35	desert	deserted, solitary, lonely, uninhabited
6:32,47	ship	boat
6:33	outwent	went ahead, passed them up
6:35	far passed	i.e. quite late
6:39	companies	full military units
6:40	ranks	single unit or groups of soldiers
6:43	fragments	leftovers, pieces, small bits
6:48	contrary to	hostile, oppose, against
	toiling	working, laboring, putting effort into
	the fourth watch of the night	3-6 A.M.
6:50	troubled	frightened, upset
6:51	sore amazed	very surprised, stunned, shocked
6:53	passed	crossed
6:55	bed	pallets – cots, stretcher
6:56	besought	asked, pleaded, begged
	whole	healthy, well, strong
7:4	brazen	brass like, copper, shiny brown metal
7:6	hypocrites	imposter, poser, fraud, pretender
7:7	doctrines	teaching, rules, instruction
7:9	reject	refuse, turn down
7:13	delivered	handed down, passed
7:15,20,23	defile	dirty, dishonor, disgrace, spoil
7:18	perceive	understood, comprehended, "got it"
7:19	draught	butt, anus – literally the drain pipe
	purging	eliminating, cleaning, washing, purifying
	meats	foods
7:20	defiles	dirty, dishonor, disgrace, spoil
7:22	lasciviousness	sexual abandon, out of control lust
	blasphemy	irreverence, disrespect, slander, evil speaking
7:24	would	wanted to
7:26	besought	asked, pleaded, begged
	devil	demons, evil spirit, bad supernatural force
7:27	filled	satisfied, content, full
	meet	fitting, proper, expected, the right thing
7:28	crumbs	leftovers, extras
7:29,30	devil	demons, evil spirit, bad supernatural force
7:32	beseech	begging, plead, ask with intensity

MARK

	impediment	speech problem(s), stutter, mumble
7:35	string	ability, control, vocal cords
7:36	charged	ordered, warned, commanded
8:3	divers	various, different
8:8	were filled	satisfied, content, full
	meat	food
8:10,13,14	ship	large boat
8:11	tempting	testing, tease, lure, draw away
8:12	verily	surely, truly, honestly, yes, correct
8:15	charged	ordered, warned, commanded
	leaven	a substance added to bread that made it rise, puff up, i.e. evil teaching
8:17	perceive	understood, comprehended, "got it"
8:22	besought	asked, pleaded, begged
8:24	as	like
8:30	charged	ordered, warned, commanded
8:32	rebuke	correct, criticize, yell at, scold
8:33	savor	regard, care about, value, understand
8:35	My	i.e. the Lord Jesus Christ's
8:36	profit	benefit, helpful, useful, valuable
9:1,12,41	Verily	surely, truly, honestly, yes, correct
9:2	transfigured	changed, morphed, appeared differently
9:3	raiment	clothing, garments, apparel
	fuller	launderer, clothes cleaner
9:5	tabernacles	tent, dwelling place, sacred building
9:6	sore	very, greatly, badly
9:8	save	except, besides, other than
9:9	charged	ordered, warned, commanded
9:12	set at nothing	utterly despised – treated with contempt
9:13	listed	wished, wanted, hoped for
9:15	saluted	a formal greeting, say hello, hi there, recognize
9:18	pineth away	wither, lose a lot of weight, become skinny
9:19	faithless	unbelieving, doubting
	suffer	put up with, endure, tolerate
9:20	tore	convulsed, pulled at
9:25	charge	ordered, warned, commanded
9:26	rent	convulsed, tear, ripped, shred, pull apart, open
	sore	terribly, badly

MARK

9:29	forth	out, went, left
9:30	would not	was unwilling, refused
9:33,34	disputed	discussed, debate, argue, find faults
9:34	held their peace	kept silent, didn't speak or say a word
9:37	Him, Me	i.e. Father, Jesus
9:38	devils	demons, evil spirit, bad supernatural force
9:40	on our part	for us
9:42	offend	cause to stumble, sin, done wrong, hurt someone
9:43	maimed	crippled, permanently injured, handicapped
9:43,44,45,46,48	quenched	put out, or stopped
9:44,46,48	worm dies not	skin worm, maggot; conscience, memory continuously gnaws away at you
9:45	halt	lame, crippled, handicapped
9:47	offend	cause to stumble, sin, done wrong, hurt someone
9:49	salted with fire	tested/prepared, preserved, tenderized
10:1	he was wont	his habit, custom, routine
	wont	his habit, custom, routine
10:4	suffered	permitted, allowed, let happen
10:5	precept	rule, doctrine, instruction
10:13	rebuked	corrected, criticized, yelled at, warn
10:14	Kingdom	family of God, realm, domain
10:15,29	Verily	surely, truly, honestly, yes, correct
10:23	How hardly	with difficulty, effort
10:26	out of	beyond, past
10:28	Lo	behold, because, therefore
10:30	a hundredfold	100 times more
10:33	delivered	turned over, given up
10:34	mock	taunting, make fun of, laugh at, disrespect
	scourge	whipped, punishment, plague, curse, pestilence
10:36	would you	do you want
10:43	minister	servant, attendant, preacher
10:44	chiefest	first in rank, influence, honour
10:45	ministered	attended, served, cared for
10:48	charged	sternly ordered, warned, commanded
	hold his peace	be quiet, don't speak, remain silent
	a great deal	loudly, more
10:49	Be of good comfort	take courage, be strong
10:50	rose	jumped up, got up, risen

MARK

10:52	whole	well, healthy
11:2	colt	a young horse, not fully grown
11:4, 5	loose	unbind, untie, set free, let go
11:7	cast, him	put, placed
	him	i.e. the donkey's back
11:8	way	road, path, small street
	scattered	spread, distribute, tossed
11:12	morrow	next day, tomorrow
11:13	haply	by chance, in case, maybe
11:17	nations	groups, tribes, peoples
11:18	doctrine	teaching, rules, instruction
11:23	Verily	surely, truly, honestly, yes, correct
12:1	parables	story, myth, riddle/puzzle
	let it	rented, loaned, leased
	winefat	winepress, a place where wine was made & sold
12:1,2,7,9	husbandmen	someone that took care of agriculture (plants, trees, vines, etc.), gardening, landscaping
12:2	season	harvest
12:3	empty	without, not having, empty-handed
12:4	handled	treated, attended, cared for
12:6	reverence	worship, revere, pay respect to
12:8	lord	owner
12:13	catch	trap, snag
12:14	lawful	proper, correct, authorized
	tribute	tax, money owed to the government
12:15	hypocrisy	insincerity, poser, fraud, pretender, two-faced
	tempt	trials, test, tease, lure, draw away
12:16	superscription	signature, writing, engraving
12:17	Render	give, pay, provide
12:19,20,21,22	seed	descendants, offspring, children
12:24,27	err	make mistakes, be wrong, fail
12:28	reasoning	arguing, dispute, debate
	perceiving	knowing, recognizing, understanding
	first	foremost, chief, top-dog
12:34	kingdom	people, citizens, children of God
12:38	doctrine	teaching, rules, instruction
	salutations	a formal greeting, hello, hi there
12:39	uppermost	chief, first, best

MARK

12:40	devour	eat up, consume, destroy
	pretence	pretend, fake, to put on an act, deceive
12:41	beheld	observed, watched
12:42	mites	the very smallest bronze or copper coin
	which…farthing	small amount of money (a farthing equaled about 1/2 of a penny)
12:43	Verily	surely, truly, honestly, yes, correct
	they	others
12:43,44	cast	put, placed, deposited
13:6,21,22	Christ	Messiah, the Anointed One
13:8	divers	various, different
13:11	Ghost	God's Spirit, supernatural force/ power
	premeditate	plan, rehearse, make-up in advance
13:14	abomination of desolation	disgusting, sick, forbidden, offensive (the Muslim Mosque of Omar that was built on the Temple Mount, over/near the Jewish Holy Temple)
13:17	woe	trouble, danger, look out! – a warning
	give suck	nurse, breast feed
13:19	affliction	tribulation, trial, pain, suffering
13:22	seduce	lead astray, entice, tempt, tease, lure
	elect	chosen, special, singled out
13:28	parable	story, myth, riddle/puzzle, illustration
13:30	Verily	surely, truly, honestly, yes, correct 14:1
	unleavened	yeast-free
	craft	stealth, deception being sneaky
14:2	meat	food
	spikenard	an expensive plant from the Himalayas (India) used to make perfume
14:4	indignation	anger, temper, destructive rage verging on madness
14:5	pence	a Roman coin/money worth one days wages/pay
	murmured	complain, fuss, whine, grumble
14:6	work	deed, act, outcome/product
14:9,18,25,30	Verily	surely, truly, honestly, yes, correct
14:12	unleavened	yeast-free
	killed	sacrificed, butchered
14:21,62	Son of man	a prophet, a chosen person i.e. Jesus

	that man	i.e. Judas
14:24	shed	poured out, given, supplied
14:27,29	offended	cause to stumble, sin, done wrong, hurt someone
14:31	vehemently	harshly, hotly, fiercely, powerfully
	wise	way, happened like this
14:33	sore amazed	struck with terror, shocked, stunned
	very heavy	in anguish or distress
14:41	hour	time, moment
14:43,48	staves	clubs, sticks, poles, bats
14:44	token	signal, cue, clue
	safely	under guard, watched, supervised
14:45	was come	arrived, showed up
14:47	smote	struck, hit, smacked, punched
14:50	foresook	left, abandoned
14:51	laid hold on	seized, grab
14:54	afar off	at a distance
14:55	sought	kept trying, attempting
14:57	certain	some, individuals i.e. certain people
14:59,60	witness	testimony, talks about, tells, testifies
14:62	right hand of power	in charge, position of power and authority
14:63	rent	tear, ripped, shred, pull apart, open
14:64	blasphemy	irreverence, disrespect, slander, evil speaking
	guilty	deserving
14:65	buffet	slap, push around, punch
	servants	officers, government workers
14:70	speech	accent, dialect
15:8	to desire	request i.e. asking
	ever	always
15:11	moved	stirred up, excited, motivated
15:15	content	satisfied, happy, fulfilled
15:18	salute	a formal greeting, say hello, hi there, recognize
15:19	smote	struck, hit, smacked, punched
	reed	cane, stick
15:20	mocked	taunting, make fun of, laugh at, disrespect
15:21	compel one	forced, made, threatened
15:25	third hour	9:00 A.M.
15:28	fulfilled	made true, brought to pass, made happen
	numbered with	

	transgressors	sinners, wrong-doers, criminals, gangsters
15:29	railed	verbally abused, yelled at, screamed at
15:32	reviled	criticized, bad mouthed, cursed, put downs
15:33	sixth hour	12 noon
	ninth hour	3 P.M.
15:38	rent	tear, ripped, shred, pull apart, open
15:39	Son of God	Messiah i.e. Jesus
15:42	sabbath	rest day, day off, seventh day of the week
15:43	craved	hungered, lusted, wanted badly
15:44	marveled	amazed, blown away, wow!
	any while dead	dead a long time
15:46	sepulcher	tombs, graves, crypts
15:47	beheld	saw, observed
16:1	sabbath	rest day, day off, seventh day of the week
16:2,9	first day	i.e. Sunday
16:2,3,5,8	sepulcher	tombs, graves, crypts
16:4	great	large, big
16:7	before	ahead of, in front of
16:13	residue	others, who's left over, excess, surplus
16:14	meat	eat, dine, have a meal
16:17	My name	Jesus, Messiah
	tongues	languages, dialects

LUKE

1:2	word	teaching/sayings/doctrines of the Lord Jesus Christ
1:3	The-oph-i-lus	the person Luke addressed his Gospel and the book of Acts to
1:5	course	priestly division, offices, roles
1:7,18	well	advanced, far along
	stricken	run down, weak, old
1:8	executed	finish, perform, complete, fulfill
1:9	lot	turn, time, duty
1:20	dumb	mute, can't speak
1:22	beckoned	called, motioned to come, signaled
1:25	reproach	shamed, ruined reputation, humiliation
1:27	espoused	engaged, pledged
1:29,41,44	salutation	a formal greeting, hello, hi there
1:32	Him…David	God prophesied that one would come/be born in the future that would be the greatest king ever, and he would be an ancestor of King David
1:36	barren	childless, not able to have children, unfertile
1:40	saluted	a formal greeting, say hello, hi there, recognize
1:42	blessed are you	special, unique, favored among women
1:50	fear	revered, respected, trembled, dread
1:52	low degree	lowly status, humility, poor
1:55	seed	descendants, offspring, children
1:56	abode	live, residence, make home, dwell
1:61	kindred	relatives, family
1:62	called	named
1:63	writing table	small board to write on – like a chalk/white board
1:65	noised	heard, broadcast, published, spoken, rumored
1:69	horn	emblem of strength, influence, power, force
1:70	spoke by the mouth	predicted, foretold, told them in advance
1:72	covenant	agreed, made a deal, promised
1:77	remission	forgiveness, removal, taking away
1:78	dayspring	daybreak, sunrise, early morning
1:80	waxed	grew, increased, became
2:1,2	taxed	registered for taxation

LUKE

2:4	house	estate, household, i.e. family
	lineage	bloodline, ancestry, family line
2:5	espoused	engaged, pledged, promise to wed
2:7	swaddling	clothes used to wrap infants, baby blanket
2:8	abiding	remaining, dwell, hang out, inhabit, live
2:9	sore	very, greatly, badly
2:10	tidings	news, report
2:11	city of David	i.e. Jerusalem
2:17,34,40	Child	i.e. Jesus
2:19	pondered	thought about, reasoned, daydreamed
2:24	turtle doves	small pigeons; derived from the noise of its sad cooing; offered as sacrifices by very poor people
2:25	consolation	answer to prayer, comfort, encouragement
2:25,26	Ghost	God's Spirit, supernatural force/ power
2:32	lighten	inform, bring life, give understanding
2:33	marveled	amazed, blown away, wow!
2:36	lived with a husband seven…virginity	married for seven years before her husband died
2:39	performed	completes, carries out, accomplishes
2:40	waxed	grew, increased, became
2:44	company	group, crowd, associates
	kinsfolk	relatives, family
2:46	doctors	teachers, scholars, professors
2:51	subject to	obedient
3:1	tetrarch	a governor, co-ruler, small-time prince
3:7	generation of vipers	offspring of cunning, malignant, wicked men-deceivers
3:9	root	foundation, strength
	trees, tree	symbol of man, Nations & Israel
3:11	impart	given, supplied, awarded, passed on to
	meat	food
3:12	publicans	tax collector/gatherers
3:13	Exact	collect, force to pay
	appointed	due, owed
3:15	the Christ	Messiah, the Anointed One
	mused	meditated upon, pondered, thought about
3:16	with	in
	latchet	leather thong or strap used to fasten a shoe or

LUKE

		sandal on the foot
3:16,22	Ghost	God's Spirit, supernatural force/ power
3:17	purge his floor	clean, empty, clear-out
3:19	reproved	corrected, criticized, yelled at, warn
3:22	descended	came down, visited
3:23	began…thirty years	turned thirty years old
4:1	Ghost	God's Spirit, supernatural force/ power
4:2	tempted	trials, test, tease, lure, draw away
4:2,+	devil	demons, evil spirit, bad supernatural force
4:7	worship	kneel before, bowed before, pray, respect, adore
4:9	pinnacle	the top of the building, the tallest point
4:19	acceptable year	an era of grace, mercy and acceptance had come
4:25	widows…Israel	a lot of women whose husbands had died
4:29	headlong	headfirst, drop him on his head over the cliff
4:38	besought	asked, pleaded, begged
5:3	prayed	asked, requested
	thrust	pushed, launched
5:4	left	stopped, finished, quit
5:4,9	draught	net-casting i.e. catch
5:5	toiled	worked, labored, put effort into
5:6	enclosed	caught, trapped
5:7	beckoned	called, motioned to come, signaled
5:11	forsook	left, gave up, walked away from
5:12	besought	asked, pleaded, begged
5:14	charged	ordered, warned, commanded
5:15	fame	report or rumor, news
	infirmities	sickness, illness, disease
5:17	doctors	teachers, scholars, professors
5:18	taken	became, got, obtained
5:19	tiling	roof tiles, shingles, rafters
5:19, 24	couch	pallet, cot, stretcher, temporary bed
5:21	reason	arguing, dispute, debate, talk
5:22	perceived	understood, comprehended, "got it"
	reason	think, consider, ponder
5:23	Whether	which
5:26	fear	revered, respected, trembled, dread
5:27	receipt of custom	book or ledger that kept the records of
	collected taxes	

LUKE

5:27,29,30	publican	tax collector/gatherers
5:30	murmured	complain, fuss, whine, grumble
5:31	whole	well, healthy
5:36	makes a rent	tear, ripped, shred, pull apart, open
	agrees not	inconsistent i.e. doesn't match
5:37	perish	die, end i.e. be of no use
6:1,2,5,6,7,9	sabbath	rest day, day off, seventh day of the week
6:1	corn	grain
6:1,4	rubbing them in their hands	either they were taking the husk off the corn, or the corn was dried and they were breaking off the individual kernels to eat
6:2,9	lawful	proper, correct, authorized
6:4	showbread	ceremonial bread used in religious service
6:8	stand	come, attend, present, show
6:10	restored whole	made well, healthy
6:18	vexed	anger, annoy, bother, harass, frustrate
6:19	virtue	power, force, energy
6:20,21,22	Blessed	fortunate, lucky, favored
6:21	filled	satisfied, content, full
6:22	hate	despise, detest, reject, revile
	evil	bad reputation, infamous, scandalous
6:24,25,26	woe	trouble, danger, look out! – a warning
6:24	consolation	answer to prayer, comfort, encouragement
6:28	despitefully	cruelly, unfairly, mean
6:29	cloak	cape, coat, long coat with a hood
6:35	again	in return, to be paid back
6:38	mete withal	measure, pay, give, disperse, deal out
6:41,42	mote	speck, splinter, small piece of dust/dirt
	beam	a piece of wood, lumber, house-building material
6:41	perceive	understood, comprehended, "got it"
6:42	hypocrite	actor behind a mask; imposter, poser, fraud, pretender
6:43	corrupt	rotten, spoil, pollute, change for the worse
6:44	bramble	thorn bush, hedge
6:48,49	vehemently	harshly, hotly, fiercely, powerfully
7:2,6	centurion's	Roman officer's (in charge of 100 men)
	ready	about

7:3	beseeching	begging, plead, ask with intensity
7:4	instantly	earnestly, diligently
7:5	nation	Israel i.e. Jewish people
7:6	under my roof	my house, home
7:8	set	placed, put before
7:10	whole	well, healthy, healed
7:13	compassion	mercy, pity, sympathy, kindness
	Weep	cry, wail, mourn
7:14	bier	casket, the funeral couch the Jews carried their dead to burial
7:16	fear	revered, respected, trembled, dread
7:17	rumor	report, story, news, gossip
7:18	showed	told, explained, reported
7:21	infirmities	sickness, illness, disease
	plagues	disease, sickness, disaster, curse, punishment
7:22	gospel	good news, the story of Jesus
7:23	blessed	happy, special, unique, favored
	offended	cause to stumble, confuse, upset i.e. doubtful of
7:25	raiment	clothing, garments, apparel
	appareled	arrayed, outfitted, dressed up, styling
7:27	he	i.e. John The Baptist
7:28	least	smallest, unimportant
7:29	publicans	tax collector/gatherers
7:30	rejected	refused, turned down
7:31	this	present, current
7:32	piped	upbeat, uptempo i.e. played wedding music
	mourned	sad, slow i.e. played funeral music
7:33	devil	demons, evil spirit, bad supernatural force
7:35	justified	statement of innocence, free from sin
7:36	desired	asked, questioned, wanted
7:36,37	meat	ate, dined, had a meal
7:37	alabaster	a type of stone material used for perfume bottles
7:38	anointed	an oil, lotion or spirit/force used to bless, dedicate, or consecrate by pouring or applying
7:38,46	ointment	oil, lotion, crème, salve
7:39	bidden	invited, asked, requested
	prophet	someone that speaks for God, represents God – either predictions of the future or warnings

LUKE

7:49	sat at meat	ate, dined, had a meal
8:2+	devils	demons, evil spirit, bad supernatural force
8:4,9,10,11	parable	story, myth, riddle/puzzle
8:13	rock	i.e. solid foundation
	temptation	test, tease, lure, draw away
8:14	perfection	maturity, excellence, complete
8:15	with patience	slowly, surely i.e. endures
8:17	made manifest	display, demonstrate, bring out, show
8:18	heed	listen to, obey, pay attention to
8:19	press	crowd, cram, huddle
8:22,37	ship	boat
8:23	they were filled	i.e. the boat was
	jeopardy	danger, trouble
8:24	rebuked	corrected, criticized, yelled at, warn
8:27	ware	wore, dressed in
	abode	live, residence, make home, dwell
8:28	beseech	begging, plead, ask with intensity
8:29	fetters	shackles, chains, hand-cuffs, restraints
8:30	Legion	(varied over time from) 120- 7000 demons
8:31,32,37,38	besought	asked, pleaded, begged
8:31	deep	abyss, ocean
8:32,33	swine	pigs, hogs
8:33	choked	drowned
8:39	published	proclaim, report, tell, testify
8:42	thronged	crowded, pushed and shoved
8:43,44	issue	period, menstrual cycle
8:44	stanched	stopped, ceased, held back
8:45	press	crowd, cram, huddle
8:46	virtue	healing power, force, energy
8:47	hidden	concealed, stashed, put away, secret
8:48,50	whole	well, healthy
8:51	save	except, besides, other than, only
8:52	bewailed	cried, wept, moaned, agonized
8:55	meat	food
8:56	charged	ordered, warned, commanded
9:1,42,49	devils	demons, evil spirit, bad supernatural force
9:3	staves	clubs, sticks, poles, bats
	scrip	A small bag or wallet used to carry money,

		usually fastened to the belt
9:4	abide	remain, dwell, hang out, inhabit, live
9:6	gospel	good news, the story of Jesus
9:7	perplexed	troubled, confused, uncertain
9:9	desired	wished, wanted, hoped for
9:12	wear away	i.e. get late
9:13	meat	food
9:17	filled	satisfied, content, full
9:20	Christ	Messiah, the Anointed One
9:21	straitly charged	firmly ordered, warned, commanded
9:22,41	suffer	endure, put up with, tolerate
9:29	raiment	clothing, garments, apparel
9:31	decease	dying, death
9:33	tabernacles	tents, temporary houses/huts
	knowing	comprehending, understanding
9:34	feared	were afraid, frightened, scared
9:37	beseech	begging, plead, ask with intensity
9:39	hardly	with difficulty, barely
	foams again	drooled, spit turned into foam in his mouth
9:40	besought	asked, pleaded, begged
9:41	faithless	unbelieving
	perverse	rebellious, perverted, crooked, wicked; unfair
	suffer	endure, put up with, tolerate
9:42	rebuked	corrected, criticized, yelled at
	tore him	spasms, convulsions, shook uncontrollably
9:44	hands	power, authority, strength
9:45	feared	were afraid, frightened, scared
9:46	reasoning	arguing, dispute, debate
9:47	perceiving	knowing, comprehending, understanding
9:48	My, Me	i.e. Jesus
	Him	Father
9:51	steadfastly	firmly, solid, unmoving
	set His face	made up mind i.e. decided
9:52,53	face	appearance, presence or arrival
9:54	consume	destroy, devour, eat up, destroy
9:56,58	Son of man	a prophet, a chosen person i.e. Jesus
9:60	dead	spiritually dead, separated from God i.e. unbelievers

LUKE

10:1	face	in advance, under his observation
10:4	purse	money bag
	scrip	A small bag or wallet used to carry money, usually fastened to the belt
	salute	a formal greeting, say hello, hi there, recognize
10:6	the son of peace	a welcome spirit, friendliness, acceptance
10:8	receive	welcome, invite, treat nicely
10:11	notwithstanding	nevertheless, anyway, whatever
10:12,14	tolerable	bearable, OK, alright, so-so, satisfactory
10:13	Woe	trouble, danger, look out! – a warning
	repented	change one's mind & purpose; regret, guilt
10:17	devils	demons, evil spirit, bad supernatural force
10:18	behold	look, see, observe
10:21	prudent	careful, good judgment, common sense, wise
10:22	Me	i.e. Jesus
	Son	i.e. Jesus
10:23	Blessed	happy, fortunate, special, unique, favored
10:25	tempted	test, tease, lure, draw away
10:30	raiment	clothing, garments, apparel
10:33	compassion	mercy, pity, sympathy, kindness
10:40	cumbered about	burdened with, tired, burdened, stressed
10:41	careful	anxious, concerned, worried
11:1	ceased	stopped, ended, concluded
11:4	lead	bring, push
	temptation	test, tease, lure, draw away
11:14,15,18,19,20	devil	demons, evil spirit, bad supernatural force
11:14	dumb	mute, can't speak
11:16	tempting	test, tease, lure, draw away
	sought	begged, pleaded, asked
11:17	desolation	destroyed, ruined, empty
11:18,19	Be'el'ze-bub	demon, messenger of Satan (literally it means "lord of the flies" – the king of corruption – which is ironic as Jesus was the author of life)
11:20	finger	authority, force, authority
11:22	spoils	plunder, loot, stolen goods, money
11:24	unclean	impure, dirty, filthy, unacceptable
11:24,25,26	he	i.e. the evil spirit

LUKE

11:26	him	i.e. evil spirit
11:27	paps	breasts, nipples
11:31	queen	i.e. queen of Sheba
	utmost	remote, far away, distant, high
11:32	condemn	judge, sentence, find guilty, cursed
11:34	single	healthy, whole, without injury
	evil	sick, unhealthy, corrupted
11:35	heed	listen to, obey, pay attention to
11:37	besought	asked, pleaded, begged
	meat	food
11:38	marveled	astonished, amazed, blown away, wow!
11:39	ravening	hungry, starving, bloodthirsty, violent
11:42,43,44,46,	woe	oh no, oh my; a cry of grief, sadness
11:42	rue	a shrubby plant about two feet high, of strong medicinal virtues
11:43	uppermost	choice, best, V.I.P., "box seats"
11:44	appear not	don't show, hidden, unseen, camouflaged
	woe	trouble, danger, look out! – a warning
11:45	reproach	insult, shame, ruin reputation, humiliate
11:46	lade	burden, beat down, make life difficult
11:47,48	sepulchers	tombs, graves, crypts
11:51	verily	surely, truly, honestly, yes, correct
11:52	hindered	delayed, slowed down, got in the way
11:53	urge	cheered, supported, encouraged, pushed
	vehemently	harshly, hotly, fiercely, powerfully
12:1	leaven	a substance added to bread that made it rise, puff up, i.e. evil teaching
12:3	closets	inner rooms, private areas
12:5	fear	afraid, frightened, scared
	hell	a deep, dark, miserable prison for the dead whom have not believed & served God. A place of never-ending torment i.e. the Lake of Fire
	forewarn	tell in advance, warn ahead of time
12:6	farthings	small amount of money (a farthing equaled about 1/2 of a penny)
12:10,12	Ghost	God's Spirit, supernatural force/ power
12:16,41	parable	story, myth, riddle/puzzle
12:17,18	bestow	give, share, let have, provide

LUKE

12:18	greater	larger
12:23	meat	food, nourishment
	raiment	clothing, garments, apparel
12:25,26	taking thought	worrying, anxious, troubled
12:29	doubtful	uncertain, confused
12:32	Fear not	don't be afraid, scared, frightened
12:33	wax	grew, increased, became
	corrupts	destroys, rots, spoils, pollutes, changes for the worse
12:35	loins be girded	supported by armor i.e. body be clothed
12:37,38,43	Blessed	happy, fortunate, special, unique, favored
12:37	verily	surely, truly, honestly, yes, correct
12:37,42	meat	ate, dined, had a meal
12:38	second watch	9 pm to midnight
	third watch	midnight to 3 am
12:39	goodman	master, i.e. head
	through	i.e. into
12:42,45,46	lord	employer, boss
12:47,48	stripes	lashes; marks caused by being whipped/beaten
12:50	till	plow, dig long rows in the ground, cultivate
12:51	division	dividing, separation, split
12:55	see	feel, observe
12:56	hypocrites	actors behind a mask, phonies, pretenders
	discern	know, recognize, understand, comprehend
12:58	hale	drag, pull, force to come
13:2	Suppose	think, believe
13:5	except	unless
13:7	fig tree	symbol of people of Israel
	cumbers it	burdens, sucks life from
13:8	dung	fertilize
13:10,14,15,16	sabbath	rest day, day off, seventh day of the week
13:11	bowed	bent over, bent in half, broken, humbled
13:11,12	infirmity	sickness, illness, disease
13:12	loosed	unbind, untie, set free, let go
13:15	hypocrite	imposter, poser, fraud, pretender
13:19	waxed	grew, increased, became
13:21	leaven	a substance added to bread that made it rise, puff up, i.e. evil teaching

LUKE

	leavened	mixed with yeast, a substance added to bread that made it rise, puff up, i.e. evil teaching
13:24	strait	narrow/skinny, bottleneck, channel of water
13:31	will	wish, want to, desire, longing
13:32	devils	demons, evil spirit, bad supernatural force
	do cures	heal
13:34	brood	nest, bunch, a pile of hatched
13:35	desolate	destroyed, ruined, empty, alone
	verily	surely, truly, honestly, yes, correct
	Blessed	happy, fortunate, special, unique, favored
14:1,3,5	sabbath	rest day, day off, seventh day of the week
14:2	lawful	proper, correct, authorized
	dropsy	a disease, excessive swelling in a body part
14:7	parable	story, myth, riddle/puzzle
	chief rooms	best places, choice, V.I.P.
14:8	highest rooms	best places, choice, V.I.P.
14:8,17	bidden	ask for, called, invitation, request to come
14:9, 10,17,24	bid	invited, asked, requested
14:9,10	room	place, chamber, hall
14:10	worship	bowed before, pray, respect, adore
14:11	abased	humbled, broken, ashamed
14:12,14	recompense	pay back, payment, reward or punish
14:13	maimed	crippled, permanently injured, handicapped
14:14,15	blessed	happy, fortunate, special, unique, favored
14:14	resurrection	rising from the dead, a.k.a. the Rapture
	just	righteous, honest, fair
14:15	meat	ate, dined, had a meal
14:18	all in one consent	at the same time, unanimously
14:19	prove	try, test, verify, check out
14:21	maimed	permanently injured, handicapped
	halt	lame, crippled, handicapped
14:23	compel	force, pressure into, make someone do a thing
14:25	multitudes	group, crowd, gathering, horde
14:26	hate	abhor, despise, loathe, detest, reject
14:28	compel	force, pressure into, make someone do a thing
14:29	mock	taunting, make fun of, laugh at, disrespect
14:31	consults	consider, deliberate, determine, take counsel
14:32	ambassage	representative, greeting party

LUKE

14:33	forsakes	leaves, give up, walked away from
14:34	savor	flavor, spice, seasoning
14:35	dunghill	manure pile
15:1	publicans	tax collector/gatherers
15:2	parable	story, myth, riddle/puzzle
15:7	just	righteous, honest, fair
15:10	angels	messenger, heavenly being, guardian
	repents	change one's mind & purpose; regret, guilt
15:12	portion	quota, ration, share, piece of the pie
	living	wealth, earnings, savings, money
15:14	mighty	severe, bad, harsh
	want	need, starving, desperate situation
15:15	joined	attached, partnered with
15:15,16	swine	pigs, hogs
15:16	fain	desired, badly wanted
15:17	perish	die, cease to live
15:22	hand	finger
15:27	is come	has arrived, is here
	received	welcomed, greeted
15:28	entreated	plead, beg, to sincerely request
15:29	transgressed	misdeeds, sinned, wrong-doing, violate i.e. disobeyed
	kid	young lamb
15:31	ever	always, all the time
15:32	meet	fitting, proper, expected, the right thing
16:1	steward	manager, personal assistant
16:2,3,4	stewardship	management
16:4	resolved	settled, decided, determined
16:5	lord's	employer's, boss's
16:7	fourscore	80
16:9,11,13	mammon	money, wealth, riches, material things
16:13	hate	abhor, despise, loathe, detest, reject
16:14	covetous	greedy, never satisfied, money lovers
	derided	make fun of, mock, laugh at, disrespect
16:15	knows	understand, comprehend, "gets it"
16:15	abomination	disgusting, sick, forbidden, offensive
16:17	tittle	small mark (like the dot over the letter "i")
16:19	sumptuously	first class, expensive, plush, fancy

16:22	angels	messenger, heavenly being, guardian
16:27	him	i.e. Lazarus
16:28	testify	testify, tell about i.e. warn
17:1	woe	trouble, danger, look out! – a warning
17:2	offend	cause to stumble, sin, done wrong, hurt someone
17:3	rebuke	corrected, criticized, yelled at, warn
17:3,4	repent	change one's mind & purpose; regret, guilt
17:4	trespass	sins, does wrong/bad things
17:6	sycamine tree	a type of tree – Mulberry or Sycamore (fig)
17:7	meat	ate, dined, had a meal
17:8	sup	ate, dined, had a meal
	gird	get ready i.e. prepare
17:9	trow	think, suppose, believe
17:16	Samaritan	person of mixed blood; Jew & Gentile
17:18	save	except, beside, other than
17:19	whole	well, healthy
17:20	demanded	questioned by, interrogated
17:31	stuff	goods, possessions, belongings
17:33	preserve	save, keep, protect
17:34	two men in one bed	people slept on mats or blankets in the same room as they lived in during the day; they didn't have their own rooms and beds like we do today
17:35	grinding together	grinding up grain (wheat, barley, etc.) at a mill
18:1	parable	story, myth, riddle/puzzle
	faint	lose heart, become discouraged, tire
18:2,4	feared	revered, respected, trembled, dread
18:3,5,7,8	avenge	get even, pay back, revenge
18:5	widow troubles me	bothers, bugs, disturbs, won't leave me alone
18:6	unjust	unrighteous, unfair, dishonest
18:10,11,13	publican	tax collector/gatherers
18:14	abased	humbled, broken, ashamed
18:17,29	Verily	surely, truly, honestly, yes, correct
18:19	save	save, keep, protect
18:23,24	sorrowful	sad, broken hearted, distressed
18:24	how hardly	with difficulty, a hard time, not easily
18:30	manifold	many, a lot, extra
18:32	mocked	taunting, make fun of, laugh at, disrespect
	entreated	handled, dealt with, addressed, talked to

18:34	hidden	concealed, stashed, put away, secret
	knew	understood, comprehended, "got it"
18:39	rebuked	corrected, criticized, yelled at, warn
	hold his peace	be quiet, don't speak, remain silent
18:40	stood	stopped, stood still, froze
19:2	publicans	tax collector/gatherers
19:3	press	crowd, cram, huddle
	little of stature	tiny i.e. short
19:5,6	haste	hurry up, speed up, go faster
19:7	murmured	complain, fuss, whine, grumble
19:10	lost	unbelievers, non-saved
19:11	parable	story, myth, riddle/puzzle
19:13	occupy	do business, stay busy, active, productive
19:14	hated	abhor, despise, loathe, detest, rejected
19:17	well	good job, well done, excellent
19:19	over	boss, leader i.e. in charge of
19:20	laid	wrapped, saved
19:21,22	austere	exacting, hard, tough, no-nonsense
19:23	usury	interest
19:27	reign	rule, control, command, the boss
19:32	even	just, righteous, honest, fair
19:33	loosing	unbind, untie, set free, let go
	colt	a young horse, not fully grown
19:36	way	road, path, ground
19:37	mighty works	supernatural deeds, actions i.e. miracles
19:39	rebuke	corrected, criticized, yelled at, warn
19:40	hold their peace	be quiet, don't speak, remain silent
19:42	belong to	meant for, needed for
19:43	compass you round	go about, surround, encamp, encircle, hem in
19:43	keep	force, hold
19:44	lay you	level you, knock down
	they…another visitation	through the scriptures and prophets, people are warned to leave bad/evil places – but they often don't listen or pay attention. So, this says that a time will come when the cities they live in will be destroyed, the "stones" or the building materials will crumble to the ground (e.g. New York's Twin Towers)

LUKE

19:47	sought	tried, attempted
20:9	parable	story, myth, riddle/puzzle
	let	rented, leased, paid a fee for temporary use
20:9,10,14,16	husbandmen	someone that took care of agriculture (plants, trees, vines, etc.), gardening, landscaping
20:10	fruit	produce (fruits & vegetables)
20:10,11	empty	empty handed, without anything
20:11	entreated	treated, acted, behaved
20:13	reverence	pay respect to, admire
20:17	head of the corner	headstone or cornerstone; a block/large square stone of great importance in binding together the sides of a building (if the corner wasn't straight the walls will go up crooked etc.); the word "corner stone" is sometimes used to denote some person of rank and importance
20:18	powder	dust, crushed rock, sand
20:19	sought	attempted, tried
	perceived	knew, recognized, understood
20:20	feign	pretend, faked, put on an act, deceived
	just	righteous, honest, fair
20:22	tribute	taxes
20:25	render	give, offer, hand over
20:26	held their peace	be quiet, don't speak, remain silent
20:28	raise up seed to his brother	it was Jewish law that if a man couldn't or didn't have children, his brother/male relative had to have sex with his brother's widow for the purpose of having a child. The reason being was to provide a direct blood relative to give all the possessions to – land, animals, money, etc.
20:47	a show	pretense, show i.e. smoke-screen
21:1,2,3	casting	putting, placing
21:3,4	penury	pennies, small amount, poverty
21:8	go	move out i.e. follow
21:9	by and by	immediately, right away, very soon
21:11	divers	various, different, many
21:15	gainsay	argue, debate, speak against
21:16	kinsfolks	family, direct relatives, blood
21:17	for	on account of

LUKE

21:18	perish	lost, badly damaged, destroyed
21:20	know	recognize, understand, comprehend, "gets it"
	desolation	destruction, ruin, emptiness
21:21	countries	lands, nations
21:22	vengeance	justice, get even, pay back, revenge
21:23	give suck	nurse, breast feed
21:24	trodden	trampled, crushed or broken by being stepped upon
21:25	perplexity	puzzled, confusion, uncertain, anxious
21:28,31	come to pass	take place, happen
21:29	parable	story, myth, riddle/puzzle
21:32	Verily	surely, truly, honestly, yes, correct
21:32	This	i.e. Generation 40-70 years
21:34	surfeiting	guzzling, doing shots, drinking quickly, out of control
	unawares	suddenly, unexpected, caught off-guard
21:35	snare	trapped, caught, imprisoned, tripped up, lure
21:37	abode	dwell, live, stay, make a home
22:1,7	unleavened	yeast-free
22:4	Him	Jesus
22:5	covenanted	agreed, made a deal, promised
22:6	multitude	crowds, people, large gathering
22:8	passover	kill the lamb used for the sacrifice during a ceremony; in remembrance of an event where God's angel of death did "Passover" any person or house that was marked by blood
22:10	bearing	carrying, holding
22:11	goodman	owner, landlord
	guest chamber	dining room, banquet hall
22:19	remembrance	memorial; reminder
22:22	determined	planned, ordained, destined
	woe	trouble, danger, look out! – a warning
22:24	accounted	considered, thought out
22:25	benefactors	financial supporter, donor, generous giver
22:27	whether	who, what person
	at meat	ate, dined, had a meal
22:28	continued	stood, stayed
	temptations	trials, test, tease, lure, draw away

22:35,36	scrip	A small bag or wallet used to carry money, usually fastened to the belt
22:37	accomplished	fulfilled, brought to pass, made happen
	have an end	reach a destiny, goal, fulfillment
22:39	wont	his habit, custom, routine
22:41	was withdrawn	pull back, separated i.e. withdrew
	cast	scatter, threw, tossed
22:43	angel	messenger, heavenly being, guardian
22:46	temptation	trials, test, tease, lure, draw away
22:51	suffer you thus far	enough, that's all, no more of this
22:52	staves	clubs, sticks, poles, bats
22:63	mocked	taunting, make fun of, laugh at, disrespect
22:63,64	smote	struck, hit, smacked, punched
22:65	blasphemously	irreverently, disrespectful, slanderous, evil speaking
22:67	Christ	Messiah, the Anointed One
23:2	perverting	mislead, corrupt, twist, change for the worse
	tribute	tax, money owed to the government
23:5	fierce	strong, harsh, cruel
23:7	jurisdiction	territory, turf, area he was in control of
23:8	desirous	hopeful, eager, wishful
	season	time, period, while
23:10	vehemently	harshly, hotly, fiercely, powerfully
23:11	men of war	soldiers, warriors
	set Him at nothing	treated Him with contempt
	mocked	taunting, make fun of, laugh at, disrespect
23:12	enmity	hatred, bad blood, bitterness
23:14	perverts	mislead, corrupt, twist, change for the worse
	fault	guilt, criminal act, wrong-doing
23:16,22	chastise	discipline, punish, rebuke, reprimand, scold
23:19,25	sedition	mutiny, rebellion, undermine, work against
23:20	willing	want to, desire, longing
23:22	evil	crime, offense
23:24	gave sentence	pronounced, verdict
23:27	bewailed	wailed, grieve, mourn
	lamented	wept, was sad
23:28	weep	cry, shed tears
23:29	Blessed	happy, fortunate, special, unique, favored

LUKE

	gave suck	nurse, breast feed
23:33,39	malefactors	sinners, wrong-doers, criminals, gangsters
23:34	parted His raiment	divided His clothing
23:35	derided	make fun of, mock, laugh at, disrespect
23:36	mocked	taunting, make fun of, laugh at, disrespect
23:41	amiss	bad, wrong, unlawful
23:43	Verily	surely, truly, honestly, yes, correct
	paradise	temporary waiting place, dimension - while waiting for the Rapture
23:44	sixth hour	12 noon
	ninth hour	3 p.m.
23:48	sight	spectacle, scene
	were done	happened, occurred
	returned	left, went home
23:52	begged	asked for, pleaded, sincerely requested
23:53,55	sepulcher	tombs, graves, crypts
23:53	hewn	cut, hack, chisel, chop
23:54	sabbath	rest day, day off, seventh day of the week
24:1	first day	i.e. Sunday
24:1,2,12,22,24	sepulcher	tombs, graves, crypts
24:11	idle tales	stories, fairy tales, talking nonsense
24:13	[60] furlongs	about 2 1/2 miles (a furlong is about 1/10 of a mile; about half way around a track)
24:15	communed	talked, discussed, spent time
24:16	held, hold	held back, disabled, stopped, blocked
24:23	angels	messenger, heavenly being, guardian
24:24	even so	right, correct, exactly
24:25	fools	not understanding, unwise, hard-headed
24:27	expounded	explained, interpreted, clarified, taught
24:30,41	meat	eat, dine, have a meal
24:31	knew	understood, comprehended, "got it"
24:32	way	road, path, trail
	opened	explained, made clear, revealed, taught
24:35	known	recognize, understand, comprehend, "gets it"
24:38	thoughts	doubts, worrying, anxious, troubled
	hearts	soul, one's innermost being i.e. mind
24:39	handle	touch, feel
24:46	behoved	necessary, required, had to happen

24:47	nations	other countries
	repentance	to change one's mind & purpose; regret, guilt
24:49	tarry	stay, hesitate, wait, delay, put off
	endued	given, supplied, awarded
24:53	Amen	this is true, yes, so be it, let it be

JOHN

1:1	In the beginning	start of everything, at the first
1:1,14	Word	logos, i.e. thoughts then sayings of God
1:3	All things	all: sun, earth, waters, mankind
1:5	comprehended	understood, mentally grasped
1:7,8,9	Light	i.e. Jesus
1:8	He	i.e. John the Baptist
1:11	own	the Jews i.e. own people
1:13	not of blood	not through sexual acts (a spiritual birth)
	will	want, desire, longing, plan
	but of God	God's will, desire
1:15	was	i.e. existed
1:25	that Christ	Messiah, the Anointed One
1:27	latchet	leather thong or strap used to fasten a shoe or sandal on the foot
	unloose	untie, take off
1:30	for He was before me	existed; Jesus (as a thought in God's mind) was the first or beginning of the creation of God (Revelation 3:14)
1:31	made manifest	revealed, made visible, made known
1:33	Holy Ghost	God's Spirit, supernatural force/ power
1:34	bore record	witnessed, observed and wrote about
1:38	dwell	live
1:39	tenth	4 pm
1:40	Him	i.e. the Lord Jesus
1:42	stone	petros; a little pebble or rock
1:47	guile	dishonesty, falsehood, fraud, deceit, baloney
1:51	Verily	surely, truly, honestly, yes, correct
	hereafter	at this time, very soon, right away, right away
2:2	called	invited, asked to attend, selected
2:3	wanted	needed, desired, wished for
2:4	Woman, what have I to do with you? My hour is not yet come	two points exist here: Jesus' relationship with his mother was changing and clarified (he was not actually her and Joseph's son, he was virgin born or created without the physical sexual act – so he calls her "woman" instead of "mother");

		and he also uses this phrase to imply that she overstepped his boundary by asking him to use his powers for a personal benefit, instead of healing/saving people – he was on the earth at that time to heal and save, not create personal wealth.
2:6	firkins	3 firkins=about 25 gallonlons each
2:8,9	governor	manager, supervisor, ruler, manager
2:11	miracles	supernatural, unusual event; wonder
	manifested forth	revealed, made visible, made known
2:15	scourge	whipped, punishment, plague, curse, pestilence
2:17	zeal of your house	the crazy behavior of the religious person
	has eaten me up	bothers, saddens, disturbed
2:20	rear	build, construct
2:24	commit	entrust, rely upon, hold responsible
3:3,5,11	Verily	surely, truly, honestly, yes, correct
3:3	again	anew, second time
3:10	master	teacher, tutor, mentor, revered leader
3:12	earthly	worldly, human
3:17,18	condemn	judged, sentenced, found guilty, cursed
3:20	reproved	exposed, correct, scold, show the error of
3:21	made manifest	revealed, made visible, made known
3:22	tarried	stayed, waited, delayed, put off
3:30	increase	become more important, grow great
3:32	testifies	bears witness, talks about, tells, testifies
3:32,33	testimony	witness, talks about, tells, testifies
3:36	everlasting life	never die, i.e. will live in heaven
	wrath	judgment, anger, hellfire, punishment
	abides	dwells, hangs out, inhabits, lives
4:3	departed	left, went back, returned
4:4	needs	has to, must, necessarily
4:5	parcel	piece of land, lot, ground, dirt
4:6	wearied	tired, exhausted
	sixth	12 noon
4:8,32,34	meat	food, nourishment
4:9,40	Samaritans	person of mixed blood; Jew & Gentile
4:10,11	living water	eternal life
4:19	perceive	understood, comprehended, "got it"

JOHN

4:20	fathers	ancestors, family, blood-line, kin
4:27	marveled	surprised, amazed, blown away, wow!
4:31	prayed	urged, asked, begged
4:36	reaps	gets, harvest, collect, gather, pick/pluck
4:38	bestowed	give, share, let have, provide
4:40	tarry	stay, hesitate, wait, delay, put off
4:46,49	nobleman	wealthy, influential, important i.e. official
4:47	besought	asked, pleaded, begged
4:48	Except	unless, other than
4:52	amend	get better, heal
	seventh hour	i.e. 1 pm
5:2	market	gate, area
	Hebrew tongue	the Hebrew language, what the Jews spoke
5:3,7	impotent	weak, feeble, without strength, powerless
5:3	halt	lame, crippled, handicapped
	withered	muscled weakened i.e. paralyzed
5:4	angel	messenger, heavenly being, guardian
	troubled	stirred, moved
5:4,6,9,11,14,15	whole	well, healthy, healed
5:5	infirmity	sickness, illness, disease
5:9,10,16,18	sabbath	rest day, day off, seventh day of the week
5:10	lawful	proper, correct, authorized
5:10,11,12	bed	pallet, cot, temporary bed
5:16	sought	asked, pleaded, begged, enquired, looked for
5:19,24,25	Verily, verily	surely, truly, honestly, yes, correct
5:20	marvel	act surprised, be amazed, shocked, blown away
5:21,22,23	Son	i.e. Jesus
5:24	death to life	earthly death, life in heaven
5:25	Son of God	Jesus
5:26	life	the source of life, eternal life
5:27	execute	finish, perform, complete, fulfill
5:29	resurrection of life	to live again, rising from the dead, a.k.a. the Rapture
	damnation	judgment
5:31	bear witness..myself	talk about myself, brag, blow my own horn (for a matter to be considered several people had to agree, testify)
5:39	Search	look at, investigate, research

	scriptures	sacred, holy writings; religious texts/books
	for	because
5:47	his writings	Pentateuch i.e. Genesis-Deuteronomy
6:6	drive	test, show, demonstrate
6:7	pennyworth	Roman coin/money – worth one days wages/pay
6:11	would	wanted, desired
6:12,13	fragments	leftovers, pieces, small bits
6:13	to them that	i.e. that which the people
6:15	perceived	understood, comprehended, "got it"
6:16	even	evening, after sunset
6:19	furlongs	20-30 furlongs=about one mile (a furlong is about 1/10 of a mile; about half way around a track)
6:21	received	took, brought, accepted
6:22	save	except, besides, other than
6:24	shipping	boats, traveled by water
6:26,32,47,53	Verily	surely, truly, honestly, yes, correct
6:27	Labor	work
6:27,55	meat	spiritual food
6:28,30	work	do, perform, accomplished
6:29	you believe on Him	admit belief in Jesus
6:32	not that bread from heaven	not the manna that was eaten in the wilderness or natural/man-made bread – a spiritual food
6:34	evermore	always, forever
6:41,43	murmured	complain, fuss, whine, grumble
6:46	save	except, besides, other than
6:49	manna	a small bread-like food that tasted like honey, like a cracker or very small tortilla
6:52	strove	fought, rebelled against, worked hard at
6:56	dwells	dwell, live, stay, make a home, settled
6:57	by	because of
6:60	hard	harsh, offensive
	hear	understand, comprehend, "get it"
6:63	quickens	strengthen, energize, bring to life
6:70	a devil	evil, wicked, bad
7:1,30	sought	desired, wanted, wished for
7:5	neither	not even, nor

JOHN

7:7	hate, hates	abhor, despise, loathe, detest, reject
7:9	abode	dwell, live, stay, make a home, settled
7:12	murmuring	secret discussion, complain, fuss, whine, grumble
7:13	fear	afraid, frightened, scared
7:16	doctrine	teaching, rules, instruction
7:18	unrighteousness	injustice, unlawful, disobedient
7:20	devil	demons, evil spirit, bad supernatural force
7:22,23	sabbath	rest day, day off, seventh day of the week
7:23	whit	every bit, completely, all parts
7:32	murmured	complain, fuss, whine, grumble
7:35	dispersed	scattered, spread
	Gentiles	non-Jewish people/races
7:36	come	go, follow
7:39	Ghost	God's Spirit, supernatural force/ power
7:49	knows	recognize, understand, comprehend, "gets it"
	law	Pentateuch, Torah i.e. law of Moses
8:2	again	back, returned
8:5	stoned	killed, punished by throwing stones
8:6	tempting	trials, test, tease, lure, draw away
8:10	condemned	judged, sentenced, found guilty, cursed
8:13,14	record	witness, history, account
8:15	judge after flesh	guess using human faculties (mind, emotions)
8:18	witness	talks about, tells, testifies
	bears	gives, shows, produces
8:28	lifted up	crucified, nailed to a cross; public execution
8:30,31	on	in
8:33	seed	descendants, offspring, children
	bondage	slavery, servitude
8:34	commits	does, performs, carries out
8:34,51,58	Verily, verily	surely, truly, honestly, yes, correct
8:35	abides	dwells, hangs out, inhabits, lives
8:41	fornication	illegallon sex outside of marriage, immoral, dirty; also describes a union or relationship to something other than God/His rules
8:42	If God were your Father, you would	this speaks to bloodline and the spirit of a thing - "after its kind" – if they were God's children

	love me	they would have the same spirit and would therefore both know and love Jesus
8:44	lusts	desires, wants, hungers for
	abode	live, residence, make home, dwell
8:46	convinces	convicts, persuades
8:48	Samaritan	person of mixed blood; Jew & Gentile
8:48,52	devil	demons, evil spirit, bad supernatural force
8:51,52	keep	respects, obey, follow, adhere to
8:52	taste	experience
8:55	be liar like to you	it's a play on words – they said they knew God and did not, he did know God and if he said he didn't he would lie
8:58	I am	the Eternal God; Holy Spirit in a man
9:3,8	that	so that
	manifest	display, demonstrate, bring out, show
9:4	work	do, act, perform
9:6,11	spittle	spit, saliva
	anointed	an oil, lotion or spirit/force used to bless, dedicate, or consecrate by pouring or applying
9:14,16	sabbath	rest day, day off, seventh day of the week
9:16	keeps	respects, obey, follow, adhere to
	division	difference of opinion
9:22	feared	were afraid of, frightened, scared
9:27	wherefore	why, is it because
9:28	reviled	criticized, bad mouthed, cursed, put downs
9:31	hears no sinners	doesn't listen to bad people; doesn't answer the prayers of evil doers
10:1,7	Verily, verily	surely, truly, honestly, yes, correct
10:4+	sheep	obedient, followers of Jesus i.e. believers
10:6	parable	story, myth, riddle/puzzle
10:8	hear	listen to, hearken, pay attention
10:9,10,11	I am	guard, gatekeeper; i.e. Jesus
10:9	find pasture	a good place to eat, food
10:10	abundantly	a lot, plentiful, extra
10:11,12,14,15	shepherd	guardian, protector, leader
10:12	wolf	enemy i.e. Satan
	hireling	servant, paid laborer, worker
10:17	lay down	give up, death on the cross

	take it again	raised and living
10:19	sayings	words, speech, stories, teachings
10:20,21	devil	demons, evil spirit, bad supernatural force
10:24	make us to doubt	keep us in suspense
10:31,32,33	stone	kill/punish by throwing stones
10:33,36	blasphemy	irreverence, disrespect, slander, evil speaking
10:39	sought	tried, attempted, wanted
10:40	abode	dwell, live, stay, make a home, settled
11:6	abode	live, residence, make home, dwell
11:8	sought	tried, attempted
11:12	shall do well	get better, heal, will recover
11:18	furlongs	15 furlongs=1/2 mile (a furlong is about 1/10 of a mile; about half way around a track)
11:20	sat sill in the house	stayed/remained in the house, didn't go out
11:21,32	not died	would not have
11:31	hastily	quickly, speedily, in a hurry
11:33	troubled	concerned, worried, distressed, sad
	groaned in the spirit	to be in emotional turmoil, moan, cry, sigh
11:44	Loose	unbind, untie, set free, let go
11:46	went their ways	left, dispersed, returned
11:55	purify	cleanse, wash, scrub, make holy
11:56	sought they	looked for a way, tried, attempted
12:3	spikenard	an expensive plant from the Himalayas (India) used to make perfume
12:4	which should	who would
12:5	pence	Roman coin/money –worth one days wages/pay
12:6	bag	money purse, wallet
12:11	away	left, departed, switched
12:21	desired	wished, wanted, hoped for
	would	want to
12:24	Verily, verily	surely, truly, honestly, yes, correct
12:25	hates	abhor, despise, loathe, detest, reject
12:28	glorified	praised, talk well about, honored
12:29	angel	messenger, heavenly being, guardian
12:31	the prince	i.e. Satan
12:34	abides	remain, dwell, hang out, inhabit, live
	lifted up	put to death by crucifixion
12:46	abide	remain, dwell, hang out, inhabit, live

12:50	everlasting	very old, ancient, been around a long time
13:2	devil	demons, evil spirit, bad supernatural force
13:5	wipe	dry
	girded	equipped, fastened, put on, got dressed up
13:7,12,17	know	recognize, understand, comprehend, "gets it"
13:10	save	except, besides, other than
	whit	bit, all, completely
	but not at all	i.e. except Judas
13:13	well	correctly, proper, right
13:16,20,21,38	Verily, verily	surely, truly, honestly, yes, correct
13:22	doubting	uncertain, confused
13:24	beckoned	called, motioned to come, signaled
13:25	lying on Jesus breast	resting his head on his chest, leaned against
13:25+	Lord	master, ruler; deity (Jesus or God)
13:26,27,30,36	sop	a piece of bread, used for dipping in sauce or gravy
13:27	That	What, the thing
13:28	intent	purpose, the point, reason
13:29	bag	money bag, purse, wallet
14:8	sufficed	enough, satisfied
14:12	Verily, verily	surely, truly, honestly, yes, correct
14:16	Comforter	Holy Spirit
	abide	remain, dwell, hang out, inhabit, live
14:18	comfortless	as orphans, alone, no support
14:21	keeps	respects, obey, follow, adhere to
14:21,22	manifest	revealed, made visible, made known
14:30	the prince of this world	i.e. Satan
15:1	husbandman	someone that took care of agriculture (plants, trees, vines, etc.), gardening, landscaping
15:2	purges	cleans, washes, purifies
15:4,6,7,10	abide	remain, dwell, hang out, inhabit, live
15:5	without	apart, separate
15:6	withered	dry up, shrink, slowly die
15:10	keep	respects, obey, follow, adhere to
15:11	joy might be full	complete, finished, more than ever thought
15:16	ordained	authorized, chose, selected, purposed
15:17,18,23,24,25	hate	abhor, despise, loathe, detest, reject

JOHN

15:19	were of	belonged to, a part of
15:22	cloak	covering, disguise, camouflage
15:26	Comforter	Holy Spirit
16:7	expedient	necessary, required, has to happen
	Comforter	Holy Spirit
16:8	reprove	exposed, correct, scold, show the error of
	judgment	do justice, punish, revenge, sentance
16:11	prince	i.e. Satan
16:12	bear	understand, appreciate
16:13	Spirit of truth	power, force, the life of a thing – therefore something that represents or identifies with truth
16:18	cannot tell	do not understand
16:20,23	Verily, verily	surely, truly, honestly, yes, correct
16:20	lament	cry, be sad about, agonize, mourn
16:21	anguish	grief, heartache, misery
	travail	birth pains
16:24	joy	contentment, happiness
16:25,29	proverbs	symbolic or figurative sayings
16:26	for you	on your behalf
16:32	own	own home, by himself, alone
	shall be scattered	split up, spread out, all over the place
16:33	tribulation	trials, difficult times, hardships, suffering
17:6	manifested	revealed, made visible, made known
17:12	son of perdition	destruction, ruin, wickedness i.e. Judas
17:14	hated	abhorred, despise, detest, reject
17:15	keep	protect, preserve
	the evil	sin, wickedness, demonic power
17:17,19	Sanctify, sanctified	made holy, cleansed, purified
17:23	I in them	Jesus in man
	You in Me	Father in Jesus
	Perfect	maturity, excellence, complete
17:26	declared	made known, shown, demonstrated
18:2,20	resorted there	met there, vacationed, rested, hung out
18:4	come upon	arrived, showed up, happened by
18:12	band	group of soldiers
18:17	damsel	girl, young woman
18:19	doctrine	teaching, rules, instruction
18:20	ever	always

JOHN

18:23	bear witness	talks about, tells, testifies
	coat…without seam	robe made from one piece of material, custom
18:26	kinsman	family, direct relative, blood
18:30	malefactor	sinner, wrong-doer, criminal, gangster
18:37	bear witness	testimony, talks about, tells, testifies
18:39	release	set free, deliver
19:1	scourged	whipped, punishment, plague, curse, pestilence
19:2	platted	braided, woven, twisted
19:3	smote	struck, hit, smacked, punched
19:4,6	fault	guilt, criminal activity
19:10,11	power	authority, force
19:14	the sixth hour	i.e. 12 noon
19:18	in the midst	in between
19:24	rend	tear, rip, shred, pull apart
	raiment	outer clothing, garments, apparel
	vesture	clothes, garments, what you wear
19:25	bore record	witnessed, observed and wrote about, eye-witness
19:29	hyssop	a common plant (Oregano?), used like a brush/sponge
19:31	sabbath	rest day, day off, seventh day of the week
	high day	special, sacred, important
19:33	saw	knew, understood, comprehended, "got it"
19:34	forthwith	right away, immediately, instantly
19:38	for fear	were afraid, frightened, scared
	besought	asked, pleaded, begged
	leave	permission, orders to go
19:39	myrrh	an herb and mixed with wine was a pain reliever, and could cause unconsciousness
19:40	wound	wrapped, bundled (like a mummy)
19:41,42;20:1+	sepulcher	tombs, graves, crypts
20:2,13,20	Lord	master, ruler; deity (Jesus or God)
20:9	knew	understood, comprehended, "got it"
20:15	borne	carried, transported
20:19	first day of the week	i.e. Sunday
	for fear	were afraid, frightened, scared
20:22	Ghost	God's Spirit, supernatural force/ power
20:23	remit	forgive, remove, take away

JOHN

20:26	within	inside, shut in, secluded
20:27	thrust	stab, poke, jab, spear
21:1	wise	manner, way
21:3,6,8	ship	boat
21:5	meat	food
21:7	girt	wear, fasten, put on, get dressed up in
21:15,16	love	love (agapao: divine love)
		like (phileo: human love)
		lust (eros: sexual love)
21:18	Verily, verily	surely, truly, honestly, yes, correct
	girded	wrapped, covered
21:19	he	i.e. Peter
	glorify	praised, exalted, adored, revered
21:22,23	tarry	stay, hesitate, wait, delay, put off
21:23	will	wish, want to, desire, longing

ACTS

1:1	treatise	account, record, history
1:2	up	risen, ascended i.e. to heaven
1:3	passion	agonizing death, burial & resurrection
	infallible	never failing, no mistakes or errors
1:4	assembled	grouped, gathered, crowded together
1:5	baptized with the Holy Ghost	when you believe, show your belief & baptized before others, the Holy Ghost will come upon you; possessed by, controlled
1:7	seasons	events of time, periods
1:8,16	Ghost	God's Spirit, supernatural force/ power
1:8	uttermost	farthest, four corners, remote areas/regions
1:10	steadfastly	courageous, brave, determined, committed
1:12	sabbath day's journey	i.e. about a half mile
1:14	accord	agreement, united
1:16	needs	necessarily, required
1:17,18	headlong	face first, headfirst
	asunder	cut into pieces, half, divide, split
1:18	reward of iniquity	payment for his bad deed/betrayal
	bowels gushed out	ripped his stomach open, guts fell out
1:20	bishopric	office, position, job, overseer
1:22	ordained	authorized, chose, selected, purposed
1:23	surnamed	title, family/given name (Robert vs. nickname "Bo")
1:25	apostleship	position, office as a missionary
1:26	numbered with	added to, included, counted
2:3	like as of fire	that looked like fire
	sat	rested, hovered over
2:4	utterance	things to say, prophetic sayings, speech
2:4,33,38	Ghost	God's Spirit, supernatural force/ power
2:4,8,11	tongue	languages, dialects
2:6	confounded	bewildered, confused
2:10	proselytes	disciples, followers, converts, supporters i.e. Gentiles converted to Judaism
2:11	works	deeds, actions, behavior

ACTS

2:13	mocking	taunting, make fun of, laugh at, disrespect
2:14	hearken	listen to, hearken, pay attention
2:15	the third hour	9 am
2:17,18	prophesy	foretell, make a prediction, speak for God
2:20	notable	famous, well-known, special
2:23	determinate counsel	chosen group, special committee, grand jury
	foreknowledge	describes God's ability to "know" the future, and make a plan according to his will/wants
2:24	loosed the pains of death	struggles, grip, hold
	of	by
2:25	moved	shaken, upset, troubled
2:27	leave	abandon, walk away, forsake
	see corruption	undergo decay, die, decompose
2:28	countenance	"face" - appearance, expression, presence
2:29	sepulcher	tombs, graves, crypts
	patriarch	the male elder, chief, head of the family/clan
2:30	prophet	someone that speaks for God, represents God – either predictions of the future or warnings
2:31	He	David
2:36	house	estate, household, i.e. family
	assuredly	for certain, definite, positive
2:39	call	invite, request i.e. salvation
2:40	exhort	urge, encourage, warn, advise
	untoward	crooked, wicked, corrupt
2:42	doctrine	teaching, rules, instruction
2:45	parted	divided, split up, separated
2:46	meat	food
3:1	the ninth hour	3 pm
3:2	ask	beg, plead, sincerely request
3:3	an alms	a gift, charity, hand out
3:4	on	at
3:5	heed	listen to, obey, pay attention to
3:10	alms	a gift, charity, hand out
3:12	marvel you	surprised, amazed, blown away, wow!
3:15	Prince of life	i.e. Jesus the Son of God
3:16	yea	yes, sure, ok
3:18	suffer	permit, endure, put up with, tolerate

ACTS

3:21	restitution	pay back, restore, replace
3:24	foretold	tell in advance, predict
3:25	kindreds	family, direct relative, blood
	children	sons & daughters, offspring, people
	covenant	agreed, made a deal, promised
	seed	descendants, offspring, children
4:2	grieved	disturbed, upset, bothered, troubled
4:3	hold	prison, jail, cell
4:8,31	Ghost	God's Spirit, supernatural force/ power
4:9	impotent	weak, feeble, without strength, powerless
4:9,10	whole	well, healthy, healed
4:13	perceived	knew, recognized, understood
4:15	go aside out	leave, depart
	conferred	discussed, talked
4:16	notable	famous, well-known, celebrity
	manifest	revealed, made visible, made known
4:17	this name	i.e. Jesus
4:21	glorified	praised, exalted, adored, revered
4:22	above	over
	showed	performed, completes, carries out, accomplishes
4:23	let go	released, set free
4:24	lifted up their voice	prayed; request, petition, plea; communing/talking with God – this implies that God can/does hear us, talks back to us and can answer our prayers if He chooses to.
4:25	heathen	unbeliever, non-Jew i.e. Gentiles
4:34	lacked	were in need
	possessors	owners
	prices	earnings, proceeds
4:36	surnamed	title, family/given name (Robert vs. nickname "Bo")
5:2	privy	aware, know, understand
5:3,32	Ghost	God's Spirit, supernatural force/ power
5:5,10	gave up the ghost	i.e. died
5:9	tempt	trials, test, tease, lure, draw away
5:12	wrought	worked, labored, crafted, made
5:16	vexed	angered, annoyed, bothered, harassed
5:19	angel	messenger, heavenly being, guardian

ACTS

5:21	senate	council of elders a.k.a. Sanhedrin
5:22	told	reported, rumored, talked about
5:23	keepers	guards, jailors
5:24	doubted	uncertain, confused
5:26	lest	or, unless
5:27	set	stood, placed, positioned
5:28	doctrine	teaching, rules, instruction
5:33	cut to the heart	anger, convicted, felt guilty
	took counsel	conspired, plotted, talked together i.e. considered how
5:34	had	held
5:35	heed	listen to, obey, pay attention to
5:36	brought to	became, ended up
5:37	taxing	registration for taxation
	dispersed	scattered, spread out, move all over the place
5:38	Refrain	stand away, get back, seperate
	counsel	guidance, wisdom, instruction, teaching, advice
5:39	lest haply	or, unless by accident, chance
6:1	ministration	service, work, job, routine
6:2	reason	desirable, wise, smart
6:3,5	Ghost	God's Spirit, supernatural force/ power
6:8	did	performed, completes, carries out, accomplishes
6:9	disputing	arguing, debating, discussing
6:11	suborned	bribed, paid to give a false story
6:12	stirred up	provoked, aroused, challenged, angered
6:13	blasphemous	dishonor, act disgracefully, ruin the name or reputation (in this case, using God's name wrongfully by saying/claiming he was directly related to God)
	holy place	temple, religious building
6:14	customs	rites, traditions, ceremonies
6:15	angel	messenger, heavenly being, guardian
7:1	said	asked, stated
7:2	hearken	listen, pay attention, attend
7:3,19	kindred	relatives, family, tribe
7:4,5	He	i.e. God
7:5,6	seed	descendants, offspring, children

7:6	sojourn	temporarily stay, visit, live
	entreat them evil	deal harshly with them for
7:8,9	patriarchs	the male elders, chiefs, heads of the family/clan
7:10,11	afflictions	troubles, torment, sickness, suffering
7:11	dearth	famine, no food due to bad weather
	sustenance	food, help, financial aid, support
7:12	corn	grain
7:14	threescore and fifteen	i.e. 75
7:15	sepulcher	tombs, graves, crypts
7:18	arose	came to power, ascended, placed
7:19	subtilly	tricky, deceitfully, crafty, outwit
7:22	learned	educated, went to school
7:23	full forty years old	when he turned forty years old
7:26	strove	fought, rebelled against, worked hard at
7:30	expired	passed, ended, over, used up
7:30,35,38,53	angel	messenger, heavenly being, guardian
7:44	witness	witness, talks about, tells, testifies of God's presence
7:51	stiffnecked	stubborn, hard-headed, rebellious
7:51,55	Ghost	God's Spirit, supernatural force/ power
7:53	kept	obey, follow, do, practice
	disposition	delivered, given by, decreed
7:54	cut to the heart	convicted, felt guilty, sad, remorse
7:55	steadfastly	courageous, brave, determined, committed
7:57	ran upon him	attacked, jumped him
7:59	calling	Stephan was calling, praying to God
8:1	consenting	agreeing, permitting, authorizing
8:2	lamentation	sad, broken hearted, distressed
8:3	havoc	commotion, damage, trouble, problems
	haling	dragging, pulling, taking by force
8:4	they	believers, Christians, Jesus' followers
	word	teachings/sayings of Jesus, a.k.a. gospel
8:6	heed	listen to, obey, pay attention to
	did	performed, completes, carries out, accomplishes
8:7	taken	stricken, hit with
8:9,11	sorcery	magic, witchcraft
	bewitched	confused, under a spell

ACTS

8:11	regard	believe to be, consider, have a reputation
8:15,17,18,19	Ghost	God's Spirit, supernatural force/ power
8:21	lot	portion, quota, ration, share, piece of the pie
8:23	bond of iniquity	trapped in evil, crime, sin, vice, wickedness
8:26	angel	messenger, heavenly being, guardian
8:27,38,39	eunuch	either a castrated man (no testicles/balls) or, in ancient terms, any man who is impotent with women. They worked as household servants, religious specialists, government officials, and guardians of women
8:31	guide	instruct, teach, show the way
	desired	wished, wanted, hoped for
8:32	dumb	mute, can't speak
8:33	humiliation	shame, embarrassment, ruined reputation
8:34	answered	asked, inquired
9:1	yet	still, continuing
9:2	desired	wished, wanted, hoped for
	of this way	Christianity i.e. followers of Jesus Christ
9:8	no man	nothing, none, no one
9:13	saints	holy ones, purified, believers, true followers
9:14	bind	arrest, tie up, restrain
9:17,31	Ghost	God's Spirit, supernatural force/ power
9:18	as it had been scales	like scales, flakes
	forthwith	right away, immediately, instantly
9:19	received meat	ate, dined, had a meal
9:22	confounded	confused, put to shame, rattled
9:23	took counsel	made plans, conspired, plotted, talked together
9:29	disputed	discussed, debate, argue, find faults
9:31	edified	built up, strengthened, establish, made strong
	fear	revered, respected, trembled, dread
9:34	whole	well, healthy, healed
9:36	almsdeeds	charity, helping others financially
9:37	washed	prepared her body
9:38	desiring	requesting, wanting, wishing
9:39	by	around, near
9:41	saints	Christians, purified, believers, true followers
10:1	centurion	Roman soldier in charge of 100 soldiers
10:2	devout	having moral integrity or purity; avoidance of

		sin, dedicated to God
10:2,35	feared	revered, respected, trembled, dread
10:2,31	alms	a gift, charity, hand out
10:3,30	ninth hour	i.e. 3 pm
10:3,7,22	angel	messenger, heavenly being, guardian
10:5	surname	title, family/given name (Robert vs. nickname "Bo")
10:6	a tanner	a leather worker, someone that worked with animal hides
10:9	sixth hour	i.e. 12 noon
10:17	doubted	uncertain, confused i.e. questioned
10:18	were lodged	staying, living
	surnamed	title, family/given name (Robert vs. nickname "Bo")
10:22	centurion	Roman officer over 100 soldiers
10:29	gainsaying	arguing, debating, speaking against, gossiping
	intent	purpose, plan, reason
10:38,44,45,47	Ghost	God's Spirit, supernatural force/ power
10:40	openly	plainly, clearly i.e. visibly alive
10:43	remission	forgiveness, removal, taking away
10:45	they of the circumcision	i.e. the Jews
10:46	tongues	languages, dialects
	magnify	exalt, lift up, praise, worship
10:48	tarry	stay, hesitate, wait, delay, put off
11:2	contended	disputed, discussed, debated, argued, find faults
11:4	expounded	explained, interpreted clarified, taught
11:5	even to	unto
	great sheet	big sheet or blanket
11:6	fowls	birds
11:12	bid me	invited, asked, requested
11:13	angel	messenger, heavenly being, guardian
	surnamed	title, family/given name (Robert vs. nickname "Bo")
11:15,16,24	Ghost	God's Spirit, supernatural force/ power
11:18	repentance	to change one's mind & purpose; regret, guilt
11:19	persecution	attacks, hassles, bullied, given trouble
11:23	exhorted	urged, encouraged, warned, advised

ACTS

11:28	signified	indicated, revealed, informed
	dearth	famine, no food due to bad weather
11:30	it	i.e. the money
12:1	vex	anger, annoy, bother, harass, frustrate
12:3	take	seize, i.e. arrest
	unleavened	yeast-free
12:4	apprehended	arrested, caught, laid hold on
	[4] quaternions	consisted of four soldiers each, two stayed with the prisoner and two stayed outside to guard; total of sixteen
	Easter	pagan festival after Passover
12:5	church	gathering together of believers, group
12:6	kept	guarded, watched over
12:7+	angel	messenger, heavenly being, guardian
12:7	smote	struck, hit, smacked, punched
	raised	aroused, wake
12:9	true	real, genuine, factual
12:10	ward	guard, jailor, watchman
	passed on	walked
12:11	of a surety	for sure, guarantee
12:13	damsel	servant girl, girl, young woman
	hearken	listen to, hearken, pay attention
12:15	affirmed	stated, pledged, swore, kept her story
12:16	astonished	amazed, shocked, stunned, surprised
12:17	hold their peace	be quiet, don't speak, remain silent
12:18	stir	provoke, arouse, challenge, anger
12:21	arrayed	clothed, dressed, displayed
	oration	speech
12:25	ministry	service, mission, way of helpng
13:1	prophet	someone that speaks for God, represents God – either predictions of the future or warnings
	tetrarch	a governor, co-ruler, small-time prince
13:2,4,9,52	Ghost	God's Spirit, supernatural force/ power
13:5	minister	preacher i.e. as their helper
13:7,12	deputy	procounsel, judge/city official
13:7	prudent	careful, good judgment, common sense, wise
13:8	withstood	opposed, fought, resisted
13:10	subtilty	deceit, logic, wisdom, street smarts

ACTS

	devil	demons, evil spirit, bad supernatural force
	pervert	mislead, corrupt, twist, change for the worse
13:11	season	time
13:12	doctrine	teaching, rules, instruction
13:13	loosed	set sail, released, set free
13:14,27,42,44	Sabbath	rest day, day off, seventh day of the week
13:16	fear	reverence, respect, awe i.e. honor
13:17	a high arm	authority, strength, mighty power
13:18	manners	evil ways, bad behavior
13:23	seed	descendants, offspring, children
13:25	loose	unbind, untie, set free, let go
13:26	fears	revered, respected, trembled, dread
13:28	cause	reason, excuse, explanation
13:29	sepulcher	tombs, graves, crypts
13:36	fell on sleep	fell asleep, i.e. died
	served…generation	performed his God-ordained job/duties
	saw corruption	decomposed, rotted after death
13:37	corruption	decay, die, decompose, rot
13:40	lest that	that it might not, or, otherwise
13:42	besought	asked, pleaded, begged
13:43	proselytes	disciples, followers, converts, supporters
13:45	spoke against	contradicted, bad-mouthed
	contradicting	arguing, debating, speaking against, gossiping
13:48	glorified	praised, exalted, adored, revered
13:50	coasts	territory, boundary, border, districts
	devout	having moral integrity or purity; avoidance of sin, dedicated to God
14:8	impotent	weak, frail, without power
14:9	perceiving	knowing, comprehending, understanding
	steadfastly	courageous, brave, determined, committed
14:14	rent	tear, ripped, shred, pull apart, open
14:15	passions	feelings, emotions
	vanities	useless activities, pointless behaviors (e.g. asking stone statues to help them)
14:19	supposing	thinking, guessing
14:20	rose up	brought back from the dead i.e. revived
14:22	exhorting	an urging, encouragement, warning, advice
14:26	recommended	commended, suggested, advised

ACTS

14:28	disciples	believers, followers of Jesus & teachings
15:2	disputation	disagreement, argument, misunderstanding
15:4	declared	reported, stated, talked about
15:5	needful	necessary, required
	keep	respects, obey, follow, adhere to
	sect	group, gang, organization
15:8,28	Ghost	God's Spirit, supernatural force/ power
15:10	tempt	trials, test, tease, lure, draw away
	yoke	power/control over, burden or bondage, serve
15:12	wrought	worked, labored, crafted, made
15:13	held their peace	stopped speaking
	hearken	listen, pay attention, attend
15:19	sentence	judgment, verdict, punishment
15:20	abstain	hold back, avoid, do without, stay away from
	fornication	illegallon sex outside of marriage, immoral, dirty; also describes a union or relationship to something other than God/His rules
15:22	chief	leader, in charge, top dog
15:24	subverting	rebel, undermine, weaken, corrupt, sabotage
15:25	with one accord	agreement, unity i.e. as one
15:26	hazarded	risked, endangered
15:27	by mouth	directly i.e. face to face
15:29	meats	foods
15:30	multitude	group, crowd, gathering of people
	epistle	letter, message, note, directive
15:32	prophets	someone that speaks for God, represents God – either predictions of the future or warnings
15:33	tarried	stayed, waited, delayed, put off
15:34	still	awhile, yet, soon
15:38	departed	deserted, left, went away
15:39	departed asunder	separated, half, divide, split
15:40	recommended	commended, suggested, advised
15:41	confirming	strengthening, supporting
16:1	and	i.e. who
16:4	ordained	authorized, chose, selected, purposed
16:6	Ghost	God's Spirit, supernatural force/ power
16:7	assayed	thought about, considered, was deciding

ACTS

16:9	prayed	begged, pleaded, asked
16:10	assuredly gathering	concluding, believing, being persuaded
	endeavored	attempted, best efforts, good try
16:11	loosing	setting sail, casting off
16:13	sabbath	rest day, day off, seventh day of the week
	wont	his habit, custom, routine
	resorted	gathered, hung out
16:14	a seller of purple	expensive clothes seller, upscale, fancy
16:15	constrained	prevailed upon, forced, convinced
16:16	damsel	girl, young woman
	gain	profit, money-making
	soothsaying	fortune telling
16:18	grieved	disturbed, upset, bothered, troubled
16:19	hope of their gains	profits gone, money-making scheme is busted
16:22	rent	tear, ripped, shred, pull apart, open
16:23	stripes	lashes; marks caused by being whipped/beaten
	charging	commanding, ordering, warning
16:24	charge	ordered, warned, commanded
	fast	firmly fastened, solid, unmoving
16:27	been fled	escaped, got away
16:29	sprang	rushed, leapt, went after
16:33	stripes	lashes; marks caused by being whipped/beaten
16:34	meat	food
16:35	sergeants	a government official, military representative
16:36	sent	instructed, commanded, gave orders
16:37	thrust	put, sent, shoved
	secretly	privately, quietly, hush-hush
	nay	no, never, incorrect
	verily	surely, truly, honestly, yes, correct
17:2	sabbath	rest day, day off, seventh day of the week
17:3	alleging	making accusations, indicting, slander, blaming
	needs	necessarily, required
17:4	consorted	friends with, hung out, buddies
	devout	having moral integrity or purity; avoidance of sin, dedicated to God
17:5	lewd	wicked, dishonest, naughty, nasty
	baser	no honor, punks, thugs, wicked, lowdown
	assaulted	attacked, beat, mugged

ACTS

17:8	troubled	stirred up, concerned, distressed
17:12	honorable	prominent, respected
17:15	to	for
17:16	stirred	provoked, aroused, challenged, angered
	wholly	completed, fully
	idolatry	worshipping an idols or any god other than the One God (Jehovah)
17:17	disputed	discussed, debate, argue, find faults
	devout	dedicated i.e. God honoring
17:18	encountered	talked to, confronted
	babbler	speaks nonsense, idiot, lunatic, pointless talk
17:19	doctrine	teaching, rules, instruction
	whereof	of which
17:23	your devotions	worship objects, religious ceremonies
	haply	perhaps, maybe
17:29	**Godhead**	the essential nature of God, three main offices of ONE God; The more intelligent pagan Greeks no more pretended that these sculptured gods and goddesses were real deities, or even their actual likenesses than Romanist Christians do their images; and Paul doubtless knew this; yet here we find him condemning all such efforts visibly to represent the invisible God. We see similar behavior in the Greek and Roman churches that paganize the worship of the Christian Church by the encouragement of pictures and images in religious service. (In the eighth century, the second council of Nicea decreed that the image of God was as proper an object of worship as God Himself). The additional unbiblical practice of separating God into three distinct persons was also considered wrong and similar to making God into inferior parts.
17:31	Man	i.e. Jesus
	ordained	authorized, chose, selected, purposed
17:32	resurrection	rising from the dead, a.k.a. the Rapture
	mocked	taunting, make fun of, laugh at, disrespect

ACTS

18:3	craft	trade, job, skill
	wrought	worked, labored, crafted, made
18:4	sabbath	rest day, day off, seventh day of the week
18:6	raiment	clothing, garments, apparel
18:7	joined hard	was next, close to, near by
18:9	hold not your peace	do not keep quiet, speak up, talk
18:10	set on	attack, assault, beat up
18:12	insurrection	uprising, mutiny, rebellion, to attempt an overthrow
18:14	lewdness	scandalous, wicked, dishonest, naughty, nasty
18:17	cared	concerned, worried
18:18	tarried	stayed, waited, delayed, put off
	vow	pledge, promise, commitment
18:22	saluted	a formal greeting, say hello, hi there, recognize
18:25	fervent	excited, energetic, devoted, hard-working
	knowing	recognize, understand, comprehend, "gets it"
18:26	perfectly	accurately, precisely, correct
18:28	scriptures	Jewish sacred writings i.e. Old Testament
19:2,6	Ghost	God's Spirit, supernatural force/ power
19:3	To	Into
19:6	tongues	spoke forth, different dialects, languages
	prophesied	foretell, make a prediction, speak for God
19:7	all the men were	there were seventy two men
19:9	divers	various, different, many
	disputing	arguing, dispute, debate
19:10	dwelled	lived
19:11	wrought	worked, labored, crafted, made
19:12	from his body were brought to the sick handkerchiefs	pieces of cloth were taken and used for the sick to touch in belief that the Spirit of God would "rub off" on the cloth and thus heal them
19:13	exorcists	i.e. those who cast out demons
	adjure	plead, beg, to sincerely request
19:16	prevailed against	conquered, beat, defeated i.e. overcame
19:17	fear	revered, respected, trembled, dread
19:19	curious arts	witchcraft, magic
	books	books of magic, spells, sorcery
19:20	grew	increased, spread

ACTS

	prevailed	conquered, beat, defeated i.e. overcame
19:22	season	a while, period of time
19:24	no small gain	a good profit
19:27	to be set at nothing	becoming worthless
19:31	adventure himself	chance, risk going
19:35	appeased	quieted, calmed
	townclerk	city manager, public official, politician
19:37	blasphemes	uses or ruins the name or reputation of God
19:38	implead	accuse, bring charges, take the matter to court
	matter	complaint, issue
	open	available, ready, prepared
19:39	determined	settled, mind made up, positive
19:40	called in question	accused, charged, blamed
	uproar	disorder, chaos, anarchy
	concourse	disorderly conduct, public disturbance, near-riot
19:41	assembly	grouped, gathered, crowded together
20:1	ceased	quieted, stilled, were silent
20:2	exhortation	an urging, encouragement, warning, advice
20:3	abode	live, residence, make home, dwell
20:5,15	tarried	stayed, waited, delayed, put off
20:6	unleavened	yeast-free
20:7	the first day of the week	i.e. Sunday
20:9	loft	story, upstairs, inner balcony
20:12	not a little	a lot, much i.e. greatly
20:13	afoot	walk, travel on foot
20:16	hasted	hurry up, speed up, go faster
20:18	seasons	times
20:19	lying in wait	plot, conspiracy, trap
20:22	befall	happen to, become of
20:23	Save	except, besides, other than
	abide	remain, dwell, hang out, inhabit, live
20:23,28	Ghost	God's Spirit, supernatural force/ power
20:24	testify	solemnly affirm, swear, promise
20:27	shunned	hesitated, ignored, ceased
20:30	perverse	rebellious, perverted, crooked, wicked; unfair
21:2	forth	set sail
21:3	discovered	sighted, spotted, spied, found

ACTS

	unlade	unload, dumped
21:4,10	tarried	stayed, waited, delayed, put off
21:5	accomplished	finished, complete
21:7	course	voyage, trip
21:7,19	saluted	a formal greeting, say hello, hi there, recognize
21:7,8	abode	live, residence, make home, dwell
21:8	evangelist	preacher, minister, a fiery/dynamic speaker
21:11	girdle	belt
21:15	carriages	baggage
21:20	zealous	excited, energetic, hyper, hard-working
21:22	must needs	will certainly, of course, sure
21:23	vow	pledge, promise, commitment
21:25	touching	concerning, about, relating to
21:26	accomplishment	finished, complete, done
21:28	polluted	defiled, dirty, dishonor, disgrace, spoil
21:30	moved	aroused, stirred up, fired up
21:32	centurions	Roman captains of 100 soldiers
	left	stopped, ended, ceased
21:33	demanded	asked, inquired, questioned
21:34	certainty	positive, confirmed i.e. for sure
21:35	for	because of
	borne	carry, took it, suffered it, endured, hung in there
21:38	made an uproar	stirred up a revolt, created chaos
21:39	beseech	begging, plead, ask with intensity
21:40	tongue	language, dialect
22:3	verily	surely, truly, honestly, yes, correct
	zealous	excited, ambitious, energetic, hyper, hard-working
22:5	estate of the elders	gathering, council, group of leaders
22:11	could not see	i.e. was blind
22:12	dwelled	lived, stayed, abode
	devout	having moral integrity or purity; avoidance of sin, dedicated to God
22:14	Just One	i.e. the Lord Jesus Christ
22:16	tarriest	waited, delayed, put off
22:19	imprisoned	put in prison, held as a prisoner, in captivity
22:20	raiment	clothing, garments, apparel
22:24	bid	urged, invited, asked, requested

	wherefore	why, the reason/purpose
22:24,25	scourging	whipped, punishment, plague, curse, pestilence
22:26	heed	listen to, obey, pay attention to
	centurion	a soldier that was the boss of 100 soldiers
22:28	free born	not a slave i.e. born a Roman citizen
23:2	smite	beat, strike, hit, punch, slap
23:3	whited	painted white on the outside to hide the dirt, stain
	smitten contrary	as a Jew, he should not have been hit, slapped, or punched until he had officially been found guilty of a crime or violation of their laws
23:4	Revile	speak against, criticize, bad mouth
23:7,10	dissension	conflict, argument, controversy, dispute
23:9	strove	fought, rebelled against, worked hard at
23:11	cheer	encourage, support
23:12	bound themselves under a curse	took a vow, an oath with a penalty if they didn't keep their promises
23:20	perfectly	maturity, excellence, complete i.e. thoroughly
23:22	charged	ordered, warned, commanded
	showed	told, reported, rumored, talked about
23:23	third hour of the night	i.e. 9 pm
23:24	beasts	i.e. horses
23:32	morrow	next day, tomorrow
23:33	epistle	letter, message, note, directive
24:1	orator	public speaker, politician
24:2	providence	supervision, rule, governance
24:4	tedious	dull, boring, routine
	clemency	kindness, mercy, justice, patience
24:6	profane	violated, polluted, disrespected
24:9	assented	agreed, verified, conspired
24:14	heresy	religious/doctrinal rebellion or error, blasphemy
24:15	allow	accept, agree to, acknowledge
24:16	void of offense	blameless, innocent, honest
24:17	alms	a gift, charity, hand out
24:18	tumult	commotion, excitement, outcry, pandemonium
24:19	ought	something, anything, an issue, complaint
24:22	perfect	maturity, excellence, complete
	know the uttermost	decide, persuaded, sure

ACTS

24:25	temperance	self control, self-discipline
	know the uttermost	decide, persuaded, sure
24:26	the oftener	more often, common, frequent
25:2	besought	asked, pleaded, begged
25:6,10	judgment seat	court room, judges seat
25:7	grievous	terribly, sad, painful, hurtful
25:10	judged	tried, found guilty
25:11	I refuse not to die	I would accept my punishment if I were guilty
25:12	appealed	asked, questioned, second opinion
	conferred	spoken with, agreed
25:13	salute	a formal greeting, say hello, hi there, recognize
25:16	license	permission, authority
25:18	supposed	expected, presumed
25:19	superstition	fear, false belief, religious customs
25:20	doubted	perplexed, troubled, confused, uncertain
25:23	on the morrow	tomorrow, next day
	pomp	big show, flashy, showy
		place of hearing courtroom
25:26	certain	exact, precise, without doubt
25:27	withal to signify	indicate, proclaim, express
26:3	beseech	begging, plead, ask with intensity
26:9	verily	surely, truly, honestly, yes, correct
	contrary	hostile, oppose, against
26:11	compelled	force, pressure into, make someone do a thing
	strange	foreign
26:12	commission	power, authority, permission, duty
26:14	pricks	spur; cowboys, cattle herders used metal goads or sharp, pointed sticks to poke the cattle and make them move – for an animal to resist or "kick" against would mean it would only get injured – thus it was foolish and pointless to fight
	tongue	language, dialect
26:20	meet	fitting, proper, expected, the right thing
26:22	witnessing	testimony, talks about, tells, testifies
26:25	noble	excellent, virtuous, reputable, dignified
27:2,4	launched	set sail
27:7,16	under	near, close

ACTS

27:7	scarce	with difficulty, hardship, trouble
27:9	admonished	warned, advised, yelled at, threatened
27:10	hurt	danger, harm, trouble
	lading	cargo, load, shipment, goods
27:12	commodious	comfortable, fit, cozy, useful
	more part	majority, most of
	haven	hideout, safe place, sanctuary, shelter
27:13	loosing	lifting anchor, repairing
27:14	tempestuous	emotional, hysterical, wild, stormy
27:16	come by	secure
27:17	undergirding	extra support, backup
27:18	lightened the ship	threw cargo overboard
27:19	tackling of a ship	ropes, cables, winches, hoists, etc
27:20	taken away	abandoned, gave up
27:21	hearkened	listen, pay attention, attend
	loosed	set sail, released, set free
	abstinence	holding back, avoidance, doing without
27:22	exhort	an urging, encouragement, warning, advice
27:23	angel	messenger, heavenly being, guardian
27:27	up and down	back and forth
	deemed	thought, supposed, believed
	country	island
27:28	fathoms	the distance across the chest from the tip of one middle finger to the tip of the other when the arms are outstretched, five or six feet per fathom; [20] fathoms=120 feet deep
27:30	foreship	prow, bow, tip, front; forward part of the ship
	color	navy signals communication (with flags)
27:31	abide	remain, dwell, hang out, inhabit, live
27:32	her	i.e. the boat
27:33	besought	asked, pleaded, begged
	tarried	stayed, waited, delayed, put off
27:33,34,36	meat	food
27:37	souls	lives i.e. 276
27:39	creek	bay, narrow inlet of water
		into…they minded thought, decided, intended
	thrust in the ship	steered, drove, pointed
27:42	counsel	plan, conspire, plot, talked together

ACTS

28:1	Mel'I-ta	now called Malta
28:2	barbarous	non-Greek speaking person; generally rough, crude and considered "uncivilized"
28:3	viper out of the heat	a snake that had been hiding among the wood came out
28:4	vengeance	justice, get even, pay back, revenge
28:8	a bloody flux	very bad, bloody diarrhea
28:10	laded	loaded, burdened, filled
28:12	tarried	stayed, waited, delayed, put off
28:13	Pu-te'o-li	a city of Campanaia in Italy, situated on the Bay Of Naples
28:14	tarry	stay, hesitate, wait, delay, put off
28:19	constrained	held back, held down, restrained, bound
28:25	Ghost	God's Spirit, supernatural force/ power
28:27	waxed gross	fat, dull, lazy, unresponsive to God
	converted	The turning of a sinner to God. "Converted" means a person has left their old way of living/believing and has embraced the Christian faith; and in a more special sense men are converted when, by the influence of divine grace in their souls, their whole life is changed.
28:29	reasoning	arguing, dispute, debate
29:30	received	welcomed, greeted

ROMANS

1:3	seed	descendants, offspring, children
1:5	apostleship	position, office as a missionary
1:6	called	chosen, invited, asked to attend, selected
1:7	saints	Christians, believers; changed people
1:11	impart	given, supplied, awarded, passed on to
	established	strengthened, built up
1:12	mutual	similar, common, the same
1:13	fruit	sharing, benefits, blessings, rewards
1:14	debtor	under obligation, owing
1:18	hold	suppress, keep down, restrain
1:19	manifest	reveal, make visible, make known
1:20	Him	i.e. Jesus
1:21	glorified	praised, exalted, adored, revered
	vain	empty, worthless, shallow, proud
1:23	incorruptible	immortal, won't die
	corruptible	able to become sick, die, decay/rot
1:25	more	rather, other than
1:26	vile	disgusting, evil, filthy, nasty, sickening
	women …nature	three-fold change: they didn't want to have children, they wanted to act/become like men (dress, occupations, mannerisms), and they were lesbians (woman homosexuals)
1:27	recompence	pay back, payment, reward or punish
	meet	fitting, proper, expected, the right thing
	burned in their lust	sexual abandon, out of control craving
	men with men	homosexual behavior, same gender sex
	working that which unseemly	unnatural, disgusting
1:28	reprobate	unfaithful, wicked, mean, corrupt
1:29	fornication	illegallon sex outside of marriage, immoral, dirty; also describes a union or relationship to something other than God/His rules
	covetousness	envious, greedy, wants what others have, lust
	maliciousness	evil, wicked, cruel, mean-spirited
	malignity	violent, evil, bad, sick
	debate	strife, controversy, disagreement, dispute, fight

ROMANS

	malignity	malice, mean-spirit, spite
1:30	spiteful	insolent, shamefully, cruelly, unfairly, mean
	backbiters	spreads rumors, liars, gossips, false witnesses
1:31	covenant	agreed, made a deal, promised
	natural affection	male to female is natural; wanting children is natural; keeping conceived children vs. abortion is natural
2:4	longsuffering	patience, tolerance, "putting up with"
2:6	render	give up, surrender, provide
2:9	tribulation	trials, difficult times, hardships, suffering
	anguish	grief, heartache, misery
2:15	Which	Who
	the mean	bearing witness, confirm
2:17	rest in	rely on, trust, live by
2:22	abhor	detest, hate, despise
	sacrilege	dishonor, violate a holy thing or building (rob a church)
2:25	verily	surely, truly, honestly, yes, correct
2:26	righteousness	correct, proper, lawful living
3:2	oracles	words, prophecy, foretelling
3:3	faith	plan, purpose, belief
3:13	sepulcher	tombs, graves, crypts
3:15	feet…swift	quick, in a hurry, hasty, no self control
	to shed blood	kill, murder, fight, hurt someone
3:16	destruction	breaking, ruining, smashing, vandalism
	misery	heartache, heartbreak, sadness, pain
3:18	fear	revered, respected, trembled, dread
3:19	guilty	convicted, under judgment
3:20	flesh	physical body
3:22	difference	distinction, discrimination
3:25	propitiation	substitute victim; because God's laws required death for our sins, in the Old Testament He allowed a substitute to take our place (animal sacrifice) – Jesus fulfilled God's final requirement and became THE sacrifice or propitiation, accepting this act of self-sacrifice forgives our sins and allows us to live (eternal life).

ROMANS

	forbearance	forgiveness, tolerance, generosity
3:28	without	apart from, separate
3:31	make void	nullify, cancel, end
4:6,8,11,22,23,24	imputes	credits, transfers
4:7,8	Blessed	happy, fortunate, special, unique, favored
4:8	not impute sin	hold against, count, blame
4:13,16,18	seed	descendants, offspring, children
4:16	sure	certain, positive
4:20	staggered	wavered, doubted, hesitate
4:25	delivered	brought, betrayed, led captive
5:3	tribulation(s)	trials, difficult times, hardships, suffering
5:5	Ghost	God's Spirit, supernatural force/ power
5:6,8	yet	still, all the time
5:11	atonement	a sacrifice, gift offered to forgive sins (sin separated man from God, the gift forgave the sin and united them: at-one-ment, to become one again)
5:12,17,19	one man	i.e. Adam
5:13	imputed	credited, transferred
5:14	similitude	likeness
	death reigned	the boss, ruler, champion; no one beat or cheated death
5:18	One	i.e. Jesus Christ
6:6	hereafter	since then, afterward, now
6:9,14	dominion	authority, command, power over
6:11	reckon yourself to be dead indeed to sin	unaffected, it has no influence anymore
6:12	reign	rule, control, command, the boss
	lusts	desires, craving, physical/sexual hunger
6:17	doctrine	teaching, rules, instruction
6:19	members	body parts, eg eye, finger, etc.
	holiness	sanctification, clean/proper living
	infirmity	sickness, illness, disease
6:23	wages of	payment, salary, pay off, results
7:1	dominion	authority, command, power over
7:2	loosed	unbind, untie, set free, let go
7:3,4,5	married	joined, united
7:5	motions	effects, influence, current

ROMANS

7:5,23	members	body parts, eg eye, finger, etc.
7:7	You shall not covet	desire, want/crave what does not belong to you
7:8	wrought	work, labor, build, produce
	concupiscence	lust, craving, hunger, need for something (specifically unlawful sexual activity)
	without	apart from, separate
7:8,9	occasion	opportunity, chance
7:9	I was alive without the law once	one time lived without God's laws, rules
7:14	carnal	the natural, unconverted man, and his basic animal wants and needs (food, water, sex, safety, shelter)
7:15	allow	recognize, understand, comprehend, "gets it"
	hate	abhor, despise, detest, reject
7:15,19,20	would	wish, want to, desire, longing
7:16	consent	agree with, accept, recognize
7:22	inward man	the soul, heart or part of man that has eternal life if a person has accepted God's way(s)
8:6,7	enmity	hostile, fighting against, warring, bad blood
8:8	in the flesh	carnal, controlled by impulse, base desire
8:11	quicken	alive, energetic, active, powerful
8:12	debtors	under obligation, owing
8:13	mortify	put to death, deny, make no provision for
8:19	earnest expectation	anxious/sincere longing
	manifestation	display, demonstration, brought out, show
8:21	corruption	rotten, spoil, pollute, change for the worse
8:26	intercession	mediate, go-between, plead/pray on behalf of
8:27	saints	Christians, purified, believers, true followers
8:29	foreknow	describes God's ability to "know" the future, and make a plan according to his will/wants
	predestinate	plan ahead, determine to happen
8:35	tribulation	trials, difficult times, hardships, suffering
	sword	danger, violence, bloodshed
	peril	danger, trouble, risk, hazard
8:38	persuaded	convinced, sure, positive
9:1	Ghost	God's Spirit, supernatural force/ power
9:4	covenants	agreed, made a deal, promised

ROMANS

	promises	promised blessings, contract with God
9:7,8,29	seed	descendants, offspring, children
9:8	counted	considered as
9:13	hated	abhor, despise, loathe, detest, reject
9:15	compassion	mercy, pity, sympathy, kindness
9:18	hardens	makes stubborn
9:20	replies	answers, response, says
9:33	ashamed	disappointed, embarrassed
10:2	zeal	fervor, desire, enthusiasm
10:3	established	secure, insure, build, create, make
10:8	even your mouth	on your lips, just speak, make an admission/confession
10:16	report	message, news
10:18	verily	surely, truly, honestly, yes, correct
10:20	manifest	revealed, made visible, made known
10:21	gainsaying	arguing, debating, speaking against, gossiping
11:1	God forbid	"may it never be," and "I hope not"
	seed	descendants, offspring, children
11:2	makes intercession	pleads, requests, implores
11:4	bowed	kneel before, pray, respect, adore i.e. worship
11:5	remnant	leftover, remains, survivors
11:7,30,31	obtained	received, gotten
11:7	seeks	wishes, wants, would like
	blinded	hardened, deceived, confused
11:8	slumber	stupor, daze, sleep
11:9	recompense	pay back, payment, reward or punish
	table…a snare	appetites, hungers, desires will give them problems and eventually trap or control them
11:10	eyes be darkened	take away their sight, make them blind (a curse)
11:11	jealousy	to be jealous, angry, envious
11:13	office	ministry, position
11:14	emulation	jealousy, the desire to copy or be like
11:15	casting away	reject, ignore, not accepting
	receiving	accept, take in, embrace, hold
11:17	fatness	richness, wealthy, blessing
11:20	high-minded	proud, arrogant, self-important
	fear	revered, respected, trembled, dread
11:21	natural branches	direct descendants, blood-born i.e. the Jews

ROMANS

	heed	listen to, obey, pay attention to
11:22	severity	harshness, wrath, fury
11:25	mystery	hidden truth
11:26	Deliverer	i.e. The Lord Jesus Christ
11:27	covenant	agreed, made a deal, promised
11:28	touching	concerning, relating to, about
	the election	chosen, special, singled out
11:30,31	believed	obeyed, accepted, followed
11:32	concluded them	counted, considered, judged
11:34	counselor	adviser, teacher
11:35	recompensed	pay back, payment, reward or punish
12:1	beseech	begging, plead, ask with intensity
	present	offer, give, provide
12:2	conformed	changed, shaped, become like
12:4,5	members	body parts
12:9	dissimulation	hypocrisy, pretense, faking
12:11	slothful in business	lazy, slow, worthless, slacker
12:12	instant	urgent, immediate, up-to-date
12:13	distributing	giving, sharing, helping out
	necessity	needs (typically food, clothing, shelter)
12:16	conceits	ability, talent, intelligence, smarts
12:17	Recompense	pay back, payment, reward or punish
12:19	place to wrath	let it go, don't take action
13:1	soul	inner person, emotion, life-force, being, life
	higher powers	governmental authorities – police, military
	ordained of	established by, authorized, chose, selected
13:2	damnation	condemnation, judgement, cursed
	ordinance	rules, authority, command
13:4,6	minister	servant, helper, preacher
13:4	bears not the sword in vain	armed with weapons for a purpose, to defend and punish
13:6,7	tribute	tax, money owed to the government
13:7	custom	tolls, tax
13:10	ill	wrong, bad, evil, harm
13:12	far spent	almost gone, depleted, used up
13:13	honestly	properly, correctly, rightly
	chambering	sexual indulgence, immorality
	wantonness	sexual abandon, out of control lust

ROMANS

13:14	lusts	desires, craving, physical/sexual hunger
	provision	opportunity, chance, food, fuel
14:1	doubtful	questionable, uncertain
	disputations	disagreements, arguments, debates
14:5	persuaded	convinced, sure, certain
	esteems	favors, loves, honors, respects
14:9	revived	came back to life, rose from the dead
14:13	stumbling-block	something to trip over (a rock, a tree stump) be offended by
14:15,17,20	meat	food
14:15	charitably	in love, kindly, considerate
14:16	evil spoken	given a bad name, ruin reputation, slander
14:17	Ghost	God's Spirit, supernatural force/ power
14:18	acceptable	pleasing
14:19	edify	build up, strengthen, establish, make strong
14:23	damned	condemned, despised, judged, curse
15:1	infirmities	weaknesses, sickness, illness, disease
15:2	edification	process of building up, strengthening
15:5	consolation	encouragement, support, reward
15:6,9	glorify	praised, exalted, adored, revered
15:11	laud	praise, honor, cheer, applaud
15:12	trust	hope, believe, have confidence
15:13,16	Ghost	God's Spirit, supernatural force/ power
15:14	admonish	warn, advise, yell at, threaten
15:18	wrought	accomplished, worked, labored, crafted, made
15:22	hindered from	delayed in, kept back, stopped
15:24	Whensoever	Whenever
15:25	minister	serve, help, attend, preach
15:26	saints	Christians, purified, believers, true followers
15:27	verily	surely, truly, honestly, yes, correct
	carnal	earthly, basic animal instinct/desire
15:30	beseech	begging, plead, ask with intensity
15:31	accepted of	well received by, befriended
15:33	Amen	finished, so be it, yes
16:2	as becomes	in a manner worthy of
	whatsoever business	whatever matters, anything, activity
	succorer	protector, guardian, caregiver
16:4	laid down	risked, jeopardized

ROMANS

16:5+	Salute	a formal greeting, say hello, hi there, recognize
16:5	well-beloved	greatly loved, special
16:10	approved in household	accepted, welcomed, recognized
16:12	salute	a formal greeting, say hello, hi there, recognize
16:13	his mother and mine	she was like a mother, cared for me like a mother
16:15	saints	Christians, purified, believers, true followers
16:17	beseech	begging, plead, ask with intensity
	doctrine	teaching, rules, instruction
16:18,19	simple	unsuspecting, harmless, innocent, naive
16:20	bruise	crush, smash, injure
16:23	chamberlain	treasurer, financial , manager
16:25	establish	build up, strengthen, make strong
	mystery	hidden knowledge
16:26	manifest	revealed, made visible, made known

1 CORINTHIANS

1:1	apostle	a special position, office as a missionary
1:2	sanctified	set apart, made clean, right living
1:4	I thank God on your behalf	thankful for you, thankful I know you
1:5	utterance	things to say, prophetic sayings, speech
1:7	come behind in no gift	aren't cheated, up to date, have all that is available
1:8	confirm	firmly establish, support, strength
1:10	beseech	begging, plead, ask with intensity
1:11	declared	told, reported, rumored, talked about
	contentions	fights against, disputes, opposition
1:15	in my own name	Christians i.e. my disciples
1:17	none effect	no power, no influence
1:18	preaching…cross	talking about Jesus and the need for salvation
	to them that perish	people that don't want to change, turning from
	foolishness	sin is stupid, pointless
1:20	disputer	someone that likes to debate, argue, find faults
1:20,21,22	wisdom	learning, knowledge
1:27	confound	confuse, puzzle
1:28	base	lowly, animal-like, thug
1:31	glories, glory	boasts, brag about, show off, gloat
2:4	enticing	persuasive, crafty, tricky, well-spoken
2:6	perfect	full-grown, mature, complete
2;6,13	wisdom	learning, knowledge, understanding
2:7	mystery	hidden, in a veiled manner, not yet revealed
	ordained	predetermined, chose, selected, purposed
2:10	deep things	deeper meaning, advanced topics/material
2:13	Ghost	God's Spirit, supernatural force/ power
2:14	receives	accepts, acknowledges, embraces, believes
	discerned	judged, i.e. understood, comrehended
3:1,3,4	carnal	earthly, basic animal instinct/desire
3:3	envying	jealousy, rivalry
3:6	Apollos	a friend and co-worker of Paul; a learned Jew from Alexandria and knowledgeable in the scriptures
3:9	husbandry	someone that took care of agriculture (plants,

I CORINTHIANS

		trees, vines, etc.), gardening, landscaping
3:10	master builder	architect, chief foreman, designer
3:13	manifest	revealed, made visible, made known
	try	test
3:14	thereupon	on top of, directly on (like a layer)
3:15	so as	by, through, because of
3:17	defile	dirty, dishonor, disgrace, spoil
3:20	vain	empty, worthless, shallow, proud
4:1	ministers	serves, cares for, peaches
	mysteries	hidden truths, unrevealed scriptural meanings
4:2	stewards	managers, personal assistants
4:4	by	of, through
4:5	manifest	revealed, made visible, made known
4:5, 11	counsels	guidance, wisdom, instruction, teaching, advice
4:8	would	wish, want, like to do
4:9	spectacle	street show, comedy act, something to laugh at
4:10	despised	without honor, hated, rejected
4:11	buffeted	beaten, slap, push around, punch
4:12	reviled	criticized, bad mouthed, cursed, put downs
4:13	defamed	made fun of, mocked, laughed at, disrespected
	offscouring	trash, scum, low-life
4:16	beseech	begging, plead, ask with intensity
	followers	imitators, disciples, students
4:18,19	puffed up	proud, arrogant, self-important
5:6	glorying	boasting, bragging
	leavens	puffs up, inflates
5:6,8	leaven	a substance added to bread that made it rise, puff up, i.e. evil teaching
5:7	Purge	Clean, empty out, dump
5:7,8	old leaven	old nature, unconverted heart i.e. sinful person
5:8	leaven	a substance added to bread that made it rise, puff
5:9	company	group, crowd, associates
5:9,10	fornicators	people that have illegallon sex outside of
marriage,		
		immoral, dirty; also describes a union or relationship to something other than God/His rules
5:10	needs	necessarily, must, required

I CORINTHIANS

5:11	railer	big mouth, trash talker, noisy, argumentative
	extortioner	blackmailer, loan sharks, money/payday lenders
	eat	accompany, associate, hang out with
6:1	unjust	unfair, false, unrighteous (non-Christian)
6:1,2	saints	Christians, purified, believers, true followers
6:4	least esteemed	of no account, unimportant , i.e. poor, weak
	pertaining	relating, are about, deal with
6:5	speak to your shame	your actions are a disgrace, shameful, embarrassing
6:7	defraud	cheat, con, rip-off, double-cross
6:9	effeminate	men that act soft, dainty, lady-like
6:10	revilers	criticizers, bad mouthers, rowdy mob
6:11	sanctified	set apart, made holy, cleansed, purified
6:13	Meats	foods
6:18	Flee	avoid, run from
6:19	Ghost	God's Spirit, supernatural force/ power
7:1	to touch a woman	any sexual contact (hug, kiss, etc)
7:3	render	give to, provide, supply
	due benevolence	sexual relations, intimacy
7:4	of	over
	wife has not power of her own body	as a married woman, she has to make decisions with her husband – not alone
7:5	defraud	cheat, rip-off, hold out on - (not have sex with)
	incontinency	lack of self-control, overpowering sexual drive/need
7:7	I would that all men were…as I myself	I wish everyone were as I, unmarried and able to do so without sin; single and totally dedicated to serving God without distraction
7:9	contain	control themselves; power over sexual urges
	burn	sexual hunger i.e. with uncontrolled passion
7:11,12	put away	divorce
7:11	reconciled	brought back, reunited, hook up again
7:12	has a wife that believes not, and she be pleased to dwell with him, let him not put her away	a Christian can get divorced if married to a non-Christian, or they can choose to stay together
7:14	sanctified	set apart, made holy, cleansed, purified

I CORINTHIANS

	unclean	impure, dirty, filthy, unacceptable
7:17	ordain	direct, command, authorized, purposed
7:19	keeping	respects, obey, follow, adhere to
7:20,24	abide	remain, dwell, hang out, inhabit, live
7:22,23	servant	bond slave, laborer
7:27	loosed	unbind, untie, set free, let go
7:28	trouble in the flesh	distractions, sexual difficulties, pregnancy
7:31	fashion	structure, scheme
7:32	without carefulness	free from concern, no worries, peaceful
7:32,33,34	cares	concerns, worries
7:35	snare	trap, noose, i.e. restraint
7:36	*The whole verse.....*	a father had authority over his family, specifically his unmarried daughters. Once a girl became a woman (had her period/menstruation, sexual maturity) he could allow her to marry or not – he had to consider many factors (the right man, her financial security, and her type/intensity of sexual passion/drive). If she were hot-blooded, trying to keep her unmarried would backfire and most likely would end up very unhappy, distracted and likely to have sex outside of marriage
7:37	keep his virgin	doesn't let her marry, keeps her from marrying
7:38	he that gives her not in marriage does better	remaining unmarried (if possible/beneficial) is best
8:1	puffs up	arrogance i.e. fills with pride
	edifies	builds up, strengthens, establishes, makes strong
8:7,11	knowledge	understanding, wisdom
8:8,13	meat	food
8:9	heed	listen to, obey, pay attention to
	liberty	freedom, not forced, choice
8:10	sit at meat	meal i.e. eat
	emboldened	encouraged, assured, confident
8:13	offend	cause to stumble, sin, done wrong, hurt someone
9:2	seal	proof, evidence

I CORINTHIANS

9:3	answer	defense, account, prove
9:4,5	not power	no right, not permitted
9:6,12,18	power	the right, allowed, permitted
9:6	forbear	avoid, not have to, cease, stop
9:7,18	charges	expenses, costs
9:10	partaker	take part, share, participate
9:11	carnal	earthly, basic animal instinct/desire
9:12	suffer	endure, put up with, tolerate
	hinder	delay, slow down, get in the way
9:13	partakers	helper, associate, member, aide
9:15	void	empty, barren, without
9:16	woe	trouble, danger, look out! – a warning
9:17	dispensation	commission, assignment, role, part
9:18	Verily	surely, truly, honestly, yes, correct
9:19,20,21,22	gain	win, get
9:23	be partaker	take part, share, participate
9:24	obtain	get, earn i.e. win the prize
9:25	strives for the mastery	trains/competes athletically and to win
9:26	uncertainly	without aim, no purpose
	beats the air	swing and miss, throw a punch into the air
9:27	subjection	under control, a servant, obedience
	a cast-away	disqualified, failure, disgraced
10:1	be ignorant	not know, uninformed
10:3	spiritual meat	supernatural; God-sent/provided birds for food
10:4	spiritual drink	supernatural; God-sent/provided water out of a rock
	Rock	Petras
	followed	accompanied, joined
10:6	lust	crave, hunger, want badly
	lusted	craved, hungered, wanted badly
10:7	idolaters	heathens, a non-Jew, persons that worshipped idols or any god other than the One God (Jehovah)
10:9	tempt	trials, test, tease, lure, draw away
10:10	murmur	complain, fuss, whine, grumble
10:11	admonition	warning, advising, yelling at, threatening
10:12	heed	listen to, obey, pay attention to
10:18,21,30	partakers	take part, share, participate

I CORINTHIANS

10:20,21	devils	demons, evil spirit, bad supernatural force
10:23	edify not	do not build up, don't strengthen or support
10:24	wealth	well-being
10:25	shambles	meat market, food stalls
11:1	followers	imitators, faithful disciples
11:4	prophesying	foretelling, making a prediction, speak for God
11:6	shorn	shaved bald, all hair cut off as a symbol/shame
11:12	is of	i.e. originate(s) from
1:13	comely	proper, seem right, appropriate
11:14	shame	dishonor, disgrace, humiliate
11:19	heresies	religious/doctrinal rebellion or error(s), blasphemy(s)
	manifest	revealed, made visible, made known
11:22	have not	poor, lacking money or material goods
11:25	supped	ate, took a meal, had dinner
	testament	agreement, covenant
11:29	discerning	wise, understanding, comprehend
11:33	tarry	stay, hesitate, wait, delay, put off
11:34	condemnation	judgment, sentenced, found guilty, cursed
12:1	ignorant	unaware, uninformed, not knowing
12:3	Ghost	God's Spirit, supernatural force/ power
12:5	differences	varieties, kinds
	administration	ministries, jobs, talents
12:7	withal	by
12:9	faith by…same spirit	the Holy Spirit is God's force or energy, it gives all Christians certain special abilities – though all have "faith", some have an extra amount
12:10	divers	various, different
	tongues	languages, dialects
12:11	dividing	distributing, sharing, splitting up
	severally	more than one, several, multiple, extra
12:12+	members	body parts
12:13	baptized…one body	initiated, joined, made a part of the "body of Christ" that is a mystical group united by faith and spirit
12:22	Nay	On the contrary, not so, rather
	more feeble	weaker, less capable
12:23	bestow	give, share, let have, provide

I CORINTHIANS

12:24	tempered	united, combined, assembled
12:25	schism	division, split, disruption, lack of unity
12:28	diversities	different kinds, various
12:28,30	tongues	languages, dialects
12:31	covet	seek, want, crave, lust for
13:1,8	tongues	languages, dialects
13:1	tinkling cymbal	like a wind chime, just making a sound for no reason
13:1,2,3,4,8,13	charity	love, care, concern
13:2,9	prophecy	forth-telling or fore-telling
13:3	bestow	give, donate, distribute, hand out
13:4	puffed up	proud, arrogant
	vaunts	boast, brag, talk big, act tough
13:5	evil	wrong, bad, wicked
13:11	thought	reasoned, ponder, consider
14:1	charity	love, care, concern
14:1,3,4,5,22,31	prophecy	forth-tell or fore-tell
14:2+	tongue	language, dialect
14:3	to edification	for building up, strengthen, make strong
	exhortation	an urging, encouragement, warning, advice
14:4,5,12,17,26	edifies	building up, strengthen, make strong
14:6,26	doctrine	teaching, rules, instruction
14:8	uncertain	indistinct
	to the battle	for war
14:9	into the air	to yourself, to no advantage, pointless
14:10	signification	meaning
14:11	voice	language, words, spoken
14:16,23	unlearned	uneducated, non-believers
14:17	verily	surely, truly, honestly, yes, correct
14:20	malice	evil, wicked, cruel, mean-spirited
14:25	manifest	revealed, made visible, made known
14:26	doctrine	teaching, rules, instruction
	edifying	builds up, strengthening, establish, make strong
14:27	by course	in turn
14:30	hold his peace	be quiet, don't speak, remain silent
14:31	comforted	support, encouragement
14:38	ignorant	not knowing

I CORINTHIANS

14:39	covet	greedy, wanting, lust
14:40	decently	properly
15:5	Ce'phas	Peter
15:6,18	fallen asleep	i.e. dead
15:9	meet	fitting, proper, expected, the right thing
15:10	bestowed	placed, given, shared
15:14,17	vain	empty, worthless, shallow, proud
15:17	raised	raised from death, resurrection
15:20	slept	died & buried
15:27	manifest	revealed, made visible, made known
15:28	subdued	subjected, controlled, defeated, tamed
15:30	jeopardy	danger, at risk
15:33	communications	companions, friends, buddies
15:40	celestial	heavenly, spiritual, angelic
	terrestrial	earthly, natural
15:45	soul	inner person, emotion, life-force, being, life
15:51	mystery	secret, unrevealed truth
15:52	trump	trumpet, bugle, brass horn
15:53,54	corruptible	perishable, able to die, decompose/rot
	incorruption	without sin, immortal
15:55	grave	death
15:58	steadfast	faithful, reliable, trustworthy
16:1,15	saints	Christians, purified, believers, true followers
16:2	first day of the week	i.e. Sunday
	gatherings	collections, donations, offering
16:3	liberality	generous donation, cash offering, financial help
16:4	meet	fitting, proper, expected, the right thing
16:7	tarry	stay, hesitate, wait, delay, put off
16:11	conduct	bring, escort, transport
16:13	quit you	act, be, perform
16:14	things	doings, actions, behavior
	charity	love, thought of others, unselfishly
16:15	beseech	begging, plead, ask with intensity
	addicted	devoted, completely given/dedicated
16:19	salute	a formal greeting, say hello, hi there, recognize
16:22	An-ath'e-ma	accursed
	Mar'an-a'tha	the Lord is coming

II CORINTHIANS

1:1	apostle	missionary, "one sent", chief disciple
	saints	Christians, purified, believers, true followers
1:4	tribulation	trials, difficult times, hardships, suffering
1:5,6	consolation	comfort, peace, rest
1:6	effectual	successful, skillful, talented
1:7	steadfast	faithful, reliable, trustworthy
1:8	ignorant	not knowing, uncertain
	pressed…measure	overwhelmed, stressed, burnt-out
1:11	bestowed upon	give, share, let have, provide
1:12	simplicity	mental honesty, innocence
	had our conversation	manner of life, behavior, actions
1:16	brought	helped, assisted, aided
1:17	did I use lightness	subtilty, deception
1:17,18,19,29	yea, yea	yes, true
	nay, nay	no, false
1:22	earnest	pledge, down payment, advance
1:24	dominion	authority, command, power over
2:1	heaviness	sorrow, grief
2:2	sorry	sad, feel bad, remorseful
2:4	affliction	troubles, torment, sickness, suffering
2:7	swallowed up	overwhelmed
	contrariwise	the opposite, instead of
2:8	beseech	begging, plead, ask with intensity
2:11	ignorant	unaware, uncertain, unknowing
2:13	rest	relief, peace
2:14	manifest	revealed, made visible, made known
2:14,15,16	savor	fragrance, aroma, scent
2:17	corrupt	rot, spoil, pollute, change for the worse
3:2	epistle	letter, message, note, directive
3:3	manifestly	openly, plainly, clearly
3:4	trust	confidence, belief, faith
3:6	ministers	servants, caretakers, helpers, preachers
3:7,8,9	ministration	ministry, working, function, action
3:10	respect	part, way
	excels	exceeds, goes beyond, better than

II CORINTHIANS

3:11	is done	fades, eliminated
3:12	plainness	boldness, directness
3:13	untaken away	not removed, remaining, left in place
	veil over his face	covered his face so people wouldn't stare
3:17	Liberty	freedom, choice
4:1	faint	lose heart, become discouraged, tire
4:2	manifestation	open showing, reveal, demonstrate
4:3	hidden	concealed, stashed, put away, secret
4:7	we have treasure in earthen vessels	the treasure is salvation & eternal life, it is kept within us, in our hearts (natural bodies)
4:8	perplexed	puzzled, confused, uncertain, anxious
4:10,11	manifest	revealed, made visible, made known
4:15	redound	increase, multiply, exceed, be greater than hoped
4:17	affliction	troubles, torment, sickness, suffering
5:2	be clothed upon with our house which is from heaven	our heavenly, spiritual, angelic body
5:18	reconciliation	resolution, reunion, bring peace
6:1	beseech	begging, plead, ask with intensity
6:2	succoured	helped, nurtured, nourished
6:4	ministers	servants, caretakers, helpers, preachers
6:5	stripes	lashes; marks caused by being whipped/beaten
	imprisonments	put in prison, held as a prisoner, in captivity
	tumults	brawls, fights, riots, commotions
6:6	longsuffering	patience, tolerance
	Ghost	God's Spirit, supernatural force/ power
	unfeigned	pure, innocent, uncomplicated, simple
6:7	deceivers	liar, con artist, false witness i.e. imposter
6:11	mouth…open	we are freely saying we support, love, etc.
6:12	you are straitened in our own bowels	the thought of your situation/circumstances hurts us deeply, we are pained inside
	bowels	emotions, feelings i.e. affections i.e. compassion
6:13	recompence	pay back, payment, reward or punish
	enlarged	generous giving i.e. big hearted
6:15	concord	harmony, friendship, union
	Be'li-al	followers of, or actually *the* fallen angel/demon "Bel." Be'li-al is translated "lawlessness"— and follows a rabbinical tradition which interpreted

		it as "beli 'ol" the one who has thrown off the yoke of heaven. Belial was accordingly considered the opponent of the rule of God; that is, Satan, or the antagonist of God.
	Infidel	unbeliever, faithless, heathen, non-Christian
6:17	unclean	impure, dirty, filthy, unacceptable
7:1	fear	revered, respected, trembled, dread
7:2	frauded	taken advantage of, deceived, cheated
7:4	glorying	boasting, brag about, show off, gloat
7:7	fervent	excited, ambitious, devoted, hard-working
7:8	repent	change one's mind & purpose; regret, guilt
	epistle	letter, message, note, directive
	season	time, period
7:9	receive damage	suffer loss, hurt, harmed
	sorry after a godly manner	guilt for doing wrong, inspired by God vs. long-term shame/guilt that is a memory and eats away at us
7:11	selfsame	the same, similar, just like
	indignation	anger, temper, destructive rage verging on madness
	yea	yes
	approved	shown, proven, demonstrated
	clear	innocent, not guilty
7:14	ashamed	embarrassed
8:1	do you to know	make known to you, reveal, show
8:2	affliction	troubles, torment, sickness, suffering
8:3	of themselves	i.e. of their own accord
8:4	ministering	support, service, help, preach
8:7	abound	excel, overflow
8:10	expedient	profitable, necessary, important
	forward	willing, desiring, wanting
8:12	willing mind	zeal, desire; the want to do something vs. force
8:17	exhortation	an urging, encouragement, warning, advice
8:22	oftentimes	many times, a lot
9:1	touching the	concerning, relating
	ministering to	teaching, preaching, helping, serving
	superfluous	unnecessary, don't need
9:2	forwardness	readiness, desire

II CORINTHIANS

	provoked	aroused, challenged, angered
9:3	boasting in vain	uncalled for, not deserving, can't back play
9:5	exhort	an urging, encouragement, warning, advice
	bounty	gift, surplus, profits
9:6	bountifully	generously, overboard, gives a lot
9:7	necessity	under compulsion
9:10	ministers	supplies, helps, serves gives, provides
9:12	administration	rendering, giving, supplying
	want	need, necessity, "basics"
	saints	Christians, purified, believers, true followers
9:13	experiment	proof, working, trying
	ministration	service, support, help, provision
9:14	long	yearn, wants, desires
9:15	unspeakable	indescribable, awesome, fantastic
10:1,2	beseech	begging, plead, ask with intensity
12:2	base	meek, humble, simple
10:4	carnal	earthly, basic animal instinct/desire
10:5	high	proud, exalted, arrogant
10:6	revenge	justice, get even, pay back, revenge
10:8	edification	process of building up, strengthening
10:9	terrify	frighten, scare, upset
10:10	contemptible	despicable, shameful, low-down
10:12	not wise	without understanding, dumb, foolish
10:16	boast	brag about, show off, gloat
10:17	glories, glory	lift up self, arrogant
10:18	commends	recommends, praises, brags about
11:2	espoused	engaged, promised, joined
	godly jealousy	deeply care about, spiritual concern
11:4	another	different, other
11:5	whit	every bit, completely, all parts
	chiefest	greatest, most important, leading
11:6	rude	unskilled, rough
	manifest	revealed, made visible, made known
11:7	abasing	humbling, breaking, chastising
	freely	without charge, willingly, unselfishly
11:13	apostles	followers, disciples of Jesus, missionaries
11:14	transformed	changed, converted
11:15,23	ministers	servants, caretakers, helpers, preachers

II CORINTHIANS

11:18,30	glory	boast, brag about, show off, gloat
11:19	suffer	endure, put up with, tolerate
11:20	taken of	enslave, trapped, snared
	exalt	put you down and make himself look good at your expense
11:21	reproach	insult, shame, ruin reputation, humiliate
	whereinsoever	in whatever way
11:23,24	stripes	lashes; marks caused by being whipped/beaten
11:26	perils	dangers, troubles, risks, hazards
11:27	watchings	sleepless nights, nightly prayers
11:28	care	concern, worry, responsibility
11:30	needs	necessities, required
	infirmities	sickness, illness, disease
11:32	desirous	hopeful, eager, wishful
	apprehend	arrest, catch, lay hold on
12:1	expedient	necessary, required, has to happen
12:1,5,6,9,11	glory	boast, brag about, show off, gloat
12:2	above	before, i.e. more than
12:4	lawful	permissible, proper, correct, authorized
	utter	speak, talk, tell
12:5,9	infirmities	weaknesses, sickness, illness, disease
12:6	forbear	refrain, stop, withhold
12:7	buffet	torment, punish, push around
12:11	chiefest	top, leader, best known, most popular
12:12	wrought	performed, worked, labored, crafted, made
12:13,14	not burdensome	not a burden, self-supporting
12:15	more I love you, the less I be loved	his love was expressed in his correction/scolding of them for wrong-doing, this they didn't enjoy and often got mad – but they needed it and he gave (like a parent-child/teen relationship)
12:16	crafty	sneaky, tricky, wise, out-wit
12:17,18	make a gain	take advantage, benefit
12:19	edifying	building up, strengthen, make strong
12:20	tumults	commotion, excitement, outcry, pandemonium
	backbiting	spreads rumors, lying, gossiping, false witness
12:21	bewail	cry, weep, moan
	lasciviousness	sexual abandon, out of control lust
13:3	you-ward…not weak	for your sakes I tell you the straight truth and

II CORINTHIANS

		point out your faults that you might change your ways and be better Christians
13:5,6,7	reprobates	unfaithful, wicked, mean, corrupt
13:9	we are glad when we are weak	if our suffering and hardships make you stronger, we are happy you do well
13:10	sharpness	harsh, cruelty, i.e. sarcasm?
	power	authority, force, strength
	edification	building up, strengthen, make strong
13:11	perfect	maturity, excellence, complete, complete
13:13	saints	Christians, purified, believers, true followers
	salute	a formal greeting, say hello, hi there, recognize
13:14	communion	fellowship, talk, discuss, spend time with
	Ghost	God's Spirit, supernatural force/ power

GALATIANS

1:6	marvel	amazed, blown away, wow!
	another	a different, alternate
1:7	pervert	mislead, corrupt, twist, change for the worse
1:8	angel	messenger, heavenly being, guardian
1:8,9	accursed	banned, forbidden, illegallon, cursed
1:11	certify	assure, guarantee, promise
	after	according to, relating to
1:13	conversation	way of life, behavior, actions
1:16	heathen	nations, non-Jew, pagan
	conferred	talked with, discussed, met, chatted
1:18	abode	live, residence, make home, dwell
1:24	glorified	praised, exalted, adored, revered
2:2	lest	unless, or, otherwise
2:4	unawares	suddenly, unexpected, caught off-guard
	secretly	stealthfully, privately
2:7	contrariwise	opposite, "on the other hand"
2:8	effectually	successfully, skillfully, talented
	wrought	worked, labored, crafted, made
2:9	heathen	nations, non-Jew, pagan
2:13	likewise	also, just like, similar to
	dissimulation	hypocrisy, pretense, faking
2:16	flesh	physical man, the body
2:21	in vain	needlessly, pointlessly, futile
3:4	many things	much, more, a lot
3:5	ministers	provides, cares for, serves
3:6	accounted	reckoned, credited
3:7	which are of	who have, belonging to, a part of
3:8	heathen	nations, non-Jew, pagan
	nations	people, groups by tribe or selection
3:9	faithful	believer, followers of Jesus
3:10	works of the law are under a curse	Jesus' death ended the need to follow the law of the Old Testament, he also ended the "curse" all mankind lived under (trying to measure up and do everything right) – so, to live by the law is to choose to continue under the curse vs. grace & freedom

3:13	made a curse for us	all of mankind's sins were put on Jesus, he took the full penalty and took away the curse at his death
	tree	cross
3:15,17	covenant	agreed, made a deal, promised
3:15	confirmed	ratified, proven, vindicated
	disannuls	cancels, takes away, ends, voids
3:16,29	seed	descendants, offspring, children
3:19	wherefore then serves the law	why did people once keep the law then?
3:20	mediator	a go-between, pleads on behalf of, advocates, or is a lawyer
3:22	concluded	shut up, ended, finished
4:1,7	servant	slave, laborer
4:2	tutors	guardian, caretaker, specially assigned teacher
	governors	managers, those in charge, having authority
4:4	made	born, created, gendered
4:5	receive…adoption	adoption meant more than becoming a son or daughter in a different family – it was a formal ceremony where even a biological child was given approval and authority, after they had been properly trained and were found worthy and reliable. This process wasn't possible until Jesus died and sent back His spirit to make us live in a way that was acceptable and pleasing to him.
4:6	Ab'ba	father, papa, dad
4:7	servant	slave, laborer
4:11	vain	without result, pointless
4:12	beseech	begging, plead, ask with intensity
	injured	wronged, hurt, violated
4:14	temptation	trials, test, tease, lure, draw away
	angel	messenger, heavenly being, guardian
4:17,18	zealously	ambitious, energetically, hyper, hard-working
4:19	travail	labor, pain, work hard, toil, difficulty
	be formed	take shape, show himself more, can be seen more
4:20	voice	tone, sounds, noises

GALATIANS

4:22	bondmaid	literally a female slave, a companion that is not a wife nor a prostitute – but here it means a woman that is totally committed to Christ
4:24	allegory	comparison, myth, parable, storytelling
	covenants	agreed, made a deal, promised
	genders	leads, starts, begins
4:25	answers	corresponds, parallels, connected
5:2	profit	benefit, helpful, useful, valuable
5:3	debtor	owes, under obligation
5:9	leaven leavens	i.e. wrong doctrine mixes in, changes
5:10	minded	reminded, thought about, memory jogged, idea
5:11	the offense	stumbling block
	ceased	stopped, removed, eliminated
5:15	bite	fight, argue, attack
	consumed	destroy, devour, eat up, destroy
5:17	contrary	hostile, oppose
	flesh lusts against Spirit	fights, wars, is in competition
5:18	led by Spirit	Jesus' spirit leads and controls your life, desires
	not under the law	don't have to follow "rules" since the Spirit in you will tell you what to do and help you do it
5:19	manifest	evident, revealed, plain to see
	lasciviousness	sexual abandon, out of control lust
5:20	variance	at odds, disagree, fighting, at war
	emulations	jealousy, the desire to copy or be like
	heresies	religious/doctrinal rebellion or error(s), blasphemy(s)
5:21	revellings	parties, celebrations, like Mardi Gras
5:23	temperance	self control, even tempered, patient
5:24	affections	passions, desires, animal instincts
5:26	vain glory	empty praise, earthly awards
6:1	fault	trespass, sins, does wrong/bad things
6:5	burden	load, struggles, problems
6:6	communicate to	share with, be generous
6:8	corruption	destruction, spoil, pollute, change for the worse
6:12	constrain	hold back, hold down, restrain, bind
6:13	keep	respects, obey, follow, adhere to
6:13,14	glory	boast, brag about, show off, gloat

EPHESIANS

1:1,15	saints	Christians, purified, believers, true followers
1:4	foundation	beginning, start, created
1:5	predestinated	planned ahead, determined to happen, preappoint
1:8	prudence	carefulness, good judgment, common sense
1:10	dispensation	historical period, time frame, era
1:11	predestinated	planned ahead, determined to happen, preappoint
1:13	gospel	good news, the story of Jesus
1:14	earnest	promise, pledge, down payment
1:19	to us-ward	towards us, us
2:1,5	quickened	made alive, energetic, active, powerful
2:2	prince	i.e. Satan, the devil
2:3	conversation	manner of life, behavior, actions
2:4	wherewith	by, having, where, as
2:10	ordained	planned, purposed, decided
2:12	aliens	foreigners, strangers, outcasts
	covenants	agreed, made a deal, promised
2:14	partition	wall, divider, vale; veil of the temple - thick curtain that separated two of the holiest rooms in the temple
2:15,16	enmity	hatred, bad blood, bitterness
2:19	saints	Christians, purified, believers, true followers
2:22	habitation	dwelling, house, place to live
3:1	prisoner..Jesus Christ	a person that is totally committed to Christ; obeys every command
3:2	dispensation	commission, assignment, role, part
	you-ward	toward you
3:3,4	mystery	hidden truth
3:7	minister	servants, caretakers, helpers, preachers
	effectual	successful, skillful, talented
3:8,18	saints	Christians, purified, believers, true followers
3:10	manifold	many, a lot, extra
3:11	purpose, purposed	plan, intent, goal, design
3:13	faint	lose heart, become discouraged, tire
	tribulations	trials, difficult times, hardships, suffering

EPHESIANS

3:18	comprehend	understand, recognize, "get it"
3:20	above	beyond, more than
3:21	glory	honor, praise, acclaim
4:1	beseech	begging, plead, ask with intensity
	vocation	job, occupation, work
4:2	lowliness	humble, broken, submissive
	forebearing one another in love	caring about others more than yourself
4:3	Endeavoring	attempting, best efforts, trying
4:4	even	just, righteous, honest, fair
4:11	evangelists	preacher, minister, a fiery/dynamic speaker
4:12	perfecting	completing, maturing, ripening
	saints	Christians, purified, believers, true followers
	ministry	teaching, education, discipleship
4:12,16,29	edifying	building up, strengthen, make strong
4:13	perfect	maturity, excellence, complete
4:14	doctrine	teaching, rules, instruction
	sleight	trick, cheat, deception, bad deal
	craftiness	cleverness, sneaky, tricky, deceptive
4:17	vanity	futility, empty, pointless
4:18	alienated	estranged, an outcast, abandoned, left out
4:19	lasciviousness	sexual abandon, out of control lust
4:22	conversation	manner of life, behavior, actions
4:26	wrath	judgment, anger, hellfire, punishment
4:27	Neither give place to the devil	don't let him in our life (through bad thoughts, bad sights/pictures or wrong actions)
4:29	corrupt	dirty, foul, nasty, indecent (a.k.a. cussing)
	communication	speech, discussions, talk
4:31	clamor	uproar, racket, noisy
	malice	evil, wicked, cruel, mean-spirited
5:1	followers	believers, disciples
5:3	saints	Christians, purified, believers, true followers
	covetousness	envious, greedy, wants what others have, lust
5:5	whoremonger	a person that often uses prostitutes; pays for sex
	idolater	heathen, a non-Jew, person that worshipped idols or any god other than the One God (Jehovah)
5:6	vain	empty, worthless, shallow, proud

EPHESIANS

5:7	partakers	take part, share, participate
5:8	sometimes	formerly, once, used to be
5:10	acceptable	pleasing, satisfying
5:11,13	reprove, reproved	exposed, correct, scold, show the error of
5:13	manifest	revealed, made visible, made known
5:15	circumspectly	in a complete circle around; meaning to see something from all sides, have all the facts
5:18	filled with	controlled by, satisfied, overcome
5:21,22	Submitting	subordinating, yielding, giving control to
5:21	fear	revered, respected, trembled, dread
5:26	sanctify	set apart, made holy, cleansed, purified
5:27	blemish	mark, blot, stain
5:29	nourishes	feeds, strengthens, builds up
	cherishes	cares for, loves, pampers
5:31	cause	reason, purpose
5:32	mystery	hidden truth
5:33	particular	individually, separate, alone
	reverence	reverence, respect, awe
6:4	provoke	make angry, get going, motivate, stir
	wrath	judgment, anger, hellfire, punishment
	nurture	discipline, correction, care
	admonition	warned, advised, yelled at, threatened
6:5	fear	revered, respected, trembled, dread
	singleness	sincerity, undivided, loyall
6:6	eye-service	only while someone is watching, hypocrite
	men pleasers	do something to gain approval or favors, scam
6:9	forbearing	giving up, refraining from
	Master	lord, owner
6:11,13	whole armor	all available spiritual weapons; power
6:11	wiles	tricks, cheats, deception, bad deals
6:12	rulers	devils in charge, strong demons
	principalities	kingdoms, governments, earthly powers
6:14	girt	belted, outfitted, supported
6:15	gospel of peace	God's Word, Bible
6:16	quench	put out, extinguish
	darts	arrows, i.e. shots
6:17	helmet of salvation	meaning put salvation on your head, in your thoughts, in your mind

EPHESIANS

6:19	utterance	speech, conversation
	mystery	hidden truth
6:20	ambassador	representative, spokesman, leader
	bonds	chains, restaraints

PHILIPPIANS

1:1	deacons	servant of the people, caretaker, helper
1:6	perform	completes, carries out, accomplishes
1:7	meet	fitting, proper, expected, the right thing
	partakers	helper, associate, member, aide
1:8	record	witness, testimony, account
	bowels	emotions, feelings i.e. affections i.e. compassion
1:12	fallen	turned, left, drifted away
	furtherance	progress, advancement, benefit
1:13	manifest	revealed, made visible, made known
	palace	mansion, military headquarters
1:14	waxing	grew, increased, became
1:16	contention	fights against, disputing, opposition
1:18	pretense	pretend, fake, to put on an act, deceive
1:19	supply	providing, giving
1:23	in a strait	stuck, falter, in a jam
1:27	fast	firmly fastened, solid, unmoving
1:28	terrified	frighten, scare, upset
	token	sign, indicator
	perdition	destruction, ruin, wickedness
2:1	bowels	emotions, feelings i.e. affections i.e. compassion
2:3	vainglory	pride, personal gain or glory, recognition
2:6+	God	the Almighty, Supreme Deity, Father
2:8	fashion as a man	in a human body, a natural man vs. spirit
	obedient to death	always obedience, even when he was asked to give his life
2:12	fear	revered, respected, trembled, dread
2:14	murmurings	complain, fuss, whine, grumble
2:15	harmless	innocent, not guilt, without blame
2:19,20	state	condition, situation, form
2:20	like-minded	similar, alike, kindred spirit
2:22	proof	evidence, reputation, credentials
2:23	presently	immediately, now, right away
2:15	ministered	helped with, served, cared for
2:26	full of heaviness	distressed, sad, down
2:29	reputation	high regard, esteem
3:1	dogs	non-Jew; Gentiles (unbelievers)

PHILLIPPIANS

3:1, 2	concision	a play on words – similar to "circumcision" which is what the Jews were called, but this term means to castrate (cut off the testicles/balls). Paul is saying that the Jews may as well castrate themselves because cutting of any flesh isn't what makes a person live clean – it is the Holy Spirit "circumcising" the heart and cutting away any extra "flesh" or sin/evil etc.
3:8	dung	poop, crap, waste
3:10	conformable	conformed, to be like or have the same experience
3:12	apprehend	seize, grasp, take hold of
3:14	mark	goal, target
4:2	beseech	begging, plead, ask with intensity
4:3	entreat	plead, beg, to sincerely request
	yoke-fellow	fellow worker, team mate
4:5	moderation	gentleness, even-tempered, self-control
4:6	careful	anxious, concerned, worried
	supplication	prayer, request, petition, plea
4:8	honest	honorable, decent, respectable
4:11	respect of want	desperate, as if I have to have something
4:12	abased	humbled, broken, ashamed
4:12,17,18	abound	have abundance, increase, do very well
4:14	communicate	share, charity, be kind, give
	affliction	troubles, torment, sickness, suffering
4:18	odor	fragrance, smell, scent
4:21,22	salute	a formal greeting, say hello, hi there, recognize
	saint(s)	Christians, purified, believers, true follower

COLOSSIANS

1:2,4,12,26	saints	Christians, purified, believers, true followers
1:12	meet	fitting, proper, expected, the right thing
1:16	principalities	kingdoms, governments, earthly powers
1:17	consist	hold together, kept, remain
1:18	preeminence	in charge, control, seniority, power
1:20	reconcile	restore harmony to, mediate
1:23	grounded	established, built up, solid
1:23,25	minister	servants, caretakers, helpers, preachers
1:25	dispensation	commission, assignment, role, part
1:25	fulfill	bring to pass, i.e. fully preach
1:26,27	mystery	hidden truth
1:26	manifest	revealed, made visible, made known
1:28	perfect	maturity, excellence, complete
2:4	beguile	cast a spell, deceive, trick, trap
	enticing	seduce, tempt, tease
2:5	order	good discipline, management, rule
2:7	abounding	become rich, successful, growing strong
2:8,15	spoil, spoiled	capture, snare, catch
2:8,20	rudiments	basics, principles
2:10	principality	kingdom, government, earthly power
2:13	quickened	made alive, energetic, active, powerful
2:14	contrary	against, opposing, not on our side
2:15	spoiled principalities	defeated kingdoms, governments, earthly powers
	triumphing	winning, being victorious, beating
2:16	let no man judge you in meat, drink or holyday	don't sin/do bad things, follow your own heart in matters or things that aren't clearly forbidden in scriptures, Bible
	Sabbath	rest day, day off, seventh day of the week
2:18	beguile	trick, deceive, seduce
	puffed up	inflated with pride, arrogant
2:19	Head	Christ
	which	whom
	increases	grows, improves
2:20	ordinances	rules, doctrines, ceremonies

COLOSSIANS

	dead with Christ	no longer "living" by the Old Testament laws, rules and therefore "dead" to those things
2:22	doctrines	teaching, rules, instruction
2:23	humility	humble, broken, submissive
3:5	mortify	put to death, put down, subdue
	inordinate	excessive, overboard, unreasonable, unnatural
	concupiscence	lust , craving, desire for what is forbidden
3:8	blasphemy	irreverence, disrespect, slander, evil speaking
3:12	elect	chosen, special, singled out
	bowels of mercies	emotions, feelings i.e. affections i.e. compassion
3:13	quarrel	complaint, fight, argument, debate
3:14	charity	love, care, concern, good deeds
3:16	admonishing	warning, advising, yelling at, threatening
3:18	submit	yield, surrender, serve
3:22	eye service	only while someone is watching
	men pleasers	kiss up, doing something to gain approval
	singleness	focus, dedication, single purpose/goal
	fearing	revered, respected, trembled, dread
4:4	manifest	revealed, made visible, made known
4:7	state	affairs, condition, wishes, directions
4:8	estate	circumstances, condition, situation, form
4:10,15	salutes	a formal greeting, say hello, hi there, recognize
4:12	fervently	ambitious, energetically, devoted, hard-working
4:13	zeal	excitement, energetic, hyper, hard-working
4:16	epistle	letter, message, note, directive
	Laodicea	a city in Asia Minor that was destroyed by earthquake, for a while it had a thriving, successful church in it that was led by St. Paul – the name translated means "the people's rights"
417	heed	listen to, obey, pay attention to
4:18	salutation	a formal greeting, hello, hi ther

I THESSALONIANS

1:4	election	being chosen, special, singled out
1:5,6	Ghost	God's Spirit, supernatural force/ power
1:6	followers	imitators, disciples, believers
2:1	entrance	coming, visit
	in vain	a failure, pointless, meaningless
2:2	entreated	mistreated, abused, disrespected
2:3	deceit	error, false, incorrect
	exhortation	an urging, encouragement, warning, advice
	guile	dishonesty, falsehood, fraud, deceit, baloney
2:4	allowed	approved, agreed, OK
	tries	examines, judges, proves
2:5	covetousness	greed, lust, hunger for more & more
2:7	cherishes	loves, cares for, takes care of, pampers
2:8	imparted	given, supplied, awarded, passed on to
2:9	travail	labor, pain, work hard, toil, difficulty
2:9	chargeable	a burden, problem, concern
2:10	unblamably	blameless, without fault, good character
2:11	exhorted	an urging, encouragement, warning, advice
	charged	implored, ordered, warned, commanded
2:13	cause	reason, sake, purpose
2:15,19	contrary	against, opposing, not on our side
2:16	fill	heap, pile up
	uttermost	last, end
2:17	endeavored	attempted, best efforts, good try
3:1,5	forbear	hold back, not go forward, withhold, suffer
3:3	thereunto	for this, to, for
3:4	verily	surely, truly, honestly, yes, correct
	tribulation	trials, difficult times, hardships, suffering
3:5	tempter	Satan, the devil, evil spirits
3:6	tidings	news, report, word, greetings
	charity	love, care, concern
3:8	fast	firmly fastened, solid, unmoving
3:9	render	give, provide, offer
3:11	direct	guide, show, lead, instruct
3:12	abound	overflow, exceed, increase

I THESSALONIANS

3:13	saints	Christians, purified, believers, true followers
4:1,10	beseech	begging, plead, ask with intensity
4:2	commandments	instructions, precepts, teachings
4:3,4	sanctification	set apart, made holy, cleansed, purified
4:4	possess his vessel	control his body, self-control, discipline
4:5	concupiscence	lust, craving, hunger, need for something (specifically unlawful sexual activity)
	Gentiles	unbeliever, non-Jew
4:6	defraud his brother	cheat, trick, con, rip-off
4:8	despises	rejects, disregards
4:11	study	learn, practice
	commanded	instructed, taught
4:12	lack of nothing	all you need, no wants, satisfied
	walk honestly	live and act honestly, be truthful
4:13	ignorant	unsure, unaware, not knowing
4:13,14	asleep, sleep	dead, cease living/breathing
4:15	prevent	precede, hinder, hold back
4:16	archangel	powerful, high-ranking angel
4:18	comfort	encourage, support, calm
5:1	seasons	times, dates, periods
5:2	perfectly	maturity, excellence, complete
5:3	travail	birth pains, groaning, labor
5:4	overtake	surprise, catch off-guard
5:10	should	may, likely
5:11	comfort	encourage, support, calm
	edify	building up, strengthen, make strong
5:12	beseech	begging, plead, ask with intensity
	labor	work, preach/teach, minister
	admonish	urging, encouragement, warning, advice
5:13	esteem	hold, respect, revere, give honor
5:14	feeble-minded	faint hearted, slow-witted
5:15	evil for evil	wrong for wrong, revenge, pay back
5:16	evermore	always
5:19	quench	Extinguish, put out, stop, hold back
5:21	fast	firmly fastened, solid, unmoving
5:22	abstain	hold back, avoid, do without, stay away from
5:27	charge	order, warn, command

II THESSALONIANS

1:3	meet	fitting, proper, expected, the right thing
	charity	love, care, concern
	abounds	become rich, successful, grow strong
1:4	glory in	speak proudly of, respect, revere
1:4,6	tribulations	trials, difficult times, hardships, suffering
1:5	manifest	visible, evident, plain to see
1:6	recompense	pay back, payment, reward or punish
1:10	saints	Christians, purified, believers, true followers
1:11	delusion	lie, deceit, error
2:1	beseech	begging, plead, ask with intensity
2:2	shaken in the mind	confused, uncertain, lose focus and commitment
2:3	falling away first	stop doing what is right, lose enthusiasm slowly
	son of perdition	destruction, ruin, wickedness, antichrist
2:7	iniquity	evil, crimes, sin, vice, wickedness
	lets, let	restrains, restrain, holds back
2:8	consume with the spirit of His mouth	the spirit of His mouth is His Word, already spoken/written that prophesies of Satan and his followers destruction – when the time comes, the "illumined" or seen/fulfilled words will come to pass and consume (completely destroy), e.g. this principle can be seen in Genesis where God says "Let there be light" and light appears.
2:9	him	anti-christ, religios imposter
2:10	deceivableness	deceit, dishonesty, lies, untruthfulness
2:11	delusion	unbelief, deception, trick
	they	unbelievers, non-Christians
	a lie	what is false, not true
	busybodies	spreads rumors, liars, gossipers, false witnesses
2:12	damned	condemned, sentenced, found guilty, cursed
2:13	bound	obliged, required, determined
2:14	obtaining	gaining, getting, recieving
2:15	fast	firmly fastened, solid, unmoving
	epistle	letter, message, note, directive
3:1	free course	no restraints i.e. spread rapidly
	glorified	praised, exalted, adored, revered

II THESSALONIANS

3:4	touching	concerning, relating to, about
3:6	tradition	teaching, religious history
3:7	us	i.e. our example
	disorderly	undisciplined, chaotic, unruly
3:8	wrought	worked, labored, crafted, made
	travail	labor, pain, work hard, toil, difficulty
	chargeable	a burden, obligation, indebted
3:9	power	authority, right, permission
3:11	walk	live, conduct self
3:12	exhort	an urging, encouragement, warning, advice
3:14	word	instruction, teachings
	company	group, crowd, associates
3:15	admonish	warn, advise, yell at, threate
3:16	by all means	in every way, any way
3:17	salutation	a formal greeting, hello, hi there
	which is the token	my mark, my style, signature
	espistle	letter, memo, note, directive

1 TIMOTHY

1:3	besought	urged, asked, pleaded, begged
	charge	ordered, warned, commanded
	doctrine	teachings, rules, doctrines, instructions
1:4	minister	servants, caretakers, helpers, preachers
	edifying	building up, strengthen, make strong
1:5	end	goal, target
	charity	love, care, concern
	unfeigned	pure, innocent, uncomplicated, simple
1:6	swerved	gone off course, left the path
	jangling	talks nonsense, liar, gossip, false witness
1:7	affirm	state, pledge, swear, keep same story
1:9	disobedient	rebellious, stubborn, disagreeable
	man-slayers	murderers, killers
1:10	whoremongers	a person that often uses prostitutes; pays for sex
	men-stealers	kidnappers, slave-traders
	perjured	liar, false witness, dishonest
1:13	blasphemer	irreverence, disrespect, slander, evil speaking
	injurious	someone that hurts others, with words or actions
1:15	faithful	trustworthy, honest, respectful
1:18	war	fight, struggle
1:19	Holding	Keeping, possessing
1:20	I have delivered to Satan	takeout from behind the protection of the church, a person is left to defend themselves against the Mental, emotional and spiritual attacks of the devil
2:1	intercessions	mediate, pleading/prayer on behalf of
	exhort	an urging, encouragement, warning, advice
2:4	will have	wish, want to, desire, longing
2:5	mediator	negotiator, go-between, advocate, lawyer
2:6	testified	witnessed, talks about, tells, account
2:7	verily	honesty, genuineness, faithfulness
2:8	lifting up holy hands	worship, prayer, respect
2:9	shamefacedness	humble, broken, submissive
	sobriety	serious, no-nonsense, dependable
2:11	silence	quietly, without talking/teaching

1TIMOTHY

	subjection	submission, yield to, obey
2:12	suffer	endure, put up with, tolerate
	usurp	take away, rip-off, overthrow
2:13	formed	created, made
2:14	transgression	sinned, wrong-doing, violate i.e. disobeyed
2:15	charity	love, care, concern
3:2	blameless	above reproach, without fault
3:3	given	addicted, regularly, frequently
	striker	fighter, violent
	brawler	fighter, argumentative, bad-tempered, crabby
3:3, 8	filthy lucre	money, wealth, material things
3:4	rules	manages, leads
	subjection	control, submission, orderly
3:5	house	estate, household, i.e. family
3:6	novice	new convert, inexperienced, beginner, rookie
	lifted up	proud, puffed up, arrogant
3:6,7	devil	demons, evil spirit, bad supernatural force
3:7	reproach	insult, shame, ruin reputation, humiliate
	snare	trapped, caught, imprisoned, tripped up, lure
3:8	double-tongued	hypocrites, false, deception
	deacons be grave	serious, business-like, no-nonsense
3:10	proved	try, test, verify, check out
3:11	slanderers	making accusations, telling lies, blaming
3:13	used the office of a deacon	served, worked, labored
	degree	standing, position, office
3:16	mystery	hidden truth
	Manifest	revealed, made visible, made known
4:1,6,16	doctrines	teaching, rules, instruction
4:1	devils	demons, evil spirit, bad supernatural force
4:2	conscience seared with a hot iron	numb, hardened, calloused, can't feel guilt branding iron
4:3	meats	foods
4:5	sanctified	set apart, made holy, cleansed, purified
4:6	minister	servants, caretakers, helpers, preachers
	nourished up	mentally nourished, educated
4:6,13,16	doctrine	teaching, rules, instruction
4:7	exercise	train, condition, practice

1TIMOTHY

	profane	violate, pollute, disrespect
4:9	faithful	trustworthy, reliable, honest
4:12	despise	look down on, hate
	conversation	manner of life, behavior, actions
	charity	love, care, concern
4:13	attendance	attention, focus
	exhortation	warn, correct, encourage i.e. preaching
4:14	by prophecy	foretelling, prediction
	presbytery	elders, council, church leaders
4:15	Meditate	Think, ponder, contemplate
4:16	heed	listen to, obey, pay attention to
5:1	entreat	plead, beg, to sincerely request
5:5	desolate	destroyed, ruined, empty, alone
	supplications	prayers, requests, petitions, pleas
5:7	give in charge	command, announce
5:8	house	estate, household, i.e. family
	infidel	unbeliever, faithless, heathen, non-Christian
5:9	taken into the number	put on a list, served, cared for
5:11	wax wanton	sexual abandon, out of control lust, crazy
5:12	faith	pledge, commitment, belief
5:13	tattlers	liars, gossips, false witnesses, spread rumors
5:14	guide	keep, lead. oversee
	adversary	enemy, non-believers
	reproachfully	disapprovingly, shamefully, with contempt/hate
5:16	charged	burdened, ordered, warned, commanded
5:17	the word	teaching, preaching
	doctrine	teaching, rules, instruction
5:18	muzzle	tie the mouth up so it couldn't eat
5:21	charge	instruct, ordered, warned, commanded
	elect	chosen, special, singled out
	preferring one before another	favoritism, special treatment
5:22	partaker	helper, associate, member, aide
5:23	no longer water	water alone, by itself
	often infirmities	frequent/regular sickness, illness, disease
5:24	they follow after	show up later, seen at later time
5:25	manifest	revealed, made visible, made known
6:1	under the yoke	bondage, trapped, enslaved, influenced

1TIMOTHY

	doctrine	teaching, rules, instruction
	blasphemed	irreverent, disrespected, slandered, evil speaking
6:2	despise	belittle, mock, hate
6:3	consent	agree to, permit, allow
	wholesome	healthy, helpful, truthful, correct
6:4	surmisings	thoughts, reflections, predictions, statements
6:4	proud	conceited, lifted up, arrogant
	doting about	dwelling on, focus on, obsess over
	railings	abusive talk, verbal abuse
	surmisings	questions, speculation, guesses
6:5	perverse disputings	constant friction, tension, arguing
	destitute	deprived, lacking, missing
6:8	raiment	clothing, garments, apparel
6:10	erred	make mistakes, sinned, acted badly
6:11	meekness	gentleness, kind, easy-going
6:13,17	charge	command, instruction
6:14	unrebukable	needing no correction, without fault or blame
6:15	Potentate	ruler, important person, officials
617	high-minded	conceited, proud, arrogant
6:18	willing	desires, wants to, ok with, doesn't mind
	communicate	share, charity, give
6:20	profane	ungodly, hurtful, unhelpful; (dirty/crude jokes)
	vain	empty, worthless, shallow, proud

II TIMOTHY

1:3	pure	clean, holy, innocent
1:5	unfeigned	pure, innocent, uncomplicated, simple
1:6	stir up...gift of God	get fired up, excited again, renewed
1:7	fear	timidity, worry, anxious
	a sound mind	mentally healthy, sane, logical
1:10	manifest	revealed, made visible, made known
	gospel	good news, the story of Jesus
1:12	cause	reason, purpose
1:13	fast	firmly fastened, solid, unmoving
1:14	committed	entrusted, rely upon, held responsible
	Ghost	God's Spirit, supernatural force/ power
1:15	be turned away from	deserted, left, walked away
1:17	sought	searched, looked for, went after
	diligently	faithfully, carefully, with effort, hard work
1:18	ministered to	served, helped, cared for
2:4	wars	fighting, battles, struggles
2:5,24	strive	compete, war, fight against, wrestle
2:5	masteries	athletic victories, success
2:6	husbandman	someone that took care of agriculture (plants, trees, vines, etc.), gardening, landscaping
	partaker	take part, share, participate
2:8	seed	descendants, offspring, children
2:9	bonds	shackles, handcuffs i.e. prison chains
2:10	elect's	chosen, special, singled out
2:11	faithful	trustworthy, true, honest
	dead	alive no more, earthly desires cease
2:12	reign	rule, control, command, the boss
2:13	believe not	are faithless, doubtful
	abides	remain, dwell, hang out, inhabit, live
2:14	charging	warning, instructing, ordering
	subverting	rebel, undermine, weaken, corrupt, sabotage
2:15	Study	Be diligent, be informed, educate, learn
2:16	profane and vain	ungodly, hurtful, unhelpful; (dirty/crude jokes)
	babblings	talking nonsense, lies, gossip, false witness
2:17	canker	disease, rot, gangrene, leprosy

II TIMOTHY

2:19	sure	firm, solid, stable
	iniquity	evil, crimes, sin, vice, wickedness
2:21	purge	cleanse, empty, get rid of
	sanctified	set apart, made holy, cleansed, purified
	meet	fitting, proper, expected, the right thing
2:22	lusts	desires, craving, physical/sexual hunger
	charity	love
2:23	unlearned	ignorant, simple, naïve
	gender strifes	produces/creates controversy, dispute
2:26	snare	trapped, caught, imprisoned, tripped up, lure
3:1	perilous	dangerous, troublesome, risky, hazardous
3:2	blasphemers	revilers, irreverence, slander, evil speaking
	lovers of their own	selfish, only concerned with own happiness
	covetous	envy, greed, lust, wanting what is not yours
3:3	incontinent	without self-control, overpowering emotions, drives/needs
3:4	high-minded	conceited, proud, arrogant, cocky
3:6	laden	overwhelmed, tired, burdened, stressed
	divers	various, different
3:8	reprobate	unfaithful, wicked, mean, corrupt
3:9	manifest	revealed, made visible, made known
3:10,16	doctrine	teaching, rules, instruction
3:10	charity	love
3:12	seducers	imposters, schemers, con artists
	wax worse and worse	progress from bad to worse
3:17	perfect	maturity, excellence, complete
4:1	charge	ordered, warned, commanded
	quick	alive, energetic, active, powerful
4:2	instant	ready, prepared
	exhort	an urging, encouragement, warning, advice
4:2,3	doctrine	teaching, rules, instruction
4:3	itching ears	follow their own desires and will look for teachers who will tell them whatever they want to hear (scratch their itch)
4:4	fables	story, myth, fairy-tale
4:5	make full proof	demonstrate, convince by actions
4:6	departure	death, dying

II TIMOTHY

4:7	course	race, destiny, purpose, job
4:8	His	i.e. the Lord Jesus Christ's
4:9	Do your diligence	make haste, be diligent
4:11	profitable	benefit, helpful, useful, valuable
4:14	reward	repay, punish, avenge
4:15	ware	on guard, careful, watchful
	withstood	opposed, fought, stood against
4:17	notwithstanding	nevertheless, but
4:19	salute	a formal greeting, say hello, hi there, recognize
4:21	your diligence	your best, make an effort, try hard

TITUS

1:1	elect	chosen, special, singled out
1:3	manifested	revealed, made visible, made known
1:5	ordain	authorize, choose, select, purpose
1:6,7	blameless	above reproach, honorable, good reputation
1:6	faithful	believing, respectful, keeps God's command
	unruly	out of control, disobedient, disrespectful
1:7,11	filthy lucre	dishonest gain, wealth, material things
1:7	striker	fighter, brawler, violent
1:8	temperate	having self control, even tempered, patient
	doctrine	teaching, rules, instruction
	gainsayers	opposition, debaters, fault finders
1:10	they of the circumcision	i.e. Jews
1:11	subvert	rebel, undermine, weaken, corrupt, sabotage
1:12	slow bellies	lazy gluttons, pigs
1:14	fables	myths, stories
1:16	abominable	disgusting, sick, forbidden, offensive
	reprobate	unfaithful, wicked, mean, corrupt
2:1	become	are fitting to, apply, represent
2:1,7,10	doctrine	teaching, rules, instruction
2:2,4	sober	serious, business-like, no-nonsense
2:2	charity	love, giving, helping
2:5	discreet	sensible, careful, wise
	blasphemed	dishonored, irreverent, disrespected, evil speaking
2:6,9,15	exhort	an urging, encouragement, warning, advice
2:6	sober minded	self control, calm, careful
2:7	uncorruptness	integrity, purity, honesty
	gravity	dignity, seriousness
2:8	contrary	hostile, oppose, not believing
2:10	purloining	stealing, theft, ripping things off
	fidelity	faith, trustworthiness, honesty
2:12	soberly	sensibly, calmly, carefully
2:14	iniquity	evil, crimes, sin, vice, wickedness
	peculiar	special, unique, one of a kind

TITUS

2:15	rebuke	corrected, criticized, yelled at, warn
3:1	principalities	rulers, leaders
	powers	authority, force, strength
3:2	no brawlers	non-contentious, peaceful, easy going
	meekness	gentleness, kind, easy-going
3:3	divers	various, different, many
	lust	enslaved to various desires, cravings
	malice	evil, wicked, cruel, mean-spirited
3:5	Ghost	God's Spirit, supernatural force/ power
	washing of regeneration	the act of water baptism
3:8	affirm constantly	repeat, remind, tell again
3:9	strivings	disputes, discussions, debates, arguments
	vain	empty, worthless, shallow, proud
	contentions	fights against, disputes, opposition
3:10	heretic	someone that believes or teaches religious/doctrinal rebellion or error, blasphemy
	admonition	repeatedly, over & over, warned, advised, yelled at, threatened
3:11	subverted	mislead, corrupt, twist, change for the worse
3:12	determined	decided, made up my mind
3:13	wanting	lacking, missing, in need of
3:14	ours	i.e. our people
	maintain	practice
3:15	salute	a formal greeting, say hello, hi there, recognize

PHILEMON

1:5	saints	Christians, purified, believers, true followers
1:6	communication	expression, demonstration, actions
1:7	consolation	comfort, peace, support
1:7,12,20	bowels	emotions, feelings i.e. affections i.e. compassion
1:8	enjoin	cautioned, warned, command, instructed
	convenient	proper, fitting, right
1:9	prisoner of Jesus	a person that is totally committed to Christ; obeys every command
1:9,10	beseech	begging, plead, ask with intensity
1:10	bonds	restraints, handcuffs i.e. prison chains
1:11	unprofitable	not beneficial, unhelpful, not useful
1:12	bowels	emotions, feelings i.e. affections i.e. compassion
1:13	bonds of the gospel	while in prison for Jesus sake, on His and/or the gospel's behalf
	stead	behalf, place, position
1:17	receive	welcome, accept, treat
1:19	albeit	yet, though, although
1:20	joy	benefit, happiness, satisfaction
1:22	given	restored, brought, sent
1:23	salute	a formal greeting, say hello, hi there, recognize

HEBREWS

1:1	divers	various, different, many
	sundry times	different, various times through history
1:2	worlds	universe, planets
1:3	purged	cleansed, washed away, removed
1:4,5,7,13	angels	messenger, heavenly being, guardian
1:6	Begotten	Child, conceived, born
1:7	ministers	servants, caretakers, helpers, preachers
1:8	scepter of	a symbol of the king's power, authority;
	righteousness	it looked like a club or band-leaders baton
		justice, blameless, faithful
1:11	wax	grew, increased, became
1:12	vesture	clothes, garments, what you wear
1:14	ministering	serving, helping, caring for
2:1	slip	drift away, fall, fail
	earnest head	really pay attention, take seriously
2:2,5,7,16	angels	messenger, heavenly being, guardian
2:2	steadfast	solid, unmoving i.e. binding
	recompence of reward	pay back, payment, reward or punish
2:4	divers	various, different, many
	Ghost	God's Spirit, supernatural force/ power
2:5,8	subjection	control, dominion
2:6	visit	care for, meet, befriend
2:9	grace	gift, mercy, kindess
2:10	became	was proper for, needed of, required
	captain	author, pioneer, in charge
	perfect	maturity, excellence, complete
2:11	sanctifies	set apart, made holy, cleansed, purified
2:14	Forasmuch	since, while
2:16	verily	surely, truly, honestly, yes, correct
	seed	descendants, offspring, children
2:17	behooved	necessary, required, had to happen
	pertaining	relating to, concerning, relevant
2:18	tempted	trials, test, tease, lure, draw away
	succor	protect, guard, give care and attention
3:1,14	partakers	take part, share, participate

HEBREWS

	profession	confession, statements, spoken beliefs
3:3	glory	praise, recognition, honor
3:3	He who has built the house	house builder, master builder, architect
3:5	verily	surely, truly, honestly, yes, correct
3:6	fast	closely, firmly, tightly
3:8,9	temptation	trials, test, tease, lure, draw away
3:10	err	make mistakes, sin, act badly
3:12	departing	turning away, leaving, backsliding
3:13	exhort	an urging, encouragement, warning, advice
3:14	steadfast	firmly fastened, solid, unmoving
3:15	provocation	testing, trials i.e. rebellion
3:16	provoke	rouse to anger, challenge, taunt
3:17	grieved	disturbed, upset, bothered, troubled
	carcasses	bodies
3:18	believe not	were disobedient, didn't obey God
4:1	fear	were afraid, frightened, scared i.e. be careful
4:2	gospel	good news, the story of Jesus
	mixed	combined, joined with
4:3	if they shall enter into	hypothetical; God says "if", when in reality he always planned to do it
4:6	it	Gospel, word of God
	unbelief	disobedience, lack of faith
4:8	Jesus	Joshua (NT name is Jesus)
4:10	ceased	rested, stopped
4:12	quick	alive, energetic, active, powerful
	marrow	the substance inside of bones; essence
	asunder	separate, divide, cut in two
	soul	inner person, emotion, life-force, being, life
	discerner	judges, recognizes, understands, comprehends
4:13	not manifest	hidden, secret, covered up
4:14	fast	firmly fastened, solid, unmoving
	profession	confession, statements, spoken belief
4:15	infirmities	sickness, illness, disease, weakness
5:1	ordained	authorized, chose, selected, purposed
5:2	out of the way	sinners i.e. wayward
	compassed with	

	infirmity	beset with weakness, full of problems
5:5	glorified	praised, exalted, adored, revered
5:7	feared	reverence, awe i.e. showed respect to God
	supplications	prayers, requests, petitions, pleas
5:9	being made perfect	mature, excellence, complete i.e. having completed his goal
5:11	uttered	spoken, taught
	dull	slow, stubborn, difficult to teach
5:12	oracles	Gods words, prophecies, commands, instructions
5:12,14	meat	solid food, adult food
5:13	everyone..uses milk	simple, basic knowledge of scriptures/teachings
	unskilled	weak, not experienced, defenseless
	babe	newcomer, just starting off, rookie
5:14	exercised	trained, skillful, well developed
6:1,2	doctrine	teaching, rules, instruction
6:1	perfection	maturity, excellence, complete
6:4	Ghost	God's Spirit, supernatural force/ power
6:5	world	age, kingdom, new creation
6:6	renew	revive, bring back
6:9	persuaded	convinced of, strong belief
	of	concerning, for
	accompany	go with, part of
6:10	ministered to	served, helped, cared for
6:12	slothful	lazy, slow, worthless, slacker
	followers	imitators, disciples, members
6:15	endured	waited, put up with, tolerated
6:16	verily	surely, truly, honestly, yes, correct
6:17,18	immutablilty	never changing, consistent, always the same
6:19	sure	firm, solid, faithful
6:20	forerunner	lead, prepare the way before, messenger
7:3,6	descent	genealogy, family tree, heritage
	abides	remain, dwell, hang out, inhabit, live
7:4	patriarch	male elder, chief, head of the family/clan
	spoils	plunder, loot, stolen goods, money
7:5	office…priesthood	job of being a priest, minister, religious leader
7:5,18	verily	surely, truly, honestly, yes, correct
7:6	counted	traced, associated, included
7:6,8,9	tithes	tenth portions, ten percent, 1 out of every 10

HEBREWS

7:7	better	greater, more important
7:8	witnessed	testimony, talks about, tells, testifies
7:10	yet	still
7:12	necessity	require, must, need
7:13	pertains	belongs, relates
	gave attendance	served, worked
	sprang	rose up, came from
7:15	similitude	similarity, likeness, image, copy
7:16	carnal	old testament law that governed natural mans actions/behavior
7:17,21	Mel-chis'e-dec	of unknown birth, was prophet, priest, King
7:18	disannulling	canceling, ending, putting away, rejecting
7:20,21	an oath	pledge, promise, commitment
7:21	swore	pledged, vowed, promised, gave an oath
7:22	surety	guarantee, ransom, down payment
	testament	unconditional agreement, contract, promise
7:24,25	ever	forever, always
7:25	uttermost	completely, fully, entirely
7:26	became	is proper for, was required or needed
7:27	once	i.e. once for all
7:28	makes	appoints, ordains, positions
	have infirmity	are weak, sick, ill, problems, troubles
8:1	sum	main point, summary, conclusion
8:2	pitched	set up, established, built
8:3	ordained	authorized, chose, selected, purposed
8:6	more excellent	superior, better
8:6,7,8,9,10,13	covenant	agreed, made a deal, promised
8:11	Me	God, the Lord i.e. Jesus
8:12	iniquities	sins, crime, evildoing, immorality
8:13	waxes	grew, increased, became
	vanish away	disappear, end, be finished
9:1	verily	surely, truly, honestly, yes, correct
	ordinances	regulations, policies, rules
	worldly	earthly, man-made
9:1,4	covenant	agreed, made a deal, promised
9:2,3,21	tabernacle	tent (with 2 chambers)
9:2	showbread	ceremonial bread used in religious service

HEBREWS

	sanctuary	temple, religious building, holy site 9:3,8
	Holiest of all	Holy of Holies
9:4	censer	an incense burner, something to burn incense in
9:5	particularly	in detail, specifically
9:6	ordained	prepared, planned, destined
	first tabernacle	Holy Place
	accomplishing	perform, completes, carries out
9:8	Ghost this signifying	Spirit thus showing
	made manifest	disclosed, revealed, made visible, made known
9:10	meats	food
	divers	various, different, many
	carnal ordinances	fleshly, natural laws
9:13	sanctifies	set apart, made holy, cleansed, purified
9:13,14	purifying, purge	cleansing, cleanse, empty, wash away
9:14	spot	defect, blemish, small mark
9:15	transgressions	misdeeds, sinned, wrong-doing, violate i.e. disobeyed
9:16,17,18,20	testament	will, statement, directives
9:16,17	testator	reference to a person's "last will and testament" – when someone leaves a thing or makes a promise, they must die to fulfill their last wishes. E.g. if I give you my car, you don't get it till I die
9:18	dedicated	verified, signed i.e. confirmed
9:19	precept	rules, doctrines, instructions
9:20	of	bound, given i.e. which seals
9:22	remission	forgiveness, removal, taking away
9:23	patterns	examples, original version, type
	purified	cleansed, washed clean, made holy
9:24	figures	anti-types, i.e. representatives
9:26	world	age
10:1	shadow	outline, reflection, general idea
	image	likeness, actual thing, object
10:2	purged	cleansed, washed, purified
	conscience	awareness, innate sense of right-wrong
10:3	remembrance	reminder, memorial
10:5,8	would	desire, want, ask

HEBREWS

10:10,14	sanctified	set apart, made holy, cleansed, purified
10:12	this man	i.e. the Lord Jesus Christ
	After	when
10:13	expecting	waiting, anticipating
10:15	Ghost	God's Spirit, supernatural force/ power
10:16,29	covenant	agreed, made a deal, promised
10:19	boldness	confidence, faith, positive attitude
10:20	consecrated	dedicated i.e. prepared
10:21	high	great, lead, chief
10:23	fast	firmly fastened, solid, unmoving
10:25	forsaking	giving up, leaving, walking away from
	exhorting	an urging, encouragement, warning, advice
10:27,31	fearful	terrified, afraid, frightened, scared
10:27	adversaries	enemies, opponents, bad guys
10:28	despised	rejected, hated, didn't accept
	Moses's law	the Old Testament laws (the first five books of the Bible – "Pentateuch")
10:29	trodden under foot the Son of God	disrespect, despise, reject Jesus and his sacrifice
	done despite	insulted, opposite, regardless
10:30,35	recompense	pay back, payment, reward or punish
10:33	gazing stock	street show, comedy act, something to laugh at
10:34	compassion	sympathy, kindness, mercy
	spoiling	plunder, loot, steal, rip-off
	goods	property, money, possessions
10:35	reward	payment, benefit
10:36	patience	endurance, calmness, the ability to wait
10:37	tarry	stay, hesitate, wait, delay, put off
10:39	perdition	destruction, unbelief, damnation
11:1	substance	assurance, thing, fact
	evidence	conviction, proof
11:2,4	it	i.e. faith
11:2	obtained	gained, received, granted
11:3	worlds were framed by the word of God	God spoke/commanded and the worlds (universes) were made and set in order
11:5	translated	transferred, moved, transported, raised
11:7	fear	revered, respected, trembled, dread
	heir	a family member, direct relative, blood that

HEBREWS

		inherits (takes over) everything
11:9	tabernacles	tent, dwelling place, sacred building
11:11	judged	considered, believed, trusted
11:12	as good as dead	past her prime i.e. by age close to death
	innumerable	many, a lot, countless, too many to count
11:13	persuaded	convinced, certain, had no doubts
	pilgrims	temporary residents, visitors, tourists
11:14	plainly	clearly, definitely
11:15	mindful	thinking, considering, visualizing
11:17	tried	tested, proven, challenged
	begotten	born
11:18	seed	descendants, offspring, children, heir
11:22	mention	spoke, talked about, told
11:25	season	short time, moment, little while
11:26	recompence	pay back, payment, reward or punish
11:27	forsook	left, gave up, walked away from
11:29	assaying	attempting, trying
11:30	compassed about	go about, surround, encamp, encircle
11:31	perished	died, killed
11:33	wrought	work, labor, build, produce
11:34	quenched	extinguished, put out, stopped
	waxed	grew, increased, became
11:36	mockings	taunting, make fun of, laugh at, disrespect
	scourgings	beatings, whippings, punishment
11:37	asunder	cut into pieces, half, divide, split
11:39	report	testimony, witness, talks about, tells, testifies
11:40	provided	planned, given, supplied
	perfect	maturity, excellence, complete
12:1	compassed about	go about, surround, encamp, encircle
	beset	assaulted, attacked, surrounded
	patience	endurance, steadiness, a good pace
12:2	author	chief leader, pioneer, starter, originator
	despising	thinking little of, hating
12:5,6,8,11	chastening	discipline, punishment, rebuke, reprimand
12:6	scourges	whipped, punishment, plague, curse, pestilence
12:9	subjection	submission, obedience, under authority
12:9,28	reverence	pay respect to, admire
12:10	verily	surely, truly, honestly, yes, correct

HEBREWS

	pleasure	judgment, desire, will
12:11	exercised	trained, worked, conditioned
12:12	lift up	uphold, support strengthen
12:15	diligently	carefully, with best effort
12:16	profane	godless, disrespectful
	meat	food
12:19	entreated	plead, beg, to sincerely request
12:20	beast touch the mountain	an animal walked or grazed past a certain point/spot on the mountain God designated holy or sacred; there were certain off-limit areas
12:24	covenant	agreed, made a deal, promised
12:25	Him	God, Lord i.e. Jesus
13:2	entertain	receive, help, be charitable, treat well
	angels	messenger, heavenly being, guardian
	unawares	suddenly, unexpected, caught off-guard
13:3	bonds	in jail or prison
	adversity	trouble, difficulties, trials
13:4	undefiled	kept pure, clean, proper
	whoremongers	a person that often uses prostitutes; pays for sex
13:5,7	conversation	manner of life, behavior, actions
13:7	end	result, product, outcome
13:9	divers	various, different, many
	doctrines	teaching, rules, instruction, ideas
	profited	benefit, helpful, useful, valuable
13:11	sanctuary	temple, religious building, holy site
13:12	sanctify	set apart, made holy, cleansed, purified
13:13	reproach	insult, shame, ruin reputation, humiliate
13:15	fruit of our lips	i.e. praise, worship, adoration
13:17,24	rule	leadership, ministerial positions
13:17	grief	unhappiness, sadness, lacking enthusiasm, eg a burden or chore
13:18	conscience	the soul or some part of us that distinguishes between what is morally good and bad; heart, gut, small voice
13:19,22	beseech	begging, plead, ask with intensity
13:20	covenant	agreed, made a deal, promised
13:22	suffer	endure, put up with, tolerate
	exhortation	an urging, encouragement, warning, advice

HEBREWS

13:24	Salute	a formal greeting, say hello, hi there, recognize

JAMES

1:1	abroad	all over, everywhere, in many places
1:2	divers temptations	various trials, test, tease, lure, draw away
1:3	entire	complete, whole
	wanting	lacking, missing
1:5	upbraids	reproach, defy, taunt, yell at, scold
1:6	wavers	doubting, hesitates, uncertain
1:8	double minded men	hypocrite, imposter, poser, fraud, pretender
1:9	low degree	humble circumstances, simple, average
1:12	temptation	trials, test, tease, lure, draw away
1:13	with	by, of
1:14,15	lust	desire, hunger, crave, want badly
1:15	finished	full-grown, complete, accomplished
1:16	err	make mistakes, be wrong, fail, led stray
1:17	variableness	variation, changes, differences
1:20	wrath	judgment, anger, hellfire, punishment
	works	achievements, deeds, actions
1:21	superfluity	excess, abundance, overflowing
	naughtiness	evil, immorality, wickedness
	engrafted	implanted, inserted, injected
	save	deliver, preserve, rescue
1:23,24	beholding	seeing, looking at
1:23	glass	mirror
1:25	continues	remains, keeps going
1:26	religious	God-fearing, church going, makes claims of faith
	bridles	controls, holds back
	vain	empty, worthless, shallow, proud
1:27	not defiled	faultless, clean, pure
	visit	care for, go to, help
	affliction	troubles, torment, sickness, suffering
2:1	Lord	master, ruler; deity (Jesus or God)
2:2	assembly	meeting, group, gathering, crowd
	goodly apparel	fine clothes, expensive clothing, designer labels
	vile raiment	poorly dressed, rags, rough clothing
2:3,9	respect	special attention, better treatment

JAMES

2:3	gay	nice, fancy, expensive
2:5	Hearken	listen, pay attention, attend
2:6	despised	disliked, hated, put off by
	judgment seats	courtrooms
2:7	blaspheme	irreverence, disrespect, slander, evil speaking
2:10	offend	cause to stumble, sin, done wrong, hurt someone
2:12	do	act, behave
2:13	rejoices	triumphs, is better than, greater
2:14	faith	belief, knowledge of/about
2:15	destitute	poor, broke, without money, ghetto
2:17	being alone	by itself, not accompanied by, eg if you said I was alive and had no pulse or breath, it would be a lie
2:19	devils	demons, evil spirit, bad supernatural force
	tremble	shudder, worry, are afraid
2:21	wrought	worked, labored, crafted, made
2:23	imputed	credited, counted for, believed
2:24,25	justified	statement of innocence, free from sin
3:1	condemnation	judgment, sentenced, found guilty, cursed
3:2	bridle	control, hold back, be in charge of
3:3	turn about	steer, drive, control
3:4	fierce	strong, harsh, cruel
	governor lists	pilot desires, wants i.e. goes where he wants it to
3:5,6	member(s)	body part(s)
3:6	iniquity	evil, crimes, sin, vice, wickedness
	defiles	dirty, dishonor, disgrace, spoil
3:7	tamed of mankind	men have tamed, subdued all animals
3:9	similitude	similarity, likeness, image, copy
3:11	place	opening, area
3:13	endued	given, supplied, awarded
	conversation	manner of life, behavior, actions
	meekness	gentleness, kind, easy-going
3:14,16	strife	controversy, disagreement, dispute, fight
3:14	glory	boast, brag about, show off, gloat
3:15	sensual	the human nature with its appetites and passions
3:16	confusion	disorder, chaos, lacking order
3:17	partiality	favoritism, preferential treatment
	hypocrisy	deception, poser, fraud, pretender, two-faced

JAMES

4:1,3	lusts	desires, craving, physical/sexual hunger
4:1	members	body parts
4:3	amiss	bad, wrong, unlawful
4:8	double minded	doubters, wavering, uncommitted, hypocrites
4:9	afflicted	troubled, tormented, sick, suffering
	heaviness	gloom, depression, sadness
4:13	Go to	come, how
	such a city	move to a new city and start a business
4:14	even a vapor	like a mist, fog
	what shall be on	what will happen the next day tomorrow
4:15	For that	instead, rather, really
4:16	boastings	arrogance, bragging, show off, gloating
5:2	corrupted	rotten, spoil, pollute, change for the worse
5:3	cankered	damaged, tarnished, rusted
	heaped	stored up, piled, accumulated
5:4	hire	contract, pay workers wages
	fraud	cheat, trick, con, rip-off
5:5	wanton	sexual abandon, out of control lust, crazy
5:7	husbandman	someone that took care of agriculture (plants, trees, vines, etc.), gardening, landscaping
5:8	establish	strengthen, build up, support
5:9	grudge	resent, dislike, want revenge
5:11	end	end-result, conclusion
	Lord	i.e. Lord's action
5:12	condemnation	judgment, sentenced, found guilty, cursed
5:13	psalms	hymns, praises
5:15	save	heal, make better
5:16	effectual	effective, successful
	avails	benefits, helps, is powerful
5:17	like	the same, similar
	space of	time period
5:18	heaven	sky, clouds, space above the earth
	brought forth	produced, gave up, provided
5:19	err	make mistakes, be wrong, fail, led astray
5:20	converts	turns, changes
	soul	inner person, emotion, life-force, being, life
	hide	cover, wash clean, forgive

1 PETER

1:1	strangers	foreigners, temporary residents
1:2	Elect	chosen, special, singled out
1:3	begotten	created, born i.e. through spiritual birth
	lively	living, energetic, active
1:4	incorruptible	imperishable, enduring, lasting
1:5	kept	obeyed, followed, were faithful to
1:6	manifold	many, a lot, extra
	temptations	tests, trials, difficult times
1:7	be tried with fire	God uses tests to purify and strengthen us; like fire melts metals (gold/silver) and purifies them, taking out dirt and unwanted metals
1:9	end	outcome, results
1:10	diligently	faithfully, carefully, with effort, hard work
1:11	signify	show, manifest, declare, testify
1:12	Ghost	God's Spirit, supernatural force/ power
	angels	messenger, heavenly being, guardian
	look into	understand, experience, participate in
1:14	fashioning	conforming, following after, imitating
1:15	conversation	manner of life, behavior, actions
1:16	it is written	recorded, stated, declared i.e. in the Scriptures
1:17	sojourning here	temporary stay (on this earth)
1:18	vain conversation	traditions, folklore, customs
	received	inherited, transferred, taught
1:20	verily	surely, truly, honestly, yes, correct
	manifest	revealed, made visible, made known
	unfeigned	pure, innocent, uncomplicated, simple
2:1,22	guile	deceit, dishonesty, trickery
2:2	desire	long after, wish, want, hope for
	sincere	pure, straight, unmixed
2:3	gracious	kind, pleasant, generous
2:4	disallowed	rejected, resisted, not allowed
2:5	lively	living, energetic, active
	a holy priesthood	counsel, group of priests, ministers, religious leaders
2:6	elect	chosen, special, singled out

I PETER

	confounded	confused, mix up, perplex, disappoint
2:8	stone of stumbling	something to trip over (a rock, a tree stump) be offended by
2:9	chosen	selected, elect, special, singled out
	a peculiar	special, unique, God's own
2:10	were not a people	not chosen/ not elected by God
	the people	chosen, selected
	obtained	received, granted
2:11	beseech	begging, plead, ask with intensity
	strangers	foreigners, outsiders
	pilgrims	temporary residents, wanderers, explorers
	lusts	desires, craving, physical/sexual hunger
2:12	conversation	manner of life, behavior, actions
	behold	observe, look on, watch
2:13	ordinance	institution, traditions, ceremonies
2:16	liberty	freedom, choice
	cloak of maliciousness	pretext/reason for evil, wicked, cruel, mean-spirited
2:17,18	fear	revered, respected, trembled, dread
2:18	froward	crooked, perverse, wicked; unfair, mean
2:19	thankworthy	admirable, commendable, excellent
2:20	buffeted	slap, push around, punch
2:22	did	committed, performed
2:24	tree	cross, crucifix
	stripes	lashes; marks caused by being whipped/beaten
2:25	Shepherd	caretaker, pastor i.e. Christ
	Bishop	leader, overseer, boss
	astray	wander, get lost, leave path
3:1,5	subjection	submission, yield, surrender
3:1	conversation	manner of life, behavior, actions
3:2	chaste	clean, pure, untouched, a virgin
	fear	revered, respected, trembled, dread
3:3	adorning	decorating, dressing up, putting on jewelry
	plaiting	braiding, fancy hairdos
	of putting on apparek	arrayed, outfitted, dressed up, styling
3:4	not corruptible	imperishable, everlasting, enduring
3:9	contrariwise	opposite

I PETER

3:11	eschew	hate, avoid, stay away from
	ensue	follow, run after, pursue
4:3	wrought	worked, labored, crafted, made
	lasciviousness	sensuality, sexual abandon, out of control lust
	abominable	disgusting, sick, forbidden, offensive
	revellings	parties, celebrations, like Mardi Gras
	banquetings	drinking, bar hopping, going to clubs
4:5	quick	alive, energetic, active, powerful
4:6	cause	purpose, make happen
4:7	sober	clear minded, sane, alert
	watch to prayer	be serious, prepared and ready; pray a lot
4:8	fervent	excited, ambitious, energetic, devoted, hard-working
4:9	grudging	complaining, murmuring
4:10	manifold	many, a lot, extra
4:11	oracles	utterances, prophecies
	minister	serve, caretake, help, preach
	dominion	authority, force, strength
4:12	fiery trial	difficult tests, temptations i.e. painful ordeal
	try	tried, tested, searched, examined, known
4:13	partakers	participants, members, sharing
4:14	happy	contented, peaceful
	evil spoken	insulted, gossiped about, slander
	glorified	praised, exalted, adored, revered
5:1	partaker	take part, share, participate
5:2	constraint	compelled, force, under pressure
	filthy lucre	love of money, corrupted by wealth
	ready	willing, able
5:4	chief Shepherd	head pastor, caretaker i.e. Christ
	stablish	build up, strengthen, establish, make strong
5:7	care	anxiety, concern, worry
5:9	steadfast	firmly fastened, solid, unmoving
5:9	accomplished	imposed upon, finished, complete
5:10	stablish	build up, strengthen, establish, make strong
5:13	salutes	a formal greeting, say hello, hi there, recognize
5:14	kiss of charity	friendly kiss on the cheek or back of the neck as a greeting or way of saying goodbye

II PETER

1:1	obtained	received (by allotment)
1:3	pertain	relates/applies to, connected with
1:5	virtue	goodness, strength, power
	diligence	earnestness, attention, hardwork
1:6	temperance	self-control, discipline, patience
1:7	charity	love, care, concern
1:8	abound	overflow, excel, increase
	barren	lazy, unproductive, useless
1:9	purged	cleansed, emptied, washed
1:10	Wherefore	therefore, instead
	election	choosing, calling
	fall	stumble, fail, not succeed
1:13	meet	fitting, proper, expected, the right thing
1:13,14	tabernacle	tent, i.e. earthly body
1:15	decease	death, dying
1:16	cunningly	inventive, inwrought, skillful, expert craftsman
1:17	excellent glory	heavenly realm, a dimension where god lives
1:19	day star arise in our hearts	"Morningstar" (actually the planet Venus) is seen in the early hours of the day when it is darkest – thus we look for Jesus (the day star) to rise in our dark hearts and give us light, hope etc.
1:20	private	individual, independent i.e. one man's
1:21	Ghost	God's Spirit, supernatural force/ power
2:1	secretly	craftily, privately, deceptive
	damnable	destructive, evil, wicked
2:2	pernicious	destructive, dangerous, wicked, evil
2:3	covetousness	envious, greedy, wants what others have, lust
	feigned words	words molded or formed (as needed), made up
2:4	chains	shackles, restraints, bonds
2:5	the eighth person	Noah was one of eight people that escaped destruction in the great flood
2:6	after	later, following
2:7,8	vexed	anger, annoy, bother, harass, frustrate
2:7	conversation	manner of life, behavior, actions
2:9	temptations	trials, test, tease, lure, draw away

II PETER

2:10	government	authority, power, control
	presumptuous	arrogant, cocky, over-confident
2:11	railing	slanderous, cruel, mean-spirited
2:13	sporting	parties, celebrations, like Mardi Gras
2:14	beguiling	cast a spell, deceive, trick, trap
2:16	dumb	voiceless, mute, can't speak
	forbad	forbidden, prohibited, banned
2:17	tempest	storm, wind, upheaval, disturbance
2:18	allure	entice, attract, bait
	lusts	desires, craving, physical/sexual hunger
	wantonness	unbridled lust, sexual abandon
2:19	servants	slaves, laborers, workers
2:20	pollutions	idolatry, worship/veneration of false gods
2:22	sow	pig, hog
	mire	muck, mud, slime, pigsty
3:1	beloved	dear ones, precious, cherished
3:3	scoffers	make fun of, mock, laugh at, disrespect
	lusts	desires, craving, physical/sexual hunger
3:4	fell asleep	died, passed away
3:6	overflowed with water	the great flood, Noah's flood
3:7	perdition	destruction, ruin, wickedness
3:9	slack, slackness	slow, delaying, lazy, neglectful
3:11	dissolved	destroyed, ended, finished, concluded
	conversation	manner of life, behavior, actions
3:12	fervent	excited, ambitious, energetic, devoted, hard-working
3:15	account	consider, bear in mind, understand
5:8	vigilant	attentive, alert, wide awake, watchful

1 JOHN

1:2	manifested	revealed, made visible, made known
1:3,5	declared	tell, spoken about, reported
1:6	do	practice, live, keep, act on
2:1	advocate	mediator, go-between, plead on behalf of, lawyer
2:2,4:10	propitiation	substitute victim; because God's laws required death for our sins, in the Old Testament He allowed a substitute to take our place (animal sacrifice) – Jesus fulfilled God's final requirement and became THE sacrifice or propitiation, accepting this act of self-sacrifice forgives our sins and allows us to live (eternal life).
2:5	verily	surely, truly, honestly, yes, correct
2:6+	abides	remain, dwell, hang out, inhabit, live
2:7	old commandment	nothing new, been around
	from…beginning	had all along within the Old Testament law
2:9,11	hates	abhors, despise, detest, reject
2:11	darkness has blinded his eyes	unbelief, sinfulness has caused eyes (or soul/ heart) to become blind and unable to "see" the truth
2:13,14	wicked	evil, devils i.e. Satan
2:16,17	lust	strong desire, hunger, want
2:19	manifest	revealed, made visible, made known
2:20	unction	anointing, anything smeared on, lotion, ointment – prepared from oil and aromatic herbs
2:22	denies	rejects, won't acknowledge/confess/accept
2:26	seduce	lead astray, entice, tempt, tease, deceive
3:4	transgression of the law	lawlessness, criminal, evil
3:5,8	manifested	revealed, made visible, made known
3:6,24	abides	remain, dwell, hang out, inhabit, live
3:7,8,10	devil	demons, evil spirit, bad supernatural force i.e.Satan
3:9	commit	practice, do, perform

I JOHN

3:11	message	commandment, teaching, instructions
3:13	marvel not	don't be: surprised, amazed, blown away
3:13,15	hate	abhor, despise, detest, reject
3:15	whosoever	who ever, someone, he/she/they
3:17	bowels	emotions, feelings i.e. affections i.e. compassion
3:18	tongue	talk, speech, communication
	deed	action, behavior
3:22	keep	respects, obey, follow, adhere to
4:1	beloved	dear friend, darling, close associate
	try	tried, tested, searched, examined, known
4:4	he	devil, demon, negative supernatural force/energy
4:5	hears	listens to, obeys, identifies with
4:6	spirit of error	lies, deception, dishonesty
4:9	manifested	revealed, made visible, made known
4:10	propitiation	substitute victim; because God's laws required death for our sins, in the Old Testament He allowed a substitute to take our place (animal sacrifice) – Jesus fulfilled God's final requirement and became THE sacrifice or propitiation, accepting this act of self-sacrifice forgives our sins and allows us to live (eternal life).
4:14	testify	witness, testimony, talks about, tells
4:15	confess	admit, acknowledge, claim to believe/ belong to
4:17,18	perfect	maturity, excellence, complete
4:17	boldness	confidence, assurance, peace of mind
4:18	torment	punishment, anxiety, worry, suffering
4:20	hates	despises, abhors, detests, rejects
5:1,18	begotten	born
5:2,3,21	keep	respects, obey, follow, adhere to
5:3	grievous	terribly, sad, painful, hurtful
5:6	water	baptism
5:7	these three agree as one	related, inter-connected, intertwined
5:8	spirit	Holy Spirit
	the water	Baptism, showing others our belief
	Blood	shed blood of Jesus, sanctification, holiness, sacrifice

I JOHN

5:9	testified	witnessed, testimony, talks about, tells, account
5:13	believe on the name	faith, confidence, acceptance
5:14	confidence	assurance, boldness, strong belief
5:17	a sin not to death	actions or behaviors that won't damn/curse the soul forever
5:18	begotten	born
	wicked one	evil, devil, demon, negative and evil force/spirit

II JOHN

1:1,13	elect	chosen, special, singled out
1:2	dwells	lives, abides, resides
1:5	beseech	begging, plead, ask with intensity
1:7	deceivers	liar, con artist, false witness
1:8	wrought	worked, labored, crafted, made
1:9	abides	remain, dwell, hang out, inhabit, live
	doctrine	teaching, rules, instruction
	has not	i.e. belongs not to, not united, doesn't possess, false claim
1:10	partaker	take part, share, participate
	neither bid him God speed	saying "God bless you" or "God speed" (which meant have a safe trip) was a greeting the Christians gave each other and John says not to treat a false person like he is a brother
1:11	bids	announces, proclaims, states, makes a wish
1:13	children	followers, believers
	elect sister	chosen, special, singled out

III JOHN

1:2	prosper	be rich, successful, healthy
1:4	children	followers, believers, Christian
1:6	bring forward	help, support, continue
	charity	kindness, hospitality, generosity
1:9	preeminence	lead, in charge, be in front
	Diotrephes	a church leader and maybe the pastor; and though there should be respect to such a leader over the church, this was carried too far, and this man, wanted more, and ruled the people with force and cruelty
1:10	prating against	talk nonsense about, tell a lie, slander, false accusations
	casts	puts, places, sets
1:12	record	witness, report, account, story
1:14	salute	a formal greeting, say hello, hi there, recognize

JUDE

1:1	sanctified	set apart, made holy, cleansed, purified
	preserved	save, keep, protect
1:2	exhort	an urging, encouragement, warning, advice
1:3	diligence	faithfulness, carefulness, effort, hard work
	common	standard, ordinary, available to all, accessible
	contend	fight for, defend, oppose with force
1:4	ordained	authorized, chosen, selected, purposed
	condemnation	judgment, sentenced, found guilty, cursed
	unawares	suddenly, unexpected, caught off-guard
	lasciviousness	sensuality, sexual abandon, out of control lust
1:6	angels	fallen, disobedient messenger, heavenly being, guardian
	first estate	position, circumstances, condition, situation
	everlasting chains	eternal bonds, imprisonment
1:7	going after	
	strange flesh	unnatural ways, perversion
	vengeance	justice, get even, pay back, revenge
	fornication	illegallon sex outside of marriage, immoral, dirty; also describes a union or relationship to something other than God/His rules
1:8	dominion	authority, command, power over
	dignities	important person, high-ranking, rulers, leaders
1:9	contending	disputing, arguing, fighting
	devil	demons, evil spirit, bad supernatural force i.e.Satan
	accusation	complaint, indictment, judgment
1:10	brute	without reason, non-thinking, a dumb animal
1:11	Woe	trouble, danger, look out! – a warning
	gainsaying	arguing, debating, speaking against, gossiping
1:12	spots	defects, stains, blemishes
	charity	love, care, concern
1:13	raging	fierce, menacing, savage, violent
	foaming out	exposing their own sin, shameful behavior
1:15	convince	convict, persuade
1:16	murmurers	complainers, whiner, grumbler

JUDE

	mouth speak great swelling words	boast, brag, talk big, act tough, arrogant
1:18	mockers	irreverent, disrespectful, skeptics, unbelievers
	lusts	desires, craving, physical/sexual hunger
1:19	they	unbelievers, sinners
	separate	leave, don't associate, depart from
	sensual	the human nature with its appetites and passions
1:20	Ghost	God's Spirit, supernatural force/ power
1:22	difference	distinction, uniqueness, seperate
1:23	spotted	stained, blemished
1:24	faultless	blameless, without fault, good character
1:25	dominon	authority, command, power over

REVELATION

1:1	Revelation	uncovering, exposition, unveiling
	shortly	soon, right away, in the near future
1:3	blessed is he..reads	reading these words will be a blessing
	prophecy	foretold statement, prediction, what God said through a man
1:5	first begotten	born
	of the dead	after dying, raised from the dead, resurrected to a new life
1:7	which pierced Him	The Jews –as a people they crucified Him
	wail	cry, weep, be sad about, mourn
1:8	Alpha and Omega	the first and last letters in the Greek alphabet – this means that Jesus is the beginning and end of God's plan
1:9	tribulation	trials, difficult times, hardships, suffering
	patience	ability to wait, not be in a hurry
	isle	island, land surrounded completely by water
1:13	girt	wear, fasten, put on, get dressed up in
	golden girdle	a thick belt made with woven, embroidered gold
1:15	feet like to fine brass	very shiny, polished
	burned in a furnace	glowing, shining, like heated metal
1:16	countenance	"face" - appearance, expression
1:17	fell at his feet	fainted, collapsed, passed out
1:18	key to hell	the key symbolized power & control – so once Jesus rose from the dead he had power & control over hell (Hell: a deep, dark, miserable prison for the dead whom have not believed & served God. A place of never-ending torment i.e. the Lake of Fire)
2:1	angel of the church	an angel is a messenger, either a special man or a heavenly being – in this case the messenger, leader of/to the church
2:3	fainted	wearied, grown tired, quit
2:7	midst of the paradise of God	paradise in the new Heaven & Earth - a reference to the Garden of Eden
2:8	first and last	this phrase describes a principle – Jesus was the

REVELATION

		first and last of everything good God has done. He was the first thought, the first of creation (as a spiritual being), the first to rise from the grave in his own power, the first to conquer death, the first sinless man, etc.
2:9	tribulation	trials, difficult times, hardships, suffering
	poverty (but…rich)	lacking material things (money, etc.), but had a lot of faith and blessing
	blasphemy	dishonor, act disgracefully, ruin/use the name or reputation of God
2:10	tried	tested, proven; see if you are faithful and trustworthy
	a crown of life	a crown is a symbol of success – those that overcome the trials and temptations of life through faith in Jesus will have "won" and be awarded eternal life
2:11	the second death	judgment day
2:13	hold fast	held on to, didn't forsake or deny the name of Jesus in all they did (preached, baptized, healed, lived)
	martyr	those who have proven the strength and genuineness of their faith in Christ by undergoing a violent death
2:14,20	fornication	illegallon sex outside of marriage, immoral, dirty; also describes a union or relationship to something other than God/His rules
2:17	hidden manna	secret bread, mysteries, private insights
2:19	charity	kindness, hospitality, generosity
2:20	notwithstanding	regardless, despite, nevertheless
	Jezebel	being a type of political system that corrupted the elect nation of Israel (now the Christian), she brought in idolatry and killed off the true religious person
	prophetess	someone that speaks for God, represents God – either predictions of the future or warnings
2:21	space	an opportunity, chance, a short time

REVELATION

2:22	I will cast her into a bed	a situation, circumstance where she will be in intimate/sexual contact with others
2:23	reigns	ability to reason, think, make decisions
2:24	depths	teachings, doctrines, mysteries of its religion
2:25	give…morning star in our hearts	"Morningstar" (actually the planet Venus) is seen in the early hours of the day when it is darkest – thus they looked for Jesus (the day star) to rise in their dark hour and give light, hope etc.
2:27	vessels of a potter	clay/ceramic pots, bowls, glasses
	shivers	pieces, fragments, slivers
3:1	seven spirits of God	the "angels" or messengers that these spirits controlled, gave power to; these seven were the leaders of the various Christian eras/"churches" (Revelation chapters 2-3). These seven are reflections of the One Holy Spirit (some use the example of God's spirit shining like light through a prism/Jesus and seven rainbow colors/spirits come out on the other side.
3:4	defiled…garments	dirtied, soiled, ruined (their testimonies/faith)
	walk…white	clean, pure, washed completely
3:7	the key of David	the key symbolized power & control – David was promised his offspring would always sit on the throne and rule Israel; so symbolically overcomers are given this "key" and they will be rulers – kings and priests
3:9	synagogue of Satan	church, religion, gathering, followers of wrong/non-biblical beliefs
3:15	would…cold or hot	make a choice, serve God or not, don't be a hypocrite or false Christian
3:16	spew	spit, vomit, throw up
3:18	tried	tested, proven; see if you are faithful and trustworthy
	eye salve	eye drops, medicine to clear up the infection that is causing them to see unclearly or not at all
3:19	chasten	discipline, punish, rebuke, reprimand, scold
	zealous	excited, ambitious, energetic, hyper, hard-

		working
3:20	sup	eat, take a meal, have dinner
4:3	sardine stone	a flesh-colored precious gem stone; a.k.a. sardius
4:6	sea of glass	if you could imagine looking up through the floor a frozen pond or glass floor, above the floor was a throne or large chair where God was sitting above everything
	full of eyes before and behind	the eyes were the "Angels" or messengers that could "see" the future/were prophets; these seven were the leaders of the various Christian eras (Revelation chapters 2-3).
4:7	third beast	see Ezekiel Chapter 1 Verse 4-21 for detailed explanation
5:2	loose the seals	seals were like wax stamps that were placed on documents to signify they were official and authentic; hot wax was melted on the seams to seal the document and then a ring with a name or symbol (like our signature) was smashed into the wax leaving its impression. Once the correct person received the document/scroll, the seals could be broken or "loosed" and the document, message opened
5:6	stood a lamb as it had been slain	this was a symbol of Jesus, the lamb of God – slain/killed to take away our sinches He had
been		
		sitting on a throne (the Throne of Mercy), His blood covering it and hiding our sin – in this scene He is standing, which means that there was no blood on the Mercy Seat and therefore the days of grace were over – the End of Time is at hand and judgment is near.
	seven	the number seven in the Bible means complete or finished, like the earth was created in seven days, etc.
	seven horns	these different "sevens" are all the same, just explained or represented in different ways – like here seven horns: a horn means influence,

REVELATION

		power, force.
	seven eyes	(see above Chapter 4 Verse 6) eyes represent the ability to see the future and hear from God (prophetic) , and also watch out for danger to be able to warn.
5:8	four & twenty elders	twenty-four notable leaders, like a council. Twelve of the elders were from the Old Testament and were made up of the Tribes of Israel (Judah, Gad, etc.) and the other twelve were from the New Testament Disciples of Jesus Christ. (Mark, John, etc.)
6:5	balances	scales, instrument used to measure/weigh
6:6	hurt not the oil and the wine	oil=holy spirit; wine=stimulation (from revelation of God's Word). God is telling the demonic forces that they can test & even kill the Christians, but they won't be able to do away with the Holy Spirit or the fact that God would reveal His truths and the truths would bless, heal, encourage, etc.
6:8	fourth part …earth	25% of the earth would suffer
6:10	avenge	get even, pay back, revenge
6:11	should be killed as they were	this scene is showing the Jews that have died are "under the altar" (some area in Heaven), and they are asking how long until they are avenged (a Christian wouldn't ask for vengeance) – they are told that a future wave of killing of Jews is yet to come (during the Great Tribulation period) and they would all be avenged.
6:12	sackcloth of hair	rough clothing, rags, woven dress-like outfit made of hair became as blood turned red, looked red
6:13	untimely figs	figs or fruit fall off the tree on their own when they are ripe (when its time) – but a strong wind can knock off fruit
6:14	departed as a scroll	changed quickly, was blacked out, disappeared
7:9	no man…number	countless, a lot, a very large amount
	kindreds	family, direct relative, blood
	tongues	languages, dialects

REVELATION

	palms in their hands	a palm branch, a big leaf that looked like a fan – whenever a king would come into town the people would lay them in the street and the king would ride over them (like the red carpet treatment for celebrities).
7:17	living fountains	the "waters" of eternal life
8:3,5	censer	an incense burner, something to burn incense in
8:7	mingled	mixed, blended, joined
8:11	wormwood	wormwood means bitter, and the effects of this "star" which represents an angel/messenger is that 30% of the earth's water sources would be poisoned/contaminated
8:12	shone	didn't shine, couldn't be seen
8:13	woe	trouble, danger, look out! – a warning
	inhabiters	residents, citizens, those that lived in that area
9:4	in their foreheads	on their forehead
9:6	death shall flee from them	life during the Great Tribulation will be so bad that people will want to die
9:9	breast plates	battle armor placed over the chest area; made up of metal or leather
9:12	woe	trouble, danger, look out! – a warning
9:17	jacinth	the color red on a black background
9:21	sorceries	deception, spells, witchcraft
	fornication	illegallon sex outside of marriage, immoral, dirty; also describes a union or relationship to something other than God/His rules
10:3	seven thunders	after the angel descends to earth, he speaks/ gives a message and reveals what was hidden in the scrolls (after the seals were opened). Once that message is revealed people can accept the truths, or reject them – if they reject the truth & mercy, the truth "thunders" and judges them.
10:9	make…belly bitter	stomach-ache, troubled
11:9	kindreds	family, direct relative, blood
11:1	reed like to a rod	thin stick or cane used to measure things
11:5	manner be killed	killed by fire
11:12	ascended	raised, went up, flew up into air
11:18	wrath	judgment, anger, hellfire, punishment

REVELATION

12:1	clothed with the sun	the woman is Israel as a nation, she is clothed in God's power and spirit
	moon under her feet	the moon is the Bride of Christ
	head twelve stars	the twelve stars are the twelve Tribes of Israel
12:2	travailing	labor, pain in child birth, struggled
12:4	third part of the stars of heaven	before man was created, Satan led a rebellion of angels in heaven where 1/3 of the angels were banished
	woman…deliver	Israel was about to bring forth a child-king Jesus
12:5	man-child caught up	Jesus raised from the dead and ascended to Heaven
12:7	dragon	originally Satan, but he takes different forms and lives/inspires different people and kingdoms – this dragon is the Roman Nation 2000 years ago
12:8	place found	Satan and his angels were not allowed in heaven
12:14	two wings of a great eagle	an eagle symbolically is a prophet, but here Israel receives two witness/wings or two different prophets – one with the spirit or Elijah and the other Moses
12:16	the earth opened her mouth…flood	Israel escapes destruction, is protected by God for 3 1/2 years of Great Tribulation
12:17	remnant of the seed	leftover, remains, survivors
13:1	beast rose…sea	beast=power; it rose from the sea=masses
13:10	patience	long-suffering, endurance, ability to wait
13:11	out of the earth	beast=power; it rose from the earth=unpopulated area
14:2	harping	playing the harp, an instrument with twelve strings
14:5	guile	dishonesty, falsehood, fraud, deceit, baloney
14:10	indignation	anger, temper, rage verging on madness
14:11	smoke of their torment	the smoke from their fiery hell
14:14	sickle	sharp, cutting farm instrument used for harvest
14:15	reap	harvest, collect, gather, pick/pluck
14:16	thrust in	Jesus during judgment time is reaping or gathering the souls of all the sinners
14:19	vine of the earth	an angel during judgment time is also reaping

REVELATION

		or gathering the souls of all the sinners
14:20	furlongs	1600 furlongs=50 miles (a furlong is about 1/10 of a mile; about half way around a track)
15:2	mingled	mixed, blended, joined
	his mark	the beast's (Satan's) identifying mark
15:6	the seven plaques	the evil disasters that came to the earth after each seal was opened, the truth revealed, and then rejected by most people
	girded	equipped, fastened, put on, got dressed up
16:2	noisome	troublesome, hurtful, painful, destructive
16:3	every living soul died in the sea	all life in the sea died (Mediteranean Sea)
16:8	scorch	burn, consume, destroy by sun & heat
16:9	repented	to change one's mind & purpose; regret, guilt
16:10	gnawed	bit, chewed
16:21	talent	about 100 pounds
	plague of the hail	punishment, disaster of chunks of ice falling to the Earth, symbolically God was "stoning" the people of the Earth for their spiritual adulteries/ unfaithfulness to him
17:1	great whore	the religious system that arose out of Babylon, then from Pagan Rome, and finally the Roman Church
17:3	names of blasphemy	irreverence, disrespect, lies; using the name of God incorrectly or without authority
17:4	arrayed	clothed, dressed, put on
	decked	adorned, fully decorated from head to toe
17:5	abominations	disgusting, sick, forbidden, offensive
17:6	martyrs	those who have proven the strength and genuineness of their faith in Christ by undergoing a violent death
17:8	ascend	climb, go up, proceed forward
	perdition	destruction, ruin, wickedness
17:9	seven mountains	the famous "Eternal City of Seven Hills" – also known as Rome
17:10	short space	for a little time, briefly
17:11	is of the seven	comes from the line or order of the other seven
18:2	hateful bird	because Babylon is fallen, its inhabitants will die

REVELATION

		and the vultures will come out to feed
18:3	waxed rich through the abundance	become very rich by selling/trading fancy goods
18:4	partakers	helper, associate, member, aide
18:7	glorified	praised, talk well about, honored
18:11	mourn	cry, be sad, agonize, be in distress
	merchandise	products, goods, stuff to buy
18:12	thyine	similar to the pine tree; a soft, aromatic wood
18:13	ointments	lotions, creams, makeup
8:14	dainty	expensive, exotic, fancy
18:15	stand afar off	far away, at a great distance
18:17	trade by sea	the oceanic shipping trade, the large cargo containers that carry good/product from all over the world
19:3	Alleluia	Praise the Lord
19:6	voice…many waters	all the prophets and ministers through history
	omnipotent	all powerful, without limitations
19:9	marriage	the final and full uniting of Jesus and his Bride that is made up of all the Christians over 2000 years
19:13	vesture	clothes, garments, what you wear
19:15	out of his mouth goes a sharp sword	the sacred, holy Word
20:2	bound him a thousand years	his influence and power is stopped and not allowed out
20:3	loosed a little season	is free for a very short period of time
20:8	deceive	lie, con, try to rip off
20:12	the book of life	the book that has all the names written down of those people that have believed in Jesus and His mission, and have been given eternal life
21:2	adorned	decorated, dressed up, covered with jewelry
21:8	abominable	disgusting, sick, forbidden, offensive
	murderers	cutthroats, killers, robbers, gangsters, thugs
	whoremongers	a person that often uses prostitutes; pays for sex
	sorcerers	those that use deception, witchcraft, cast spells
	idolaters	heathen, a non-Jew, person that worshipped idols or any god other than the One God (Jehovah)

REVELATION

	liars	dishonest people, spreaders of rumors, gossipers, false witnesses
21:15	reed	thin stick or cane used to measure things
21:19	garnished	decorated, dressed up, designed
21:21	twelve gates were twelve pearls	each of the twelve city gates were made either from one giant pearl or were overlaid and/or decorated with many, many pearls
21:27	no wise shall enter	forbidden, not allowed to enter, off limits
22:15	sorcerers	those that use deception, witchcraft, cast spells
	whoremongers	a person that often uses prostitutes; pays for sex
	idolaters	heathens, a non-Jew, persons that worshipped idols or any god other than the One God (Jehovah)
22:16	root…offspring	Jesus is the root=source of life, the beginning of the creation, yet he is also the offspring=child of God
22:19	the book of life	the book that has all the names written down of those people that have believed in Jesus and His mission, and have been given eternal life

APPENDIX A

The Plan of God – Salvation

What will happen after you die?

If you suddenly died and found yourself standing before God's Judgment Throne, what would you say to Him? Since He demands absolute perfection, what would you say to convince Him to let you enter His perfect, undefiled Kingdom where there is ***no sin***?

In this generation of 'enlightenment', people want you to believe that 'sin' is an obsolete concept. They say it doesn't matter what you believe... that "truth is relative"... that all that matters is if you're a good person. Well... it sounds okay on talk shows, it doesn't offend anyone, and it makes everyone feel good. [After all, that pesky guilt thing can really interfere with you having a good time!] And that would be okay ***if*** we never ***had to die*** in order to find out who's right and who's wrong. That brings me to the purpose of this Addendum. I want to convince you that...

All Gods and faiths are not equal!
Whoa! I can hear you gasping in disbelief. In this 'New Age' of knowledge and tolerance, people don't want to hear that they may be headed for certain destruction. And they surely don't want to hear that they're sinners. What they refuse to understand is that the Bible says...

Truth, by definition, must be exclusive!
All world religions are not the same. Either one is right and all the others are wrong... or they're ***all*** wrong! But one thing is certain: they ***cannot all be right***! Either Jesus is God or He's not! You cannot remain neutral on that point...

I want you to know that the Gospel of Jesus Christ is ***all-inclusive***! You're just as worthy of God's free gift of salvation through faith in Jesus Christ as anyone else. Being a 'good' person won't cut it — but giving up and letting Jesus Christ do it for you is ***the Key*** that opens Heaven's doors to you!

What must I do to be saved?

"Faith is hard because it is so easy.
It is difficult because there is no difficulty in it.
And it seems obscure simply because it is so clear."
Charles Spurgeon

I think the hardest thing for us to understand about salvation in Christ is that it doesn't depend on anything **we** do. It all depends on **who** God is — **His** faithfulness — and what He has already done.

We are so performance-oriented that we don't know **how** to respond to that! From kindergarten on through high school, college, and the workplace, we're evaluated and rewarded — or punished — based on our **performance**. In the workplace, we strive for promotions and raises — all based on our **performance**. People acknowledge us, or fail to acknowledge us, based on how we **perform**.

So, when someone tries to tell us we can't do anything to **earn** our salvation, it's so totally opposed to everything we've ever been taught that we don't know how to receive it. Many either reject it outright (because, after all, **nothing** in this life is free) or we **say** we believe and accept it — but all the while, we continue to **work** for our salvation.

We think that if we fail, God won't love us anymore. We think that we have to add something to what Christ did, just to make sure.

It's been said that there are really only **two** religions: "DO" and "DONE". All other religions require you to work for salvation. But have you ever wondered how you **know** for sure when you've done enough? Christianity — that is, faith in Christ, **not** religion — is the **only** religion that tells you upfront, "*You can't save yourself! Don't even try!*"

The Bible says, *"As many as received Him (Christ), to them gave He power to become the sons of God, even to them that believe on His name."* (John 1:12) The Bible also says, *"And this is the testimony: God has given us eternal life, and this life is in His Son. He who has the Son has life; he who does not have the Son of God does not have life."* (1 John 5:11,12) **Could it be any clearer?**

St. Peter was asked one time what was needed to be saved, he replied "Repent, and be baptized every one of you in the name of Jesus Christ for the remission of sins, and ye shall receive the gist of the Holy Ghost…" (Acts 2:37-39) The moment you open your heart to Jesus Christ and place your complete trust in Him — and Him alone — as the **only** one who can save you, then God promises to write your name in the Book of Life and reserve a place for you in heaven.

Jesus said, "*He that hears My word, and believes on Him who sent Me, has everlasting life, and shall not come into condemnation; but is passed from death to life.*" (John 5:24)

You can receive this **free** gift by simply admitting that you are a sinner (that means you haven't kept God's laws). Then, you pray and ask Jesus Christ to work this life-giving miracle in your life. If you don't know what to pray, here's a suggested prayer you can use to guide you. Remember . . . it's your **heart** that matters, not the words.

"Father God, I admit that I am a sinner and I cannot save myself. I believe that Jesus was sent from You, that He died for my sins, and that He rose from death to give me new life. I repent of my sins and ask Jesus to come into my heart and take control of my life. Thank you for saving me. Now, Father, teach me Your ways and Your will as I start this journey of a new life in Christ. Amen.

If you prayed that from your heart, and you **truly** believe that the only way you can be saved is through Jesus Christ, then you are saved! You are starting on a journey that won't always be easy, but Christ promises to give you the Holy Spirit who will help you become born again and He will be there with you every step of the way.

APPENDIX B

Water Baptism

Water Baptism - A Witness to the World

"Then cometh Jesus from Gallonilee to Jordan unto John [John the Baptist], to be baptized of him. But John forbad Him, saying, "I have need to be baptized of Thee, and comest thou to me?" And Jesus answering said unto him, "Suffer it to be so now; for thus it becometh us to fulfill all righteousness." Then he consented. And Jesus when he was baptized, went up immediately out of the water, and behold, the heavens were opened and He saw the Spirit of God descending like a dove, and alighting on Him; and lo, a voice from heaven, saying, "This is My beloved Son, with Whom I am well pleased." (Matthew 3:13-17 KJV)

The English word *baptize* is derived from the original Greek word of the New Testament which literally meant to *immerse in water*. As the Scriptures above make clear, Jesus Christ considered baptism to be an important act, so much so that He insisted on it when John hesitated to baptize Him. Jesus' baptism was then done in The Jordan River. Jesus' baptism was of course done solely to set an *example* for the repentant, since He had absolutely nothing to repent of, and absolutely no sins to be forgiven. But why is baptism in water important? Why wouldn't Jesus take "no" for answer, even with Himself?

An Act Of Sincere Repentance

Those who repented were always baptized in water:

> "Behold, I send my messenger before thy face, who shall prepare thy way before thee; the voice of one crying in the wilderness: Prepare ye the way of the Lord, make his paths straight" John did baptize in the wilderness, and preach the baptism of repentance for the forgiveness of sinches And there went out unto him all the land of Judea, and all the people of Jerusalem; and they were baptized by him in the river Jordan, confessing their sinches" (Mark 1:2-5 KJV)
>
> "Baptism, which corresponds to this, now saves you, not as a removal of dirt from the body but as an appeal to God for a clear conscience." (1 Peter 3:21 RSV)

Water Baptism and The Holy Spirit

With repentance and baptism comes The Holy Spirit:

> "Repent, and be **baptized every one of you in the name of Jesus Christ** for the remission of sins, and ye shall receive the gist of the Holy Ghost..." (Acts 2:37-39)
>
> "And as they went on their way, they came unto a certain water: and the eunuch said, See, here is water; what doth hinder me to be baptized? And Philip said, If thou believest with all thine heart, thou mayest. And he answered and said, I believe that Jesus Christ is the Son of God. And he commanded the chariot to stand still: and they went down both into the water, both Philip and the eunuch; and he baptized him. And when they were come up out of the water, the Spirit of the Lord caught away Philip, that the eunuch saw him no more: and he went on his way rejoicing." (Acts 8:36-39 KJV)
>
> "Paul said, "John's baptism was a baptism of repentance. He told the people to believe in the one coming after him, that is, in Jesus." On hearing this, they were **baptized into the name of the Lord Jesus**. When Paul placed his hands on them, the Holy Spirit came on them, and they spoke in tongues and prophesied." (Acts 19:4-6 KJV)
>
> "Then Peter said, "Can anyone keep these people from being baptized with water? They have received the Holy Spirit just as we have." So he ordered that they be **baptized in the name of Jesus Christ**." (Acts 10:47-48 KJV)

A Symbol Death, Burial and Resurrection

Baptism symbolizes the death (of the old self, by repentance), burial (by immersion in the water) and resurrection (the coming up out from under the water) to those who repent:

> "Or don't you know that all of us who were baptized into Christ Jesus were baptized into his death? We were therefore buried with him through baptism into death in order that, just as Christ was raised from the dead through the glory of the Father, we too may live a new life. If we have been united with him like this in his death, we will certainly also be united with him in his resurrection." (Romans 6:3-5 KJV)

"and you were buried with Him in baptism, in which you were also raised with Him through faith in the working of God, who raised Him from the dead." (Colossians 2:12 RSV)

An Important Step Toward Salvation

To set an example, Jesus insisted upon water baptism for Himself. Christians should do no less for themselves:

> "You are all sons of God through faith in Christ Jesus, for all of you who were baptized into Christ have clothed yourselves with Christ. There is neither Jew nor Greek, slave nor free, male nor female, for you are all one in Christ Jesus. If you belong to Christ, then you are Abraham's seed, and heirs according to the promise." (Gallonatians 3:26-29)
>
> "Whoever believes and is baptized will be saved; but whoever does not believe will be condemned." (Mark 16:16 KJV)

A Witness to the World!

One reason for water baptism is that it is a symbolic picture to the world of our decision to serve God, become a part of the Christian community and *especially* the new birth. In Romans 6:3,4 we read:

"Know ye not, that so many of us as were baptized into Jesus Christ were baptized into his death? Therefore we are buried with him by baptism into death: that like as Christ was raised up from the dead by the glory of the Father, even so we also should walk in newness of life."

By being baptized, a person testifies that he has been saved and is right with God. His immersion signifies to God and to those who witness his baptism that he is dead to the world. He is buried with Christ in baptism, and then rises to walk in newness of life. The work of regeneration has already been performed in his heart. Water baptism is an outward demonstration to others of what has happened withinch

Those who have been baptized in water can look back upon it as a landmark in their spiritual walk. And because they obeyed another of Jesus' commands, they can expect to grow spiritually as a result of it. ***Then as the scriptures declare, we should be baptized in the name of Jesus Christ, being immersed under water as a sign that we believe Jesus died for our sins, was buried and then was raised in newness of life.***

APPENDIX C

The Names of God – His Identity & Character

Isn't God's name "God" or "Lord" or "Lord Almighty"?
No, "God" and "Lord" are ***not*** His name; they are titles. The God of the Bible — the God of Abraham, Isaac, and Jacob (later changed by God to Israel) — is ***the*** God of many gods, ***the*** Lord of many lords.

What difference does it make what name I use?
In the Bible, a name was more than just a label; it was an ***identity***, a ***selfness***, an ***exactness***. For example...

- The name Jacob meant "over thrower" or "deceiver". Genesis 27:36a: "*And he said, 'Is not he rightly named Jacob? for he hath supplanted me these two times:'* "
- Later, God changed Jacob's name to Israel, which means "princely contender with God". Genesis 32:28: "*And he said, 'Thy name shall be called no more Jacob, but Israel: for as a prince hast thou power with God and with men, and hast prevailed.'* "
- The name Nabal meant "fool". 1 Samuel 25:25: "*For as his name is, so is he; Nabal is his name, and folly is with him.*"
- The name Jabez meant "pain" or "sorrowful". 1 Chronicles 4:9: "*...his mother called his name Jabez, saying, 'Because I bare him with sorrow.'* "

Therefore, the names God uses for Himself in the Bible reveal His characteristics — ***who*** He is, ***what*** He is, and what He ***does***. When the Bible uses the phrase "the name of God" or "in the name of the Lord", it refers to His ***total person*** — all that He is.

God's ***name*** is excellent and majestic, as in Psalm 8:1: "*Yahweh, our Lord, how majestic is Your name in all the earth, who has set your glory above the heavens!*"

As you get to know God by His names, your view of Him will change. He will become bigger, more majestic, more holy, more able to meet every one of your deepest needs, and more worthy of your heartfelt devotion and worship. God knows each of us by name. Shouldn't we know Him by His?

"Hallowed be Your name..."?
"*Our Father which art in heaven, Hallowed be Your name...*" (Matthew 6:9)

To hallow God's name means to set it apart, to exalt it as being worthy of ***absolute devotion*** and ***reverence***.

- Nehemiah 9:5b: "Stand up and bless Yahweh your God from everlasting to everlasting; and blessed be your glorious name, which is exalted above all blessing and praise."
- Exodus 20:7: "You shall not take the name of Yahweh your God in vain, for Yahweh will not hold him guiltless who takes his name in vainch"
- Leviticus 22:32: "You shall not profane My holy name, but I will be made holy among the children of Israel. I am Yahweh who makes you holy."

Is God's name really that important? I mean, really... who cares?
God cares!

God is quite serious about ***how***, ***when***, ***where***, and ***why*** His name is used.

- God wants people to know ***Him*** by knowing His name!
  At least 16 times God says that His reason for doing certain things was so people would "know [His] name", "fear [His] name", or that His name would be "declared":
  - Exodus 9:16: "but indeed for this cause I have made you stand: to show you My power, and that My name may be declared throughout all the earth;"
  - Psalm 9:10: "Those who know Your name will put their trust in You, for You, Yahweh, have not forsaken those who seek You."
  - Jeremiah 16:21: "Therefore, behold, I will cause them to know, this once will I cause them to know My hand and My might; and they shall know that My name is Yahweh."
  - Malachi 4:2: "But to you who fear My name shall the sun of righteousness arise with healing in its wings. You will go out, and leap like calves of the stall."
  - *See also* 1 Kings 8:42-43; 2 Chronicles 6:33; Nehemiah 1:11; Psalm 61:5, 83:18, 86:11; Isaiah 52:6; Jeremiah 29:3; Ezekiel 20:44, 36:23, and 39:7.
  -
- God cares deeply about ***where*** and ***in whom*** His name dwells!
  More than 50 times God refers to a place for His "name to dwell" or His name being in a person or place:
  - Exodus 23:21: "Pay attention to him, and listen to his voice. Don't provoke him, for he will not pardon your disobedience, for My name is in him."
  - Deuteronomy 16:11: "and you shall rejoice before Yahweh your God . . . in the place which Yahweh your God shall choose, to cause His name to dwell there."
  - Nehemiah 1:9: "but if you return to Me . . . yet will I . . .bring them to the place that I have chosen, to cause My name to dwell there."

- 2 Chronicles 7:14: "if My people, who are called by My name, shall humble themselves, and pray, and seek My face, and turn from their wicked ways; then will I hear from heaven, and will forgive their sin, and will heal their land."
- *See also* Exodus 20:24; Numbers 6:27; Deuteronomy 12:11, 14:23, 16:2, 16:6, 26:2; Ezra 6:12; 2 Samuel 7:13; 1 Kings 5:5, 8:16-19, 8:29, 9:3, 11:36; 2 Kings 21:4, 21:7, 23:27; 1 Chronicles 22:8-10, 28:3; 2 Chronicles 6:5-10, 6:33, 7:16, 7:20, 33:4, 33:7; Numbers 1:9; Isaiah 43:7, 63:19, 65:1; Jeremiah 7:10-14, 7:30, 14:9, 15:16, 25:29, 32:34, 34:15; Daniel 9:18-19; and Amos 9:12.
-

- God cares about His name's ***reputation***!
  At least 19 times God references doing something for the sake of His name:
  - 1 Samuel 12:22: "For Yahweh will not forsake His people for His great name's sake, because it has pleased Yahweh to make you a people to Himself..."
  - Psalm 23:3: "He restores my soul. He guides me in the paths of righteousness for His name's sake."
  - Ezekiel 20:22: "Nevertheless I withdrew My hand, and worked for My name's sake, that it should not be profaned in the sight of the nations, in whose sight I brought them forth."
  - *See also* 1 Kings 8:41; 2 Chronicles 6:32; Psalm 25:11, 31:3, 79:9, 106:8, 109:21, 143:11; Isaiah 48:9, 66:5; Jeremiah 14:7, 14:21; Ezekiel 20:9, 20:14, 20:44, and 36:22.
- God cares about ***how*** His name is used!
  More than 30 times God says, not only that ***He*** is holy, but that His ***name*** is holy or worthy of glory:
  - 1 Chronicles 16:10: "Glory you in his holy name; Let the heart of them rejoice who seek Yahweh."
  - Psalm 29:2: "Ascribe to Yahweh the glory due to his name. Worship Yahweh in holy array."
  - Psalm 111:9: "He has sent redemption to His people. He has ordained His covenant forever. His name is holy and awesome!"
  - Isaiah 57:15: "For thus says the high and lofty One who inhabits eternity, whose name is Holy: I dwell in the high and holy place, with him also who is of a contrite and humble spirit, to revive the spirit of the humble, and to revive the heart of the contrite."
  - *See also* Leviticus 20:3, 22:2, 22:32; 1 Chronicles 16:29, 16:35, 29:16; Nehemiah 9:5; Psalm 30:4, 33:21, 97:12, 99:3, 103:1, 105:3, 106:47, 138:2, 145:21, 148:13; Isaiah 12:4, 47:4; Ezekiel 20:39, 36:20-22, 39:7, 39:25, 43:7-8; and Amos 2:7.
- And finally, God simply cares about people ***knowing His name***!
  The phrases "My name" and "Your name" (apart from the other more specific verses already provided) appear at least 58 times:

- Exodus 3:15: "God said moreover to Moses, "You shall tell the children of Israel this, 'Yahweh, the God of your fathers, the God of Abraham, the God of Isaac, and the God of Jacob, has sent me to you.' This is my name forever, and this is my memorial to all generations."
- Leviticus 19:12: "'You shall not swear by my name falsely, and profane the name of your God. I am Yahweh."
- 2 Samuel 7:26: "Let Your name be magnified forever, saying, Yahweh of hosts is God over Israel..."
- Isaiah 42:8: "I am Yahweh, that is My name; and My glory will I not give to another, neither My praise to engraved images."
- 1 Chronicles 17:24: "Let Your name be established and magnified forever, saying, Yahweh of Hosts is the God of Israel..."
- 2 Chronicles 14:11: "...help us, Yahweh our God; for we rely on You, and in Your name are we come against this multitude..."

It's obvious that these aren't mere casual references to God's name, but that He cares deeply about ***how***, ***when***, ***where***, and ***why*** His name is used. As Christians, shouldn't we care just as much about how we address and worship the Most High God?

Still don't understand why it's important to know God's names?
The purpose of man — the reason we were created — is to worship and glorify God. "Whether, then, you eat or drink or whatever you do, do all to the glory of God" (1 Corinthians 10:31). In order to truly worship and glorify God, we must not only know ***about*** Him, but we must know Him ***personally*** based on what we know about Him.

The word "*glory*" in the Greek New Testament is "*doxa*", which means an opinion, estimation, or reputation in which one is held. It refers to all that we give to God as praise, thanksgiving, obedience, reverence, and service — because of who He has revealed Himself to be and what He does (past, present, and future.

The many names God gives us about Himself in the Bible impart to us revelations of His ***character***, His ***works***, and His ***relationship*** to us. It's in the knowing and understanding of these names that we gain greater insight, love, respect, and reverence for who He is.

The Messiah has a name: Jesus (Y'shua). So, also, the God of the Old Testament has revealed Himself by a name. I believe, as Bible Scholar T. E. McComiskey so rightly wrote, "a blessing is lost when no attention is paid to the difference in usage of a title and the actual name of the God of Israel."

YHWH / Jehovah (The Self-Existing One"

יהוה

The name YHWH is used more than any other name in the Bible.
Of all the names of God, the one which occurs most frequently in the Biblia Hebraica (Hebrew Bible) is the Tetragrammaton (from the Greek: "word with four letters"), which is spelled (in the Hebrew alphabet) י(yodh) ה(heh) ו(vav) ה(heh) or, reading right-to-left, יהוה(YHWH). It is the distinctive ***personal*** name of the God of Israel. YHWH (written as "LORD" in most English Bibles) means "**the self-existent one**" and denotes God's **personal name** and His **eternality** ("**I AM**"). It is often used in relationship to God as a personal Redeemer and Covenant-keeper. (Interestingly, "*Yodh*" is the smallest letter in the Hebrew alphabet, and it always and only refers to YHWH.)
Most litterateurs agree that the Tetragrammaton is a form of the Hebrew root "*Havah*" ("*to be*" or "*to exist*"). Thus, YHWH becomes "**He who brings into being**" (compare Exodus 3:12 and 14: "*I will be with you*" and "*I will be who I will be*").

According to the Jewish Encyclopedia, the Tetragrammaton appears 6,828 times in the Biblia Hebraica. Other Bible scholars say the name appears approximately 5600 times in the Hebrew Scriptures, while yet another source claims the name is used more than 7000 times in the Old Testament and 1000 times in the New Testament. Regardless of which numbers are correct, we cannot overlook the fact that God obviously wants us to know His name, likely for what it reveals about who He is!

God desires us to understand the manner of His character; He wants us to know, not only His name, but to know Him through His name!

Used more than any other name in the Bible, YHWH is first seen in Genesis 2:4: "This is the history of the generations of the heavens and of the earth when they were created, in the day that YHWH God made earth and the heavens."

However, God did not reveal Himself to mankind as YHWH until Exodus 3:14 when God said to Moses, "I AM WHO I AM," and "You shall tell the children of Israel this: 'I AM has sent me to you.' "

Then later in Exodus 6:2-3, He said to Moses: "I am YHWH; and I appeared to Abraham, to Isaac, and to Jacob, as God Almighty; but by My name YHWH I was not known to them."

From the choice of words in the above-referenced Scriptures, it's obvious that God desires us to understand the manner of His character; that He wants us to know, not only His name, but to know **Him *through*** His name!

Exodus 14:4 further supports the view that the name YHWH embodies aspects of God's character. It says: ". . . *and the Egyptians will know that I am YHWH.*" It isn't likely that God intended in this declaration that they would simply learn the name of the Hebrew God. There is a strong element of Divine self-disclosure within it.

The modern spelling includes vowels to assist in pronunciation. Many pronounce YHWH as "*Yahweh*" (Yä-wá) or "*Yahveh*" (Yä-vá); but the exact pronunciation has been lost to us for several centuries.

Some people render the four-letter name as "Jehovah".
God's personal name was so sacred to most Jews that they didn't want to write or even speak it for fear of violating the commandment "You shall not take the name of Yahweh your God in vain, for Yahweh will not hold him guiltless who takes His name in vain," (Exodus 20:7) and "You shall not profane My holy name, but I will be made holy among the children of Israel. I am Yahweh who makes you holy." (Leviticus 22:32)

Thus, the Jewish practice was to read "*Adonai*" (Hebrew "Adonay"), meaning "*Lord*", in place of "*YHWH*" (Adonai means ***master*** or ***sovereign ruler*** and generally denotes ***authority*** and ***position***). And they often read "*Elohim*" in place of the Hebrew compound name "*YHWH Adonay*" to avoid the duplication of Adonay (Elohim means ***mighty one*** or ***strong one***"; it denotes the ***power*** and ***pre-eminence*** [conspicuous glory] of God).

To remind the reader that he was not to pronounce "*YHWH*" but instead was to read the word as "*Adonay*", they placed the vowels of Adonay (a-o-a) under the Tetragrammaton YHWH, thus creating יְהוָֹה. The first English translators who transcribed God's name into English had no reason to believe that the vowel points of יְהוָֹה might be incorrect, so they transcribed "YaHoWaH" into English just as it was written.

Today the English transcription "Jehovah" is used by many English-speaking Protestant Christians and also by Jehovah's Witnesses. Most modern scholars, however, believe that "Jehovah" is an implausible rendering, based on their belief that the written form יְהוָֹה (read normally, "Yehovah") was only intended to indicate to the reader of the Bible in Hebrew to pronounce it "Adonai".

The American Standard Version (ASV) of the Bible uses the name "Jehovah" 5818 times, whereas most other English versions, unfortunately, continue to translate "YHWH" as "LORD" (capital letters), not to be confused with "Lord"

(Adonai/Adonay). The King James Version of the Bible uses the word "LORD" 5557 times.

Regardless of the editorial decision of substituting "LORD" for "YHWH" or of using the name "Yahweh" or "Jehovah", we must keep in mind that Yahweh or YHWH is the name that ***God*** used in revealing Himself to His ancient people. In reading the text of the Old Testament, it is my hope that we would develop an affection for usage of the name itself over such usages as "God" or "Lord" (*see* Exodus 3:15; Psalm 102:15-16; Psalm 113:1-4; Psalm 135:1-6; Psalm 148:13).

Adonai..&..Elohim (Lord)

אֲדֹנָי אלהים

Did you know that Adonai and Elohim are *plural* Hebrew nouns?
Two common names of God in the Biblia Hebraica (Hebrew Bible) are "Adonai" which is Hebrew for "Lord", and "Elohim" which expresses concepts of divinity (i.e., "God"). Technically, the word "Adonai" is the plural form of "Adon", meaning "my lord"; and the name "Elohim" is the masculine plural form of "Eloha".

The singular Adon was used by the Phoenicians for their pagan god Tammuz and is the origin of the Greek name Adonis. The ordinary feminine singular word "Eloha" refers to the pagan polytheistic notion of multiple gods, or to powerful men or judges (Exodus 21:6 "...then his master [Eloha] shall bring him to God, and shall bring him to the door or to the door-post, and his master [Eloha] shall bore his ear through with an awl, and he shall serve him for ever.").

Since Adonai and Elohim are written in the plural form, many Christians have used this as a foundation on which to build the Christian doctrine of the Trinity. However, while these names are written in the plural form, they regularly employ singular verbs in Hebrew grammar and are singular in usage. Therefore, acting as singular nouns with singular verbs, many believe these names represent a plural of ***majesty***, perhaps pointing out that this ***one God*** embodies ***all*** the attributes of the many pagan gods worshipped by other peoples. (For a more detailed discussion of the name "Elohim", see the article titled "El — Eloha — Elohim" below)

Adonai (Hebrew: Adonay) was used as a substitute for the name Yahweh (YHWH).
The Tetragrammaton YHWH appears approximately 6000 times in the Hebrew Scriptures. To avoid violating the commandment "You shall not take the name of Yahweh your God in vain" (Exodus 20:7), sometimes Adonai was used as a substitute for Yahweh (YHWH) or the vowels "a-o-a" were inserted between the letters "YHWH" to remind people to not pronounce the name "Yahweh".

Adonai (Lord) means "**master**", "**owner**", or "**sovereign ruler**" and generally denotes the authority and position of God. Adonai is first used in Genesis 15:2 where Abram asked, "*Lord Yahweh [Adonai], what will You give me, seeing I go childless...?*" The word Adonai, in reference to God, occurs 300 times in the Old Testament — especially in Isaiah, Ezekiel (200 times), and Daniel (10 times in the 9th chapter). It is usually written "Lord" in most English Bibles, "Jehovah" in the American Standard Version (ASV) of the Bible, and "Yahweh" or "Lord". Primarily, the name Adonai stresses man's relationship to God as his **Master**, **Authority**, and **Provider**. Some examples of where the name "Adonai" is used...

- Genesis 18:1: Yahweh [Adonai] appeared to him (Abraham) by the oaks of Mamre, as he sat in the tent door in the heat of the day.

- Joshua 5:14: He said, "*No; but as prince of the host of Yahweh [Adonai] am I now come.*"
- Joshua fell on his face to the earth, and did worship..."

- 1 Samuel 1:15: Hannah answered, "*No, my lord, I am a woman of a sorrowful spirit: I have drunk neither wine nor strong drink, but I poured out my soul before Yahweh [Adonai].*"
- Psalm 68:32: Sing to God, you kingdoms of the earth! Sing praises to the Lord [Adonai]! *Selah.*
- Isaiah 6:1-4: In the year that king Uzziah died, I saw the Lord [Adonai] sitting on a throne, high and lifted up; and His train filled the temple . . . One called to another, and said, "*Holy, holy, holy, is Yahweh of Hosts! The whole earth is full of His glory!*" The foundations of the thresholds shook at the voice of Him who called, and the house was filled with smoke.
- *See also* Exodus 4:10; Judges 6:15; 2 Samuel 7:18-20; Psalm 8, 114:7, 135:5, 141:8, 109:21-28.

The name "Elohim" is the first of God's names used in the Bible.
Elohim is the name of God that occurs first in Scripture in Genesis 1:1: "In the beginning God [Elohim] created the heavens and the earth." The name occurs 2,570 times in the Old Testament: 32 times in Genesis; and almost exclusively in Ecclesiastes, Daniel, and Jonah. Elohim was often used in place of "YHWH Adonai" to avoid duplication of the name "Adonai" whenever the Hebrew compound name "*YHWH Adonai*" appeared in Scripture.

The name "Elohim" is used in Scripture when emphasizing God's **might**, His **creative power**, and His attributes of **justice** and **rulership**. It denotes the power and pre-eminence (conspicuous glory) of God and is especially used in relation to God's sovereignty, creative work, and mighty works for Israel. Variations of this name include "El", "Eloha", "Elohai" (my God) and "Elohaynu" (our God). In the Pentateuch the name "Elohim" portrays God as the **transcendent Being**, the **Creator** of the universe.

Some examples where the name "Elohim" is used...

- Deuteronomy 5:24: ...Yahweh our God [Elohim] has shown us His glory and His greatness, and we have heard His voice out of the midst of the fire...
- Deuteronomy 8:15: [Elohim]...led you through the great and terrible wilderness, in which were fiery serpents and scorpions, and thirsty ground where was no water; who brought you forth water out of the rock of flint;
- Psalm 68:1: Let God [Elohim] arise! Let His enemies be scattered! Let them who hate Him also flee before Him.
- Isaiah 6:8-11: I heard the Lord's [Elohim's] voice, saying, "*Whom shall I send, and who will go for Us?*" Then I said, "*Here I am. Send me!*" He [Elohim] said, "*Go, and tell this people, 'You hear indeed, but don't understand; and you see indeed, but don't perceive.*" . . . Then I said, "*Lord [Elohim], how long?*" He answered, "*Until cities are waste without inhabitant, and houses without man, and the land becomes utterly waste...*"
- Isaiah 45:18: For thus says Yahweh [Elohim] who created the heavens, the God who formed the earth and made it, who established it and didn't create it a waste, who formed it to be inhabited: "*I am Yahweh; and there is no one [Elohim] else.*"
- Isaiah 54:5: "For your Maker is your husband; Yahweh of Hosts is his name: and the Holy One of Israel is your Redeemer; the God of the whole earth [Elohim] shall He be called."
- Jeremiah 32:27: "Behold, I am Yahweh, the God [Elohim] of all flesh: is there anything too hard for Me?"

El — Eloha — Elohim (The Almighty God)

אלהים אלוה אל

Apart from the name "Yahweh", it may be argued that the name "Elohim" says more about the God of Israel than any other name. Certainly, all that the name embodies deserves more deliberation.

The name "Elohim" contains the concept of ***creative*** and ***governing power***, of ***omnipotence*** and ***sovereignty***. When God is presented in relation to His creation and to the peoples of the earth — especially in the Pentateuch — the name "Elohim" is used most often. In the name "Yahweh", on the other hand, are represented the high ***moral attributes*** of God which are revealed only to humankind and the angels.

The root word "El" or "Eloha"

In order to gain a greater understanding of the meaning of the name "Elohim", it's important to first examine its origin and usage. Unfortunately, the precise development of the word "Elohim" is unknown. There are many theories, but most Bible scholars believe it is derived from the shorter word "El" (meaning ***mighty***, ***strong***, or ***prominent***) or the Hebrew form "Eloha". The use of "Eloha" is rare, occurring only in poetry and late prose, mainly in Job. The word "El", however, is itself translated "God", "God Almighty", and "Mighty God" approximately 250 times and frequently in circumstances which especially indicate the ***great power*** of God. For instance...

- It is the name "El" under which God made His great promises to Abraham in Genesis 17:1 — "When Abram was ninety-nine years old, Yahweh appeared to Abram, and said to him, "I am God Almighty [El]. Walk before Me, and be blameless," and to Jacob in Genesis 35:11 — "God said to him, 'I am God Almighty [El]...' "
- It is also one of the names given to the promised Messiah in Isaiah 9:6 — "For to us a child is born, to us a Son is given; and the government shall be on His shoulder: and His name shall be called Wonderful, Counselor, Mighty God [El], Everlasting Father, Prince of Peace."
- *See also* Genesis 7:1, 28:3, 35:11; Numbers 23:22; Joshua 3:10; 2 Samuel 22:31-32; Nehemiah 1:5, 9:32; Isaiah 9:6; Ezekiel 10.

"Elohim" is a designation as well as a proper name

"Elohim" is more than just a proper name for God. It's also an appellative or designation of all that the name embodies. For example, in the frequent expression, "LORD your God" (or "Yahweh your God"), *LORD* (*Yahweh*) functions as the *proper name*, while *God* functions as the *designation* of deity. Throughout the first two chapters of the Bible, Elohim is used most often as a proper name. After Exodus 3 the name begins to occur with increasing frequency as a *designation*, that is, "the God [Elohim] of," or "your God [Elohim]". The word denotes God as ***the*** supreme deity of a person or people.

More about the plurality of "Elohim"

Though Elohim is a plural word, it does not denote more than one entity or being. It is clear that the scriptures teach that we should worship only one God. In Deuteronomy 6:4, God calls out, “Hear, O Israel: The LORD our God is one LORD.” In the New Testament, in Mark 12:29, THE Lord Jesus Christ also says, “The first of all the commandments is, Hear, O Israel; The Lord our God is one Lord.”

...the plural word "Elohim" teaches us that no finite word can adequately define the infinite personality of God.

As mentioned above, when referring to the God of the Bible, the *plural* name "Elohim" is always accompanied by *singular* verbs, adjectives, and pronouns. For instance...

- Deuteronomy 32:39 — "See now that I, even I, am He [Elohim], there is no god [Elohim] with Me." (If the plural word "Elohim" used plural verbs and pronouns, the verse would read: "See now that <u>We</u> . . . <u>are</u> Elohim, there <u>are</u> no Elohim with <u>Us</u>.")
- Isaiah 40:28 — "Have you not known? Have you not heard? The everlasting God [Elohim], Yahweh, the Creator of the ends of the earth, does not faint, neither is weary; there is no searching of His understanding." (If using plural verbs and pronouns along with the plural "Elohim", the verse would read: "...The everlasting Elohim, Yahweh, the Creator<u>s</u> . . . <u>do</u> not faint, neither <u>are</u> weary; there is no searching of <u>their</u> understanding."
- *See also* II Kings 19:4, 16; Psalm 7:9, 57:2; Isaiah 45:5, 45:22.

Many Bible scholars object to the idea of the Trinity in the word "Elohim" and they suggest that the plural is only a plural of ***majesty***, such as used by rulers and kings. Other scholars call it a plural of ***intensity***. They argue that the Hebrews often expressed a word in the plural to give it a stronger meaning (such as in Isaiah 6:3 with "Holy" being expressed three times). As one theologian points out, the use of the plural "only implies (even in the plural of majesty) that the word in the singular is not full enough to set forth all that is intended."

Thus, whether plural of majesty... plural of intensity...the plural word "Elohim" teaches us that no finite word can adequately define the infinite personality of God.

As Nathan Stone wrote: "There is blessing and comfort in this great name of God signifying supreme ***power***, ***sovereignty***, and ***glory*** on the one hand . . . and on the other hand signifying a covenant relationship which He is ever faithful to keep. Thus He says to us, "I will be to you <u>Elohim</u>," that we may say, "My <u>Elohim</u>; in Him will I trust." (Psalm 91:2)."

ALSO AVAILABLE

America - You Will Be Destroyed! Thus Saith The Lord - and Other Amazing Prophecies

Book Description

Author R Scott Giberti, feeling compelled to warn and to inform Americans about frightening prophecies that he believes relate to their present and immediate future, has written **America: You Will Be Destroyed! - And Other Amazing Prophecies.**

Drawing from the prophecies of renowned evangelist William Branham, deemed by millions to be a prophet, Giberti in his first nonfiction book, take readers on an unforgettable journey through prophecy and current events and into the terrifying future of America.

His book is unique in that it was not written as a personal attack on Hillary Clinton or a commentary on her various scandals. In fact, Giberti does not seem to have a political axe to grind. He is on a mission – seven events were foretold in 1933, two remain unfulfilled: Will Hillary Clinton become America's first dictator, and can America escape destruction?

America is at a crossroads and has a date with destiny, yet is deserving of a final warning. Read his book to find out why.

Made in the USA